Morocco 2040

DIRECTIONS IN DEVELOPMENT
Countries and Regions

Morocco 2040

Emerging by Investing in Intangible Capital

Jean-Pierre Chauffour

 **WORLD BANK GROUP**

Contents

Figures

Tables

Foreword

The new World Bank Country Economic Memorandum on Morocco, *Emerging by Investing in Intangible Capital,* is remarkable for at least three reasons:

- It is primarily a prospective report. Considering, like Fernand Braudel, that "the future cannot be predicted, but has to be prepared," this Memorandum proposes ways to build Morocco in 2040, and favors convergence with the countries of Southern Europe, a scenario dear to IPEMED since its project "Mediterranean 2030." And the stakes are high, since the per capita GDP of Morocco could reach 45 percent of that of Southern Europeans in 2040, versus 22 percent currently. It is the scenario of an emerging, politically stable country that wants to and can play the cards of youth, progress, and modernity by valuing its assets and reducing its weaknesses. This scenario is optimistic, but the projections of the World Bank rely on a realistic diagnosis of Morocco in 2016.
- Moreover, this report has the merit of favoring only one strategic variable: the accumulation of intangible capital. Gone are the complex scenarios and planning in which the variables (labor, capital, foreign trade, laws, regulations, and so on) multiply and interfere, leaving policymakers to face difficult choices. This report contains one single directive: to promote a sustainable increase in the productivity of the Moroccan economy through a greater accumulation of intangible capital. The phase of physical capital accumulation, initiated in particular by the "Plan Emergence," needs to be complemented by a phase of intangible capital accumulation. For Morocco, action must be taken to improve the quality of jobs (through education and training), strengthen market support structures, transform public institutions and services, and nurture social capital (parity between men and women, modernization of the law, and so on). In short, we must not only continue creating new things, but also improve the quality of those things that already exist, so that present and future generations benefit from the conditions conducive to higher, sustainable, and inclusive job-creating growth. According to His Majesty the King, in a speech in July 2014, this policy of improving the intangible could become "the fundamental criterion for the elaboration of public policies." This is in line with the foundations of the economy already spelled out by Jean Bodin: "There is neither wealth nor strength but men."

- Finally, this Memorandum projects Morocco into the industrial revolution of the 21st century, that of the digital and collaborative economy. In the age of the Internet, the world in which young people evolve promotes the digitalization of exchanges, the sharing of objects and functions, and the emergence of new economic paradigms (collaborative economics, short supply chains, and so on). These are the parameters of the economy of the future. It is the transition from the economy of having to the economy of being. I recall, when I was a young professor in the 1970s and 1980s, the remarks made by a president of the Economic and Social Council in Paris: "Soon the divide will no longer be between those who have and those who don't but between those who know and those who don't know."

By placing youth, education, health, and training at the heart of Morocco's development model for years to come, the World Bank Memorandum also calls for a renewal of the "rules of the game." Let's hope that the Kingdom partners, starting with Europe, anticipate these major changes in order to better prepare for them.

I enjoyed reading this report. I hope you will do the same.

Jean-Louis Guigou
President of the IPEMED

Preface

Ten years after the publication of the last World Bank Country Economic Memorandum for Morocco, the 2017 book, *Morocco 2040: Emerging by Investing in Intangible Capital*, documents the major economic and social strides made by Morocco in recent decades and analyzes the obstacles that the country must overcome to ensure that the economic catch-up process underway in the country can be accelerated and will pave the way for sustainable economic convergence and the improved well-being of the entire population. With these accomplishments under its belt, Morocco has set its sights on achieving the legitimate goal of accelerating its economic convergence with developed countries in the decades ahead and becoming the first non–oil-producing North African country to attain emerging country status.

To examine the possible pathways to achieving this convergence, this Memorandum first assesses Morocco's economic and social performance over the past 15 years, before looking ahead to 2040 (that is, the next generation), and analyzing the economic scenarios that could double Morocco's current rate of convergence with Southern European countries (France, Italy, Portugal, and Spain). A virtuous yet realistic scenario suggests that Morocco's per capita GDP (in purchasing power parity) could reach almost 45 percent of that of a southern European country such as Spain by 2040; the rate currently stands at a mere 22 percent.

The Memorandum then presents the economic policies and political economy conditions that could contribute to this virtuous scenario of accelerated economic convergence. This scenario is based on sustained increased productivity of the Moroccan economy through greater accumulation of intangible capital, which relates to the quality of the institutional, human, and social capital of countries. To that end, the Memorandum also seeks to provide ways to address the issue raised by His Majesty, King Mohammed VI, in his Throne Speech of July 2014 regarding the manner in which intangible capital could become the "fundamental criterion in the development of public policies so that all Moroccans may benefit from their country's wealth."

Acknowledgments

This book was prepared by a team led by lead author Jean-Pierre Chauffour (Lead Economist), under the supervision of Auguste Tano Kouame (Practice Manager) and Marie-Françoise Marie-Nelly (Country Director for the Maghreb).

The lead World Bank team was composed of Diego Angel-Urdinola (Senior Economist), Kamel Braham (Education Program Leader), Dorothée Chen (Health Specialist), Safaa El-Kogali (Practice Manager), Khalid El-Massnaoui (Senior Economist), Roberto Foa (Consultant), Caroline Krafft (Consultant), Andrea Liverani (Sustainable Development Program Leader), Mariem Malouche (Senior Economist), Eva Maria Melis (Counsel), Philippe de Meneval (Trade and Competitiveness Program Leader), Patrick Mullen (Senior Health Specialist), Emre Ozaltin (Senior Economist), Paul Scott Prettitore (Senior Public Sector Specialist), Elisabeth Sandor (Consultant), and Fabian Seiderer (Lead Public Sector Specialist).

Several colleagues provided general research assistance: Hind Arroub (Consultant), Abdoul Gadiry Barry (Consultant), Saad Belghazi (Consultant), Morgane Breuil (Consultant), Rachid M. Doukkali (Consultant), Asma El Alami El Fellousse (Consultant), Arthur Foch (ICT Policy Specialist), Johan Grijsen (Consultant), Jamal Guennouni (Consultant), Abderrahmane Lahlou (Consultant), Daniela Marotta (Senior Economist), Jean-Philippe Mas (Consultant), Carlo Maria Rossotto (Lead ICT Policy Specialist), and Gabriel Sensenbrenner (Lead Economist). Salma Daki (Consultant), Amina Iraqui (Consultant), Fatima Ezzahra Kinani (Consultant), and Jules Porte (Consultant) analyzed and presented the data.

No publication can reach its potential readers without production and communication support. Jewel McFadden (Publishing Associate) supervised the editorial and publication aspects of the book, with support from Rumit Pancholi (Project Manager) and his team. Marcelle Djomo (Project Coordinator) coordinated the translation of the report into English, and the consultancy Interpreters Morocco coordinated the translation of the executive summary into Arabic. Manuella Lea Palmioli (Customer Service Representative) used her designing talent to prepare the cover and page layout for the report. Muna Abeid Salim (Senior Program Assistant) and Abdurrahman Bashir Karwa (Program Assistant) were responsible for ensuring professional administrative support services, and

Ibtissam Alaoui (Communications Officer) ensured overall communication and dissemination of project information.

The authors express their sincere appreciation to Hafez Ghanem, World Bank MENA Vice President, as well as Simon Gray (former World Bank Country Director for the Maghreb), Marie-Françoise Marie-Nelly (World Bank Country Director for the Maghreb), and Shantayanan Devarajan (MENA Chief Economist) for their sound advice and invaluable support throughout the preparation of the report. The authors also thank the MENA sector managers, in particular Enis Baris, Najy Benhassine, Benoit Blarel, Safaa El-Kogali, Aurora Ferrari, Ernest Massiah, Jean Pesme, and Hisham Waly for their support and that of their teams throughout the project.

The book benefited greatly from comments from the review committee, established at the design stage and composed of Uri Dadush (Senior Associate, Carnegie Endowment for International Peace), Ivailo Izvorski (Practice Manager, World Bank), Adesinaola Odugbemi (Senior Communications Officer, World Bank), and Alexandria Valerio (Senior Economist, World Bank); and at the preliminary report stage, composed of Mohamed Chafiki (Director of Studies and Financial Forecasts, Moroccan Ministry of Economy and Finance), Sébastien Dessus (Lead Economist, World Bank), Ishac Diwan (Visiting Scholar, Paris School of Economics), Ivailo Izvorski (Practice Manager, World Bank), and Hedi Larbi (Visiting Scholar, Harvard Kennedy School). The authors of the report benefited from insightful comments from various regional experts, many of whom submitted written remarks. The authors mention in particular Nicolas Blancher (Mission Chief, International Monetary Fund), Kamel Braham (Program Leader), Kevin Carey (Lead Economist), Quy-Toan Do (Senior Economist), Arthur Foch (ICT Policy Specialist), Afef Haddad (Country Program Coordinator), Michael Hamaide (Senior Country Officer), Mélise Jaud (Economist), Andrea Liverani (Sustainable Development Program Leader), Philippe de Meneval (Trade and Competitiveness Program Leader), Carlo Maria Rossotto (Lead ICT Policy Specialist), and Dorte Verner (Lead Agriculture Economist). The writing and clarity of the book were also greatly improved by the attentive and meticulous review of the final report by Ibtissam Alaoui (Communications Officer), Kamel Braham (Education Program Leader), Auguste Tano Kouame (Practice Manager), and Marie-Françoise Marie-Nelly (Country Director for the Maghreb).

Preparation of the book benefited from close consultation with the Economic, Social and Environmental Council (CESE); the Bank Al-Maghrib (BAM); and the High Commission for Planning (HCP). The team extends special thanks to Nizar Baraka (President of the CESE), Abdellatif Jouahri (Governor of BAM), and Ahmed Lahlimi (High Commissioner, HCP), as well as their colleagues Driss Guerraoui (Secretary General, CESE), Mohamed Taamouti (Director of Studies and International Relations, BAM), and Abdelhak Allalat (Director of National Accounts, HCP) for their availability and valuable cooperation.

Other prominent individuals helped refine the report through extremely fruitful and enriching exchanges on a number of themes in the report during the period 2014–16. The following must be mentioned in particular (in alphabetical order): Fouad Abdelmoumni (Secretary General of Transparency, Maroc), Aziz Ajbilou (Secretary General of the Ministry of General Affairs and Governance), Abdelali Benamour (Chair of the Competition Council), Mohammed Benayad (Secretary General of the Ministry of Foreign Trade), Miriem Bensalah Chaqroun (Chair of the General Confederation of Moroccan Enterprises), Mohamed Berrada (professor emeritus at the University Hassan II Casablanca), Mohammed Boussaid (Ministry of Economy and Finance), Mohamed Chafiki (Director of Studies and Financial Forecasts, Ministry of Economy and Finance), Zouhair Chorfi (Director General of the Customs and Excise Administration), Karim El-Aynaoui (Director of the OCP Policy Center), Nouh El-Harmouzi (Director of the Arab Center for Scientific Research and Humane Studies), Mohamed El-Kettani (Chief Executive Officer of Groupe Attijariwafa Bank), Habib El-Malki (Chair of the Centre Marocain de Conjoncture), Tarik El-Malki (lecturer and researcher at the Institut supérieur de commerce et d'administration des entreprises), Jaouad Hamri (former Director of the Office des Changes), Rupert Joy (Ambassador and Head of the European Union Delegation), Omar Kabbaj (Advisor to His Majesty King Mohammed VI), Jawad Kerdoudi (Chair of the Moroccan Institute for International Relations), Said Khairoun (President of the Committee of Finance and Economic Development, House of Representatives), Ayache Khellaf (Director of Economic Forecasting and Prospective Studies at the HCP), Driss Ksikes (Director of the HEM Business School Research Center), Abdelghni Lakhdar (Economic Advisor to the Head of Government), Raul de Luzenberger (Deputy Head of the European Union Delegation), Jean-Luc Martinet (Member of the French Chamber of Commerce and Industry in Morocco), Redouane Mfadel (journalist, Luxe Radio), Mohamed Tawfik Mouline (Director General of the Royal Institute of Strategic Studies), Said Mouline (Director General of the National Agency for the Development of Renewable Energy and Energy Efficiency), Marta Moya Díaz (Chief of Section, European Union Delegation), Abdelaziz Nihou (Economic Advisor to the Office of the Prime Minister), Driss Ouaouicha (President of Al Akhawayn University), Youssef Saadani (Director of Economic Studies at the Caisse de Dépôt et de Gestion), Nadia Salah (Editorial Director, Groupe Eco-Medias), Marie-Cécile Tardieu (Head of the Economic Unit at the Embassy of France), and Faouzia Zaâboul (Treasury Director at the Ministry of Economy and Finance).

The team also extends heartfelt thanks for the care and attention that the Secretaries General of the different ministries gave to the draft of this book at the presentation of the Executive Summary on June 30, 2016, and then through the series of written comments and constructive suggestions coordinated by the Ministry of General Affairs and Governance and submitted by the Ministry of the Interior; the Ministry of Economy and Finance; the Ministry of Agriculture and Fisheries; the Ministry of National Education and Vocational Training; the Ministry for Higher Education, Scientific Research and Professional Training; the Ministry of Infrastructure, Transport and Logistics; the Ministry of Industry,

Commerce, Investment and Digital Economy; the Ministry of Health; the Ministry of Energy, Mines, Water and Environment; the Ministry for Solidarity, Women, Family and Social Development; the Ministry of Employment and Social Affairs; the Ministry of Public Service and Modernization of the Administration; the High Commission for Planning; and Bank Al-Maghrib.

The book was also greatly enriched by the numerous opportunities during the preparation phase for information sharing with representatives from the government, civil society, and academia. The authors are particularly appreciative of the many organizers of conferences, workshops, and seminars for the opportunity to present the key themes of the book over the past two years. At the beginning of 2014, issues associated with the promotion of an open society for a prosperous and resilient economy were presented (in chronological order) to the Economic, Social and Environmental Council (CESE); the World Bank Country Office during a workshop on the job market; the High Commission for Planning (HCP); the OCP Policy Center; the Rabat School of Governance and Economics (EGE); the Forum de Paris–Casablanca Round; the HEM Business School Research Center (CESEM); a seminar at the Moroccan Parliament House of Councilors; the University Hassan II Casablanca; the French Chamber of Commerce and Industry in Morocco (CFCIM); a conference organized with the Ministry of Economy and Finance on trade openness in Morocco; and the General Confederation of Moroccan Enterprises (CGEM). In the fall of 2014, issues associated with intangible capital were likewise presented to CESE, the International University of Rabat (IUR), the National School of Public Health (ENSP), the Al Akhawayn University in Ifrane, the Association of Women Entrepreneurs in Morocco (AFEM), the OCP Policy Center, the Attijariwafa Bank Foundation, the Moroccan Institute for International Relations (IMRI), the Arab Center for Scientific Research and Humane Studies (CAS-ERH), the Centre Marocain de Conjoncture (CMC), the delegation and member states of the European Union, the international symposium on Morocco's development model organized in Skhirat by the Ministry of Economy and Finance, and during two interministerial meetings organized by the Ministry of General Affairs and Governance in Rabat in June and October 2016.

The authors sincerely appreciate all of the contributions and support received, but in no way suggest that the various experts and institutions consulted are necessarily in agreement with the analysis and findings of the book, for which the authors assume full responsibility.

The book is based on a series of World Bank reports prepared in parallel with it and a series of working papers and notes prepared specifically to inform the book.

Chapters 1 and 2, on Morocco in 2016 and in 2040, respectively, are based on working notes about "La comptabilité de la Croissance au Maroc" and "Les Scénarios de croissance du Maroc à Moyen Terme," prepared by Youssef Saadani, Khalid El Massnaoui, and Jean-Pierre Chauffour and on the working note, "Contribution économique de la surexploitation des eaux souterraines au Maroc," prepared by Rachid M. Doukkali and Johan Grijsen.

Chapter 3, on market support institutions, is based on the working paper, "Un défi décisif pour l'investissement et l'emploi au Maroc : renforcer le cadre institutionnel pour une application équitable des règles entre les acteurs économiques," prepared by Philippe de Méneval and Morgane Breuil; the working paper, "Are Minimum Wages and Payroll Taxes a Constraint to the Creation of Formal Jobs in Morocco?" prepared by Diego F. Angel-Urdinola, Abdoul Gadiry Barry, and Jamal Guennouni; and the report, "Trade and EU Integration: Strengthening Morocco's Competitiveness," prepared by a World Bank team under the oversight of Jean-Pierre Chauffour (World Bank 2013, Report No. AUS4799). This chapter is also based on the working note, "Le haut débit: plate-forme de l'économie numérique et enjeu critique pour le développement du Maroc," prepared by Arthur Foch and Carlo Maria Rossotto.

Chapter 4, on public services and institutions, is based mainly on the working paper, "Etat de Droit, Justice et Capital Immatériel" prepared by Paul Scott Prettitore, Eva Maria Melis, and Jean-Pierre Chauffour and the working paper, "Gouvernance des Services Publics," prepared by Fabian Seiderer, Elisabeth Sandor, and Jean-Pierre Chauffour. This chapter is also based on the working note, "Modernisation de l'administration et réformes de la fonction publique," prepared by Khalid El-Massnaoui and Jean-Pierre Chauffour.

Chapter 5, on human capital, is based on three working papers on (i) "Education," prepared by Kamel Braham, Youssef Saadani, and Jean-Pierre Chauffour; (ii) "Health," prepared by Dorothée Chen, Patrick Mullen, Emre Ozaltin, and Jean-Pierre Chauffour; and (iii) "Early Childhood Development," prepared by Safaa El-Kogali and Caroline Krafft.

Chapter 6, on social capital, is based on the report, "Morocco: Mind the Gap—Empowering Women for a More Open, Inclusive, and Prosperous Society," prepared by Daniela Marotta and Paul Scott Prettitore (World Bank 2015, Report No. 97778) and on the working note, "Nurturing Morocco's Social Capital: Trust, Civic Cooperation, and Association," prepared by Roberto Foa, Andrea Liverani, and Jean-Pierre Chauffour.

About the Author

Jean-Pierre Chauffour is Lead Economist for the Maghreb countries in the Middle East and North Africa Region at the World Bank. Since joining the World Bank in 2007, Mr. Chauffour has held various senior assignments, including Advisor in the International Trade Department and Lead Economist in the Poverty Reduction and Economic Management Network, specializing on issues related to economic competitiveness, regionalism, and economic integration. Prior to joining the World Bank, Mr. Chauffour worked for 15 years at the International Monetary Fund, where he held various positions, including Mission Chief in the African Department and Head of Office and Representative to the World Trade Organization and United Nations in Geneva. He also spent two years in Brussels as a Senior Economist in the Directorate for Economic and Financial Affairs at the European Commission. Over his career, Mr. Chauffour has worked and provided economic policy advice in many emerging countries, most extensively in the Middle East, Africa, and Eastern Europe. His main centers of interest are economic development, macroeconomic management, and economic freedom. He started his career as a macroeconomist with the Paris-based Centre d'Etudes Prospectives et d'Informations Internationales (CEPII).

Mr. Chauffour holds master's degrees in Economics and Money, Banking, and Finance from the Panthéon-Sorbonne University in Paris. He is the author of *The Power of Freedom: Uniting Human Rights and Development* (Cato Institute, 2009) and co-editor of *Preferential Trade Agreement Policies for Development: A Handbook* (World Bank, 2011) and *Trade Finance during the Great Trade Collapse* (World Bank, 2011). His most recent book, on the aftermath of the Arab Spring, is entitled *From Political to Economic Awakening in the Arab World: The Path of Economic Integration* (World Bank, 2013).

Overview

Morocco has made undeniable progress over the past fifteen years not only in the economic and social spheres, but also in the areas of personal freedoms and civil and political rights. These achievements are evident in the country's economic growth performance, increase in wealth, improvements in the population's average standard of living, the eradication of extreme poverty, universal access to primary education, the overall improved access to basic public services, and significant public infrastructure development. These achievements have enabled the Kingdom to launch a process of economic convergence with Southern European countries (France, Italy, Portugal, and Spain).

While many economic indicators are on the right track, one continues to lag: the integration of young people into the society. With roughly only one in two young people between the ages of 25 and 35 years employed in a job that is often informal and insecure, youth employment poses a daunting challenge. Morocco must also contend with the need to meet a less immediate demand that is nonetheless as pressing as the demand for jobs: the desire of young people to quickly attain a standard of living similar to that enjoyed in more developed countries. However, the economic convergence process set in motion since the early 2000s has been slow, particularly compared to the process in other emerging countries that have managed to significantly bridge the gap. Although Morocco's political situation has improved since 2011, the aspirations of Morocco's youth for a better future are ever-present.

In this context, what economic and political economy conditions would enable Morocco to improve growth significantly and sustainably, with a view to creating quality jobs for the greatest number of people and converging more rapidly, over the course of a single generation, toward income and wealth levels in the most advanced countries? This is the question that *Morocco 2040: Emerging by Investing in Intangible Capital* seeks to answer, by beginning with an assessment of Morocco's recent economic performance and its prospects for 2040, and then outlining the economic reforms that could facilitate the achievement of an ambitious, albeit realistic, scenario to double Morocco's current rate of convergence with Southern European countries.

In 2016, the following stylized facts characterized the Moroccan economy:

- The economic and social progress made over the past decade cannot be taken for granted. On the supply side, the major investment effort—primarily made by the central government and state-owned enterprises—has not yet generated significant productivity gains and can hardly be replicated in the coming years without endangering macroeconomic stability. On the demand side, growth has been mainly driven by domestic consumption against a backdrop of increased public, corporate, and household debts.

- Morocco's process of structural transformation reveals three basic trends: difficulty allocating unskilled labor owing to weak industrialization dynamics overall, despite resounding successes in a number of emerging sectors (e.g., automotive, aeronautics, and renewable energies); difficulty allocating skilled labor owing to the slow upgrading of productive structures and, in particular, demand for middle and senior management; and difficulty allocating talent resulting in weak entrepreneurial drive. Poorly structured, small, and largely domestic in nature, Moroccan businesses are not very enterprising or innovative.

Morocco in 2040. Attaining and maintaining a high level of inclusive economic growth and quality job creation over a 25-year period is one of the major political and economic challenges facing Morocco. A review of possible scenarios raises the following salient points:

- Demographic transition, the urbanization of society in the context of decentralization ("advanced regionalization"), and higher levels of education are three structural trends currently at work in society that provide a unique window of opportunity for catch-up growth. In particular, the low dependency ratio (share of under-15s and over-65s in the total population) projected through 2040 is a real demographic windfall.

- However, these structural trends are not enough to trigger a sustainable upturn in growth. To avoid the "middle-income trap," Morocco would need to achieve and, more importantly, sustain for at least one generation higher productivity gains than in the past.

- The scenario that extrapolates the trends observed over the 2000–15 period (strong fixed capital accumulation, modest job creations, and low productivity gains) is based on a capital accumulation dynamic that is hard to sustain from a macroeconomic standpoint: the investment rate cannot continue to grow indefinitely. Without an upturn in productivity gains, growth can only slow. The sluggish economic growth in recent years could be interpreted as a harbinger of this slow convergence scenario.

- Productivity gains are the cornerstone of a robust growth that is viable in the long run and able to improve the well-being and prosperity of Moroccans while strengthening peace and social stability. The accelerated economic convergence scenario assumes a 2 percent increase in total factor productivity per year and an increase in the employment rate of the working age population from 45 percent in 2015 to 55 percent in 2040, driven mainly by an increase in the current persistently and extremely low female employment rate of roughly 23 percent. The cumulative effect of higher productivity and employment rates would be a stronger, sustainable trend growth of at least 4.5 percent per year through 2040.

- Doubling productivity gains to 2 percent per year for several decades is a major challenge as it assumes an overhaul of production structures and substantial efficiency gains. Additional productivity gains will not come solely from new produced capital, but from a greater effort to accumulate more intangible assets, that is, human, institutional, and social capital. Growth in productivity and intangible capital are largely linked and the Moroccan economy's growth path and the people's increased well-being by 2040 will be determined on the basis of these two key variables.

- In refocusing its public policy priorities on the development of its intangible capital, Morocco would naturally adjust its development strategy and improve the governance of its sectoral policies.

What pathways must Morocco take to achieve economic emergence? A sustainable scale-up of total factor productivity cannot come from a single reform, however ambitious it may be. In other words, building Morocco's intangible capital will necessarily take different forms. It must seek to advance a social contract aimed at strengthening institutions, refocusing government action on its sovereign functions, developing human capital, and strengthening social capital with a view to promoting an open society.

Investing in market support institutions:

- Allocate capital more competitively. Important efficiency gains could be achieved by the removal of existing economic distortions. Morocco could act in the following three strategic areas to unlock innovative drive: strengthen competition and tackle rent seeking; better inform and further involve economic players, especially local actors, in the decisions that concern them; and promote a culture change in business and innovation.

- Allocate labor more efficiently and inclusively. Estimates suggest that overhauling the labor code would significantly raise economic participation and employment, especially formal employment for young people and women, and reduce unemployment without jeopardizing wages. The reform could seek to significantly relax labor regulations, improve income security for workers, and strengthen the effectiveness of active labor market policies.

- Increase integration into the global economy and global value chains. Greater integration of Morocco into the global economy would entail an end to the "anti-export bias" that continues to be endemic to the institutions and policies governing Morocco's exchange system, including a more flexible exchange rate regime, the liberalization of capital controls, lower tariff and nontariff barriers to trade, better trade facilitation, and an improved investment regime. The prospect of an ambitious deep and comprehensive free trade agreement (DCFTA) with the European Union and its embedded potential for modernizing Morocco's rules and regulations constitutes a strategic objective with a strong transformational potential for the Moroccan economy.

Investing in public institutions and services:

- Strengthen the rule of law and justice. Morocco should act to implement the new rights enshrined in the 2011 Constitution and the Justice System Reform Charter and introduce the necessary additional relevant provisions to quickly send a strong signal of real change, with a view to improved security of persons and property and improved contract certainty.

- Modernize the civil service. The reform pathways for the civil service generally taken around the world seek to decentralize human resource management responsibilities, empower administrators, increase the flexibility of the recruitment and career development policies, encourage individual and collective performance, and, more generally, streamline the administration. Morocco's priorities would be to decentralize government, reform the civil service by effectively introducing the notions of performance and results into human resources management, reduce the administration's operating costs through a tighter rein on staffing levels and the wage bill, and engage in more general strategic thinking on the very notion of the civil service in the 21st century.

- Improve public service governance. Strengthening public service governance entails putting the user at the center of the system as beneficiary and regulator and, in particular, giving more voice to users, systematically informing and reporting to the public, simplifying and bringing decisions closer to the users, and testing and evaluating new approaches to public service.

Investing in human capital:

- Place education at the heart of development. For the education reform to be effective, it will have to be realistic and selective. It should tackle major constraints in a "shock therapy" approach designed to trigger an "educational miracle," that is, a huge improvement in the Moroccan students' level of education. This would require a complete overhaul of the education system, improved teacher recruitment and training, the adoption of a new brand of public school governance, the development of alternative educational options (charter schools, school vouchers, and home schooling), and the promotion of 21st century skills, in particular through greater use of information and communications technologies in schools.

- Invest in health for better economic health. In support of the government's strategy and with a view to strengthening the other key dimension of human capital, the reform's priority areas should seek to extend medical coverage and adapt health care services, mobilize and improve the allocative efficiency of health care spending for primary health care, and, at the same time, significantly improve health system governance to guarantee the efficiency of the new resources by holding all actors more accountable, remobilizing health care staff, and introducing an integrated health information and management system.

- Develop early childhood care and education. Whether from the point of view of human rights, equal opportunities, or economic efficiency, an effort must be made to ensure that all Moroccan children benefit from improved care and development during early childhood. This calls for major public information activities and awareness-raising campaigns on the importance of early childhood development, improved coordination of government support policies and programs, additional quality investments in pre-primary education, and the provision of more information to parents on responsible parenting, especially with respect to fathers.

Investing in social capital:

- Achieve gender equality. Morocco has a long way to go to improve access to economic opportunities and empowerment for women. Public policies can be designed to both combat gender inequalities and promote economic growth. They could be based on three major pillars: open up economic opportunities for women; encourage women's empowerment, agency, and autonomy; and systematically mainstream gender equality into public policies and continue the process of modernizing the law.

- Encourage greater interpersonal trust. A country has a fairly small range of means available to build its social capital as no one can dictate the general level of trust among people, any more than they can dictate the way people live, relate to one another, and work together. Social capital is a by-product of perpetual or inherited structural factors that are hard to change (geography, history, and culture). Nevertheless, studies have shown that it is possible to raise the level of social capital by ensuring greater respect for and improved application of the rule of law, promoting a sense of civic duty and exemplarity in all decision-making spheres, encouraging engagement in associations and the development of civil society, and supporting a change in attitudes and sociocultural norms through targeted information campaigns.

In its epilogue, the book discusses the political economy conditions that could bring about a new, ambitious reform process. The question discussed is no longer "what should be done" but rather "how it should be done." How can the identified reforms be implemented in ways that significantly improve the social well-being of Moroccans? What are the forces that can foster a superior economic equilibrium and improve social well-being? This generally requires enhancing the understanding and application of "the rules of the game" or adopting and implementing new rules where necessary:

- The book speculates that, even in the absence of changes to "the rules of the game" strictly speaking, informing the actors (enterprises, households, and citizens) of the causes and consequences of the public policies adopted, sharing new concepts and ideas, and discussing the existing rules of the game may shift the equilibrium among the various components of the society and thus engender the desired change in the actors' positions (such as education reform). Increasing the level of knowledge, scaling up accountability and transparency, and encouraging policy evaluation are three mechanisms that enable players to constantly revise their positions.

- Where an improved understanding of the rules of the game is not enough to alter the actors' positions and the equilibrium, the book speculates that two exceptional circumstances would be able to change the rules of the game and promote Morocco's accelerated transition toward a more open society: the swift and thorough implementation of the spirit and principles of the 2011 Constitution and the equally swift and thorough implementation of an ambitious deep and comprehensive free trade agreement (DCFTA) with the European Union.

Table O.1 summarizes the main economic and institutional policy areas that could pave the way for Morocco's economic emergence, based on the analysis in the book. These policies are separated into short-term policies (those that can be immediately executed) and longer-term policies (those that require more preparation or cannot be immediately executed). These recommendations are generically formulated, in accordance with the book's objective, to map out the broad economic policies in the various areas related to intangible capital. To achieve their objectives, the recommendations must also necessarily be refined and deepened through adequate sectoral dialogue.

Table O.1 The Pathways to Emergence

Short-term policies	*Long-term policies*
Strengthen market support institutions	
Capital allocation:	***Capital allocation:***
- *Eliminate government and public enterprise payment arrears* and take the necessary steps to ensure that payment times comply with the legislation to avoid penalizing business cash flow.	- *Promote and ensure the strict separation of public and private interests* to combat conflicts of interest and ensure the good governance of a modern State.
- *Speed up value-added tax (VAT) credit refunds* to reinstate the economic neutrality of VAT.	- *Strengthen fair competition and tackle rent seeking* by increasing the regulatory authorities' autonomy and powers and reducing visible rents (land, approvals, licenses, authorizations, etc.) and invisible rents (regulatory loopholes).
- *Strengthen institutional public policy making and monitoring and evaluation mechanisms,* especially for sector policies, for systematic evaluation of the economic relevance of the different incentives, subsidies, and other tax expenditure.	- *Improve the cost of and access to industrial property* by clarifying, streamlining, and improving the transparency of the regulations and providing a planned, less expensive supply.
- *Strengthen public-private dialogue to better inform and involve economic players upstream in the decisions that concern them* by including local and regional government representatives and the entire private sector (large corporations, small and medium enterprises, very small enterprises, and unincorporated entrepreneurs). In particular, use the decentralization process underway to more effectively include local public and private players in a regionalized approach to economic development.	- *Step up promotion of a business culture change by promoting a culture of entrepreneurship* and innovation in national education and the administration so that private sector development reforms are understood, sustained, and owned.
- Refocus government actions strictly in the public sphere and reconsider its interventions aimed at promoting investment (investment agreements, tax and other incentives, free zones, etc.), and the role and governance of the key public actors financing the economy (Caisse de dépôt et de gestion, Hassan II Fund, etc.).	- *Encourage the development of the Casablanca stock exchange* as an alternative business finance instrument to the banking system. Assist the modernization of business accounting and the development of popular shareholding.
Labor allocation:	***Labor allocation:***
- *Improve the governance, effectiveness, and efficiency of the employment and skills promotion policies* with the adoption of output-based monitoring and evaluation systems; the outsourcing of employment and training services on program contracts; and the inclusion of the unskilled population in the active labor market policies according to demand and the current and foreseeable needs of the private sector.	- *Increase labor market flexibility by adapting the labor code* to the needs of a changing economy, including hiring and firing conditions, working hours, remuneration of overtime, etc.
- *Introduce minimum wage plans suited to regional and sector particularities* in order to attract low-productivity workers to the formal sector and provide them with social security coverage.	- *Improve social security financing transparency and efficiency* to free up fiscal space to be able to finance a universal unemployment benefit system, improve worker protection, and facilitate the mobility of labor.

table continues next page

Table O.1 The Pathways to Emergence (continued)

Short-term policies	Long-term policies
International integration:	**International integration:**
- *Adopt a flexible exchange rate system* to enable the dirham to achieve its market-clearing price.	- *Continue to relax currency controls to guarantee the dirham's full convertibility* and increase Morocco's attractiveness to investors and international operators.
- *Lower tariff and nontariff trade barriers* by launching a new plan to reduce and bind most-favored nation tariffs, by reducing the number of tariff lines for which the applied rates continue to exceed Morocco's bound rates, and by gradually aligning customs duties for all partners.	- *Gradually liberalize agricultural trade,* which remains protected behind quotas and high customs duties, and rationalize nontariff measures and their related procedures.
- *Facilitate trade* by improving commercial import-export logistics, clarifying and automating procedures, and improving regional connectivity, especially for maritime freight.	- *Negotiate an ambitious deep and comprehensive free trade agreement (DCFTA) with the European Union* to promote greater freedom of movement of goods, services, capital, and persons and hence better position Morocco on the European Single Market and in worldwide competition, including by means of improving the integration of Morocco into the global value chains.
- *Reform the investment regime* by phasing out certain restrictions on foreign ownership of capital in some sectors (transport services, insurance, professional services, etc.) while ensuring that the incentives used to attract foreign investors do not prevent local integration.	
Strengthen institutions and public services	
Rule of law and justice:	**Rule of law and justice:**
- *Fully implement the new rights* provided for by the Constitution and the Justice System Reform Charter.	- *Improve the justice system,* in particular to guarantee procedural fairness (individuals' fundamental rights and security of person) and fair criminal justice (impartiality and corruption control).
- *Guarantee the protection of contracts,* particularly by streamlining performance procedures and processes, including improving the settlement of disputes with the administration (redress and judgment lead time and enforcement time) and encouragement to go to arbitration.	- *Improve security of private property* by passing a single property law, encouraging the registration of land transactions with the land registry, guaranteeing the protection of land rights, and clarifying the expropriation system, including its transparency.
Public administration:	**Public administration:**
- *Reform the administration's human resources management* by effectively introducing the notions of competence, performance, and outcomes as core elements in the central and local government employee hiring, management, and promotion process.	- *Reduce operating costs and improve the administration's efficiency* ("value-for-money") with the diligent implementation of the new Budget Framework Law (LOLF) to control staffing levels and the wage bill, assign line ministries the management of their personnel appropriations, and redeploy administrative staff under the advanced regionalization process in keeping with local staffing needs.
- *Embark upon the advanced regionalization process* by systematically deconcentrating decisions and organizing a real, gradual transfer of decision-making powers and resources and means corresponding to the appropriate local and regional levels (subsidiary principle).	- *Adapt the civil service regulations to the standards of good management and governance practices,* in the context of across-the-board modernization of the administration based on advanced regionalization and the redefinition of the different government levels' strategic missions, the development of delegated management services in partnership with the private sector, and shared cross-cutting administrative services.

table continues next page

Table O.1 The Pathways to Emergence (continued)

Short-term policies	Long-term policies

Public service governance:

- *Improve civil participation in public management* by implementing new constitutional rights (petitions, legislative motions, public consultations, etc.) and introducing a full user grievance filing and management system.

- *Improve the administration's internal and external local and national transparency and accountability,* with the effective implementation of the access to information reform, the new performance-based budgetary reform, the development of e-administration, and anticorruption measures.

Public service governance:

- *Effectively implement the decentralization/deconcentration process as part of advanced regionalization,* by transferring new competencies under contract, overhauling the transfer and equalization system, deploying the necessary technical and human resources, and setting up a local service performance monitoring and evaluation system.

Strengthen human capital

Education:

- *Revise the curriculums and teaching methods* for the school to convey positive, open values, guarantee the learning of basic skills, and encourage vocational training with real employment prospects.

- *Improve teacher recruitment, training, motivation, and assessment* in order to attract competent applicants with strong potential to the teaching profession and develop suitable evaluation and coaching systems to improve the performance of working teachers.

- *Continue to develop the use of information and communications technologies (ICTs)* at school to facilitate and evaluate the learning of basic skills, aid teacher training, and support the sound management of establishments.

Education:

- *Adopt a new brand of public school governance* by refocusing it on providing better service to students, mainly with (i) a review of all the education system players' roles, responsibilities, and regulations governing their positions; (ii) learning evaluations and the dissemination of these evaluations for greater player responsibility and the promotion of quality; and (iii) the involvement of students' parents, especially fathers, in school life.

- *Develop alternative educational options* entirely consistent with the government's mission to provide quality education for all children while promoting freedom of choice and innovation (charter schools, school vouchers, etc.).

- *Develop "21st century skills" in education* (collaboration, communication, social and cultural dexterity, a sense of civic duty, and ICTs) and develop creativity, critical thinking, and adaptability.

Health:

- *Improve health system governance,* and put patient needs back at the heart of the system, by giving responsibilities to all players, ensuring compliance with the rule of law and discipline in health establishments, remotivating health personnel, and creating an integrated health information and management system.

- *Extend and harmonize universal medical coverage and adapt health care services* in the context of a coherent overall vision to facilitate access to basic care for all, avoiding having to deal with the catastrophic financial consequences of diseases.

Health:

- *Improve allocative efficiency* by investing specifically in primary health care establishments, successfully reforming results-based programmatic budgeting, developing prevention and early detection programs for noncommunicable diseases, and developing mobile health services, in particular for disadvantaged and isolated populations.

table continues next page

Table O.1 The Pathways to Emergence *(continued)*

Short-term policies	*Long-term policies*
Early childhood:	*Early childhood:*
- *Conduct public information and awareness campaigns on the importance of early childhood development*, and address early childhood care as an important public health issue (postnatal care, immunization, nutrition, etc.).	- *Involve parents and families, especially fathers, and raise their awareness of the importance of their active, positive participation in early childhood development and care*, by means of parental stimulation and attention, among others.
- *Establish a central body in charge of early childhood development matters*, which will be tasked with defining the country's vision and objectives, developing a strategy to meet these objectives, and evaluating progress made.	- *Scale up quality public early childhood policies and investment* in association with the private sector as service provider for the implementation of certain policies (e.g., preschool education, immunization campaigns, etc.).

Strengthen social capital

Gender equality:	*Gender equality:*
- *Grant women precisely the same civil rights as men* in matters of inheritance, marriage (with non-Muslims), descent, divorce, and other civil code provisions.	- *Open up economic opportunities for women* by lifting the obstacles to their labor market participation and supporting female entrepreneurship.
- Systematically mainstream gender in all public policy making and implementation to effectively achieve gender equality on the ground.	- *Encourage women's empowerment and autonomy* with awareness-raising campaigns to reduce the gender gap in terms of voice and agency in the household and society in general and encourage greater political participation by women.
	- Continue modernizing the laws and encouraging a shift in attitudes and sociocultural norms, with a view to bringing about real gender equality in the society.
Interpersonal trust:	*Interpersonal trust:*
- *Improve respect for the rule of law and promote a sense of civic duty and exemplary behavior* in all spheres of government, including increasing sanctions for deviant, illegal, or uncivil behavior in order to strengthen the values of integrity, honesty, and justice in society.	- *Launch awareness-raising campaigns to encourage a shift in attitudes and sociocultural norms* toward values of freedom, collaboration, mutual respect, and a sense of civic and civil duty, and teach these values in the school curriculum.
- *Put in place suitable public policies to encourage all forms of civic and civil engagement*, especially in associations, and refrain from taking measures liable to hinder voluntary engagement in civil society (social networks, associations, media).	

A Youth in Search of Opportunities

"Any society that does not succeed in tapping into the energy and creativity of its youth will be left behind."

— Kofi Annan

Morocco has made undeniable progress over the past 15 years not only in the economic and social spheres but also in the areas of personal freedoms and civil and political rights. Since the late 1990s, Morocco has increased its growth rate after two decades of relatively weak growth, virtually doubling its per capita gross domestic product (GDP) and initiating the process to narrow the standard-of-living gap with Southern European countries. The resulting economic growth has also led to an increase in the country's total wealth and to major social achievements, with the eradication of extreme poverty, a sharp decline in the national poverty rate, increased life expectancy, and greater access to basic public services, including universal access to primary education and significant public infrastructure development (water, electricity, and transport). Based on these improvements, Morocco's per capita income grew at a more rapid pace in the early 2000s, after the implementation of several major institutional reforms aimed at opening up the society.

With respect to personal freedoms and civil and political rights, constitutional amendments in 1992 and 1996 initiated a process to democratize and modernize public institutions by establishing more representative institutions, while recognizing new economic freedoms such as freedom of enterprise. After these constitutional amendments and the fillip given to the reforms by His Majesty King Mohammed VI upon his accession to the throne in 1999, bold reforms and new laws were adopted to gradually liberalize and open up the economy, privatize a number of public enterprises, restructure the financial system, strengthen public governance and the rule of law, and guarantee a growing number of fundamental human rights. With the creation of the Equity and Reconciliation Commission in 2004, transitional justice became the instrument for establishing truth and providing redress for past injustices and human rights violations. Women's rights were significantly strengthened with the widely hailed revision of the Family Code (*Moudawana*) in 2004. These changes reflect numerous lessons and hold great promise, in view of the institutional changes made after the constitutional amendments in 2011.

With these accomplishments made, Morocco aims at achieving the status of upper-middle income country in the not too distant future and accelerating its economic convergence with developed countries. To that end, major infrastructure projects have been and are being executed, including the Tanger-Med port, the highway network, and a series of ambitious sectoral strategies covering all sectors of the economy: agriculture and fishing, energy and mining, construction and public works, manufacturing industries, and services, in particular tourism and information and communications technologies. An ecosystem network comprising integrated industrial projects is emerging around the development of phosphate mining, agribusiness, and the pharmaceutical, automotive and aeronautical industries, and other new global business lines in Morocco. Morocco's automotive industry and the Renault Group assembled close to 345,000 cars in 2016, with the next target set at 400,000 cars. In early 2016, Morocco opened the world's largest thermodynamic solar plant and has set a target of generating more than 52 percent of its energy from renewable sources by 2030. Morocco will open the first high-speed train line on the African continent in 2017 and, in 2018, the Tanger-Med port will become the largest maritime transit hub in the Mediterranean and Africa once expansion works have been completed. The ongoing establishment of the Peugeot-Citroën auto manufacturer is expected to result in the production of 90,000 engines and vehicles by 2019 before reaching the ultimate target of 200,000, thereby strengthening Morocco's position in the global automobile manufacturing industry. Morocco's goal is to rank among the world's top 20 tourist destinations with 20 million visitors by 2020. Other examples of impressive success stories and ambitious projects can be cited. In sum, Morocco has been in many respects an outlier over the past 15 years in a region of the world beset by extremely difficult political, economic, and social problems.

As these, and other, impressive success stories illustrate, many economic indicators are on the right track; however, one important indicator—the integration of young people into the society—has remained a major source of concern. The opportunities provided to young people, as well as their participation in their country's economic and social life, are one of the best indicators for evaluating the level of social cohesion in a country. In Morocco, the issue of youth employment has a quantitative dimension in the short term and a more qualitative dimension in the medium term:[1]

- In Morocco where roughly only one in two young persons between the ages of 25 and 35 has a job that is often informal and insecure, youth employment poses a daunting, short-term challenge to the future of the society. Indeed, employment conditions the achievement of other essential economic and social goals in the country: to reduce poverty and inequalities; boost individual well-being; increase the size of the middle class; promote gender equality; provide sustainable financing of community support mechanisms; and strengthen social peace.

• Morocco must also contend with the need to meet a less immediate demand that is nonetheless as pressing as the demand for jobs: the desire of young people to secure better quality jobs to enable them to attain a standard of living that can more quickly approximate the standard enjoyed in more developed countries. Even where their material circumstances have improved, young people may experience feelings of deprivation and injustice whenever they compare themselves with other reference groups or whenever public policies, particularly with respect to employment, are not in line with their expectations (Serajuddin and Verme 2012). Although Morocco's political situation has evolved greatly since 2011, the aspirations of Morocco's youth for a better future are ever-present.

Beyond these concerns—and the technical reforms needed to address them—lies the core issue of strengthening Morocco's social contract. How can the often proactive public policies translate into a much larger number of jobs that are better paying and more equitably distributed? The country's future lies in the hands of its youth—a youth that is more skilled, urbanized, and connected to the rest of the world. However, beyond the undeniable progress achieved in Morocco in recent years, in particular relative to the other countries in the region, do Moroccan youth possess the necessary skills, particularly with respect to training, to meet the challenges of the knowledge economy in an increasingly globalized society? Education is generally viewed as the top priority to be addressed for the development of Morocco (see figure I.1). Looking forward, some of Morocco's youth feel a sense of hopelessness, and many young people seek opportunities abroad to join the roughly 4.5 million Moroccans officially residing in other countries. The 2012–14 Arab Barometer showed that more than 28 percent of the Moroccan men and women surveyed are considering emigrating, primarily for economic reasons.

In view of Morocco's economic goals, international experience shows that countries rarely transition from middle-income to high-income country status, and those that have achieved this goal have often done so with tremendous effort and sacrifice.[2] The report issued by the Commission on Growth and Development noted that only 13 countries have achieved and were able to maintain an annual growth rate of 7 percent or more over a period of more than 25 years since 1950 (Commission on Growth and Development 2008).[3] Following a generally encouraging phase of rapid development and modernization of basic infrastructure, growth in scores of developing countries has now hit a "glass ceiling"; in other words, they are contending with development limitations that are largely invisible and relate to intangible assets. Thus, despite often considerable effort, public policies struggle to create adequate conditions conducive to economic convergence. Undeniable success in industry cannot obscure the difficulty of providing

Figure I.1 What Are Morocco's General Issues and Development Priorities?

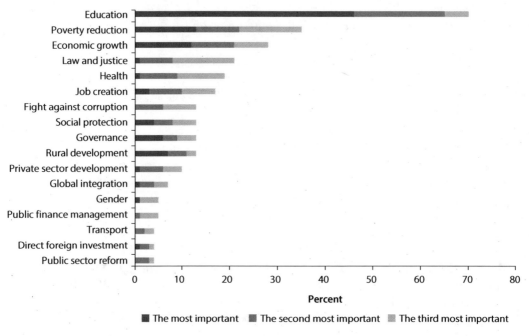

Percent

■ The most important   ■ The second most important   ▨ The third most important

Source: World Bank 2014.

greater opportunities for young people. An overly slow structural transformation of the economy is preventing this sector from absorbing the more rapid increase in college graduates. The society's institutions and organization are not evolving at a sufficiently rapid pace to create new incentives to drive sustainable development and create wealth. Urbanization is progressing without creating industrial sectors or high value-added services, a process that has been dubbed "modernization without development" (Fukuyama 2014).

In light of these international experiences, what obstacles must Morocco overcome to ensure that the groundwork laid for the economic convergence process underway in the country paves the way for sustainable accelerated economic convergence? What economic and political economy conditions would enable Morocco to significantly and sustainably increase growth, create quality jobs for the greatest number of people, and more quickly achieve the income and wealth levels of the most advanced countries? In order to identify the possible pathways for this option, *Morocco 2040: Investing in Intangible Capital to Accelerate Economic Emergence* is divided into two parts.

Part I assesses Morocco's economic and social performance over the past 15 years before looking ahead to 2040, that is, the next generation. It examines the conditions that could double Morocco's current rate of convergence with Southern European (France, Italy, Portugal, and Spain) and upper-middle-income countries (mainly the emerging economies in Southeast Asia, Africa, and Latin America).[4] It aims to answer such key questions as the following: Has economic growth in Morocco over the past 15 years created national wealth, or has it occurred to the detriment of the environment? Has it led to a reduction in poverty and inequalities? What has been the rate of convergence with developed countries in terms of economic and social indicators? Is the development model that has been followed over this period sustainable or is it beginning to sputter? Is this a model adapted to spurring a rapid structural transformation in a period marked by globalization markets, economic liberalization, and increased technology transfers? What main economic challenges must be tackled by 2040 in order to meet the expectations of Moroccan youth, particularly with respect to jobs and well-being? During this process, can Morocco benefit from windfall effects and opportunities, owing in particular to its demographic transition? What would be the economic characteristics of an accelerated convergence scenario and the implications of this scenario for the development model currently being followed by Morocco?

Part II examines the economic policies that would help make the virtuous scenario of accelerated economic convergence by 2040 a reality. As will be discussed later, this scenario requires a sustained increase in productivity in Morocco through greater accumulation of its intangible capital, which relates to the quality of the institutions, the development of human capital, and the quality of social capital in countries. World Bank reports on the wealth of nations note that economic growth that is sustainable and environmentally friendly is first and foremost composed of intangible capital accumulation (World Bank 2006, 2011). The "glass ceiling" hindering progress in nations would primarily be composed of intangible capital that is largely invisible and not easily quantifiable, such as governance, knowledge, or trust. Looking at ways to grow Morocco's intangible capital, the second part of the book seeks to answer the following questions: What measures should Morocco adopt to enable institutions supporting the market to allocate jobs and capital in a more efficient manner and ensure a more effective integration of the country into the global economy? What conditions are required to ensure that more efficient institutions and public services will help strengthen justice and the rule of law, boost the government's productivity, and improve access to and the quality of public services? How can the education and health systems and early childhood care be reformed to promote a significant boost in human capital? And lastly, how can Morocco's social capital (which underpins growth in all the other areas) be strengthened as a result of greater gender equality, increased interpersonal trust, and a stronger sense of civic duty and general interest within the society? The book therefore seeks to provide ways to address the question raised by His Majesty King Mohammed VI, in his Throne Speech of July 2014, regarding the manner in which intangible capital could become the "fundamental criterion in the development of public policies so that all Moroccans may benefit from their country's wealth."

It is important to call attention to the statistics on access by youth to jobs and economic opportunities prior to undertaking this analysis. At present, there are approximately 600,000 Moroccans aged 20 years. Close to 400,000 persons, or two thirds of this age group, have not passed the baccalaureate exam and will be low-skilled, with no great prospects for securing a decent job. It is projected that of the 200,000 young people with a high school diploma, only 50,000 will receive adequate training to secure a job in line with their expectations, while roughly 140,000 will acquire skills that have little value in the labor market. A mere 10,000 young people—less than 2 percent of the age group—will earn highly skilled degrees, thus guaranteeing attractive job and salary prospects.

In light of these statistics and the theme of this book on the economic emergence of Morocco, particular attention must be paid to the specific constraints facing four groups of young people in realizing their potential and thus making a significant contribution to efforts to boost the country's productivity. These young people have been grouped according to their qualifications and are represented through the stories of four typical individuals: Amine (young and unskilled), Nisrine (young and low-skilled), Kawtar (young and skilled), and Réda (young and highly skilled).[5] In the case of each group, there are, of course, countless other young Moroccan men and women who, irrespective of their level of education, excel in their respective field, realizing their full potential and making a major contribution to the country's value added through their work, creativity, entrepreneurial spirit, and so forth. Numerous other young people are nevertheless wrestling with major constraints and challenges in securing a job and living up to their potential to contribute to the country's economic development. These young people are the subject of this book. Understanding the source of their challenges, as well as their aspirations and frustrations, will be the first step toward finding possible solutions. This is the starting point for this book.

Amine: Young and Unskilled

Amine was born in Bouarfa, a small city in eastern Morocco, in one of the country's poorest provinces. He is the sixth child of a family of small farmers. Raised in his grandparents' house, without access to running water and latrines—the case of more than 60 percent and 15 percent, respectively, of the homes in rural areas—Amine's brothers and sisters taught him, from a very early age, the daily chores to be done to help his family, both at home and in the field.

Amine was one of the beneficiaries of the universal education policy implemented in the 1990s. Through the Tayssir program, he attended the local public school (five kilometers away). However, Amine was not really able to acquire a basic foundation in either written Arabic or French. His teacher, a young graduate who had just come from Oujda (a big city in northeastern Morocco), had no experience or training in adapted pedagogy and almost immediately found it difficult to perform his job of teaching Arabic, French, and math to students at two different scholastic levels who were put in the same class. As was the case with his brothers and sisters, Amine had no hope of overcoming the deficiencies of the public school through academic help at home, as his parents and grandparents were illiterate—a situation that applies to almost one-half of the

Moroccan rural population. In fact, no one in Amine's milieu was really interested in his education. Once his primary education ended, Amine attended secondary school in the nearby village, but the time spent traveling back and forth each day, which was even longer, combined with a feeling of failure, led him to drop out after the first year. Amine therefore joined the ranks of the 250,000 Moroccan youth who drop out of school every year without obtaining the baccalaureate.

Pushed by his parents to find a job, Amine first worked in seasonal farming and transporting merchandise at markets. However, scarce and low-paying agricultural jobs in the Bouarfa area prompted him to seek employment in Oujda and, in so doing, to join Morocco's rural exodus. Expecting to find formal employment in a factory (Amine had, for several years, heard about the country's industrial development), the young man clung to the hope of finally having a stable income and was thinking of starting a family. However, Amine soon realized that industrial companies were few and far between, did little hiring, and when they did hire, the workers were generally qualified, having obtained a baccalaureate. What Amine did not know was that industry jobs, which have never existed in large numbers in Morocco, have been on the decline for several decades and that the odds of someone with his background becoming a non-agricultural employee were a mere 1.9 percent. Amine therefore settled for odd jobs in the service industry (street vendor, parking attendant, etc.), as do more than 25 percent of the unskilled workers in urban areas. After four years of eking out a living, Amine now works on a construction site. Like the other workers, he lives on the site and manages to save some money. Discussions with his coworkers have led him to buy into the dream of a better life on the other side of the Mediterranean and he yearns to move to Europe.

Nisrine: Young and Low-Skilled

Nisrine was born in Beni-Mellal, a city with close to 500,000 residents located between the Middle Atlas and the Tadla Plain, along the highway to the imperial cities of Fez and Marrakesh. She lives with her four brothers and sisters in a working class neighborhood where her parents are clerical workers. Because she is the oldest child, Nisrine's parents have had high hopes for her since she was very young and dream of her becoming the first in the family to pursue higher education studies and then join the civil service. Knowing that the quality of instruction in the neighborhood public school was substandard, they had for some time considered enrolling Nisrine in a private school with a better reputation. In this regard, they are similar to a large number of Moroccan parents who have lost confidence in the public school system. However, without financial assistance, her parents could not continue to pay for her schooling. They nonetheless decided to pay for the private tutoring strongly recommended by her teachers. Nisrine did not pursue any extracurricular activities—neither in sports nor in the artistic or cultural fields—and there were no prominent Moroccan personalities to nurture the dreams of this young girl. After passing her baccalaureate at the makeup exam, Nisrine automatically enrolled in the law faculty of the university, along with hundreds of others who had passed this exam. Nisrine had randomly chosen this faculty as she had never met with an academic adviser—as was the case with 60 percent of Moroccan high school students—to help her develop her program of study. She nonetheless completed her university studies, unlike two thirds of the students at Moroccan universities who drop out before obtaining their degree.

Although she is hard-working and diligent, Nisrine acquired few skills during her lengthy course of studies. She lacks sound mastery of both Arabic and French, in particular. In the French placement test administered by the faculty, she obtained a beginner's score (based on the European language standard), although she had received weekly instruction in this language for 10 years as part of her formal education curriculum. Her performance was comparable to that of 70 percent of her university peers who obtain a similar or lower score. Her linguistic deficiencies pose a major obstacle to her future professional life. Nisrine's dream of joining the civil service and moving up the social ladder relative to her parents was shattered when she found that the doors of the labor market were closed. Unemployed, Nisrine joined the ranks of the 300,000 university graduates in the country seeking jobs. After an unsuccessful three-year job search, Nisrine came to realize that her university degree by itself had little value. While helping her younger brothers and sisters with their homework, she was alarmed to see that the quality of instruction had further deteriorated over time.

Nisrine decided to pay for additional training in office management and, as a result, was able to obtain a small job in a stationery shop where she works in customer relations. As is the case with four in five Moroccan workers, she has no health insurance. She has not, however, abandoned her goal of joining the civil service and has registered for a number of entrance examinations. To her, the private sector is synonymous with uncertainty, insecurity, and social instability. In fact, only the civil service offers a job for life, automatic promotions, health insurance, a pension, and access to housing loans. If she fails the entrance exam, she will likely drop out of the labor force and join the roughly 85 percent of urban women who are inactive.

Kawtar: Young and Skilled

Kawtar was born in Rabat, the capital of Morocco, into an upper-middle-class family. The daughter of two civil servants, she is the youngest of three children. Her college-educated, bilingual, and open-minded parents have always made it a priority to give their children the best possible future. Beginning with kindergarten, they chose the private school route to ensure that their three children could receive an excellent education. To afford this, Kawtar's parents made great financial sacrifices. They are members of the Moroccan middle class who find it very difficult to move ahead and who assume some debt because of deficient public services. Their sacrifices were not limited to the academic realm. Convinced that their children's future also depends on their physical, emotional, and interpersonal development, they enrolled Kawtar, at a very young age, in the swimming center, the music school, and the American cultural center. When Kawtar passed her baccalaureate examination with distinction, she was fluent in French and Arabic. She was also quite mature and responsible. Kawtar would have liked to pursue higher education management studies in Europe or the United States, but she knew that this dream was not immediately attainable. She did, however, pass the admission exam to study at a competitive, prestigious business school in Morocco, where instruction is bilingual. At the end of her highly successful course of studies, Kawtar was awarded a Master's degree in strategic marketing. She is among the 10 percent of her peers who have no reason to be concerned about the future, as the employment rate among graduates from competitive, prestigious Moroccan universities stands at 80 percent.

Talented, skilled, and passionate about her specialty, Kawtar expected to find a job easily, particularly given the number of foreign companies operating in Morocco. Unfortunately, despite having many job interviews, nothing panned out, although she was fairly satisfied with her performance. She was told either that she was overqualified or that she did not have experience. Very few managerial staff are hired in Morocco (roughly seven percent of total employment) and, unlike in other emerging countries, demand in this area is not increasing rapidly in Morocco. As she was having trouble finding a job commensurate with her education, Kawtar started to be plagued by doubt. Even though she could get a job in the civil service, that has never been her aspiration. Kawtar enjoys being challenged, using her creativity, and working in a team environment. While waiting for a better position, she decided to start a career as a customer adviser at a call center. Although she felt that she was overqualified for the call center position, Kawtar took the job because she felt obligated to her parents. She yearned to be successful in order to make sure that their sacrifices paid off. After spending a year at the call center, she finally landed a job as a teacher at a private, fairly well-regarded management school.

Réda: Young and Highly Skilled

Réda was born in Casablanca into an affluent, Moroccan bourgeois family. His father is a businessman and his mother, a physician. Réda grew up with his younger sister in a comfortable and supportive family environment and benefited from the nurturing provided by his parents and their significant financial resources. Réda's instruction—from kindergarten to the time he obtained his baccalaureate—was in a foreign education system. When he successfully completed this portion of his education, Réda was completely fluent in French, English, and Arabic and had acquired a solid skill set, from both an academic and social standpoint. While pursuing his studies, Réda played tennis, his favorite sport, with his friends, and was involved in many other activities. Réda and his friends lived a life that was very different from the vast majority of young Moroccans. They lived in a sort of parallel world. For example, Réda has never used public transportation, nor has he ever gone to a public hospital. As is the case with most Moroccan students who hold a foreign baccalaureate, Réda pursued his higher education studies outside Morocco. In his case, his family paid for his engineering studies in France at a competitive, prestigious university.

After obtaining his degree, Réda was immediately hired by a French chemical multinational company to conduct research in its research and development (R&D) department. With five years of international professional experience under his belt, Réda decided to return to Morocco to use the expertise he had gained abroad to benefit his country (Hamdouch and Wahba 2012). Given his profile and his country's needs, Réda naturally thought that he could make the biggest contribution at a university or in the R&D department of a major Moroccan company (Gibson and McKenzie 2011). Unfortunately, his plans did not come to fruition as academic research programs and structures are not attractive. On the enterprise side, Réda quickly realized that R&D and innovative functions were underdeveloped in major Moroccan companies. Only 300 patent applications are filed in Morocco every year—fewer than 10 patents per one million residents, with barely 50 being filed by private enterprises. By way of comparison, five to six times more patent applications per capita are filed in Romania and Turkey.

Réda then decided to start his own business with a foreign partner. He then faced another problem, the scope of which was unknown to him—a difficult bureaucracy and business environment. Despite the progress made by Morocco in improving a number of business environment indicators, the situation on the ground seemed to him to be quite different in terms of starting a business— obtaining authorizations, securing loans, and, in general, interacting with a government that did not seem supportive of start-ups. After abandoning the idea of becoming an entrepreneur, Réda joined his fellow graduates at a major Moroccan public consortium where he is well paid, has a job for life, and enjoys other benefits provided to public servants and employees.

Amine, Nisrine, Kawtar, and Réda

Taking into account their socioeconomic backgrounds and personal and family histories, the future will, without a doubt, be different for Amine, Nisrine, Kawtar, and Réda. Their experiences are representative of those of many of their peers and illustrate the multidimensional nature of Morocco's social disparities. While they will not know each other, they nonetheless face the same reality—problems finding a job commensurate with their potential and aspirations and, more generally, achieving upward mobility in society based on their work and merit. The factors underlying these challenges are clearly not the same for Amine, an unskilled young man, and Réda, a highly skilled young man. In fact, as will be discussed in detail below, the difficulties faced by many young people in securing a job illustrate the major obstacles to more rapid economic development in Morocco:

• The small industrial base and its inability to offer opportunities to unskilled young people from rural areas, hundreds of thousands of whom are pouring into the labor market every year.

- The poor quality of instruction, in particular inadequate mastery of languages, limited reasoning skills and independent decision-making capacity, and degrees that are not aligned with the needs of the labor market.
- Weak business demand for expertise and relatively slow pace of structural change in Moroccan industries, which is preventing this sector from absorbing the more rapid increase in university graduates.
- A system of incentives that stifles a vast pool of business talent, knowledge transfer, and wealth creation and thus stymies the improvement of the Moroccan economy.

There is the risk that a significant share of Morocco's youth may feel excluded from the current social contract. They are plagued by a sense of hopelessness, which is primarily reflected in the desire to leave Morocco and try their luck abroad. According to a European Training Foundation survey, 59 percent of young Moroccans between the ages of 18 and 29 would like to leave Morocco, with a large percentage of this group wanting to do so permanently. The job prospects for Amine, Nisrine, Kawtar, and Réda, as well as the numerous other challenges faced by the four groups of young people they represent, are directly tied to the Moroccan society's ability to come up with robust, relevant, and long-term solutions to these problems. The book is aimed at contributing to this process of reflection by proposing a framework for ambitious but realistic policies that allow for the participation of young Moroccan men and women who are currently faced with the risks of an insufficiently productive future to participate more fully in the development of their country.

Notes

1. For an in-depth analysis of the challenges facing young Moroccan men and women in the labor market and in their civic life, see the World Bank report (2012) titled "Kingdom of Morocco: Promoting Youth Opportunities and Participation."

2. For example, Landes (1998) believes that one aspect of the edifying success story of Japan's rapid industrialization in the post – World War II era that has received little attention from historians is the pain and labor that made it possible. The Japanese economic miracle was not primarily due to the efforts of the powerful Ministry of International Trade and Industry (MITI); it was the result of a work ethic, personal values, and the collective virtues of a society with abundant social capital.

3. These economies are Botswana; Brazil; China; Hong Kong SAR, China; Indonesia; Japan; the Republic of Korea; Malaysia; Malta; Oman; Singapore; Taiwan, China; and Thailand. Two other countries—India and Vietnam—were on track to join this group.

4. These two groups of comparator countries will be used throughout the book.

5. These profiles are based on various workshops, focus groups, and other consultations conducted by the World Bank with youth and women and in regions over the past few years.

References

Arab Barometer. 2017. "Morocco Five Years after the Arab Uprisings. Findings from the Arab Barometer." http://www.arabbarometer.org/.

Commission on Growth and Development. 2008. *The Growth Report: Strategies for Sustained Growth and Inclusive Development*. Washington, DC: World Bank.

Fondation européenne pour la formation et association marocaine d'études et de recherches sur les migrations. 2013. "Migration et compétences au Maroc, résultats de l'enquête 2011–2012 sur la migration et le lien entre compétences, migration et développement."

Fukuyama, Francis. 2014. *Political Order and Political Decay: From the Industrial Revolution to the Globalization of Democracy*. New York: Farrar, Straus and Giroux.

Gibson, John, and David McKenzie. 2011. "The Microeconomic Determinants of Emigration and Return Migration of the Best and Brightest." *Journal of Development Economics* 95: 18–29.

Hamdouch, Bachir, and Jackline Wahba. 2012. "Return Migration and Entrepreneurship in Morocco." Working Paper No. 666, Economic Research Forum, Giza, Egypt.

High Commission for Planning (HCP). 2009. "Les résidents étrangers au Maroc: Profil démographique et socioéconomique." Morocco.

———. 2015a. "Recensement général de la population et de l'habitat 2014." Morocco.

———. 2015b. "Activité, emploi et chômage, premiers résultats (annuel) 2014." Morocco.

Landes, David S. 1998. *The Wealth and Poverty of Nations: Why Some Are So Rich and Some So Poor*. New York: Norton.

LMS-CSA. 2014. "Enquête sur l'orientation des lycéens marocains."

Serajuddin, Umar, and Paolo Verme. 2012. "Who Is Deprived? Who Feels Deprived? Labor Deprivation, Youth, and Gender in Morocco." Policy Research Working Paper No. 6090, World Bank, Washington, DC.

World Bank. 2006. *Where Is the Wealth of Nations?* Washington, DC: World Bank.

———. 2011. *The Changing Wealth of Nations*. Washington, DC: World Bank.

———. 2012. "Kingdom of Morocco: Promoting Youth Opportunities and Participation." Report No. 68731–MOR, World Bank, Washington, DC.

———. 2014. "Morocco Country Opinion Survey Report (July 2012–June 2013)." Country Opinion Survey (COS) Program. World Bank, Washington, DC.

PART I

Morocco Today and Tomorrow

"The past resembles the future more than one drop of water another."
— Ibn Khaldoun

"The transition from the closed to the open society can be described as one of the deepest revolutions through which mankind has passed."
— Karl R. Popper

CHAPTER 1

Morocco in 2016

"One of the great mistakes is to judge policies and programs by their intentions rather than their results."

— Milton Friedman

Following the "lost" decade of the 1990s, Morocco embarked upon a relatively resilient economic catch-up process in the early 2000s. This brought an upturn in economic growth, a significant rise in income and wealth per capita, and a marked reduction in poverty. However, aside from Morocco's position in the Middle East and North Africa region, the Moroccan economy's convergence toward the Southern European countries and high-income emerging countries has remained largely incomplete in terms of both economic achievements and social progress. Moreover, the growth slowdown of recent years raises the question as to the viability of the growth model of the 2000s. Despite the government's efforts, especially in investment, in 2015 Morocco's structural transformation remained weak.

The Start of Economic and Social Convergence

Morocco has made considerable progress with economic and social development over the past 15 years. This progress set in motion a process of economic transformation, making Morocco one of the leading reforming countries in the Middle East and North Africa region. Morocco has the advantage of its strategic position: located between the European Union and Sub-Saharan Africa, it has Mediterranean roots and a long Atlantic coastline and is firmly embedded in the Arab world. Successive governments have engaged in relatively sound macroeconomic management, gradually opened up trade with regional and global partners, and launched an ambitious legal, political, and institutional modernization process with substantial political, economic, and social dimensions. Higher steady growth rates have significantly increased the country's wealth, reduced absolute poverty, and considerably improved public infrastructures (for example, water, electricity, and roads) and access to education services and other basic public services.

Faster Economic Growth

A country can only converge toward richer countries if it maintains relatively higher economic growth over a long period. From 1980 to 2000, Morocco's per capita gross domestic product (GDP) grew an average 2 percent per year, a performance similar to European countries. Yet, as Morocco's starting point was well below the European ones, this did not close the economic gap between the two, and Morocco tended to diverge from its European neighbors' situation. The 2000s marked a break as the sharp increase in growth drove the start of Morocco's convergence process.

The structural reforms conducted in the early 1990s improved Morocco's growth rate, after two decades of relatively weak growth (1980–2000). Sustained by a favorable international economic environment, until 2008, the per capita GDP growth rate stood at 3.3 percent over the 2000–15 period (see figure 1.1, panel a), narrowing the standard-of-living gap with Europe (also facilitated by the prolonged European recession that began in 2008). Inflation was brought under control, remaining at below 2 percent on average over the period. With this growth and macroeconomic stability, by 2015 Morocco had virtually doubled its per capita GDP compared to 2005 to the equivalent of US$7,360 in constant 2011 purchasing power parity (PPP) US dollars (see figure 1.1, panel b).

Faster economic growth initiated an economic convergence process toward neighboring Southern European countries (France, Italy, Portugal, and Spain). Although the average purchasing power of a Moroccan citizen (measured by per capita purchasing power parity GDP) had tended to stagnate or even regress relative to the rate in Southern European countries during the 1990s, a convergence process was under way during the 2000s (see figure 1.2). As a result, Morocco narrowed its per capita income gap by 8 to 10 percentage points with Spain and Portugal between 2000 and 2015. The gap with the other

Figure 1.1 Morocco: Per Capita GDP

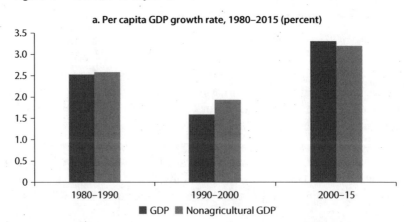

a. Per capita GDP growth rate, 1980–2015 (percent)

Source: High Commission for Planning 2016.
Note: GDP = gross domestic product.

figure continues next page

Figure 1.1 Morocco: Per Capita GDP *(continued)*

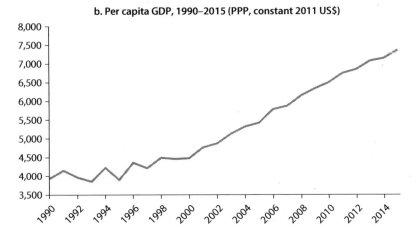

b. Per capita GDP, 1990–2015 (PPP, constant 2011 US$)

Source: World Development Indicators, World Bank.
Note: GDP = gross domestic product; PPP = purchasing power parity.

Figure 1.2 Economic Convergence of Morocco with Southern Europe
(GDP in constant 2011 PPP US$, %)

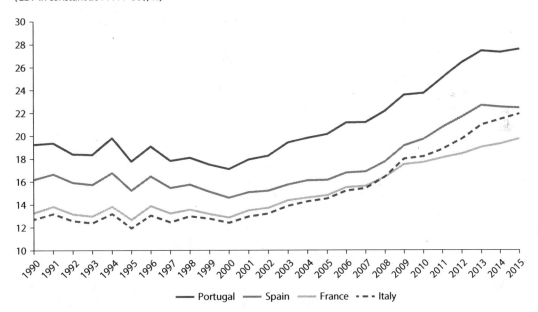

— Portugal   — Spain   ⸱⸱⸱ France   - - - Italy

Source: World Development Indicators, World Bank.
Note: Per capita GDP of Morocco relative to Southern European countries. GDP = gross domestic product; PPP = purchasing power parity.

Southern European countries was also reduced in a similar manner, suggesting that this performance was due to Morocco's efforts and not to a poor relative performance of the comparator countries.

This growth upturn was underpinned by relatively sound, prudent macroeconomic management during the period. Controlled inflation and the gradual consolidation of Morocco's public finances gave the country a current account surplus in the mid-2000s. In response to the international financial crisis in 2008, Morocco launched a countercyclical policy designed to help the sectors and social groups hit hardest by the crisis. The cost of the stimulus package, coupled with costs associated with the equalization fund, made a large hole in the budget balance, which lurched from a surplus of 0.4 percent of GDP in 2008 to a deficit of 7.3 percent of GDP in 2012. The level of public debt rose 18 percentage points of GDP in the space of six years (2008–14) to reach 64 percent of GDP. Since 2013, the government has implemented substantial macroeconomic stabilization efforts to reduce the twin deficits, keep inflation low, and rebuild the foreign exchange reserves. The International Monetary Fund has supported these efforts with two biennial agreements for the precautionary and liquidity line (International Monetary Fund 2015).

Scaled-up structural reforms, starting in the late 1990s, also stimulated growth, alongside good macroeconomic management. Morocco's per capita income picked up and grew at a more rapid pace in the early 2000s, following the implementation of several major institutional reforms to open up the economy and the society. Constitutional amendments in 1992 and 1996 initiated a process to democratize and modernize public institutions through the establishment of more representative institutions—especially the creation of a second parliamentary house elected by the municipal councils, chambers of commerce, and trade unions—while recognizing new economic freedoms such as freedom of enterprise. Following these constitutional amendments and the fillip given to the reforms by His Majesty King Mohammed VI upon his accession to the throne in 1999, bold reforms and new laws were adopted to gradually liberalize and open up the economy; privatize a number of public enterprises; restructure the financial system; strengthen public governance and the rule of law; improve access to essential public services, such as electricity, water, and education; and guarantee a growing number of fundamental human rights. These changes are rich in lessons and hold great promise, especially in view of the further constitutional changes made following the Constitutional amendment of 2011 (see chapter 2).

In a changing global environment, Morocco has embarked upon a fast-track modernization process driven by major sectoral infrastructure projects. The strategies launched in recent years have injected new momentum into strategic sectors such as agriculture, mining, energy, and industry. The implementation of the Green Morocco Plan (2008–20) has started to have tangible effects on Moroccan agriculture's restructuring and modernization. Over the 2008–15 period, the agricultural sector's growth rate hovered around 8.9 percent on average compared with 3.4 percent for the national economy. The implementation of the integrated Halieutis strategy has positioned the fisheries sector among the high export potential sectors. The mining sector development strategy, based on the modernization of the National Phosphate Company (OCP), has placed the company among the world leaders in its sector.

The country is on its way to reach the target of raising the share of renewable energies (water, solar, and wind power) to 42 percent of total energy capacity by 2020. The firm establishment of the industrial sector in the global value chains has driven the emergence of new, higher value-added industrial specializations such as automobiles, aeronautics, and offshoring. By way of example, the establishment of Renault in Tangier has made Morocco the number two vehicle manufacturer on the continent behind South Africa, and Morocco's positioning in the sector is expected to strengthen in the coming years with the impending opening of a Peugeot-Citroën group factory (Ministry of Economy and Finance 2015a). The prospect of establishing high-performance ecosystems to integrate the value chains and consolidate local relations between large corporations and small and medium enterprises (SMEs) is an integral part of the industrial acceleration plan, which was launched in 2014 and is set to create half a million industrial jobs by 2020.

Over the past decade, Morocco has undertaken a raft of reforms aimed at ensuring its successful integration into the global economy in general, and the African economy in particular, in a bid to diversify and boost its competitive export potential. Thanks to its geographic position, it has begun to strategically position itself as an economic and financial hub between Europe and the African continent. Morocco has set in motion a new strategic South-South partnership built on co-development and closer South-South cooperation to make the most of its geographical location and its historical relations with its European, American, Gulf, and Mediterranean trade partners. While trade between Morocco and the African continent is still low in absolute terms, it has quadrupled over the past decade to reach US$4.4 billion in 2014 (Ministry of Economy and Finance 2015b). And there is still considerable potential to be tapped, given that Africa accounts for a mere 6.5 percent of Morocco's total trade volume (Berahab 2016). "National champions" have set up operations in many Central and West African countries in the banking sector (Attijariwafa Bank, BMCE, Bank of Africa, and Banque Populaire), telecommunications (Morocco Telecom), insurance, energy, the food industry, and real estate, as well as in East Africa (Ethiopia, Madagascar, and Tanzania) with recently agreed megaprojects. The financial platform Casablanca Finance City Authority is currently in place to attract international investors and provide them with an infrastructure and suitable conditions for their activities in North Africa, West Africa, and Central Africa. Moroccan foreign direct investment in Sub-Saharan Africa is also booming (Amadeus Institute 2015).

A decade of macroeconomic stability, gradual reforms, and relatively good economic performance has also made Morocco more resilient to external shocks. Morocco suffered like other emerging countries from the 2008 global financial crisis, even though the country's limited financial integration on international financial markets cushioned the direct contagion effects. More serious were the impacts of the food and oil crisis that followed. With the price of crude oil (Brent) at more than US$110 per barrel on average in 2011 and 2012 and no national oil production, Morocco was confronted with a major deterioration in its terms of trade. This deterioration was exacerbated by a significant rise in the food import bill made necessary by severe drought in the country at the very moment that food prices were soaring, especially the price of wheat. With its large exposure to European Union trade, Morocco was negatively affected by the shockwaves of the eurozone crisis, especially the sovereign debt crises in Italy, Spain, and other countries in the region and the ensuing slowdown in economic growth. Morocco nonetheless took up these challenges without falling into economic recession or financial destabilization.

Increase in National Wealth

GDP growth over the past 15 years alone does not reveal the complete picture of Morocco's economic progress. Growth in the country's national wealth also needs to be taken into consideration. First, GDP growth does not account for the net creation of wealth and its sustainability. When a new output is produced at the environment's expense or on the back of unsustainable debt accumulation, the growth in wealth measured by GDP may be simply illusory. Production may well increase, but it also destroys existing natural resources, is environmentally damaging, and increases financial liability, none of which are considerations included in the calculation of GDP. Second, GDP growth reveals nothing about a country's capacity to convert growth into well-being, especially economic, social, and environmental welfare. For example, although the growing number of road traffic accidents drives up GDP owing to the medical care and car repairs they necessitate, these accidents obviously do not improve the population's quality of life or well-being. Conversely, GDP does not take into account nonmarket productive activities for charity, self-help, and solidarity purposes or domestic production. More generally, GDP does not factor in important aspects of human development and the quality of life such as life expectancy, level of knowledge and education, participation in economic and political life and governance, and the level of equity in the distribution of wealth (see box 1.1). This makes the GDP concept inadequate as an instrument to measure development (and therefore an incomplete instrument for guiding economic policy making). This limitation is especially

---

Box 1.1 From the Concept of GDP to the Notion of Wealth

The debate on the relevance of GDP as a measurement of economic development is nothing new. The Stiglitz-Sen-Fitoussi Commission (Stiglitz, Sen, and Fitoussi 2009) reported that it was time for statistical systems to focus more on measuring the population's well-being than economic production and that these measurements of well-being should be reported on in a context of sustainability (Stiglitz, Sen, and Fitoussi 2009). In particular, one of the Commission's key recommendations is to consider the wealth of nations, that is, growth in assets and liabilities, jointly with income and consumption: "Income and consumption are crucial for assessing living standards, but in the end they can only be gauged

box continues next page

Box 1.1　From the Concept of GDP to the Notion of Wealth *(continued)*

in conjunction with information on wealth. A household that spends its wealth on consumption goods increases its current well-being but at the expense of its future well-being. The consequences of such behavior would be captured in a household's balance sheet, and the same holds for other sectors of the economy, and for the economy as a whole. To construct balance sheets, we need comprehensive accounts of assets and liabilities. Balance sheets for countries are not novel in concept, but their availability is still limited and their construction should be promoted. Measures of wealth are central to measuring sustainability. What is carried over into the future necessarily has to be expressed as stocks—of physical, natural, human, and social capital. The right valuation of these stocks plays a crucial role, and is often problematic."

---

conspicuous because the level of development attained already satisfies basic material needs.

Development is fundamentally a process of net wealth accumulation—the produced, natural, and intangible capital that is the source of income and well-being of populations. Measuring changes in comprehensive wealth therefore points to whether policy, broadly conceived, is producing increases in well-being—what economists would term *social welfare* (see box 1.2). Empirical studies on growth in the wealth of nations in the 1970–2013 period find that it is not the more tangible assets in the form of natural or produced capital that dominate the wealth of countries, but their intangible assets—the accumulation of institutional, human, and social capital (World Bank 2011, 2016). In addition, experience shows that intangible capital tends to increase as a share of total wealth as countries climb the development ladder. Among the member countries of the Organisation for Economic Co-operation and Development (OECD), for example, intangible capital reportedly accounts for more than 80 percent of national wealth. In the less developed and middle-income countries like Morocco, the share of intangible capital is believed to be between 50 and 70 percent. In other words, rich countries appear to be largely wealthy because of the quality of their public institutions, human capital, and of the social contract and trust within societies. This observation forms the backbone of this book and the main framework for understanding the Moroccan economy in 2016, its outlook for 2040, and the main reforms to be conducted in the medium term (see part 2).

In line with GDP growth, Morocco's total wealth also expanded rapidly during the 2000s. Total wealth per capita (in constant dollars) reportedly rose nearly 2.8 percent per year on average from 1999 to 2013, increasing from US$28,663 to US$43,535. With few natural resources (with the exception of possessing the world's largest phosphate reserves), Morocco's wealth accumulation was dominated by an increase in produced and intangible capital. It is estimated that the stock of fixed capital (machinery, equipment, structures, and urban land) rose more than 80 percent while the stock of intangible capital

Box 1.2 The Total Wealth of Nations and Its Components

In 2006, the World Bank published a report titled *Where Is the Wealth of Nations? Measuring Capital for the 21st Century* on calculating wealth in more than 120 countries at the turn of the millennium. Methodologically, intangible capital is calculated as a residual, as the difference between the country's total wealth—itself the discounted value of the country's sustainable future consumption—and the sum of the other three components of wealth, that is, (i) produced capital corresponding to the estimated value of machinery, equipment, and structures in addition to urban land; (ii) natural capital made up of natural energy resources (for example, oil, gas, or coal), mining resources (for example, gold, silver, copper, or phosphate), farmland and pastureland, timber and other forest resources, and natural protected areas; and (iii) the country's net foreign assets (see figure B.1.2.1). This first report from the World Bank was updated in 2011, and the new edition is expected in 2017, showing the growth in the wealth of nations from 1970 to 2013.

In addition to these reports, the World Bank launched a global partnership in 2010 to promote a multipurpose conceptual framework to understand the interactions between economy and environment and to describe the stocks of environmental assets and their variations. This partnership, known by its English acronym of WAVES (Wealth Accounting and Valuation of Ecosystem Services), covers a broad coalition of United Nations specialized agencies, member states, and nongovernmental organizations and academics who work together to develop natural capital accounting and methodologies to measure the value of the services provided by a country's many ecosystems. The ultimate aim of this partnership is to promote sustainable development by ensuring that natural resources are mainstreamed into economic planning and national economic accounts.

Figure B.1.2.1 The Components of the Wealth of Nations

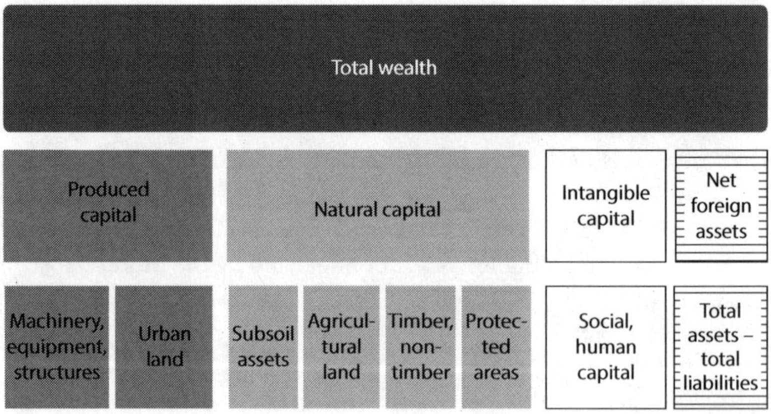

Sources: World Bank 2006. See also Hamilton and Clemens 1999; Dasgupta and Mäler 2000; Asheim and Weitzman 2001; Ferreira and Vincent 2005; Ferreira, Hamilton, and Vincent 2008.

Figure 1.3 Morocco: Growth in Total Wealth per Capita and Components, 1990–2013

(constant 2010 US$)

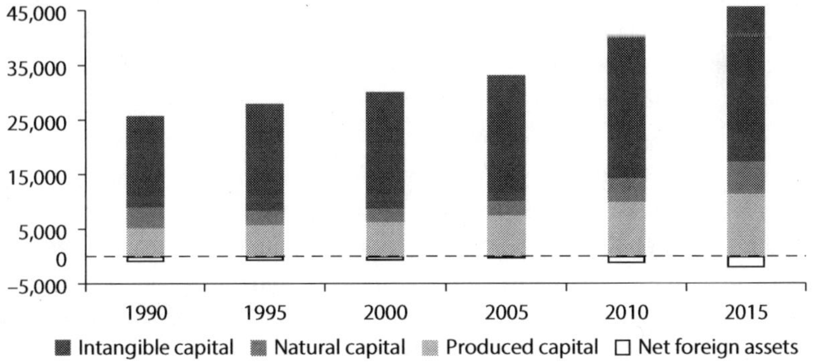

■ Intangible capital   ■ Natural capital   ■ Produced capital   ☐ Net foreign assets

Source: World Bank data set on the wealth of nations.

increased 33 percent, a trend that confirms the priority placed on fixed capital accumulation during the period (see figure 1.3). A recent joint study by the Economic, Social, and Environmental Council (CESE) and the Bank Al-Maghrib (2015) confirms this growth estimate (see box 1.3).[1]

The ongoing accumulation of intangible capital indicates, however, a major social capital deficit in Morocco (see figure 1.4). An analysis of the breakdown of intangible capital into its three main subcomponents (human capital, institutional capital, and social capital) is not an exact science. Various methodological approaches, all highly imperfect, can be developed to understand the nature and composition of the intangible capital of nations. On the basis of the assumption that intangible capital is made up of human capital, institutional capital for the good governance and smooth running of public institutions and market support institutions, and a more permanent effect corresponding to each country's social capital, Morocco's social capital, like all developing countries, is found to be largely negative, at around US$60,000 per capita (see box 1.3). In other words, the developing countries' low level of intangible capital[2] may well be due to a lack of human and institutional capital as measured by the standard education and governance indicators, but is probably due mainly to a social environment hampering the realization of potential. Chapter 6 examines this major conclusion.

This social capital shortfall has profound implications for the impacts of the different development policies. It explains why the impact of reforms that appear to be effective in one situation fall short of expectations in another situation. In the case of Morocco, it suggests that the country's intangible capital could be significantly developed by improving the education system's effectiveness and the quality of the health system, improving the rule of law and justice, improving the business climate, and increasing economic freedoms, but that the effects of these policies could be increased tenfold if these improvements were accompanied by an increase in social capital (see box 1.4). However, social

Box 1.3 Growth in Morocco's Wealth and Its Components, 1999–2013

The contributions of the different categories of assets (natural, produced, intangible, and their many subcomponents) to Morocco's total wealth in the 1999–2013 period were evaluated by Bank Al-Maghrib with the technical assistance of the World Bank (Economic, Social, and Environmental Council and Bank Al-Maghrib 2015). Bank Al-Maghrib's analysis drew on the methodology developed by the World Bank in its *Wealth of Nations* publications (World Bank 2006, 2011), but tailored and extended it to cover some important Moroccan characteristics, including the existence of sizeable fishery resources.

The measure of total wealth is built upon the intuitive notion that with no new income, an individual or a country could only sustain future consumption by drawing down its outstanding wealth. Accordingly, and in line with economic theory, total wealth is estimated as the present value of future consumption. Future consumption is calculated on the basis of current sustainable consumption; in other words, it is adjusted by a level of saving that is adequate to offset the depreciation of produced capital, investments in human capital (such as education expenditures); depletion of mineral, energy, and forest resources; and damage from local and global air pollutants. Total wealth calculation thus takes the country's adjusted net savings (ANS) or genuine savings into account. In the case of Morocco, the ANS was extended to include the potential overexploitation of fishery resources.

Measuring tangible capital stocks—produced and natural—is a complex task. Produced capital is an estimate of the stocks of machinery, equipment and structures (including infrastructure), and urban land. These stocks are derived from historical investment data using the perpetual inventory model: the sum of gross investments minus the depreciation of produced capital. In contrast to produced capital, natural resources are special economic goods because they are not produced but yield economic profits—rents. Morocco's natural capital stocks are calculated as the net present value of the rents they are able to produce over time on the basis of existing physical stocks, world prices, and local costs. This is the maximum an investor would be willing to pay for the stocks. Physical natural stocks cover energy resources, mineral resources (bauxite, copper, gold, iron, lead, nickel, phosphate, silver, tin, and zinc), timber resources, nontimber forest resources, crop land, pastureland, and protected areas.

Intangible capital includes estimates of human, social, and institutional capital that cannot be directly measured. It is calculated as a residual, that is, the difference between total wealth on one hand and the sum total of produced capital stocks, natural resources, and net foreign assets on the other. By construction, it captures all those assets that are unaccounted for in the estimates of produced and natural capital and net financial assets. Intuitively, it covers human capital (that is, the skills, knowledge, and health embodied in the labor force), institutional capital (the rule of law, property regime, and other elements of governance), and social capital (the trust among people in a society and their ability to work together for a common purpose). Social capital can be interpreted as a more permanent capital embodied in a nation's history, geography, and culture.

Figure 1.4 Breakdown of Middle-Income Countries' Intangible Capital, 2005–11
(constant 2010 US$)

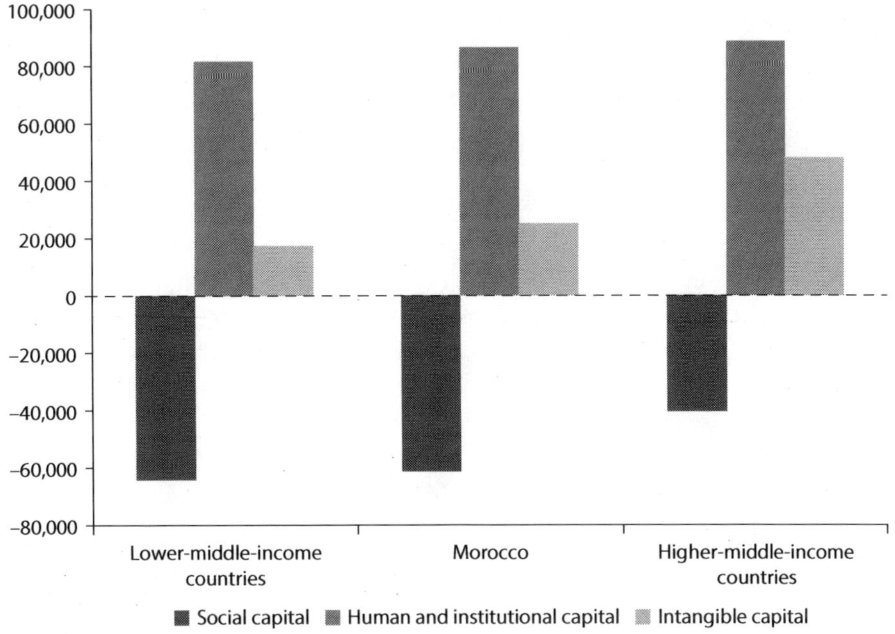

Source: World Bank estimates.

capital, embodied as it is in a country's history, geography, and culture, is hard to change. It is impossible to dictate an increase in interpersonal trust or civic cooperation in society. Yet, even though it is hard for the usual economic policies to encompass social capital, it can actually be improved. This theme will be revisited at the end of this book.

Poverty Reduction and Social Progress

With annual per capita GDP growth of 3.3 percent from 2000 to 2015, Morocco started to share the benefits of growth and significantly reduced its poverty level. According to the 2014 household survey data, extreme poverty has been eradicated in Morocco (see table 1.1). Between 2001 and 2014, the percentage of the population living below the national poverty line (US$2.15 per day in PPP) fell significantly from 15.3 percent to roughly 4.8 percent. However, poverty remains endemic in rural areas, where it posted a marginal downturn since 2011. The population's vulnerability (people living just above the poverty line) also decreased nationally, but remains high in rural areas at nearly 19.4 percent of the population. Over the period under consideration, the well-being of the bottom 40 percent of Moroccans grew both in absolute terms (the well-being of the poor improved) and relative terms (the well-being of the poor improved relative to that of the nonpoor), pointing to an increase in shared prosperity.[3] In addition to a reduction in monetary poverty, growth was reflected in a reduction in

Box 1.4 Modeling the Components of Intangible Capital

The exercise consists of modeling the respective contributions of human capital, institutional capital (governance and economic freedom), and social capital to a nation's intangible capital. IC_{it} denotes intangible capital per capita in country i for year t.

- The human capital indicator is calculated on the basis of the method put forward in the World Bank report entitled *The Changing Wealth of Nations* (World Bank 2011). This indicator captures both the effectiveness of the education system and the quality of the health system in the country concerned.
- The governance indicator is also based on the World Bank approach (2011) and uses the Kaufmann, Kraay, and Mastruzzi indices (2009). This indicator measures the quality of contract enforcement, and the police and courts, including judicial independence and the incidence of crime.
- The economic freedom indicator is the one built by the Heritage Foundation and the *Wall Street Journal*. This indicator is designed to capture the effect of business regulatory efficiency by ranking nations using ten economic freedom criteria.

After studying the correlation[a] between the explanatory variables, a composite index called the "composite index of human and institutional capital," denoted $ISCHI_{i,t}$, is built on the basis of the three aforementioned standardized indicators. The general model is then written as follows:

$$IC_{i,t} = \alpha_i + \gamma_t + \beta ISCHI_{i,t} + \varepsilon_{i,t} \tag{1}$$

α_i and γ_t reflect the fixed effects and the time dummies respectively.

The sample of per capita intangible capital data and the composite index built is used to model 95 countries over a seven-year period (2005–11). Two approaches are taken to estimate equation (1): (i) a pooled model with an income dummy variable, ignoring the panel nature of the data; and (ii) a panel model with fixed effects with the introduction of time dummies.

For the first model, the estimation suggests that a unit increase in the composite human and institutional capital index is associated with a US$50,723 increase in intangible capital per capita (see table B.1.4.1). Moreover, the dummy variable coefficient is positive, which confirms the high level of intangible capital in high-income countries. For the second model, the estimation suggests that the unit increase in the composite index raises per capita intangible capital by US$7,269. The time coefficient is sizeable (approximately US$3,857) and could be considered as a proxy measure of technological progress (World Bank 2011). The estimation therefore confirms a positive relationship between a nation's technological change and an increase in the value of intangible capital.

The differences in estimates and marginal effects depending on the estimation structure chosen (pooled model or fixed-effects model) can be explained by the introduction of characteristics specific to each country in the estimation of the fixed-effects model. In other words, an isolated improvement in human and institutional capital may fail to generate all

box continues next page

Box 1.4 Modeling the Components of Intangible Capital *(continued)*

the potential beneficial impacts on intangible capital, especially in the case of developing countries. This improvement needs to go hand in hand with an increase in social capital; capital that is reflected in the panel model's fixed effects. Therefore, in addition to low levels of human and institutional capital, the lack of social capital is found to put a sharp brake on the convergence of developing countries with developed countries.

The use of principal component analysis to construct the composite index enables us to deduct the effects of variation in the different standardized indicators that have contributed to factor composition (see table B1.4.2). The three components play an important role in the growth in per capita intangible capital. One additional unit of human capital and good governance is found to increase per capita intangible capital by US$2,694 and US$2,692, respectively. A unit increase in economic freedom is also found to have a positive effect on intangible capital of approximately US$2,730 per capita.

Table B1.4.1 Estimation of the Constituents of Per Capita Intangible Capital

Variable	Pooled model	Fixed-effects model
Composite index of human and institutional capital	50,723	7,269
Income dummy	134,670	Not applicable
Time	Not applicable	3,857

Note: Number of observations: 665; All coefficients are significant at the 5 percent level; the time dummy variable is for 2011 relative to 2005; the income dummy variable concerns the high-income group.

Table B1.4.2 Effects of the Increase of the Constituents of Per Capita Intangible Capital

Variables	Coefficients
Human capital	2,694
Governance	2,692
Economic freedom	2,731

a. At this stage, a Cronbach alpha (Cronbach -1951) coefficient analysis was conducted along with a principal component analysis for factor construction.

---

multidimensional poverty, that is, a more general improvement in living conditions (Ezzrari and Verme 2012).

Access to basic infrastructure services has increased considerably over the past 15 years. Nearly 98 percent of households now have access to the electricity grid. In 2014, thousands of villages had standpipes, supplying 94.5 percent of the population with clean drinking water (compared with 61 percent in 2004). The rate of connection to the sewerage system is estimated at approximately 88 percent in the big cities. The mobile telephone penetration rate has risen considerably, from 73 percent in 2008 to 122 percent in 2013. A remarkable upturn has been posted in access to education, with the universal primary

Table 1.1 Morocco: Main Poverty and Inequality Indicators, 2001–14

	2001	2007	2011	2014
Poverty at PPP US$1.00	2.0	0.6	0.3	0.0
Urban	0.3	0.1	0.1	0.0
Rural	4.0	1.2	0.5	0.0
Poverty at PPP US$2.00	20.2	8.2	5.7	1.3
Urban	8.7	3.6	2.5	0.3
Rural	34.2	14.3	8.4	2.9
Poverty at PPP US$2.15 (national poverty line)	15.3	8.9	6.2	4.8
Urban	7.6	4.9	3.5	1.6
Rural	25.1	14.4	10.0	9.5
Multidimensional poverty[a]	–	25.1	9.8	6.1
Urban	–	9.1	2.3	1.2
Rural	–	43.6	20.2	13.5
Vulnerability	22.8	17.4	13.3	12.5
Urban	16.6	12.7	9.4	7.9
Rural	30.5	23.6	18.7	19.4
Subjective poverty[b]	–	41.8	–	45.1
Urban	–	38.6	–	40.3
Rural	–	47.2	–	54.3
Gini	40.6	40.7	–	39.5
Urban	39.1	41.1	–	38.8
Rural	31.9	33.1	–	31.7

Source: High Commission for Planning 2001, 2007, 2014 household surveys and 2015 UNDP Human Development Report.
Note: PPP = purchasing power parity; – = N/A.
a. The multidimensional poverty index is a composite index of well-being that captures the deprivations faced by households with respect to health, education, and living standards. The figures provided under the year 2007 correspond to the figures for 2004.
b. The subjective poverty index measures households' perception of how comfortably they are living, as well as the ease or difficulty with which they cover their consumption expenses.

education Millennium Development Goal (MDG) on its way to being reached by the end of 2015. Net primary enrolment ratios rose from 75 percent to 96 percent between 2000 and 2011, and similar improvements were posted at secondary education level (UNESCO 2016). The immunization of one-year-old children is virtually universal and the average life expectancy and maternal and child mortality indicators have all improved in the past ten years.[4]

Morocco has made significant progress in terms of the Human Development Index in recent decades, even though there remains a great deal of room for improvement. From 1980 to 2014, Morocco's Human Development Index score rose almost 60 percent from 0.4 to 0.63, representing average annual growth of approximately 1.3 percent. Life expectancy at birth has lengthened by 16.4 years, the average length of schooling has increased 3.2 years, and gross national income per capita has virtually doubled in the space of 34 years (see table 1.2). Given Morocco's very poor initial situation in the early 1980s, human development improvements were nonetheless more spectacular in the first half of the period than they have been in the past 15 years.

Table 1.2 Morocco: Human Development Index, 1980–2014

Year	Life expectancy at birth	Expected years of schooling	Mean years of schooling	GNI per capita (2011 PPP US$)	Human Development Index score
1980	57.6	5.9	1.2	3,490	0.399
1990	64.8	6.5	2.2	3,899	0.457
2000	68.2	8.4	3.4	4,276	0.528
2010	70.2	11.1	4.4	6,256	0.611
2014	74.0	11.6	4.4	6,850	0.628

Source: UNDP 2015.
Note: GNI = gross national income; PPP = purchasing power parity.

A Slow and Incomplete Convergence Process

Despite the accomplishments of the past 15 years, the Moroccan economy is converging slowly with neighboring Southern European economies (France, Italy, Portugal, and Spain) and high-income emerging countries (for example, Chile, Republic of Korea, Malaysia, and Turkey). Southern European income per capita remains more than four times Morocco's in PPP (see figure 1.5).[5] Morocco's current level of economic development is similar to that of Europe in the 1960s.

In Terms of Economic Convergence…

Although barely 15 kilometers separate Morocco and Spain, the average Moroccan's purchasing power (as measured by per capita purchasing power parity GDP) stands at just 22 percent of its immediate European neighbor. Even Greece, whose economy is in severe crisis, has triple Morocco's per capita income. Historically speaking, it is interesting to note that the French were posting the Moroccans' current standard of living in 1950, the Italians in 1955, the Spanish in 1960, and the Portuguese in 1965.[6] The current economic gap between Morocco and Europe could therefore be estimated at approximately a half a century. Morocco aspires to economic emergence, yet still has a long way to go, not only to join the rich countries, but also to catch up with the fast-growing emerging countries. The Moroccan people's purchasing power stands at just around 40 percent of average purchasing power in countries such as Brazil, Malaysia, Mexico, Romania, and Turkey.

To appreciate the limitations of the convergence process that started in the early 2000s, it is useful to compare the Moroccan experience with other countries that have had successful economic takeoffs. The historical analysis shows that the economic takeoff phases in these economies—whether in Asia (China; Malaysia; Republic of Korea; Taiwan, China; and Thailand), Europe (Italy, Portugal, and Spain), or Latin America (Chile)—have always featured a per capita GDP growth rate sustained at over 4 percent per year for two to three decades (see figure 1.6). For example, from 1960 to 1990, the per capita growth rate stood at 4.5 percent in Portugal, 4.6 percent in Spain, and 3.7 percent in Italy. Taking the eight best years of the 2000–07 boom cycle, Morocco's per capita growth rate stood at 3.5 percent. However, this rate was stimulated by

Figure 1.5 Morocco: Per Capita GDP in 2015, International Comparison
(2011 US$ PPP)

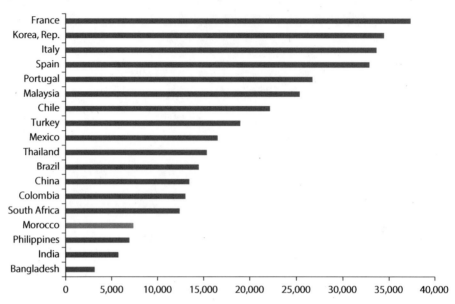

Source: WDI, World Bank.
Note: GDP = gross domestic product; PPP = purchasing power parity.

Figure 1.6 The Economic Miracles' 30-Year Boom Periods
(per capita GDP growth rate)

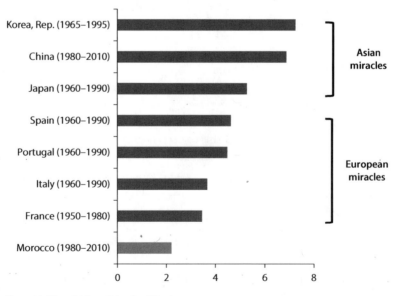

Source: Maddison database, University of Groningen.
Note: GDP = gross domestic product.

particularly favorable cyclical factors (global growth, credit boom, and development) and was unsustainable following the turning point in the cycle in 2008–09. Taking into account the entire 2000–14 period covering a full economic cycle (expansion/contraction), the structural trend of per capita growth in Morocco can currently be estimated at around 3 percent. Thus, compared with the long-term trend of 2.5 percent, the 2000s benefited from a structural growth gain of approximately 0.5 percentage points per year. At this new rate, Morocco can expect to double its per capita income every 25 years instead of every 30 years as previously projected.

On average, Morocco's growth performances explain its slower rate of convergence toward Southern Europe than observed among dynamic emerging countries. The decade of the 2000s has been one of economic convergence for all developing countries. Low-income countries and upper-middle-income countries (for example, Chile, Republic of Korea, Malaysia, and Turkey) have tended, on average, to grow more quickly and thus converge more rapidly toward high-income countries than Morocco. Morocco's growth path is more similar to that of the lower-middle-income countries than of the upper-middle-income countries (see figure 1.7). The catch-up process has been weaker than in other emerging markets in the region, such as Turkey, or countries that started with the same initial conditions in 1960, such as the Republic of Korea (see figure 1.8).

Morocco lags farther behind the dynamic emerging countries when total per capita wealth is taken into account instead of per capita GDP. Although Morocco's per capita GDP currently stands at approximately 60 percent of the upper-middle-income countries, its total per capita wealth represents barely

Figure 1.7 Per Capita GDP in Morocco and Middle-Income Countries, 1990–2015
(constant PPP 2011 US$)

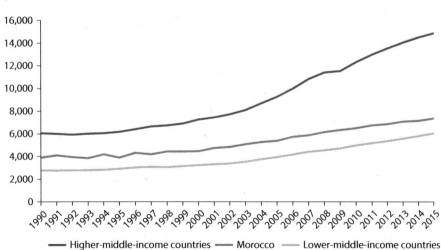

Higher-middle-income countries —— Morocco —— Lower-middle-income countries

Source: World Development Indicators, World Bank.
Note: GDP = gross domestic product; PPP = purchasing power parity.

Figure 1.8 Per Capita GDP in Morocco, the Republic of Korea, and Turkey, 1990–2015
(constant PPP 2011 US$)

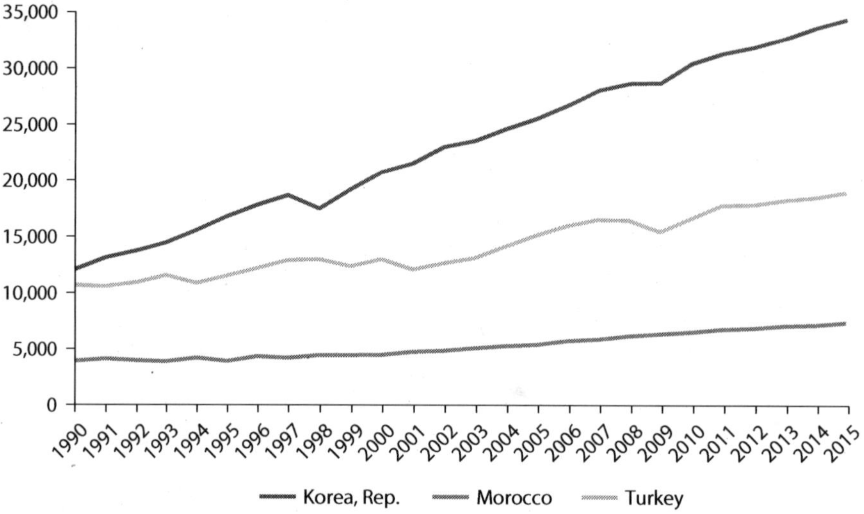

Source: World Development Indicators, World Bank.
Note: GDP = gross domestic product; PPP = purchasing power parity.

40 percent of these countries' per capita wealth. Morocco's per capita wealth grew at the same average rate as the emerging countries over the 2000–2011 period, but started from a smaller base. So although Morocco's per capita wealth increased by some US$10,000 from 2000 to 2011, the upper-middle-income countries' per capita wealth grew by approximately US$25,000 (see figure 1.9).

At the regional level, Morocco's per capita wealth is similar to the Arab Republic of Egypt, somewhat lower than Algeria, and much lower than Tunisia and Jordan. Yet the most striking and illuminating feature for each of these countries is not so much the current level of wealth as its composition. Whereas Jordan, Morocco, and Tunisia had more or less the same level of fixed capital per capita in 2011, Morocco's per capita intangible capital was less than 40 percent and 60 percent of Jordan's and Tunisia's intangible capital, respectively. Algeria paints quite the opposite picture. With negative intangible capital, Algeria is actually in an extremely difficult situation since a large proportion of the country's natural capital (essentially hydrocarbons) is not reinvested in human, institutional, or social capital, but is invested in poorly profitable fixed capital or simply consumed (see figure 1.10).

An international comparison of growth in intangible capital turns up a wealth of information for Morocco. With relatively limited natural resources and little produced capital, over 70 percent of Morocco's total wealth was made up of intangible capital in the early 2000s, placing the country well ahead of the other middle-income countries in terms of the proportion of intangible capital in total wealth (see figure 1.11). However, the share of intangible capital followed a downward trend from 2000 to 2011 as the country ramped up its fixed

Figure 1.9 Per Capita Wealth Growth and Composition, 2000 vs. 2011
(constant 2010 US$)

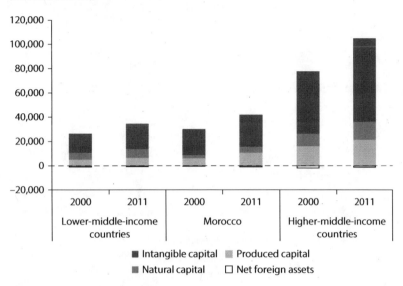

Source: World Bank data set on the wealth of nations.

Figure 1.10 Morocco: Per Capita Wealth Growth and Composition, 2011
(constant 2010 US$)

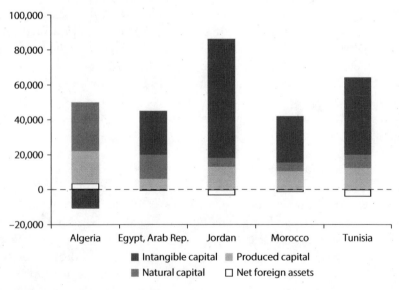

Source: World Bank data set on the wealth of nations.

capital investment effort. By 2011, Morocco's intangible capital had fallen to just 65 percent of total wealth, on a par with upper-middle-income countries. If Morocco is to converge with the wealth of the more developed countries, it will need to halt this downturn and increase its relative effort to accumulate more intangible assets in the form of institutional, human, and social capital. The

Figure 1.11 Share of Intangible Capital in Total Wealth, 2000–11
(percent)

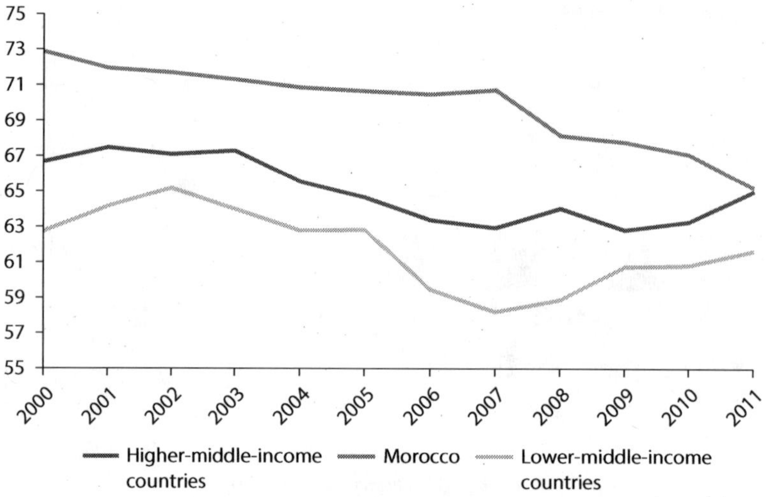

Source: World Bank data set on the wealth of nations.

dip observed in 2007, just as other middle-income countries were embarking on an upward trend, is an important stylized fact from the point of view of the country's economic prospects (see chapter 2).

Three major conclusions can be drawn from the elements presented earlier: (i) Morocco still has a huge economic gap to close with the developed and emerging countries; (ii) the rate of convergence in terms of economic growth may well have accelerated recently, but remains slow in relation to rapid economic catch-up experiences; and (iii) the convergence process appears to be particularly slow in terms of wealth accumulation, especially intangible capital accumulation.

And in Terms of Social Convergence

Analysis of microeconomic survey data finds that the economic divide between Morocco and the European countries, estimated at half a century, can also be found in terms of relative living conditions. In the area of health, for example, the child mortality rate measured in Morocco in 2015 stood at the same level as in the European countries in 1960, at approximately 24 deaths per 1,000 births (see figure 1.12). Despite substantial progress made to improve the health system and notwithstanding imports of advanced technological and medical treatments, which furthered the Moroccan people's access to much better quality goods and services than those provided to Europeans 50 years ago, the performance of the Moroccan health system as captured by the child mortality indicator is some 50 years behind European health systems. This social development divide can also be seen in terms of mobility and transport. Indeed, the car ownership rate in Morocco is lower than the rate observed in certain

Figure 1.12 Child Mortality in 2015

(per 1,000 births)

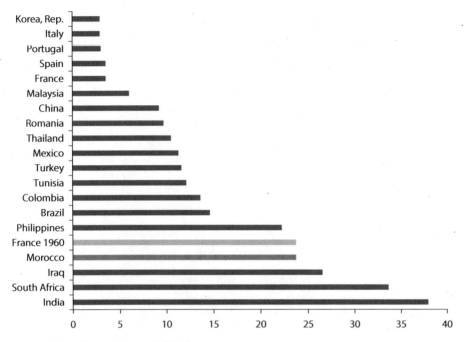

Source: World Development Indicators, World Bank.

Southern European countries half a century ago. Just 18 percent of Moroccan households own a car today as opposed to 30 percent of French households in 1960. This low rate of car ownership has a huge impact on the Moroccan population's well-being as it combines with growing urban spread and a poor public transport system. Microeconomic consumer surveys can be used to measure the Moroccan standard of living. They find that the current structure of consumer spending by Moroccan households is similar to Europe in the 1950s and 1960s. In particular, the share of food expenditure in the budget remains very high, demonstrating families' low purchasing power and the predominance of essential expenditure. Moroccans spend 40 percent of their budget on food products, compared with 35 percent for French households in 1960 and just 20 percent today (see figure 1.13).

International comparisons aside, Morocco's slow economic convergence is also evident in the considerable differences in well-being within the Moroccan population itself. Economic poverty and vulnerability remain extremely widespread as one-quarter of the rural population—approximately 3.5 million people—lives in poverty or under constant threat of falling back into poverty. Poverty is associated with harsh geographical conditions, particularly in mountainous areas, and the poor state of infrastructures, low level of access to basic services, and scant employment possibilities in the formal sector. Participants in the 2013 consultations held in Taounate province in the context of the strategic

Figure 1.13 Share of Food in the Household Budget, 2010
(percent)

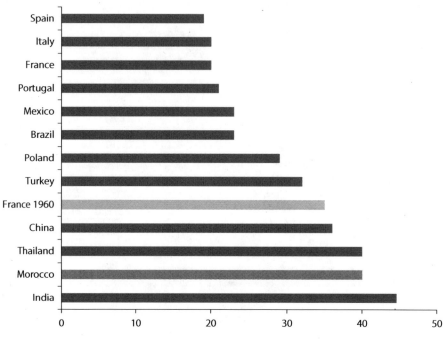

Source: Global Consumption Database, World Bank, International Finance Corporation.

partnership between Morocco and the World Bank confirmed the veracity of these problems with, for example, long distances to be covered, a lack of adequate means of transport, and large outlays by households on access to schools and health infrastructures. It was noted that children in this region set out for school before daybreak and return home after nightfall, often on foot (World Bank 2013). It was also revealed that learning inequalities were manifestly greater among Moroccan students than in other countries with, for example, a 2.5 difference in the reading scores of the top- and low-performing students, compared with under 1.5 in Southern European countries (see figure 1.14).

Despite significant economic performances and a narrowing of income inequalities in recent years, Morocco's inclusive social and human development outcomes still fail to meet the expectations of the population, well aware of multispeed development in Morocco. The implementation of the National Human Development Initiative (INDH), launched in 2005 to improve rural quality of life and tackle social exclusion in urban areas and insecurity, has resulted in significant progress for the target rural populations.[7] The Gini coefficient for Morocco reflects high levels of income inequality, although these appear to have fallen since 2007 (see figure 1.15). Following an upturn in the 2000s, inequalities reportedly returned to their late 1990s' level in 2014, according to the High Commission for Planning (HCP). Disparities in poverty rates

Figure 1.14 Reading Literacy Inequalities
(comparison between the score for the 9th decile and the 1st decile)

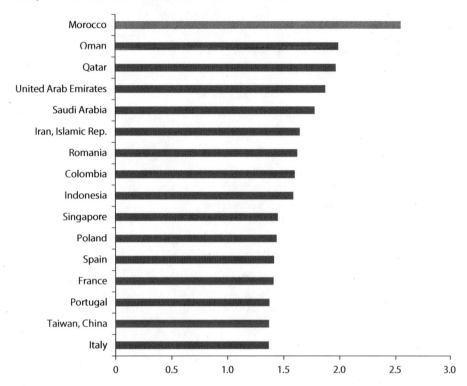

Source: UNESCO 2014.

Figure 1.15 Morocco: Gini Coefficient, 1985–2014

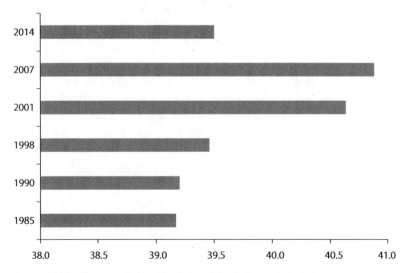

Source: World Development Indicators and High-Commission for Planning 2001, 2007, and 2014 household surveys.

across regions continue, however, to provide one measure of spatial inequalities. These regional inequalities are also striking with respect to access to human rights (Ministry of Economy and Finance 2015c). The partial narrowing of the rural-urban income gap (following regional development efforts, particularly in northern Morocco) has not eradicated the disparities: 80 percent of poverty in Morocco continues to be in rural areas, and in 2014, the urban poverty rate was 1.6 percent as opposed to 9.5 percent in rural areas. Over 19 percent of Moroccans living in rural areas are vulnerable and at risk of falling back into poverty (as opposed to less than 8 percent of persons living in urban areas). Although Morocco's cities generate nearly 75 percent of GDP, they also contain stubborn pockets of poverty and high unemployment rates. In fact, although living standards improved and poverty and vulnerability levels both declined between 2007 and 2014 in Morocco, subjective poverty, that is, one's own perception of poverty, increased from 42 percent to 45 percent across the country during this period, affecting more than 54 percent of the rural population (see table 1.1). The largest increases in subjective poverty were noted among under-25 urban youths and over-60 rural residents.

Despite major advances with access to basic infrastructure, progress overall has been uneven and certain rural and periurban regions, along with some medium-sized and small cities, still do not have access to certain infrastructure. Close to a quarter of rural households have no direct access to a road and live at least 10 kilometers away from basic health services. The share of births attended by skilled health personnel averages 63 percent in rural areas, compared with 92 percent in urban areas (World Bank, WDI). While 90 percent of urban households are connected to the drinking water network (faucet in the dwelling) and the public drainage system, rural connection rates did not even reach 40 percent in the case of drinking water and 3 percent for sanitation, with even lower rates in certain remote regions such as the Mediterranean mountainous region (HCP 2015b). Telecommunications coverage is also problematic in rural areas and the reliability, maintenance, and financial sustainability of these services remain a persistent challenge, especially at the local level. These factors combine to reduce the quality of life, productivity, and prospects of rural households.

As will be subsequently explained in more detail (see chapter 5), Morocco's human capital is struggling to develop. Illiteracy rates and disparities in access to secondary education remain high. Both education quality and learning outcomes lag far behind other countries with similar or lower income levels (see figure 1.16). Child and maternal mortality levels remain high, especially relative to the improvements in many other countries, and are falling short of MDG targets. Morocco is ranked 126th worldwide (out of 188 countries) on the Human Development Index—a composite measure of the average level of key human development components as calculated by the United Nations—behind several Middle East and North Africa countries, including Turkey (72nd), Jordan (80th), Algeria (83rd), Tunisia (96th), and Egypt (108th) (UNDP 2015).

In addition to these indicators of material and human well-being, economic gaps also give rise to "happiness gaps." "Happiness" is a subjective notion used

Figure 1.16 Ten-Year-Old Students (Grade 4) with Basic Literacy Skills
(percent)

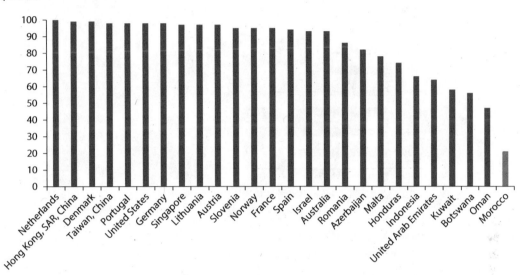

Sources: PIRLS 2011, UNESCO 2014.

by economists and measured by the degree of satisfaction with life as expressed by the people interviewed. A population's well-being is obviously a complex, multidimensional notion that cannot be reduced to a mere macroeconomic indicator. The *World Happiness Report* published annually by the United Nations has identified complementary determinants such as interpersonal trust, social support, perceived freedom, and health. Nevertheless, the analyses conducted for this book find a close correlation between a country's material wealth and its inhabitants' fulfillment: the higher a country's per capita GDP, the more people interviewed say they are satisfied with their life. So what about Morocco? Income deviations between Morocco and wealthier countries are fully reflected in the inhabitants' happiness. When the population's perceived well-being is taken into account, Morocco ranks 84th, between Montenegro and Azerbaijan, out of the 155 countries covered by the *World Happiness Report* 2017 (see figure 1.17) (United Nations 2017). This ranking is consistent with Morocco's place in the per capita GDP ranking. International data are borne out by a national well-being survey conducted by the High Commission for Planning in 2012, which confirmed that a high proportion of Moroccans are dissatisfied with their living conditions: 45 percent are not very or not at all satisfied with their life, 24 percent are fairly satisfied, and barely 30 percent are satisfied. Disposable income is a major determinant of the degree of satisfaction in the sample: the most well-off Moroccans are those who say they are the happiest and the poorest tend to consider themselves unhappy.

The lack of economic opportunities in Morocco hinders the possibility of further reducing the poverty rates and is holding back the emergence of a larger

Figure 1.17 World Happiness Index Country Rankings, 2017

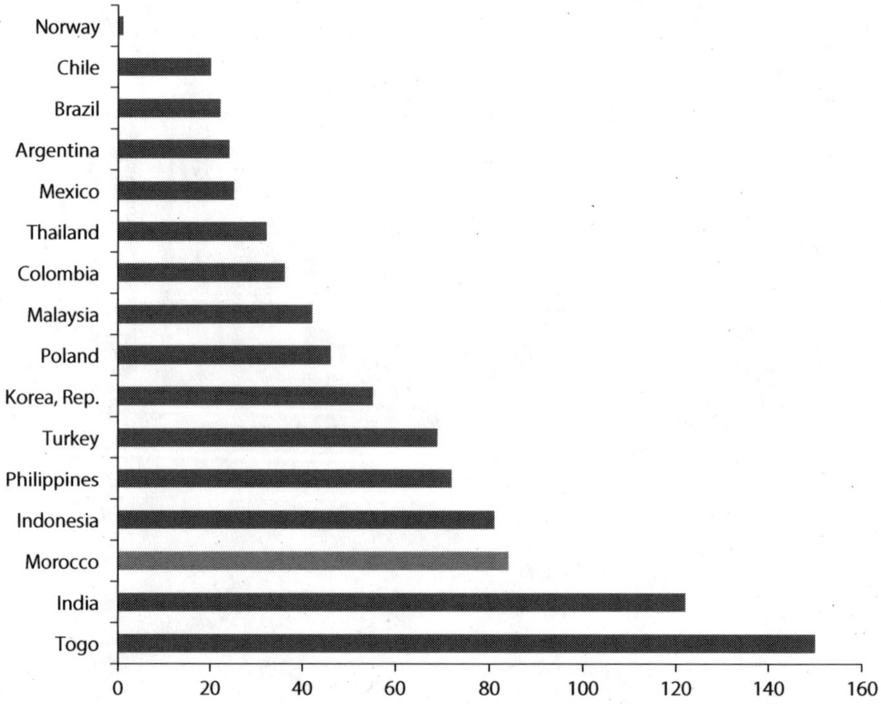

Source: United Nations, World Happiness Report 2017.

middle class. There is disagreement in the economic literature over the methodology to be used to measure the middle class. However, a household is considered
middle class if it has a per capita income of US$10 per day in 2011 PPP, which
is US$1,200 per month for a family of four (Pew Research Center 2015). Taking
the PPP conversion factor of 0.45 for Morocco, the middle class threshold would
be approximately DH 5,500 per month for a Moroccan household (see box 1.5).
This means that the middle class could currently account for around 25 percent
of the Moroccan population, and appears to be growing.[8] In 2001, this figure
stood at just 16 percent. This progress notwithstanding, Morocco's middle class
is still small relative to that of other emerging countries, where the middle and
upper classes account for 44 percent of the population on average: 40 percent in
Mexico and Thailand, 50 percent in Brazil and Turkey, and 70 percent in Malaysia
and Poland (see figure 1.18).

Nevertheless, the hypothesis of the emergence of a middle class representing
25 percent of the Moroccan population is to be treated with caution, mainly owing
to the high cost of living and the quality of public services. An alternative measurement of the middle class, taking into account the public services being provided to
the population, would significantly raise the middle-class threshold. It seems
reasonable to consider that a household is middle class when it satisfies three social
markers: (i) the capacity to purchase housing that is not public housing;

Box 1.5 What Is the Middle-Class Income Threshold?

Although all economists agree that it is important for the middle class to grow in the development process, there is no real agreement over the method to be used to measure the middle class.

One of the approaches available is to measure the middle class in relative terms on the basis of the observed income distribution. This was the approach adopted by the High Commission for Planning (HCP 2009) in a study on the middle class on the basis of data collected by the latest available standard of living survey. Middle-class households are those with a monthly income of between 0.75 times the median income (DH 2,800) and 2.5 times the median income (DH 6,736). Households that are below the lower bound are considered to be "lower class" and those above the upper bound are defined as "upper-class" households. The study's main finding is that the middle class is believed to make up 53 percent of the population, the lower class is believed to make up 34 percent of the population, and the upper class is believed to make up 13 percent of the population. This statistical method has certain advantages, especially in terms of neutrality, but it cannot evaluate social progress made during the development process. All countries, irrespective of their level of development, can say they have a large middle class on the basis of this method. In the specific case of Morocco, the bounds chosen are particularly low and include in the "middle class" socioprofessional categories considered lower-class groups by global standards. For example, a couple of unskilled employees earning the legal minimum wage (approximately DH 2,000 net wage per month) are statistically defined as middle class and could even, with a little seniority, become "upper middle class."

An alternative approach can be taken to solve this problem, whereby an absolute middle-class threshold is defined in monetary units. A study published by the Pew Research Center in 2015 considers that a household attains middle-class status with an income of US$10 per person per day (2011 PPP), or US$1,200 per month for a family of four (Pew Research Center 2015). This threshold is borne out by many other studies of developing countries (Kharas 2010). In the case of Morocco, this would correspond to a monthly income per household of 5,500 current 2014 dirhams (the 2014 census finds that the average Moroccan household has 4.2 people). On the basis of this criterion, the study estimates that 25 percent of the Moroccan population had an income higher than the middle-class threshold in 2011. In other words, 75 percent of the Moroccan population was poor or low income. This proportion rose sharply with the economic growth of the 2000s. In 2001, only 16 percent of Moroccans could claim to be middle or upper class.

Source: High Commission for Planning 2009.

(ii) the capacity to buy a low-end car; and (iii) the capacity to send children to a private school, in view of the negative view of the public school system. The simulations that are based on these three items of expenditure calculate a minimum budget of DH 10,000 per month for a family of four to be middle class.[9] The fact that the middle-class threshold is higher in Morocco than in the other emerging countries is due to public service shortcomings resulting in additional costs being

Figure 1.18 Share of the Middle and Upper Class in the Population
(household income >US$1,200 PPP, 2011)

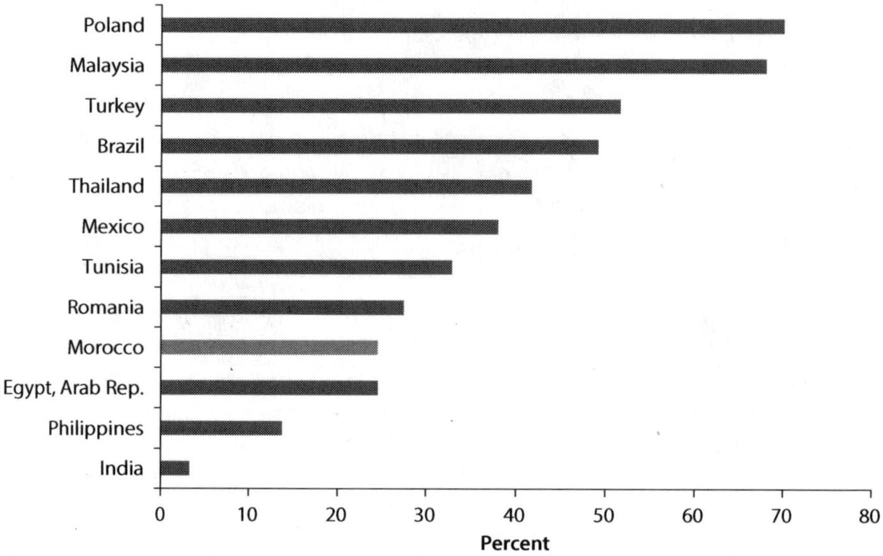

Source: Pew Research Center 2015.
Note: PPP = purchasing power parity.

borne by households: urban planning (high cost of land), education policy (high cost of private schooling for children), transport policy (poor quality public transport), and health policy (poor quality of the public health system). Studies by Moroccan analysts using a similar method produced similar findings to this threshold (Revue Economia 2009).

All of these elements point to the idea that the level set to attain middle-class status in Morocco is relatively high compared with international standards. The threshold of DH 10,000 per month for a family of four would place just 15 percent of Moroccan households in the middle and upper classes, that is, 5 million inhabitants for a total population of some 34 million (2014 census). It is interesting to note in this respect that approximately 25 percent of public administration employees earn a net monthly wage of DH 10,000 or more (Ministry of Economy and Finance 2015d). This would make the proportion of government employees in the middle class much higher than that of the other population categories (even without taking into account situations where two household members work).

This analysis of social convergence yields three lessons for Morocco: (i) the economic gap between Morocco and emerging and developed countries has concrete impacts on Moroccan well-being; (ii) despite the progress made in recent years, Moroccans' living conditions still generate a great deal of inequalities and dissatisfaction within the population; and (iii) the growth upturn observed in the 2000s expanded the middle class, which nevertheless remains small mainly owing to public service shortcomings.

The Flagging Development Model

Morocco successfully initiated a convergence process in the early 2000s, but is this convergence process sustainable? The following sections attempt to answer this question by analyzing the imbalances and vulnerabilities of the Moroccan growth model, looking at both supply and demand.

From the Unsustainable Supply…

Morocco risks quickly finding itself having to contend with the limitations of growth based on fixed capital accumulation. Morocco's growth has been analyzed on many occasions, including in previous World Bank Country Economic Memoranda and in a recent African Development Bank report, and this work has produced a clear diagnosis: Morocco's growth is primarily driven by physical capital accumulation. Morocco's economy posted an average growth rate of 4.3 percent between 2000 and 2014. According to simple growth accounting methods (see box 1.6), physical capital accumulation contributed 60 percent of this growth, labor contributed 15 percent, and total factor productivity (TFP) contributed 25 percent. If the agricultural sector is taken out of the equation, the breakdown of contributions to nonfarm GDP growth is even more enlightening: the contribution of capital is estimated at 68 percent, that of labor at 25 percent, and that of TFP at only 7 percent. Compared to the 1990s, the role of TFP has increased substantially (TFP made a negative contribution to growth in the 1990s), while the contribution of labor has decreased sharply. However, the dominance of capital in the growth dynamic has been fairly steady since the early 1970s. Productivity gains in agriculture have been higher than in industry as investment in irrigated agriculture has paid off. However, this has occurred at the cost of increasing overexploitation of groundwater in a country that suffers from a high level of water stress, despite steps taken to strengthen the water conservation policy implemented in 2008 under the Green Morocco Plan and the National Irrigation Water Conservation Program, particularly with respect to microirrigation. The following sections discuss each of the various factors of production—labor, physical capital, productivity, and degradation of the environment, in particular of "water" capital—in turn.

Small Contribution of the Labor Factor

Despite favorable demographic trends, the labor factor has contributed little to Morocco's recent growth. Morocco is enjoying a demographic dividend, with strong growth of the working age population, which increased at an average rate of some 2 percent from 2000 to 2015. However, this growth rate shows a diminishing trend: it fell from 2.5 percent in 2000 to 1.5 percent in 2015. Despite this demographic dividend, job creation has been relatively limited, which means that labor makes a small contribution to growth. The average growth of employment stood at 1 percent between 2000 and 2015, which is slower than the growth rate of the population over the age of 15. Under the circumstances,

Box 1.6 Growth Accounting

Economists usually distinguish three sources of economic growth: labor, capital, and technological progress. The third factor, which may also be called total factor productivity (TFP), measures productivity gains stemming from improvements in institutional capital, human capital,
and social capital. Technological progress is calculated as growth that cannot be attributed to
labor or capital. It is a statistical residual. It is similar to intangible capital in the literature on the
wealth of nations, which is also calculated as a statistical residual.

Growth accounting basics were laid out in the work of Solow (Solow 1957), Kendrick
(Kendrick 1961), and Denison (Denison 1962). The basic Solow growth model is a production
function with the two main factors of production, capital and labor, along with a parameter
that measures technological progress. It is a production function of the Cobb-Douglas type
with constant returns to scale:

$$Y = A \cdot K^{\alpha} \cdot L^{1-\alpha} \tag{1}$$

where Y is real GDP, K is real capital stock, L is the number of workers employed, and A is
technological progress or TFP. The parameter a denotes the share of capital in national income
and $(1-a)$ represents the share attributable to the labor factor.

The total solution of the differential equation (1) can be used to analyze the TFP growth rate
as a function of the growth rates of GDP, capital, and labor:

$$\hat{A} = \hat{Y} - \alpha \cdot \hat{K} - (1-\alpha) \cdot \hat{L} \tag{2}$$

where the caret symbol (^) represents the growth rate of the variables concerned and a the
share of capital in national income.

As is the case in many developing countries, Morocco's statistics system (HCP) does not
measure capital stock. For the purposes of this exercise, the perpetual inventory method is
used to estimate the capital stock over the period from 1980 to 2014. Capital stock at time t is
written as follows:

$$K_t = K_{t-1}(1-\delta) + I_t \tag{3}$$

where I is annual real gross investment and δ is the capital depreciation rate, which is assumed
to be constant at 5 percent over time. The capital measurement requires an investment flows
series for the whole period covered by the exercise. The 1998 base investment series is available only for the period from 1980 to 2014. Chain-linking was used to combine the data with
the former 1980 base series for the period from 1960 to 1980 in order to complete the series.

the employment rate, which is the ratio of the active workforce and the working
age population (15–65 years), has shown a declining trend, falling from more
than 48 percent in 2000 to under 43 percent in 2015 (see figure 1.19). In other
words, less than half of Morocco's working age population is contributing to
wealth creation.

Figure 1.19 Morocco: Employment Rate, 2000–15
(percent)

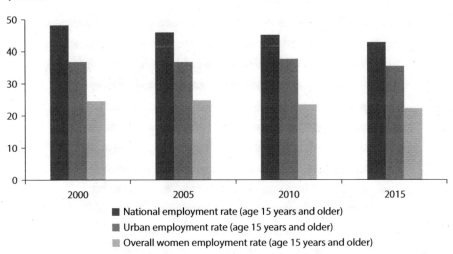

■ National employment rate (age 15 years and older)
■ Urban employment rate (age 15 years and older)
■ Overall women employment rate (age 15 years and older)

Source: High Commision for Planning 2016.

Morocco's employment rate of 42.8 percent is fairly low compared with other emerging or developed countries, where the average is 60 percent. More specifically, Morocco's economy shows a weak capacity to employ its young people between the ages of 25 and 35. The employment rate for this group stands at only 48 percent, compared with an average of 65 percent for emerging countries (60 percent in Turkey, 70 percent in Mexico and the Republic of Korea, and 73 percent in Chile). Morocco's labor market also stands out for its very low female participation rate—a mere 23 percent for the country as a whole and 13 percent in urban areas (see figure 1.20). In other emerging countries, 45 percent of working-age women have jobs. Even in countries with a tradition of low female employment, economic growth has been accompanied by an increase in the female employment rate. In Turkey, for example, the female employment rate rose from 20 percent in 2000 to 30 percent in 2014. However, Morocco has shown no real signs of women making a greater contribution to economic growth.

In aggregate, Morocco's growth has been hampered by the difficulty the economy faces in mobilizing the available human resources, particularly young people and women, and in reallocating labor across sectors rapidly to improve efficiency. Employment in rural areas has contracted with the attrition of agricultural workers and rural depopulation, but at a fairly slower pace compared with advanced or emerging countries when they were at Morocco's current stage of development. In France, for example, the farming population shrank from more than 30 percent of the workforce in the 1950s to some 10 percent in the early 1970s and 2.5 percent in 2013. In Southeast Asia and Southern Europe, the farming workforce has declined at an average annual rate of 2 percent since 1960. In Morocco, the annual decline in farming employment has been much slower,

Figure 1.20 Employment Rate for Persons Ages 15–65 Years, 2015
(percent)

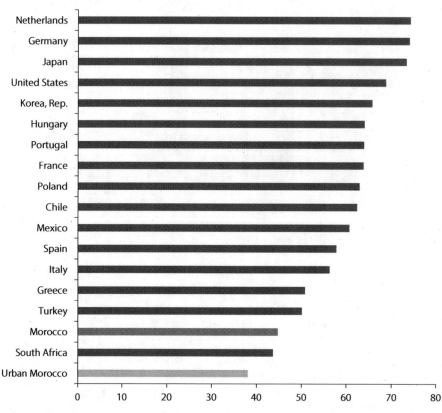

Sources: Organisation for Economic Co-operation and Development and High Commission for Planning.

at around 0.5 percent. In the future, job shedding in rural areas is expected to continue, and even pick up speed, as has been the case in every country that has undergone development. This means that job growth needs to increase in urban areas to offer opportunities for young people, women, and rural populations, and to enhance Morocco's long-term growth potential.

Large Contribution of the Capital Factor

Unlike labor, capital accumulation has made a large contribution to growth, as a result in particular of one of the highest investment rates in the world over the past decade. Over the period from 2000 to 2014, investment stood at 31 percent of GDP, as opposed to 25 percent in the 1990s. In international comparisons, Morocco stands out for its particularly high investment rate. In a selection of 30 emerging countries, Morocco ranks third behind China (43 percent) and the Republic of Korea (31 percent), and ahead of Indonesia (26 percent), Romania (28 percent), Malaysia (23 percent), and Turkey (20 percent) (see figure 1.21). In historical terms, Morocco's current level of investment is equivalent to that seen in countries that achieved "economic miracles." Investment rates in the countries

Figure 1.21 Investment (Gross Fixed Capital Formation), 2000–14
(percentage of GDP)

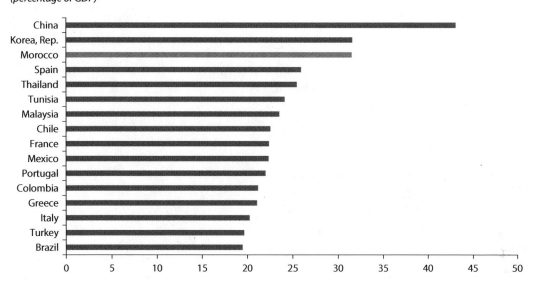

Sources: WDI, World Bank.
Note: GDP = gross domestic product.

Figure 1.22 Investment Rates in Countries That Achieved Economic "Miracles"
(percentage of GDP)

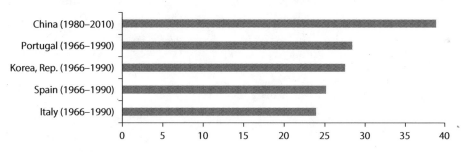

Sources: WDI, World Bank.
Note: GDP = gross domestic product.

referred to as the "Asian dragons" averaged 30 percent between 1960 and 1980. In Southern European countries, investment rates stood at 25 percent during the economic catch-up period (see figure 1.22). The main lesson to be learned from this analysis is that Morocco's investment from a quantitative standpoint has been sufficient to achieve rapid convergence.

Weak Productivity Gains

Morocco's investment effort nevertheless failed to generate productivity gains and faster growth. The growth achieved in the 2000s seems relatively modest compared with the faster pace of capital accumulation. Several emerging countries, such as Turkey and Colombia, achieved growth that is very similar to

Morocco's growth rate of 4.3 percent, but with much lower investment rates (20 percent). Other countries, such as Malaysia and the Philippines, posted growth of more than 5 percent, with maximum investment rates of 25 percent of GDP. Morocco's growth model consumes a great deal of capital to generate small productivity gains. This means that Morocco has been unable to make any significant efficiency gains, despite its structural reforms, economic openness, improved business environment, imported technologies, and increase in school enrolment rates.

International experience has clearly shown that the decisive factor for sustaining successful economic convergence is the ability to achieve productivity gains (Easterly and Levine 2001). Emerging countries cannot rely solely on capital accumulation to catch up with more advanced countries. This would require ever-increasing investment and savings rates that would ultimately be unsustainable. History has shown that the countries that manage to maintain strong and sustainable growth, without falling into the middle-income trap, are those that achieved the greatest productivity gains (figure 1.23). For example, in the countries of Southern Europe, TFP averaged 2.2 percent from 1960 to 1980 (2.1 percent in Portugal, 2.2 percent in Italy, and 2.4 percent in Spain). In the case of the Republic of Korea and Taiwan, China, growth accounting shows that productivity gains stood at some 1.7 percent per year,[10] despite very high investment rates. More recently during the 2000s, it is interesting to note that the highest productivity gains (other than China's gain of 3 percent) were achieved by the Eastern European countries that undertook major economic restructuring as part of the process of convergence with the advanced European countries (Czech Republic, 1.5 percent; Poland, 2 percent; and Romania, 2.5 percent). In contrast, all of the middle-income countries that posted weak growth showed no

Figure 1.23 Total Factor Productivity

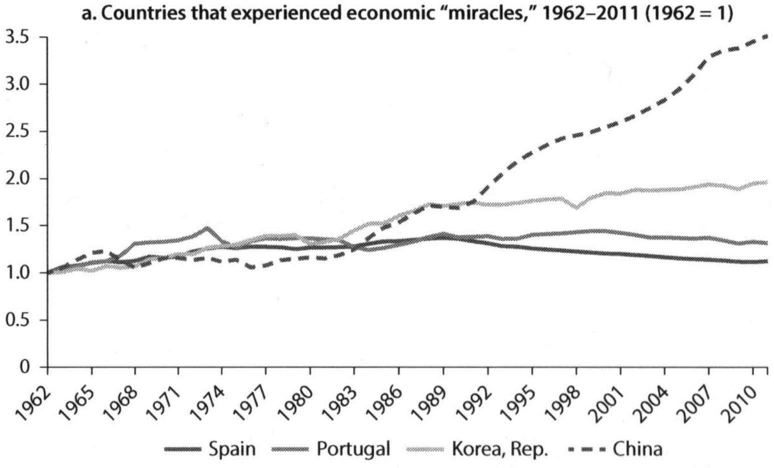

a. Countries that experienced economic "miracles," 1962–2011 (1962 = 1)

Source: Penn World Table, University of Groningen.

figure continues next page

Figure 1.23 Total Factor Productivity *(continued)*

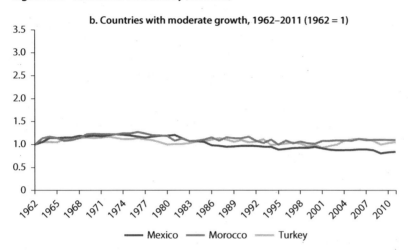

b. Countries with moderate growth, 1962–2011 (1962 = 1)

— Mexico — Morocco ⋯⋯ Turkey

Source: Penn World Table, University of Groningen.

productivity gains or negative productivity growth in the long term. This was the case for Turkey (0.1 percent) and Mexico (−0.2 percent) between 1960 and 2011. In economies where growth was primarily driven by commodities or burgeoning credit, productivity gains were weak as well (0.3 percent in Brazil and −0.9 percent in Chile).

Insufficiently high productivity gains in the Moroccan economy raise questions about the ability to sustain the growth levels achieved in recent years and thus the country's development model. It appears that in the long term, during the 1970–2011 period, the Moroccan economy did not post any TFP gains (see figure 1.23b). The efficiency level measured in 2011 was apparently the same as the level observed in 1965. In other words, even though the quantity of labor and capital in the Moroccan economy had certainly increased greatly since 1965, there was no concomitant change in efficiency in labor and capital allocation. The market institutions that are supposed to ensure efficient allocation of factors of production do not seem to have fulfilled their role in the long run. An analysis of Morocco's output performance by decade gives a glimpse of an improvement in the 2000s, with a return to positive productivity gains of about 1.2 percent (see figure 1.24). However, these gains have not been enough to sustain current growth (see box 1.7).

The low returns to capital accumulation in Morocco could be explained by the fact that the main investment effort comes from the public sector. Between 1998 and 2013, the share of investment made through the central government budget and public enterprises (the highway, train, water and sewage, and phosphates companies) is estimated to have increased from 8 percent to 14 percent of GDP, whereas private sector investment is believed to have remained stable at around 17 percent of GDP, with the exception of some upswings stemming from

Figure 1.24 Morocco: Contribution of Capital, Labor, and Total Factor Productivity to Growth

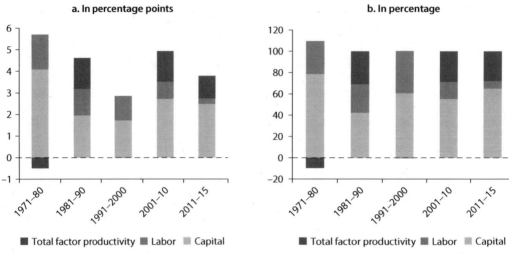

Source: World Bank.

Box 1.7 A Brief History of Productivity in the Moroccan Economy, 1960–2015

An analysis of the contribution of total factor productivity (TFP) to growth by decade high-lights the importance of government policies and structural reforms carried out over time.

In the 1960s, the large contribution of TFP to growth stems primarily from a relatively efficient allocation of resources under the first development plans that Morocco drafted after gaining independence. Allocation of limited financial resources to clearly defined pri-orities to meet the country's most urgent development needs meant that the economy derived maximum benefit from these resources. The result was a significant improvement in overall productivity. The completion of these plans set in place the infrastructure needed to overcome bottlenecks that hampered the modernization of the economy and promoted the mechanization process involving all business sectors, particularly the light processing industry and the agricultural sector. The development plans also made it possible to main-tain a stable and sustainable macroeconomic framework over the period and limit internal and external imbalances.

The highly expansionary economic policies in the 1970s were exacerbated by two oil shocks in 1974 and 1979, which explain much of the negative contribution that TFP made during this period. More specifically, the Economic and Social Development Plan (1973–77) featured large volumes of public investment expenditure (growing by an average of 18 per-cent) that was completely disconnected from the country's financial and structural absorp-tion capabilities. This plan was based on the assumption that the financial windfall from rising commodity prices, stemming from the country's main mineral export, phosphate, was likely to last. The subsequent plan (1978–1980) was based on the same assumption, despite

box continues next page

Box 1.7 A Brief History of Productivity in the Moroccan Economy (1960–2015) *(continued)*

the downward trend of phosphate prices to their pre-1974 levels. Greater use of external financing was required to pay for the completion of the government investment program included in the plans. The import substitution policy only exacerbated the economic situation further over the period, by reducing the availability of the inputs needed by the productive sector and by pushing up production costs, which, as a consequence, increased inflation. Furthermore, this period coincided with the "Moroccanization" policy affecting foreign-owned enterprises, which constituted the core of Morocco's production system. The unfortunate result of this policy was a significant reduction in the productivity of these enterprises over several years because of the lack of managerial and technical skills available to run them with the same efficiency as before. These policies deepened internal and external imbalances and exhausted the fiscal and external space, making the macroeconomic situation unsustainable and resulting in the financial crisis of the early 1980s.

Macroeconomic and sectoral reforms undertaken as part of the Structural Adjustment Program signed with the International Monetary Fund and the World Bank (1983) helped stabilize and strengthen the macroeconomic situation in the 1980s. The main objective of the reforms was to help improve macroeconomic and fiscal management. The program strengthened the resource allocation framework and rationalized government expenditure in general, and investment expenditure in particular. The program also modernized and enhanced the efficiency of the budgetary system. As a consequence, the productivity of government capital increased greatly, generating a larger contribution from TFP to GDP growth in the 1980s. It should be noted that the Structural Adjustment Program ended the way development plans used to be drawn up in rigid terms, marked by exaggerated voluntarism that was disconnected from the country's actual capacities.

The "lost" decade of the 1990s saw reforms slow down, following the positive results achieved under the Structural Adjustment Program in the previous decade. The policies carried out fell short of deepening and expanding the scope of structural adjustment reforms and building on the economic dynamic that started in the second half of the 1980s. With no formal framework for ensuring the consistency and relevance of government policies, sectoral programs turned out to be off the mark because they failed to make a clear contribution to the main development goals at that time: catching up economically, opening the economy up more to international trade, and increasing the role of the private sector in economic activity. Furthermore, such programs were often ineffective because the tools for assessing infrastructure projects were inadequate or even nonexistent. The project selection process was not based on rigorous analysis of the economic, social, and financial relevance of the programs. The objectives of the programs were often overly ambitious given the context and the country's capacities and they sometimes contradicted each other. Productivity remained weak or even negative during this period because the project selection process resulted in inefficient allocation of resources.

Over the past 15 years, Morocco has undertaken an extensive economic and political modernization process. Morocco has managed to improve management of macroeconomic and sectoral policies by introducing more competition to the political sphere. This means both that the main political parties' programs for economic and

box continues next page

Box 1.7 A Brief History of Productivity in the Moroccan Economy (1960–2015) *(continued)*

social development are more pragmatic, focusing on reform proposals, and that strategies are more relevant and more feasible to overcome the main challenges facing the
country. This management, which is more likely to conceive and implement more
appropriate reforms and policies, has led to a rapid increase in productive investment,
particularly from foreign investment, and, more important, to a vast improvement in
resource allocation. This has brought about gradual improvements in the economy's
efficiency and in TFP. However, major rigidities have persisted, with incentives that still
distort the economy and channel investment to inefficient sectors and with labor laws
that impede optimum allocation and use of human resources. This explains why the
contribution of TFP to growth, while positive, is still relatively weak.

Figure 1.25 Morocco: Composition of Investment, 1998–2014
(percentage of GDP)

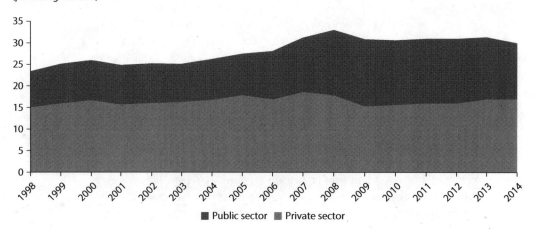

Sources: High Commission for Planning, Ministry of Finance (Rapport sur les établissements et entreprises publics).
Note: GDP = gross domestic product.

the property boom between 2005 and 2008 (see figure 1.25).[11] In 2000, private
sector investment accounted for approximately two thirds of gross fixed capital
formation in Morocco and public sector investment accounted for the remaining
third. Since 2005, the Government has undertaken many infrastructure and
facilities projects that have increased the share of public sector investment to
approximately 50 percent of total investment in Morocco. This means that the
faster capital accumulation seen in Morocco in the 2000s stems almost entirely
from a public sector investment effort.

The incentives and decision-making process for public sector investment
choices are not the same as for the allocation of private sector capital. Although
all private sector investment choices are supposed to consider return and profit-
ability, social and land-use considerations, as well as noneconomic considerations,
often motivate public sector investment choices. State-owned enterprises are

subject to soft budgetary constraints (Kornai 1986). This is hardly surprising, given that the public and private sectors implement different decision-making processes that produce equally different outcomes. On the one hand, profit seeking tends to generate innovation and a quest for efficiency, in terms of both output and resource management. On the other hand, public choice theorists (Buchanan and Tullock 1962) have shown that public policy makers may actually be motivated by public interest (or at least their perception of the public interest), as well as by self-interest or by bureaucratic interests that are sometimes at odds with proper management and good governance of public funds. Furthermore, as will be discussed in greater detail in chapter 3, government policies may distort the economics of private sector investment choices (for example, through sectoral incentives, subsidies, and other types of government intervention). These distortions may impede optimum allocation of factors of production and, ultimately, slow productivity gains.

Distortions in the allocation of capital across sectors could also help explain Morocco's weak aggregate productivity growth. Not all economic sectors are equal in terms of innovation and productivity gains. The tradables sector, which faces international competition, often has to innovate to win markets or even just to ensure its own survival. In contrast, the nontradables sector (for example, administration, construction, and domestic services) is protected from international competition and generally produces little in the way of productivity gains. The differences in the economic efficiency of these sectors can be seen in the measurements of apparent labor productivity in the sectors, defined as the ratio between the value added of a sector and the number of persons employed in that sector. For the Moroccan economy as a whole, apparent labor productivity improved by 3.7 percent per year between 2000 and 2012. In keeping with economic theory, the biggest gains were in the agricultural sector (7.5 percent), transport and communications sectors (4.5 percent), and in the other tradable goods sectors. The weakest performances were seen in the construction sector (1 percent), the hotel and catering sector (−0.5 percent), and other nontradables sectors. The industrial and trade sectors occupied the middle ground, with gains of 2.5 percent and 2 percent, respectively, depending on their openness to trade (see figure 1.26).

These sector trends elucidate the aggregate productivity trend. It seems that job creation in the 2000s was concentrated in sectors with low productivity gains. Between 2000 and 2014, Morocco's economy generated some 1.1 million non-farm jobs. Only two sectors account for more than half of these new jobs (570,000): construction and catering and hotels (see figure 1.27). Not only do these two sectors show a low level of value added per capita, with value added per worker in the construction sector standing at only 80 percent of the figure for the economy as a whole, and just 60 percent of the figure for the nonfarm economy, but they also show much lower productivity gains than other sectors. The allocation of labor by sector, which partially reflects government policy objectives, tended therefore to hamper productivity gains for Morocco's economy as a whole.

Figure 1.26 Morocco: Apparent Labor Productivity Growth Rate, by Sector, 2000–12
(percent)

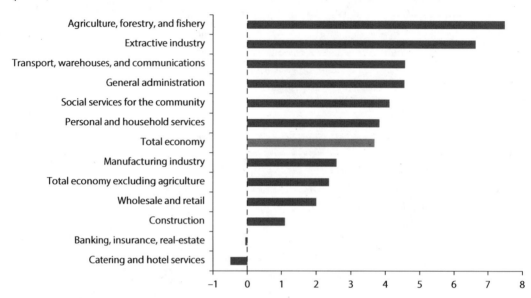

Source: High Commission for Planning.

Figure 1.27 Morocco: Net Job Creation, by Sector, 2000–12

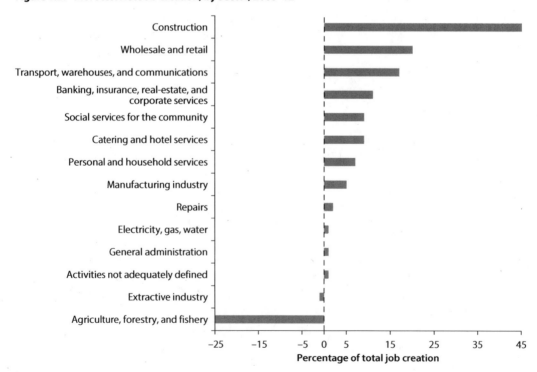

Source: High Commission for Planning.

Depletion of "Environmental" Capital

Morocco's growth has been accompanied by environmental degradation, result-ing in a wide range of costs to society (World Bank 2016). Owing to its arid and semiarid climate with limited water resources and extremely high spatiotemporal rainfall variability, Morocco is a high water stress country. Air pollution causes the accumulation of fine particles suspended in the air indoors and outdoors. Soil degradation is affecting farmland (erosion of dry cropland and the salinization of irrigated cropland) and rangeland (clearings, desertification, and degradation). Forest areas are also under strong anthropogenic pressure (clearings, fires, and other forms of overexploitation), as the current rate of reforestation is not high enough to reverse the observed degradation trend. The concentration of tourist, port, and fishing activities in certain coastal areas is exerting pressure on the living ecosystems and landscapes. The estimated cost of the various forms of environ-mental degradation to Moroccan society was approximately 3.3 percent of GDP in 2014 (see figure 1.28). This cost represents the net present value of the conse-quences of environmental degradation in 2014 over the next 25 years. This cost was assessed at three levels: social, through morbidity and mortality caused by air and water pollution; economic, through forest and rangeland production losses owing to land clearings; and environmental, through groundwater depletion and the reduced recreational value of beaches as a result of coastal degradation. The cost of environmental degradation to the Moroccan society would, however, be lower relative to the estimated 3.7 percent of GDP provided in 2000.

More specifically, the alarming depletion of water resources shows that, despite significant strides in the area of groundwater governance since the enact-ment of water law and the establishment of water basin agencies, weaknesses and deficiencies persist. Potential mobilizable water resources are estimated at 22 billion m^3 on average, of which 18 billion m^3 are surface water resources

Figure 1.28 Morocco: Cost of Environmental Degradation
(percentage of GDP)

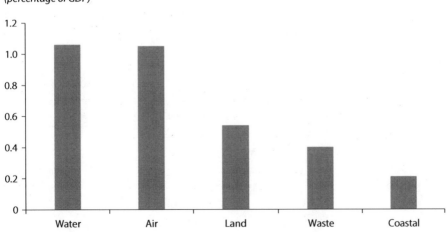

Source: World Bank 2016.
Note: GDP = gross domestic product.

Figure 1.29 Morocco: Annual Water Supply, 1946–2010
(billions of cubic meters)

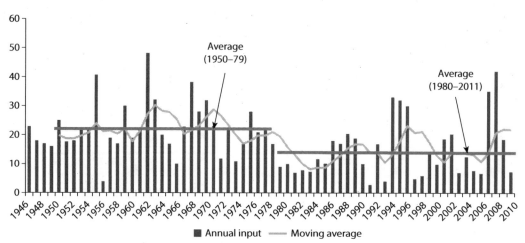

Sources: State Secretariat for Water, World Bank.

(stored in 140 dams) and four billion m³ are groundwater resources that are renewable and exploitable under acceptable technical and economic conditions (see figure 1.29).[12] Given the need to supply a population of close to 34 million inhabitants, Morocco's water potential is roughly 650 m³ per capita, placing Morocco among high water stress countries. It has been officially recognized that Morocco could experience water shortages by 2020 or 2030, regardless of the scenario selected.[13]

Despite high water stress, Morocco has made intensive agriculture a key sector for its economic and social development. Irrigation and, more specifically, surface water irrigation relying on large-scale water works has historically been the keystone of this policy. In the years following Morocco's independence, the government concentrated its action (for example, investment, exemptions, subsidies, and tariff barriers) on developing irrigated agriculture to cope with a large rural population whose main source of employment and income is agriculture and to ensure minimum food security for the country. Starting in the 1990s, agricultural policy focused more on intensive farming, which could only increase the demand for water. Paradoxically, this was the time when the first Water Law was passed to rationalize use of Morocco's limited water resources. In addition, this policy provided incentives for more fruit farms, more intensive dairy farming, and expansion of vegetable growing under glass. This led to heavy use of groundwater, which had been largely conserved up until then (Kuper, Hammani, Chohin, Garin, and Saaf 2012).

In addition to the development of modern boring techniques and lower costs, the central government played a major direct and indirect role in the use of groundwater. With a view to conserving this resource, the National Irrigation Water Conservation Program helped increase the total area equipped for localized irrigation (microirrigation) to 450,000 hectares by the end of 2015.[14] However, after several years of drought in a row, the government suspended restrictions on boring wells and even subsidized new wells and their equipment, including electric pumps. With the advent of the Green Morocco Plan, additional large subsidies were granted to localized irrigation projects.[15] In addition to direct aid and subsidies, the central government contributed indirectly to groundwater irrigation development by subsidizing the consumption of butane, thereby reducing pumping costs, at the risk of seeing an expansion of the "tomato model," an intensive, export-oriented model heavily reliant on polluting inputs and wasteful of scarce resources such as water (Akesbi 2014).

The extraordinary expansion of agriculture under this sustained irrigation policy inevitably had negative consequences for Morocco's "water" capital. As the National Water Strategy (SNE) shows, the deterioration of the water supply and overexploitation of groundwater resources have become urgent concerns for the government authorities in charge of the water sector. Overexploitation has reached alarming levels and we are now seeing depletion of all water tables by more than 860 million cubic meters per year (see figure 1.30). This obviously raises questions about the efficiency and viability of some agricultural production (Wijnen, Augeard, Hiller, Ward, and Huntjens 2012). Several measures were adopted under the SNE to improve water resource management, the outcomes of which will be evident only in the medium and long term. In 2016, for example, a new law aimed at strengthening governance in the water sector and developing nontraditional sources of water was adopted. This law seeks, inter alia,

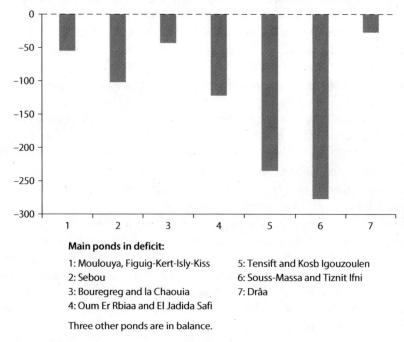

Figure 1.30 Morocco: Overexploitation of Groundwater Resources, 2011
(renewable volumes minus volumes pumped, by basin, in millions of cubic meters)

Main ponds in deficit:

1: Moulouya, Figuig-Kert-Isly-Kiss   5: Tensift and Kosb Igouzoulen
2: Sebou   6: Souss-Massa and Tiznit Ifni
3: Bouregreg and la Chaouia   7: Drâa
4: Oum Er Rbiaa and El Jadida Safi

Three other ponds are in balance.

Source: Ministry of Water and the Environment 2011.

to streamline procedures and strengthen the legal framework for the exploitation of stormwater and wastewater, the implementation of a legal framework to
desalinate seawater, and mechanisms to protect water resources against extreme
climate change phenomena.

An assessment of the economic contribution that water makes to Moroccan
agriculture shows that overexploitation of groundwater provides only a modest contribution to increasing agricultural value added (Doukkali and Grijsen
2015). In other words, the opportunity cost of marginal agricultural production is very high. At the very most, overexploitation of aquifers produces only
0.5 percent of additional GDP (see box 1.8). Groundwater resources in many
basins are being depleted without producing any significant increase in
wealth in exchange. In the case of Souss-Massa, which is most often cited as
a major hub for Morocco's agriculture, substantial groundwater overexploitation produces only 2.8 percent of the region's agricultural value added. Better
water management would prevent overexploitation of aquifers and ensure
the sustainability of groundwater resources to meet the needs of the population and ensure harmonious development of the different sectors of the
economy. Better water management would require, inter alia, alignment of

---

Box 1.8 Economic Contribution of Overexploitation of Groundwater in Morocco

The most striking aspect of a review of the economic literature on the deterioration of the
water supply and overexploitation of groundwater in Morocco is the paucity of published economic papers and research that deal with these issues. Notable exceptions are Allali (2003),
Arrifi (2012), and the World Bank (2003, 2016). This is even more striking when we realize
that Morocco is undertaking costly programs and projects to remedy or reduce pressure on
water resources.

The idea of thinking of water as economic capital is now broadly accepted, and substantial
methodological work has been carried out at the international level to attribute a monetary
value to this capital (Dickson, Levy, and Head 2014). The System of Environmental-Economic
Accounting for Water (SEEA-Water) provides a fairly comprehensive description of these
methods (UNSTATS 2013). It must be stressed, however, as the SEEA-Water shows, that these
methods make sense and can be applied only for water used in production processes, beyond
the amounts needed for basic human needs and survival. These basic survival amounts have
infinite value and do not obey economic allocation rules.

A recent economic assessment of overexploitation of groundwater in Morocco suggests
that overexploitation contributes only 0.53 percent to the country's aggregate GDP (Doukkali
and Grijsen 2015). In the Tensift region, the total contribution is estimated at 1.13 percent of
the aggregate regional value added. In the Souss-Massa region, the contribution of overexploitation of groundwater is estimated to represent 2.8 percent of the regional value added
(see table B1.8.1). In every case, the contribution is relatively modest compared with the rapid
depletion of water resources.

box continues next page

Box 1.8 Economic Contribution of Overexploitation of Groundwater in Morocco *(continued)*

Table B1.8.1 Morocco: Value-Added Generated by Overexploitation of Groundwater

	Unit	Morocco	Souss-Massa	Tensift
Use of groundwater in agriculture	Millions of m^3	3,766	606	708
Contribution of groundwater to irrigated crops valued added	Billions of Dh	14.2	2.9	1.7
Groundwater overexploitation	%	23%	46%	33%
Direct value added generated by groundwater overexploitation				
– Total	Billions of Dh	3.25	1.32	0.58
– By m^3	Dh/m^3	3.8	4.8	2.4
Multiplier		1.3	1.3	1.3
Total value added generated by groundwater overexploitation				
– Total	Billions of Dh	4.23	1.72	0.75
– By m^3	Dh/m^3	4.9	6.2	3.1
Contribution to national GDP and to regional total valued added				
– Direct value added generated by groundwater overexploitation	%	0.40%	2.16%	0.87%
– Total value added generated by groundwater overexploitation	%	0.53%	2.80%	1.13%

In light of these developments, Morocco has undertaken a massive program to remedy the situation (Ministry of Water and the Environment 2011). The main components of this program are artificial refilling of aquifers; recycling wastewater; incentives to convert from gravity irrigation systems to drip systems, which are supposed to use less water; transfers of water from basins with surpluses to basins with deficits; and seawater desalination. In addition to these investment programs, Morocco has undertaken a program to improve groundwater governance that is primarily based on the determination to give the basin agencies a stronger role and to involve groundwater users through aquifer contracts.

water prices with the average cost of supplying it, which ranges between DH 2 and DH 6 per cubic meter (DH/m^3) for dams, between DH 10 and DH 20 per cubic meter for seawater desalination, and more than DH 3.5 per cubic meter for water transferred between basins (Economic, Social, and Environmental Council 2014).

Cognizant of the myriad sectoral challenges associated with water management, the Government developed a series of strategies for climate change adaptation and water conservation. In the context of the National Environmental and Sustainable Development Charter, the National Water Plan and the reform of the water law aim to promote governance in the sector by streamlining procedures and strengthening the legal framework for the exploitation of stormwater and wastewater, the implementation of a legal framework to desalinate seawater, and strengthening of the legal framework and mechanisms to protect water resources, including holding the relevant players accountable through "aquifer contracts," with a view to reducing overexploitation of groundwater resources. As is the case in many other Middle East and North Africa countries, management of the triad of water, energy, and food security will continue to play a key role in the coming decades (Keulertz and Woertz 2016).

To the Unsustainable Demand

Morocco's growth in the 2000s was mainly stimulated by rapidly expanding domestic demand and debt (see figure 1.31). This model has now run up against three constraints that jeopardize its long-term viability: (i) the need to stabilize public debt; (ii) the need to control the development of private debt; and (iii) the need to keep external accounts close to balance. Maintaining macroeconomic stability is a prerequisite for achieving all of Morocco's other medium-term economic and social objectives. Without a stable macroeconomic environment, economic agents face much greater uncertainty, which stymies risk taking on their part and reduces their related investments and productivity gain opportunities.

Central government expenditure has expanded rapidly over the past 15 years, rising from 25 percent of GDP in 2000 to 34 percent of GDP in 2012. Most of the expansion during 2008–12 stemmed from the policy of subsidizing staple goods and petroleum prices to cope with soaring international prices. The cost of the compensation fund to the central government budget peaked at 6 percent of GDP in 2012. While this policy of protection of households' purchasing

Figure 1.31 Morocco: Contribution of Demand Components to Growth, 2008–15
(contribution to annual growth, %)

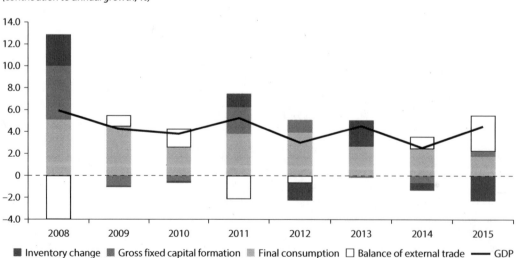

Source: High Commission for Planning.
Note: GDP = gross domestic product.

power helped underpin the growth of domestic demand, it contributed to a substantial deepening of the fiscal deficit, which reached 6.8 percent of GDP in 2012. The reform of the compensation fund initiated in 2013 did help ease pressure on government expenditure, which decreased to 28 percent of GDP in 2016, while at the same time improving the targeting and distribution of subsidies to the benefits of the poor (Verme and El-Massnaoui 2015). The fiscal deficit was further reduced to an estimated 3.9 percent of GDP in 2016, a level that allows the stabilization of the central government debt-to-GDP ratio at the current economic growth rate.

Morocco's public debt has played an important countercyclical role over time. Following a long period of fiscal consolidation that started in the 1990s, the government debt ratio had fallen substantially, to a low of 47 percent of GDP in 2008. As the fiscal deficits accumulated following the 2008 global financial crisis, the central government debt-to-GDP ratio rose by 19 percentage points of GDP in the space of 8 years to reach 66 percent in 2016. Taking into account the debt and public guarantees of all government entities and state-owned enterprises, the overall public debt amounted to 82 percent of GDP in 2016. Despite this rapid deterioration, Morocco managed to maintain the confidence of its investors and creditors. It obtained and maintained an investment grade rating from the main rating agencies. This confidence stemmed mainly from the structure of Morocco's debt, which is primarily financed on the domestic market, despite the recent increase in external financing, and from the Moroccan Government's reputation for fiscal discipline, which was underpinned by the successful reform of the compensation fund.

Although it is difficult to determine a critical threshold for government debt, several indicators suggest that the current level of Morocco's government debt is hindering long-term growth driven by public demand. First, a comparison with other countries shows that Morocco's debt ratio is much higher than the average for emerging countries, which stood at approximately 40 percent of GDP in 2014. For example, the debt-to-GDP ratio is 33 percent in Turkey, 40 percent in Romania, 47 percent in Thailand, and 50 percent in Mexico. Furthermore, the medium-term and long-term prospects point to further fiscal pressures, related primarily to the ageing population. The implied debt of Morocco's retirement system is estimated at approximately 100 percent of GDP, with half of that debt owed by the civil service retirement plan (Audit Office 2013). The pension reform adopted in 2016 is expected to help keep the Moroccan Retirement Fund (Caisse Marocaine des Retraites) afloat in the short term, which, without any parametric pension reform, is projected to exhaust its reserves by 2022. History shows that even where the context of financialization of economies differs, it bears noting that countries where the economy successfully took off had very little debt when they were at Morocco's current level of development. In Southern European countries such as Italy, Portugal, and Spain, the debt ratio was under 30 percent between 1960 and 1980. With its initial level of government debt so high and massive implied debt, Morocco does not have the same fiscal space that these countries enjoyed to stimulate their convergence. Solely by refocusing government action on its sovereign functions, continuing fiscal consolidation, and modernizing the administration can significant fiscal space be recreated.

Growing private sector debt significantly boosted recent growth, but this source of growth may also have reached its limits. One of the sectors that made the largest contribution to Morocco's growth over the past decade is property. This sector alone accounted for 40 percent of job creations between 2000 and 2014. The sector's growth was galvanized by a huge expansion of bank credit. The credit-to-GDP ratio rose from 43 percent in 2004 to 72 percent in 2012, before sharply declining starting in 2013 (see figure 1.32). Most of the growth occurred in the second half of the 2000s, when a credit boom regularly saw annual lending growth rates of more than 20 percent, with a peak of 30-percent growth in 2008. The credit boom stemmed from a combination of several favorable factors, such as lower interest rates, increased income, and the development of the financial sector. The breakdown by sector shows that the most dynamic component is property loans. The outstanding amount of such loans rose from 6.8 percent of GDP in 2000 to 26 percent of GDP in 2014. In other words, the bulk of the financial deepening in Morocco during the 2000s stemmed from the property boom. In 2014, nearly 58 percent of urban households owned their own homes, compared with 52 percent 10 years earlier.

In many countries, credit booms led to financial instability, banking crises, or credit crunches. In Morocco, after the preliminary boom, credit growth had a soft landing, which did not trigger major financial instability. Nevertheless, the build-up of risk during the boom phase did lead to an increase in bad debts a few years later.

Figure 1.32 Morocco: Bank Lending to the Private Sector, 2001–15
(percentage of GDP)

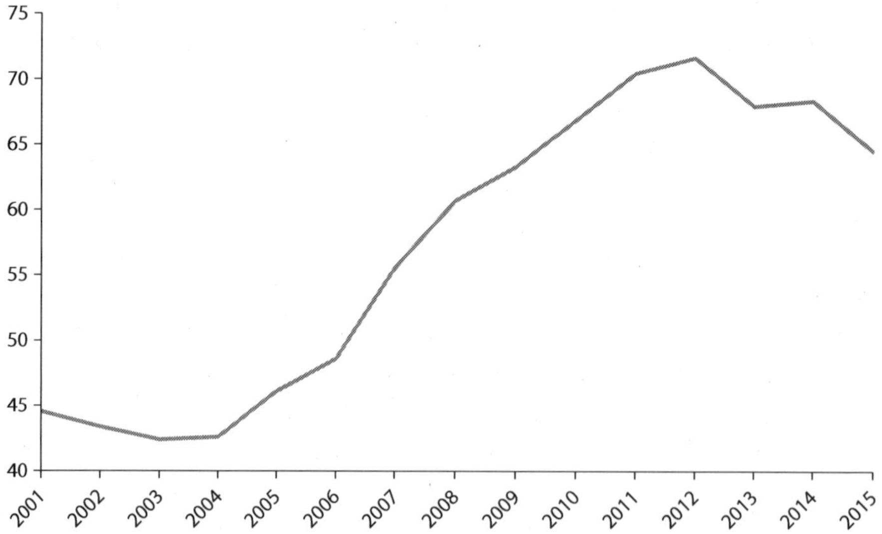

Source: World Development Indicators, World Bank.
Note: GDP = gross domestic product.

Nonperforming loans increased by 16 percent per year between 2011 and 2014, raising the bad debt ratio to 6.3 percent in 2014, compared with 4.8 percent in 2010. As the credit quality of banks' loan books declines, economic growth slows, and debts are repaid, the pace of credit growth is now slower than that of GDP growth. Credit is unlikely to play the same driving role in the future as it did in the 2000s. Morocco's private sector debt, standing at approximately 70 percent of GDP, is relatively high compared with the average ratio of around 50 percent in emerging countries (see figure 1.33). There are other factors behind the credit boom that are not reproducible: a sharp drop in interest rates, an extension of loan terms to 25 years, and the availability of unbanked savings. Morocco coped relatively well with the impact of the credit boom on financial stability, owing to the soundness of its banking system and close oversight of its bank regulator. However, other countries' experience has shown that the repetition of such episodes of massive debt accumulation significantly increases the likelihood of a financial crisis (Gourichas and Obstfeld 2011).

The combination of growing central government debt and household debt has resulted in structurally weak external accounts. The growing imbalance between public and private sector savings and investment has led to a deterioration of the domestic savings-investment balance, and thus to a large current account imbalance. Between 2008 and 2013, the current account deficit averaged 6.7 percent of GDP. The decline in oil prices since mid-2014 made it possible to reduce the current account deficit, which stood at around 6 percent of GDP in 2014 and 2 percent of GDP in 2015. However, this reduction is largely the result of cyclical factors and does not necessarily point to a structural improvement.

Figure 1.33 Bank Lending to the Private Sector, 2015
(percentage of GDP)

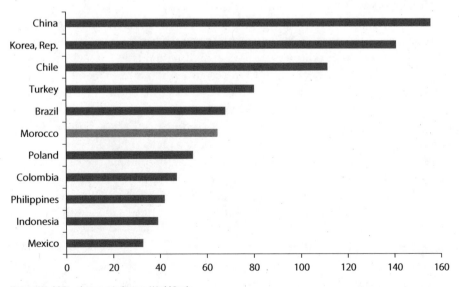

Source: World Development Indicators, World Bank.
Note: GDP = gross domestic product.

Indeed, in 2016, the current account deficit bounced back to an estimated 4 percent of GDP. In addition to a dramatic decrease in commodity prices, Morocco's current account "benefited" from slower economic growth in the country, which led to a sharp drop in the demand for imports other than energy (capital goods, semi-finished products, and, more recently, consumer goods). A further worsening of the current account deficit can therefore be expected as economic recovery causes imports to take off again. Furthermore, the Gulf countries provide Morocco with assistance equivalent to approximately 1 percent of GDP each year. This assistance is expected to continue for a few years. Taken together, these circumstances point to a larger structural current account deficit for Morocco than today's observed deficit. Even with a positive scenario of renewed growth in Europe, which would stimulate exports and transfers, Morocco's external imbalance is likely to persist at a high level.

The trade balance clearly shows the fragility of Morocco's external accounts. In 2000, the import coverage ratio stood at 64 percent. After more than a decade of growth that was largely driven by domestic demand (consumption and investment), the import coverage ratio showed a declining trend and stood at 54.8 percent in 2016. Morocco's trade deficit is now equivalent to 20 percent of GDP, compared with 11 percent in 2000. While soaring commodity prices are partly responsible for this trend, the nonenergy trade balance is the primary cause. The import coverage ratio excluding energy imports fell from 75 percent to 66 percent between 2000 and 2014. Considering the fact that soaring commodity prices also boosted Morocco's exports, such as phosphates, the deepening of the trade deficit over this period appeared to be even more marked. Tourist earnings and transfers from Moroccans residing in other countries, which are two major sources of income for Morocco, have stopped being large enough to offset the trade balance since 2008.

Morocco's structurally large external current account deficit is a major source of vulnerability that raises the issue of its viability. Morocco's balance of payments is one of the most fragile among emerging countries. From 2010 to 2014, the average emerging country's current account deficit stood at 1.5 percent of GDP, compared with 7 percent for Morocco. In a group of 25 non–oil-producing emerging countries, Morocco ranked third for the size of its current account deficit, after Jordan and Mauritius. Cumulative current account deficits are financed by growing external debt, in the form of loans or foreign direct investment (FDI). A more open and attractive Moroccan economy increased FDI flows to an average of 2.5 percent of GDP between 2000 and 2016, bringing the country into line with the other emerging countries, where FDI flows average 2.7 percent of GDP.[16] However, FDI may also create financial vulnerabilities. This is because the FDI received is in proportion to future external financial commitments to repatriate profits. FDI is important for the economy because of potential technology and know-how transfers, but it also entails future financial implications that must not be underestimated.

As a consequence of the deepening current account deficit, Morocco's net international investment position, which measures the difference between the country's external financial assets and liabilities, worsened over the past decade, increasing from the equivalent of 38 percent of GDP in 2002 to 61 percent in 2015. This is a worrying development for the country's macroeconomic stability. It is generally agreed that the critical threshold for a country's external debt, as measured by the net international investment position, stands at around 50 percent of GDP. The likelihood of a crisis becomes very strong above this threshold (Catao and Gian 2013). Morocco is approaching the critical threshold, with a net liability position that is relatively worse than the average of approximately 30 percent of GDP seen in the emerging countries. However, the risk of a crisis is somewhat attenuated by the structure of Morocco's external debt, which is dominated by FDI and official bilateral and multilateral loans, which constitute a relatively stable and low-risk source of financing. If Morocco is to maintain its macroeconomic stability in the medium term, it must restructure its current account in an orderly fashion, which means avoiding sudden swings in an unstable context. Orderly adjustment will require rebalancing the growth model, with a greater role for external demand and faster development of the tradable goods sector.

In sum, in addition to showing vulnerabilities relating to supply (poor productivity gains and job creation), Morocco's growth model is also fragile in terms of demand. A model relying mainly on domestic demand, stimulated by credit and government spending, cannot be sustainable in the long term. To ensure sounder growth, Morocco needs more balanced, export-led growth generating less debt. The worsening, volatile, and uncertain state of the regional and international environment means that Morocco cannot reasonably rely on a spontaneous increase in external demand in its traditional markets. Europe is mired in myriad crises, including managing Brexit, and the European domestic market, even if it is still the largest in the world, will not in all likelihood expand rapidly in the coming years. Morocco's strategic opening up to Sub-Saharan Africa is promising, in light of Africa's growth and development prospects (Lo 2016). However, African markets, particularly in Francophone Africa, remain small for the time being. Excluding Cameroon, Côte d'Ivoire, and Gabon, the cumulative GDP of the other 11 West and Central African countries that belong to the franc zone does not exceed Morocco's GDP. Given Nigeria's economic clout, the current opening up toward this country and East Africa provides significant economic opportunities. Morocco therefore essentially needs to continue relying on its own strengths to create the right conditions for steadier external demand, by continuing to implement its strategy to diversify target markets and promote exports. This strategy will require a faster pace of structural change in the economy.

The Challenges of a Slow Structural Transformation

The countries that are achieving or have achieved major productivity gains are the ones that have consistently managed to reallocate labor and capital to the most productive sectors and activities (McMillan and Rodrik 2011). This leads to structural transformation of the economy, as some sectors contract and others emerge. In the upper-middle-income countries, for example, the share of agriculture in the country's aggregate value added declined by an average of 20 percentage points of GDP over the past 50 years to stand at less than 10 percent of GDP in 2014. The share of industry, however, initially increased to reach approximately 30 percent of GDP in the early 1980s, before dropping off sharply in subsequent decades. In Morocco, this "structural transformation" or "creative destruction" process has been less active (Atiyas 2015). Unlike upper-middle-income countries, the share of agriculture in Morocco's GDP has declined only slightly over the past 35 years. The shares of manufacturing and services have also remained relatively stable compared with the changes seen in comparable countries (see figure 1.34).

The relative intersectoral structural stability of Morocco's economy partly obscures a more dynamic transformation in terms of intrasectoral spatialization and diversification. But this trend was not strong enough to boost the country's aggregate growth. Under the Green Morocco Plan, for example, the structural policies started to change the country's agriculture, generating real buoyancy in the sector as a result of sustained increases in agricultural investment, which was 1.7 times higher in 2014 than in 2008. The first signs of structural transformation are now perceptible with the remarkable rise in the sector's value added. Similarly, Moroccan manufacturing was highly concentrated in traditional specializations up until the end of the 1990s. The modernization process that started in 2005 revealed the duality between traditional industries that were flagging, such as the textiles and clothing industry as it sought to reposition itself on the markets, and emerging specializations, such as the automotive and aeronautics industries, the food industry, metallurgy, and pharmaceuticals. Positive dynamics within these sectors were underpinned by proactive public policies (tax incentives, subsidies, investments, and other incentives) and produced such

Figure 1.34 Morocco's Transformation Relative to Upper-Middle-Income Countries, by Sector, 1980–2014

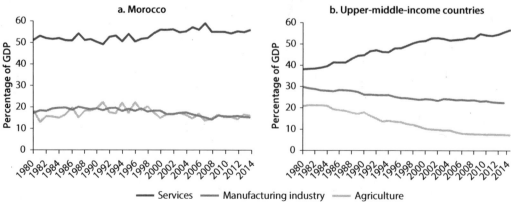

Source: World Development Indicators, World Bank.
Note: GDP = gross domestic product.

achievements as the Renault project that raised national automotive production to close to 345,000 vehicles in 2016 and created 7,100 direct jobs. However, they lack the strength and numbers to have a macroeconomic impact on growth.

Three key trends emerge when the allocation of resources is used to analyze the structural dynamics of Morocco's economy: (i) difficulty allocating unskilled labor owing to weak industrialization; (ii) difficulty allocating skilled labor owing to the slow upgrading of Morocco's economy; and (iii) difficulty allocating talent resulting in weak entrepreneurial drive. This brings us to the nub of the career problems that Amine, Nisrine, Kawtar, and Réda face.

A Difficult Industrialization Process

The history of economic development has shown us that industrialization has been a key step in most countries toward absorbing the unskilled workers leaving the agricultural sector. With very few exceptions, every country started its development process with a large rural population where most workers were employed in the agricultural sector. In 1950, agricultural jobs accounted for 44 percent of employment in Spain and 47 percent in Italy. In 1963, they accounted for 49 percent of employment in Taiwan, China; and 62 percent in the Republic of Korea (see figure 1.35). Every economic takeoff has brought with it an acceleration of rural depopulation and a major reduction in the number of agricultural workers as many of them leave the countryside to seek jobs in the city. Agricultural jobs now account for an average of only 4 percent of employment in the countries mentioned earlier. The case of Spain illustrates the scale of

Figure 1.35 Agriculture's Share of Employment, 1950–2011
(percent)

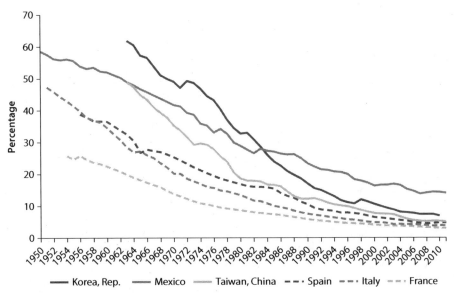

Source: Timmer, de Vries, and de Vries 2015.

Morocco 2040 · http://dx.doi.org/10.1596/978-1-4648-1066-4

this transformation: Spain had four million agricultural workers in 1950, compared with only 800,000 today. When these farm workers, who were usually poorly educated, arrived in the city, they managed to find jobs in factories, which were increasing their workforces rapidly. Jobs created in manufacturing offset the loss of agricultural jobs. A tipping point is reached when the number of factory workers exceeds the number of agricultural workers. Italy reached this point in 1966; Spain did so in 1972; Taiwan, China, in 1977; and the Republic of Korea in 1985. After the tipping point has been reached, the manufacturing workforce continues to grow until peak industrialization is achieved. At this peak, factories employ more than a quarter of the active working population. This change constitutes a stylized fact (see figure 1.36). After the peak, deindustrialization occurs and there is a trend toward a smaller share of employment in manufacturing and an increase in the share of employment in services.

When compared with these stylized facts, Morocco's industrialization process has been a difficult one. Over an extended period of time, the structural transformation of the Moroccan economy can be described as slow (El Mokri 2016). There are 4.1 million agricultural workers in Morocco today. As was the case in the advanced countries, the share of agriculture in total employment tends to diminish as part of the urbanization process (see figure 1.37). It fell from 47 percent in 2000 to 39 percent in 2014. If the trend continues in a linear fashion, agricultural jobs will account for less than 20 percent of employment by 2050. However, in contrast to the developed countries or upper-middle-income countries, Morocco's urbanization has been relatively

Figure 1.36 Manufacturing's Share of Aggregate Employment, 1950–2011
(percent)

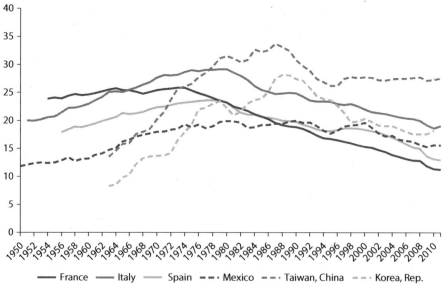

Source: 10-Sector database, University of Groningen.

Figure 1.37 Morocco: Sector Shares of Total Employment, 1999–2012
(percent)

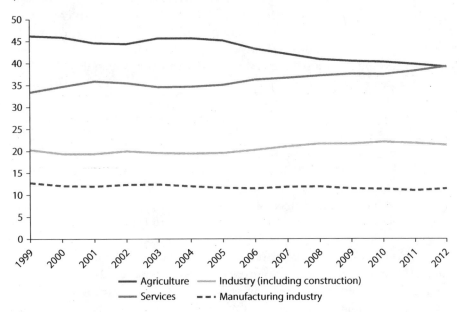

Source: High Commission for Planning.

slow and is not backed up by an industrialization process. The manufacturing share of total employment in Morocco has been declining since the late 1990s. In 2000, approximately 12 percent of workers were employed in industry, compared with only 10 percent in 2014. Manufacturing's declining share of GDP in Morocco started from a low peak of industrialization and affects many developing countries. In economic literature, this phenomenon is known as "premature deindustrialization" (Rodrik 2015). This observation is manifestly reflected in Morocco's ranking on the Economic Complexity Indicator (ECI) in 2014: 78th out of 124 countries (Hidalgo and Hausmann 2009).[17] However, it bears noting that the number of persons employed in the processing industries subsector grew steadily at an average rate of 1.4 percent between 2000 and 2014, attesting to a restructuring of the industrial landscape between the traditional sectors and certain emerging processing sectors.

And yet, the Moroccan Government introduced assertive policies to boost industrial development. The Industry Upgrade Plan and then the Emergence Plan adopted in 2004 attest to Morocco's determination to provide active support to high-potential export sectors where the country enjoys a comparative advantage, such as the automobile industry, certain offshored activities, aeronautics, the food industry, and electronics. A wide range of measures were adopted to attract foreign investors to "Morocco's Global Business Lines." These measures include the development of modern industrial parks ("integrated industrial platforms"), tax incentives, direct subsidies, cheap financing, and targeted training systems. The efforts continued with the adoption of an "Industrial Acceleration Plan" in 2014, which enhanced the existing measures by setting up an Industrial Development Fund and investments, with resources equivalent to 2 percent of GDP for the period 2014–20 in order to provide subsidies to different industries, a new incentives framework (Investment Charter) to support industrial investment, and the implementation of industrial ecosystems for the creation of a new dynamic and a new relationship between major groups and SMEs.[18]

The impetus created by this industrial policy is starting to produce results, particularly in the automotive and aeronautics industries. The opening of a massive plant in Tangier by Renault in 2011, with its output capacity of 400,000 vehicles per year, played a driving role in attracting a large number of auto parts manufacturers. The industrial base is expected to be further strengthened with the announcement in 2015 of a new plant for the Peugeot-Citroën group. There have also been encouraging developments at the aeronautics hub located near Casablanca, spearheaded by groups such as Bombardier, Safran, and Boeing. These developments bring major benefits in terms of jobs (85,000 jobs in the automotive industry and 11,000 jobs in aeronautics) and in terms of exports. Since 2014, the automotive industry has been the leading export sector in Morocco, accounting for 20 percent of the country's total exports.

In view of these positive sectoral developments, we need to analyze why industry as a whole continues to make such a feeble contribution to job creation at the national level. In 2016, the industrial sector as a whole created 8,000 jobs. However, between 2009 and 2014, more than 130,000 net industrial jobs were cut (see figure 1.38). The encouraging developments in certain "modern" industries obscure a less satisfactory situation when industry is considered as a whole. The changes underway in the industrial sector are creating jobs in new exporting businesses, but, over time, more jobs are being shed on average in traditional labor-intensive businesses. The negative net impact of these changes on employment is even more marked for unskilled workers, since the new jobs require more skills (in a cable manufacturing plant, for example, the average worker is a high school graduate). The situation is likely to change more favorably in the future. The roadmap for the SME support program (Maroc PME) provides, for example, important job creation targets, which are in line with the goals set forth in the Industrial Acceleration Plan. Thus, close to 135,000 new jobs are expected, with investments worth more than 2 percent of GDP. In the interim at the macro level, however, Morocco is experiencing an "industrial reconfiguration" rather than true "reindustrialization." In aggregate, deindustrialization is not the result of an "accounting screen"; it is a real and lasting shift (Ministry of Economy and Finance 2015e).

One of the reasons for this difficult reindustrialization is the simple fact that Moroccan entrepreneurs are not interested enough in industry. As discussed earlier, Morocco has a high investment rate, averaging more than 30 percent of GDP, and positive business creation, with between 30,000 and 40,000 new businesses each year. However, few Moroccan investors or entrepreneurs are interested in industry. Even in the most buoyant sectors, such as the automotive and

Figure 1.38 Morocco: Net Job Creation in Industry and Crafts (Excluding Construction), 2007–16

(thousands)

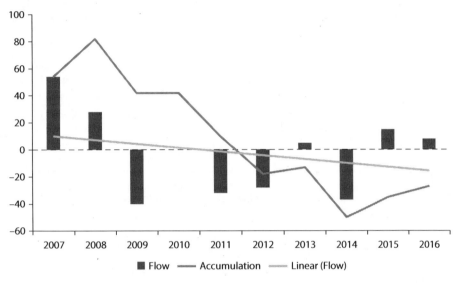

Source: High Commission for Planning notes on the job market situation.

aeronautics industries, there is limited local capital and most of the growth is driven by foreign stakeholders. For example, in the case of Renault's symbolic plant in Tangier, less than 10 percent of the first-tier suppliers that do business on a daily basis with the plant are Moroccan majority shareholders (Benabdejlil, Lung, and Piveteau 2016).[19] The local impacts relate mainly to service industries (for example, security, transport, and maintenance) and indirect purchases (such as oils and other consumables). However, the involvement of local businesses is a core element of the 2014–2020 Industrial Acceleration Plan, aimed at developing local providers, in particular second-tier ones, and facilitating the skills development of industrial enterprises.

Unlike other emerging countries, Morocco also has few joint ventures between local and foreign firms in the industrial sector. Overall, Morocco's large private sector groups invest little in industry and have only minor interests in new growth industries. In this area as well, the Industrial Acceleration Plan seeks to promote industrial partnerships involving Moroccan businesses and major international groups by providing special benefits. By way of example, under the Renault ecosystem the Industrial Acceleration Plan is supporting the execution of a large-scale, joint venture industrial project involving a local parts manufacturer and one of the world's leading automotive glass manufacturers. However, without substantial local capital, a local, autonomous industrial process struggles to get off the ground. Large domestic corporate groups have played a decisive role in the diversification of output in emerging countries that have built up sound industrial bases. The examples of Koc in Turkey, Samsung in the Republic of Korea, and Tata in India show that conglomerates make an active contribution to the industrialization of their countries by forging joint ventures with multinational groups, creating national brands, and investing in research and development (R&D) to accelerate technological adaptation and move their products upmarket. In contrast, as is the case in many emerging countries (see box 1.9), long-standing industry players are divesting from industry in Morocco and moving into other businesses, such as property development. However, the current, increasingly clear interest that major groups operating in various traditional industries are showing in promising sectors such as the automotive sector augurs well for the future.

Morocco's industrialization deficit stems from the fact that industry is less profitable than other business sectors. Incentives matter in economics. If Morocco's

---

Box 1.9 Is Morocco the Only Country Concerned by Premature Deindustrialization?

Premature deindustrialization has affected many emerging countries, and not just Morocco. The forces hampering the expansion of Morocco's industrial sector are not related solely to domestic price-competitiveness issues. Global forces are also at play. Industry accounts for a shrinking share of employment almost everywhere in the world. Deindustrialization is a normal process in rich countries, but, in the last decade, it has also started affecting most of the emerging countries, before they even have the opportunity to become industrialized. Economists cite several factors to explain this change.

- In purely statistical terms, deindustrialization is in part more of an apparent phenomenon than a real one, since industrial firms' in-house service activities are increasingly being outsourced and entrusted to specialized firms.
- In addition to the statistical aspect, the primary cause of premature deindustrialization is thought to be the emergence of China, which, owing to its size and economies of scale, is believed to have captured a very large share of global industrial output at the expense of other developing countries.
- Technology may provide another explanation. Production is increasingly automated and robots are gradually replacing human workers. According to economists Erik Brynjolfsson and Andrew McAfee in their book *The Second Machine Age* the robotics trend is just getting under way and will lead to increasing replacement of human workers by machines, particularly with the advent of 3D printing (Brynjolfsson and McAfee 2014).
- Last, the reorganization of world trade around value chains could also affect the industrial dynamics of emerging countries. The production of industrial goods is now being split up among several countries, with each producing the components for which it has a comparative advantage. Under this new configuration, emerging countries face the risk of developing a lasting specialization in the segments with low value added, without being able to move upmarket. This would ultimately limit their industrialization potential.

Morocco needs to accurately assess the global forces currently at play in order to set realistic objectives for its industrialization policy.

---

entrepreneurs and large corporate groups are shunning industry, it is because industry is less financially profitable and involves higher risks than other sectors, especially sectors that are protected from international competition. Since the late 1990s, Moroccan manufacturers have faced falling prices as international competition intensifies with the reduction of tariff barriers and China's emergence. At the same time, internal production costs for wages, services, land, etc., have increased, drastically squeezing profit margins. However, sectors that are not exposed to international competition, such as property, services, or trade, have increased their margins by raising prices, against the backdrop of rising domestic demand and expanding credit. Some government programs have amplified this movement by providing advantages and subsidies for certain sectors. More specifically, in the property market, tax incentives for developing public housing have reached 1 percent of GDP, which attracted large numbers of investors to the sector (Ministry of Economy and Finance 2015f).

The difference in profit margins between protected sectors and exposed sectors can be seen in changes in value-added prices. The value-added price in the textile and clothing sector did not increase between 1998 and 2012, whereas it rose by 50 percent in the construction sector and by 60 percent in the hotels and catering sector (see figure 1.39). Under the circumstances, economic operators, particularly many subcontractors, made the rational decision to move out of the exposed economy toward the protected economy, thus accelerating the deindustrialization process.[20] Consequently, Morocco's industry faces a critical challenge, which is to become attractive for local entrepreneurs and investors again. The downturn in the property market since 2012 is a favorable development

Figure 1.39 Morocco: Sector Deflators, 1996–2012
(index 1998=100)

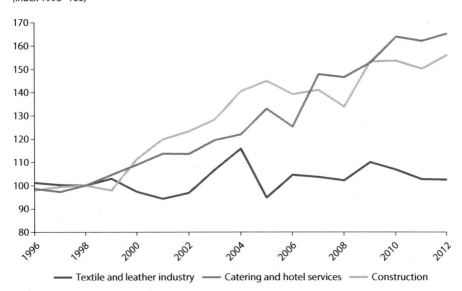

Source: High Commission for Planning.

from this perspective.[21] Morocco can therefore build on the fairly strong FDI flows to reverse the trend and create endogenous growth driven by Moroccan players to ensure a lasting takeoff of the country's industry.

Morocco's weak industrialization takes a heavy toll on economic and social development. First, it undermines the productivity of unskilled young people, who account for two-thirds of the country's young people. As noted earlier, industry constitutes the main sector where unskilled workers can achieve major productivity gains (Rodrik 2013). Yet, industry (including craft trades) currently employs only 20 percent of unskilled young men residing in urban areas. Furthermore, only 3.4 percent of these young men are employed in industrial undertakings with more than 20 employees. Another perverse effect of the lack of industrial growth is that it has a negative impact on female labor force participation. Industry, particularly the textile and agrifood industries, is the leading employer of unskilled women in urban areas. With deindustrialization, women preferred to drop out of the labor force rather than seek odd jobs. In 2010, 43 percent of unskilled urban women in employment worked in industry, as opposed to 50 percent in 2000. The lack of industrial jobs means that unskilled young workers seek odd jobs in the trade sector (30 percent) or in construction (17 percent). More than 90 percent of these unskilled young people work in the informal sector. The launch of the self-entrepreneur project that seeks to organize all informal activities into a simple and attractive regulatory framework could therefore help unleash even more private initiative.[22]

The Slow Upgrading of the Economy

The unemployment of young Moroccan graduates is often attributed to the poor quality of education provided by schools and universities. Yet, many young university-educated Moroccans are unemployed or underemployed. This means that unemployment of young graduates cannot be explained solely by the alleged poor quality of their skills; it is also linked to a lack of demand from employers for their skills. The slow pace of structural change in Morocco's industries is preventing this sector from absorbing the growing numbers of young graduates. As the authorities have noted, "the reallocation of labor from less productive sectors to more productive ones has indeed led to a moderate increase in productivity gains. However this process is still too relatively slow to have a major leveraging effect on growth over the next decade" (Ministry of Economy and Finance 2015e).

During the development process, economies undergo transformation and traditional occupations are replaced by new, more sophisticated ones. This phenomenon is occurring in developing and more advanced countries alike. In the United States, for example, an estimated 20 percent of new jobs are in fields that were nonexistent 20 years ago. By 2025, close to 50 percent of current occupations will be redundant as artificial intelligence and robotics continue to transform businesses. These new technologies usually rely on more skilled workers who do more intellectual work and fewer repetitive manual tasks. This structural transformation of employment can be seen in the growing numbers of managers and office workers. In developed countries, the share of middle managers (also referred to as "intermediary professions"—this category includes skilled professionals such as nurses and specialized technicians) and senior managers accounted on average for 10 percent of the employed population in the 1950s, compared with an average of 40 percent today. In emerging countries, such as Brazil, Poland, and Turkey, the proportion is currently around 20 percent and appears to be rising rapidly (see figure 1.40). The growth in management positions is very important as it provides opportunities for an increasingly skilled labor force. In France, for example, the increase in the number of high school graduates (more than 50 percent of labor force participants had at least a baccalaureate diploma in 2010, compared with 10 percent in 1960) was accompanied by a sharp increase in the share of management jobs (43 percent in 2010, versus 15 percent in 1960).

In Morocco, middle and senior management jobs accounted for only 7.6 percent of total employment in 2013 (14 percent in urban areas). This rate is consistent with the proportion of labor force participants with a baccalaureate or a higher degree (11 percent). However, the gap between the two percentages is likely to widen in the future. With mass extension of education, the percentage of graduates in total employment has showed steady growth of some 0.5 percentage points per year and could approach 25 percent by 2040. However, the proportion of management jobs in total employment has grown more slowly, at a rate of 0.1 percentage points per year, increasing from 6.1 percent in 2000 to 10 percent in 2010 before dipping to 7.4 percent in

Figure 1.40 Share of Middle and Senior Management Positions in Total Employment, 2008

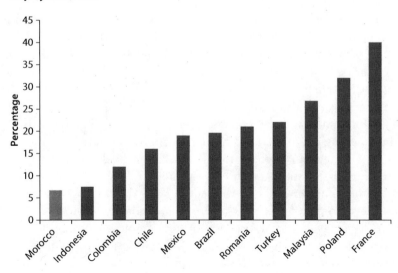

Source: International Labor Organization, ILOSTAT.

Figure 1.41 Morocco: Share of Middle and Senior Management Positions in Total Employment, 2000–14
(percent)

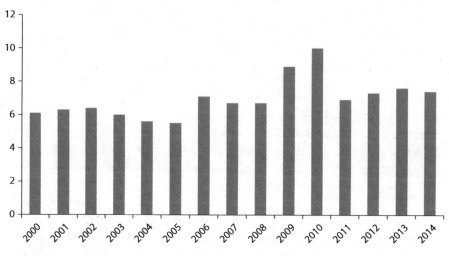

Source: High Commission for Planning.

2014 (see figure 1.41). These projections lead us to conclude that the demand for management personnel is structurally insufficient to provide opportunities for graduates entering the labor force. The slow upgrading of the economy is the main reason for this situation.

Modern, high value-added services have also been slow to emerge. In developed countries, the increase in management jobs paralleled a transformation of the structure of employment by sector. The main feature of this change has been the growth of modern services: business services, health care, and education. Many emerging countries also turn to their traditional service sectors as well as their modern service sectors as a source of employment, including well-paid jobs (Dadush 2015). In many cases, productivity in the services sector increases as quickly as, or more quickly than, in the manufacturing sector, and information technologies have made many services globally tradable, such as in the health sector, which is one of the main sources of jobs for graduates. In advanced countries, the health sector accounts for an average of 8 percent of employment, compared with 3 percent in emerging countries and only 1 percent in Morocco. This means that Morocco will need to triple employment in the health sector to attain a similar structure to such countries as Turkey (3 percent) or Brazil (3 percent). At the same time, one of the sectors with the fastest job growth during the development process is business and finance services. This sector accounts for an average of 12 percent of total employment in rich countries and 6 percent in emerging countries. In Morocco, despite substantial growth, this sector currently accounts for only 3 percent of total employment, compared with 1.5 percent in 2000. The finance and insurance sector is one of the competitive strengths of Morocco's economy, but employs only roughly 60,000 people and creates a net average of only 2,000 jobs per year. In the knowledge economy, the education sector also drives the creation of skilled jobs. This sector accounts for 7 percent of total employment in developed countries, 5 percent in emerging economies, and 3 percent in Morocco (see figure 1.42). The proportion of education professionals in total employment seems to be particularly small because Morocco's population is young and enrollment rates are increasing.

The growth of modern services has been hampered by structural constraints. As already noted, the first reason for the slow emergence of modern services is the fact that Morocco started moving toward a service economy from a relatively low level of per capita GDP, without first going through a major industrialization phase. This atypical development pattern has profound consequences for the potential growth of services. In the advanced economies, business services relied on a broad industrial base for their growth. It is estimated that more than one-third of jobs created stem from outsourcing of functions that industrial firms used to perform in house, such as, for example, accounting, maintenance and upkeep, engineering, research and development, and marketing (Berlingieri 2014). Input-output tables clearly show that industry is still the leading customer for business services. The second reason for the slow development of modern services is the weak purchasing power of Moroccan households. When the developed countries started moving toward a service economy, their per capita GDP was twice that of Morocco today. Households' purchasing power meant that consumption could transition to superior goods, such as health care, education,

Figure 1.42 Share of Modern Services in Total Employment, 2012

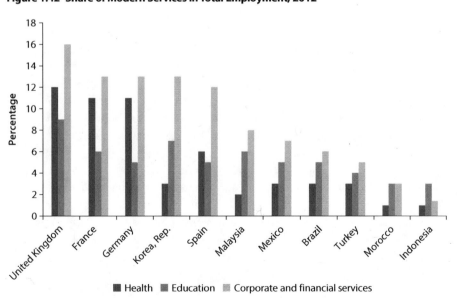

Source: ILO Statistics.

and recreation. Moroccan households still devote 40 percent of their budget to food, which was the percentage seen in European countries between 1950 and 1960. This leaves very little room for spending on other types of consumption.

The question for Morocco is whether it is possible to develop a sizeable business services sector, despite the narrow industrial base and households' weak purchasing power. Job market trends in recent years indicate that this will be a difficult challenge. Under the circumstances, one of the most promising prospects will be hosting offshored services (for example, call centers, subcontracting, outsourcing), which makes it possible to overcome Morocco's weak industrial sector by attracting foreign firms. Today, some 70,000 people work in this sector, primarily as call center employees. The objective of the Emergence Plan was to increase the number of such employees to 100,000 by 2015. This sector faces two challenges: hiring enough young employees who are fluent in more than one language and upgrading to higher value-added services to cope with keener international competition from low-cost countries.

The digital revolution makes employing young semi-skilled workers more complicated. The dissemination of new information and communications technologies (ICTs) across business sectors means that increasingly higher skill levels are required for most jobs. The "skill-biased" technologies require workers with higher levels of human capital (Autor 2010). Digitization transforms many jobs that were previously done by clerical workers (for example, data entry, processing simple transactions) into routine tasks. This transformation of jobs has led to sweeping changes on the labor market. Developed countries have seen a polarization of the job market with a downward trend in jobs for semi-skilled workers performing "routine tasks" in both industry and services. However, highly skilled occupations have seen strong growth, as have local jobs for low-skilled workers that would be difficult to automate (for example, sales people, servers, and childcare workers).

In Morocco's labor market, these changes pose major challenges with respect to demand for middle managers. This new technological context means that the emergence of a broad class of middle management employees could prove to be a more difficult process for new emerging countries than for countries that saw their economies take off in earlier decades. Many service jobs that were previously available to semi-skilled graduates are now disappearing and being replaced by new, more highly skilled jobs. One of the most striking examples is secretarial work, which significantly boosted female employment in this area in the 1960s and 1970s in today's advanced countries, accounting for up to 15 percent of women's jobs. In 2000, secretarial jobs accounted for 9.4 percent of urban female employment in Morocco. Technological change, with the advent of mobile telephones, word processing, and email, led to a sharp contraction in the number of secretarial jobs, which accounted for only 6 percent of urban female employment in 2010. This example illustrates a basic trend that affects a large number of clerical and middle-management jobs.

Digital technology is destroying semi-skilled jobs, but it is also creating new job opportunities for highly skilled workers who can join the technological revolution now underway (for example, developers, designers, researchers, analysts, and creators). However, as stressed earlier, these new jobs require high levels of human capital and a significant share of low-skilled and semi-skilled young Moroccans would be unable to fill them. We have sought to measure Moroccans' participation in the global market for new skills in order to illustrate this phenomenon, focusing on computer graphics designers, whose jobs are emblematic of the digital economy. The resulting indicator (see figure 1.43) appears to confirm the fact that Moroccans have derived relatively little benefit from the new opportunities provided by the digital economy. Technological transformation does give rise to new high value-added job opportunities, but only in countries that have a sufficiently well-trained workforce.

Weak Entrepreneurial Drive

Proper allocation of talent is critical for a country's development. In a 1990 article that has remained famous, economist William Baumol argued that every human society has entrepreneurs who are curious, driven people with a will to

Figure 1.43 Designers Registered on Dribbble.com
(per million inhabitants)

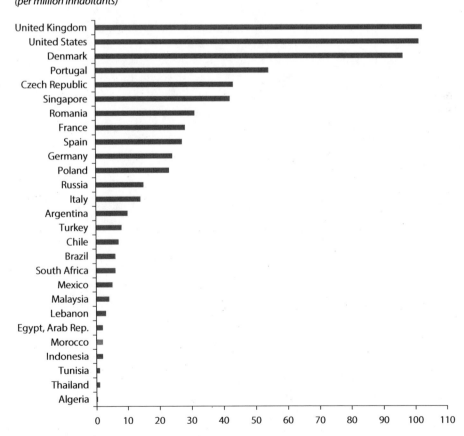

Source: www.dribbble.com.

succeed (Baumol 1990). The fundamental difference between advanced countries and developing countries lies in the nature of this entrepreneurship. Baumol
distinguishes between three types of entrepreneurship: productive, unproductive,
and destructive entrepreneurship. Prosperous countries are those that have successfully established incentives that reward productive entrepreneurship, which
promotes the creation of value, knowledge, and innovation. In contrast, less
developed countries have an incentive structure that rewards unproductive and
destructive entrepreneurship (rent seeking, corruption, low productivity).
Recent academic research has provided empirical evidence that confirms the
decisive influence of the quality of institutions on entrepreneurial drive
(Acemoglu, Johnson, and Robinson 2004). Independent courts, a democratic
model, an open economy, and competitive markets are considered to be the
types of institutions that channel behaviors into productive entrepreneurship
(see chapter 3).

Numerous entrepreneurs in Morocco establish themselves in sectors that
create little value and lack innovation, while accruing significant rents. Why
has the number of exporting firms been stagnant at only 5,300 since the early
2000s (see figure 1.44)? By way of comparison, Turkey now has 58,000 exporting firms (versus 30,200 in 2002), which is 4.7 times more than Morocco in
proportion to its population (see figure 1.45). If Morocco had the same entrepreneurial drive as Turkey, it would have some 25,000 exporting firms. Why do
so few firms manage to hire more than 20 employees? Why is the diversification
of the industrial sector taking so long, even though Morocco attracts a great
deal of FDI that brings know-how and technology with it? All three of these

Figure 1.44 Number of Exporting Firms in Morocco and Turkey, 2002–13

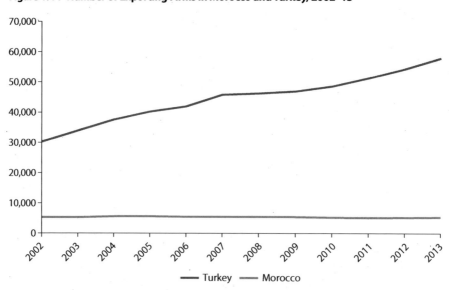

Source: Exporter Dynamics database, World Bank.

Figure 1.45 Number of Exporters in 2010
(per million of inhabitants)

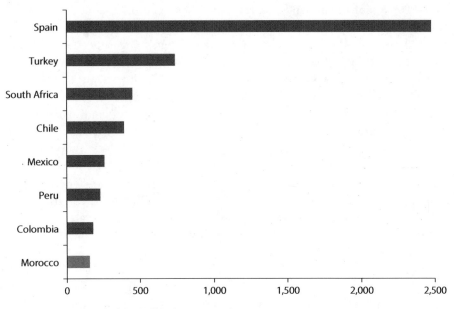

Source: Exporter Dynamics database, World Bank.

questions have the same answer: inadequate productive entrepreneurship. A recent study on entrepreneurship in Morocco revealed that, with a 4.4 percent entrepreneurship rate, the share of entrepreneurs is well below the average of 14.6 percent observed in similar economies (GEM 2015). Too few new businesses are being created each year to close the gap that has widened over time. In addition, business and other types of retail trade account by far for the largest proportion (60 percent) of nascent businesses, way ahead of industry and high value-added services.

Even though the government has made significant efforts to promote entrepreneurship through business climate reform and special financing programs for SMEs, the response from entrepreneurs has fallen short of expectations.[23] Entrepreneurs have the means to prosper without having to face competitive pressure or the need to innovate and boost performance. Many operators are protected from competition because of rents from properties, for example, or of real dissuasive barriers to entry such as administrative authorizations, licenses, and approvals. Public procurement execution is also a major source of potential distortion of competition among players (Lipson, Benouniche, Keita, and Faridi 2014). According to the available survey data, a high proportion of firms resorts to unlawful payments to win government contracts, despite the measures taken by the Government to eliminate this phenomenon. Government contracts are a source of potentially significant rents, since public procurement accounts for 17 percent of Morocco's GDP.

As is the case in many countries, property is a particularly lucrative area for rent seeking. A 2012 report issued by the Audit Office notes that more than 20 percent of the land in Casablanca has been urbanized by means of waivers. More than 500 discretionary rulings between 2005 and 2009 granted privileges to certain property developers. The report on the tax expenditure budget for 2016 reveals that the real estate sector receives the highest number of tax waivers, accounting for 22.1 percent of total tax expenditure (DH 7.1 billion). The constraints and problems posed by property in terms of urban development, urban planning, and land management pertain primarily to the complex nature of legal provisions, myriad property regimes, the low number of registered properties, and the lack of updating of the property map (World Bank 2008; Ghomija 2015). At the national conference on the State's land policy and its role in economic and social development (2015), His Majesty King Mohammed VI called for the revision and modernization of the legal provision governing public and private land, with a view to ensuring the protection and development of land capital and preventing speculation and its impact on prices.

The national conference on the State's land policy provided an opportunity to highlight the importance of significantly improving land governance in order to combat speculation and rent seeking. In the agricultural sector, the land situation is considered to be one of the main obstacles to the achievement of the agricultural development objectives, most notably improvement of agricultural productivity and increased private sector investments. In the industrial sector, the conference noted the persistent speculation in industrial land, a decrease in the supply of industrial land for investors in highly attractive economic areas, a deterioration of the infrastructure in a number of industrial zones, an increase in the price of land in areas that are extremely attractive and have strong investment demand, and the high cost of connecting industrial zones to water, electricity, and sanitation networks. In light of the foregoing, it is not surprising, indeed it is rational, that entrepreneurs shun the competitive sector, exports, and industrial production in favor of better protected and lucrative rent-seeking sectors.

The most talented Moroccans in their generation are not making their full contribution to Morocco's rapid growth. Even though its population has a relatively lower level of education than the average level in the other emerging countries, Morocco has a small group of highly skilled graduates from internationally renowned universities. Morocco has a major advantage in that the members of this elite are attached to their home country and tend to return home after receiving an education and starting their careers abroad. William Baumol's arguments lead us to question whether Morocco is taking full advantage of its most talented citizens by channeling them into productive entrepreneurship. To answer this question, we have turned to Big Data using the online professional directory, LinkedIn. We used the directory to see what has become of young graduates of leading international universities who come from emerging countries once they return to their home countries. In most emerging countries, such as Turkey, Malaysia, and Brazil, when the "best of their genera-tion" come home, the majority work in education and research, in engineering, or as entrepreneurs (see figure 1.46). Morocco stands in stark contrast to this global trend: when the "best Moroccans of their generation" come home, par-ticularly engineers, they almost always avoid the education, engineering, and research sectors. Figure 1.46 shows that the most talented Moroccan engineers hardly ever work in engineering, unlike their classmates. Yet, their comparative advantage lies in precisely those sectors, where their contribution could gener-ate major positive externalities. Instead, most of them seek jobs in manage-ment, administration, and finance. They are generally employed by large corporations or government agencies and enterprises that offer far better sala-ries and benefits than teaching or research, and without the risks inherent in entrepreneurship.

The suboptimal use of Moroccan talent leads to weak entrepreneurial drive. The main players in upgrading an economy are entrepreneurs, since they are the ones who spot opportunities, take risks, and introduce new productive activities.

Figure 1.46 The Top 10 Career Choices of Graduates from École Polytechnique and Harvard University

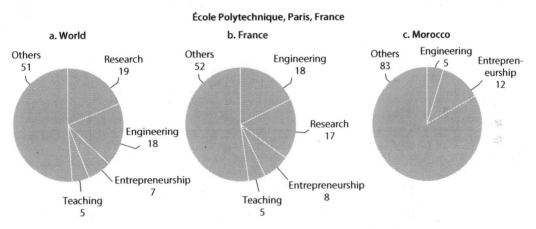

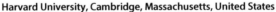

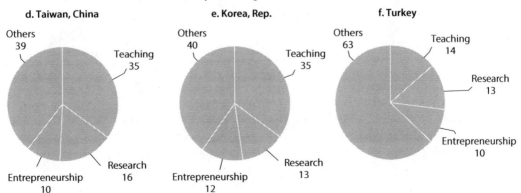

Source: LinkedIn.

Morocco 2040 • http://dx.doi.org/10.1596/978-1-4648-1066-4

Economists Ricardo Hausmann and Dani Rodrik argue that this "self-discovery" process is what drives economic development. And yet, all of the available indicators suggest that this entrepreneurial drive is weak in Morocco, not in terms of the desire to start up one's own business (which is not necessarily lower in Morocco than elsewhere), but in terms of project implementation on the ground (GEM 2015). The gap between intent and actual implementation appears to be higher among Moroccan entrepreneurs than in other emerging countries (see figure 1.47). Beyond the business environment and the state of entrepreneurial spirit, the lack of risk management tools, including those relating to fiduciary issues and personal responsibilities, is also believed to be a deterrent to business start-ups.

The lack of entrepreneurial drive results in a limited capacity to offer new products, particularly for export. Of a total of 6,000 products, Morocco exported 2,133 products in 2012 (using a filter of US$100,000 to eliminate insignificant transactions), compared with 3,500 for Romania and 4,465 for Malaysia (see figure 1.48). Over the past decade, Morocco has broadened its range of economic activities and discovered an average of 50 new export products per year. Nevertheless, this is a relatively slow pace for diversification. If this pace does not increase in the years ahead, Morocco will be on par with Romania's current diversification pace by 2040. Moroccan firms therefore rarely make forays into international markets and, consequently, do not face constant pressure to grow their businesses. Employment data show that only 10 percent of labor force participants are working in firms with more than 20 employees (17 percent in

Figure 1.47 Difference between Attempted Start-Ups and Actual Start-Ups in the Middle East and North Africa Region
(percent)

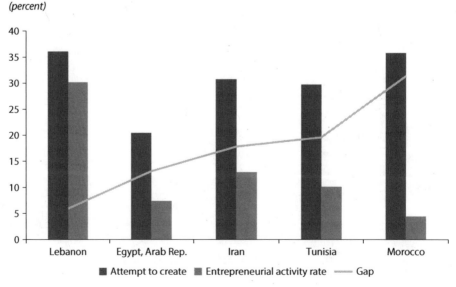

Source: Global Entrepreneurship Monitor 2015.

Figure 1.48 Number of Products Exported, 2012
(sales over US$100,000)

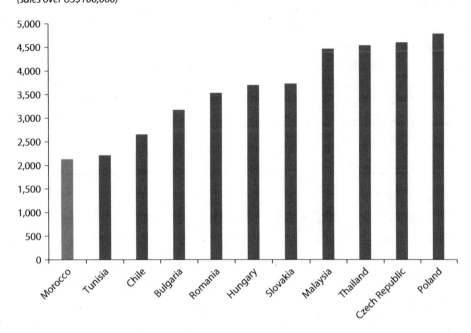

Source: Comtrade.

urban areas). This small proportion shows that, despite public policies designed to support and assist SMEs, in particular through the *Maroc PME* initiatives (Moussanada and Imtiaz), Morocco's productive sector has a small number of structured SMEs that are capable of scaling up and increasing their workforce.[24] By way of comparison, 70 percent of labor force participants in the Organisation for Economic Co-operation and Development countries work in firms with more than 20 employees.

Morocco's businesses are poorly structured, small, and largely domestic. They are also not very innovative. Moroccan residents filed only 300 patents in 2014, that is, fewer than 10 patents per million inhabitants, and barely 50 of them were filed by businesses. In contrast, Brazil had 24 patents filed per million inhabitants, Turkey had 65 patents, Poland had 124 patents, and China had 400 patents (see figure 1.49). In addition, unlike a number of other emerging countries, the new Moroccan entrepreneurs are increasingly positioning themselves in markets where many firms are already offering similar products or services. As a result, entrepreneurship is not making a substantial contribution to innovation (GEM 2015). Yet, as mentioned earlier, Morocco has no less desire to start up businesses than do other countries. The "creative" economy now plays a larger role in terms of growth, jobs, territorial inclusion, and trade in goods and services. Morocco's industrial companies operating in the creative and cultural economy have some 40,000 permanent employees, representing 7 percent of

Figure 1.49 Patent Filings by Residents, 2013
(per million inhabitants)

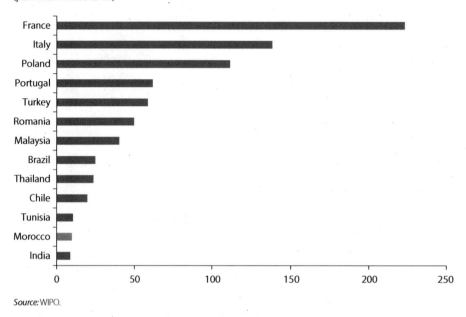

Source: WIPO.

total permanent employment in processing industries (Ministry of Economy and Finance 2016). The challenge in the future will be to channel more talented workers into entrepreneurship and the most productive jobs where they have a comparative advantage. To achieve this, it is critical to correct the existing distortions that promote economic rent seeking and establish incentives that are more favorable for the creative economy and innovation.

Notes

1. His Majesty King Mohammed VI. 2014. *Throne Speech*.
2. Bearing in mind that intangible capital represents approximately 80 percent of developed countries' total wealth.
3. The well-being of the bottom 40 percent of Moroccans improved 3.3 percent over the 2001–2007 period, compared with the per capita household consumption growth rate of 3.2 percent over the same period.
4. Life expectancy rose from 71.7 years in 2004 to 74.3 years in 2014 (WDI), and mortality rates fell more than 15 percent from 2000 to 2012 (UNDP 2012).
5. Based on the Maddison Project database managed by the University of Groningen.
6. The analysis developed in this book is based on historical series with their base year in 1998. The recent revision of the Moroccan national accounts, which adjusted Moroccan GDP by around 9 percent, only marginally alters the observed gaps.
7. The comparative analysis of the differences between 2008 and 2011 in socioeconomic characteristics of households from two groups of communes and neighborhoods—the first covered by the INDH while the second was not, but certainly comparable to the

former—revealed an increase in the average income of targeted rural households, double the rate in nontargeted communes (ONDH 2013).

8. An HCP study conducted in 2007 had put the middle class at 53 percent of the population using a method that is based on the median for consumption.

9. Based on the following vehicle expenses: DH 2,500; monthly payments on a loan for housing purchased at DH 600,000: DH 3,500; schooling for two children: DH 2,000; and other current expenditure: DH 2,000.

10. Figures derived from the University of Groningen database.

11. In the absence of a gross fixed capital formation (GFCF) series from the public sector, the public sector provided an estimate of total GFCF using annual reports on public institutions and enterprises.

12. Ministry for Water and the Environment 2009.

13. Ministry for Energy, Mines, Water, and the Environment 2016.

14. This program will be pursued until 2030 and will help conserve an estimated 2.3 billion m³ each year.

15. Joint Order No. 3417-10 of December 28, 2010.

16. Up until 2000, inward FDI for Morocco accounted for only 0.6 percent of GDP, approximately.

17. According to this indicator, which assesses the productive know-how of an economy by examining the level of sophistication and diversification of its export mix, Morocco has an intermediate level of complexity. Although the Moroccan economy is more complex, owing to a quasi-continuous trend since 2009, it is nonetheless very close to the lower bound and ranks lower than many developing countries, including countries in the Middle East and North Africa region (El Mokri 2016).

18. For more information on the Industrial Action Plan, visit the website of the Ministry of Industry, Commerce, Investment, and Digital Economy. http://www.mcinet.gov .ma/~mcinetgov/fr/content/plan-d%E2%80%99acc%C3%A9l%C3%A9ration -industrielle-2014-2020.

19. The authors of this book also note that "in the absence of local suppliers or multinational firms offering competitive prices, the Renault plant in Tangier is unique in that it integrates preassembly of components or modules, typically outsourced in accordance with international automotive industry standards. The preparation of the cockpit, and assembly of the seats, chassis, and exhaust system are therefore re-insourced and handled by the French car manufacturer itself."

20. In Morocco, outsourcing has always been the predominant business model in the textiles and clothing industry. In order to strengthen this sector's upstream phase, steps were taken subsequent to the 2008 launch of the Emergence Industrial Strategy, in particular in the finishing, printing, and dyeing segment to boost the value added of the sector's products. This repositioning was also strengthened under the Industrial Acceleration Plan launched in 2014, aimed at promoting the development of driving forces upstream in efficient textile ecosystems (spinning, weaving, knitting, finishing-printing-dyeing, fading).

21. Among other measures, the introduction of benchmark prices for property in several cities in the country, the increase of the tax on property profits, and blocking of the granting of town planning dispensations have helped to improve governance of the property sector and, consequently, to reduce rents generated by this sector and limit crowding out of productive sectors.

22. This plan has many benefits, including the simplification of start-up and closing procedures, exemption from registration in the trade registry, online payment of specific income taxes not subject to value-added tax (VAT) reduced taxation, social coverage, and exemption from seizure of the primary domicile.

23. The Imtiaz, Moussadana, and Istitmar programs managed by the National Agency for the Promotion of Small and Medium Enterprises (*Maroc PME*) seek to support investments to promote growth and employment and strengthen industrial ecosystems while providing an investment subsidy to SMEs, very small enterprises, and selected self-entrepreneurs.

24. The Imtiaz and Moussanada support and incentive programs designed to provide assistance to SMEs were evaluated by the Audit Office (2014). This evaluation revealed a number of dysfunctions pertaining to the inconsistency in the financing offered to firms, the lack of monitoring of programs by *Maroc PME*, unwarranted delays in the implementation of actions, and the absence of specific draft measures for SMEs.

References

Acemoglu, Daron, Simon Johnson, and James A. Robinson. 2004. "Institutions as the Fundamental Cause of Long-Run Growth." NBER Working Paper 10481, National Bureau of Economic Research, Cambridge, MA.

Akesbi, Najib. 2014. "Les investissements verts dans l'agriculture au Maroc." Notes de l'IFRI: Le Maghreb face aux nouveaux enjeux mondiaux.

Allali, K. 2003. "Évaluation des externalités environnementales de l'agriculture marocaine." Rapport de synthèse du Module 2. Projet FAO/The Roles of Agriculture.

Amadeus Institute. 2015. "Le Maroc en Afrique: La Voie Royale." http://www.amadeuson line.org/ftp2012/Maroc-Afrique-La-Voie-Royale-2015-Web.pdf.

Arrifi, El Mahdi. 2012. "Les ressources en eau et l'irrigation au Maroc: Contraintes et alternatives." International Conference on Desalination and Sustainability. International Desalination Association. Casablanca, 1–2 March.

Asheim, Geir B., and Martin L. Weitzman. 2001. "Does NNP Growth Indicate Welfare Improvement?" *Economics Letters* 73 (2): 233–39.

Atiyas, Izak. 2015. "Structural Transformation and Industrial Policy." Policy Perspectives 16. Economic Research Forum, Giza, Egypt.

Audit Office (Cour des Comptes). 2013. *Rapport annuel*. Morocco.

———. 2014. *Performance Audit of The National Agency for the Promotion of Small and Medium-size Enterprises (ANPME)*. Morocco.

Autor, David. 2010. "The Polarization of Job Opportunities in the U.S. Labor Market: Implications for Employment and Earnings." The Hamilton Project. Center for American Progress, Washington, DC.

Bank Al-Maghrib (BAM). 2016. *Rapport sur l'exercice 2015*. Morocco.

Baumol, William J. 1990. "Entrepreneurship: Productive, Unproductive, and Destructive." *Journal of Political Economy* 98 (5): 893–921.

Benabdejlil, Nadia, Yannick Lung, and Alain Piveteau. 2016. "L'émergence d'un pôle automobile à Tanger (Maroc)." Cahiers du GREThA, n°2016-04.

Berahab, Rim. 2016. "Structure des échanges entre le Maroc et l'Afrique: Une analyse de la spécialisation du commerce." OCP Policy Center Research Paper RP-16/07, OCP Policy Center, Rabat, Morocco.

Berlingieri, Giuseppe. 2014. "Outsourcing and the Rise in Services." Discussion Paper 1199, Centre for Economic Performance, London.

Brynjolfsson, Erik, and Andrew McAfee. 2014. *The Second Machine Age: Work, Progress and Prosperity in a Time of Brilliant Technologies*. New York: Norton.

Buchanan, James M., and Gordon Tullock. 1962. *The Calculus of Consent*. Carmel, IN: Liberty Fund.

Catão, Luis, and Gian Maria Milesi-Feretti. 2014. "External Liabilities and Crisis." *Journal of International Economics* 94 (1): 18–32.

Dadush, Uri. 2015. "Is Manufacturing Still a Key to Growth?" OCP Policy Center Policy Paper PP-15/07, OCP Policy Center, Rabat, Morocco.

Dasgupta, Partha, and Karl-Göran. Mäler. 2000. "Net National Product, Wealth, and Social Well-Being." *Environment and Development Economics* 5: 69–93.

Denison Edward Fulton. 1962. "The Sources of Economic Growth in the United States and the Alternatives before Us." *The Economic Journal* 72 (288): 935–38.

Dickson, James L., Joseph S. Levy, and James W. Head. 2014. "Time-Lapse Imagining in Polar Environments." *Earth & Space Science News* 95 (46): 417–18.

Doukkali, Rachid M., and Johan Grijsen. 2015. "Contribution économique de la surexploitation des eaux souterraines au Maroc."

Easterly, William, and Ross. Levine. 2001. "It's Not Factor Accumulation: Stylized Facts and Growth Models." World Bank, Washington, DC.

Economic, Social, and Environmental Council (CESE). 2014. *La gouvernance par la gestion intégrée des ressources en eau du Maroc: Levier fondamental de développement durable*. Morocco.

Economic, Social, and Environmental Council (CESE) and Bank Al-Maghrib. 2015. *Évolution de la valeur globale du Maroc (1999–2013)*. Unpublished report. Morocco.

El Mokri, Karim. 2016. "Le défi de la transformation économique structurelle: Une analyse par la complexité économique." Research Paper Series. OCP Policy Center, Rabat, Morocco.

Ezzrari, Abdeljaouad, and Paolo Verme. 2012. "A Multiple Correspondence Analysis Approach to the Measurement of Multidimensional Poverty in Morocco, 2001–2007." Policy Research Working Paper WPS 6087, World Bank, Washington, DC.

Ferreira, Susana, Kirk Hamilton, and Jeffrey R. Vincent. 2008. "Comprehensive Wealth and Future Consumption: Accounting for Population Growth." *World Bank Economic Review* 22: 233–48.

Ferreira, Susana, and Jeffrey R. Vincent. 2005. "Genuine Savings: Leading Indicator of Sustainable Development?" *Economic Development and Cultural Change* 53 (3): 737–54.

Global Entrepreneurship Monitor (GEM). 2015. "La dynamique entrepreneuriale au Maroc." Étude dirigée par Khalid El Ouazzani. Global Entrepreneurship Monitor and Laboratoire de recherche en entreprenariat et management des organisations.

Ghomija, Abdelmajid. 2015. "Rapport présenté lors des Assises nationales sur la politique foncière de l'État." Membre du Comité scientifique des assises.

Gourichas, Pierre-Olivier, and Maurice Obstfeld. 2011. "Stories of the Twentieth Century for the Twenty-First." *American Economic Journal: Macroeconomics* 4 (1): 226–65.

Hamilton, Kirk, and Michael Clemens. 1999. "Genuine Savings Rates in Developing Countries." *World Bank Economic Review* 13 (2): 333–56.

Hidalgo, César A., and Ricardo Hausmann. 2009. "The Building Blocks of Economic Complexity." *Proceedings of the National Academy of Sciences* 106 (26): 10570–75.

High Commission for Planning (HCP). 2009. "Etude sur les classes moyennes au Maroc." Unpublished report. Morocco.

———. 2012. "Les objectifs du millénaire pour le développement." Rapport National. Morocco.

———. 2015a. "Recensement général de la population 2014." Morocco.

———. 2015b. "Maroc entre les objectifs du millénaire pour le développement et les objectifs du développement durable: Les acquis et les défis." Morocco.

———. 2016. "Présentation des résultats de l'Enquête Nationale sur la Consommation et les Dépenses des ménages 2013/2014." Morocco.

His Majesty King Mohammed VI. 2014. *Throne Speech*. Morocco.

International Monetary Fund (IMF). 2015. "Morocco: 2014 Article IV Consultation—Staff Report." IMF Country Report 15/43, International Monetary Fund, Washington, DC.

Joint Order No. 3417-10. December 28th, 2010. Official Journal No. 5914, December 3, 2011. Morocco.

Kaufmann, Daniel, Aart Kraay, and Massimo Mastruzzi. 2009. "Governance Matters VIII: Aggregate and Individual Governance Indicators, 1996–2008." Policy Research Working Paper 4978, World Bank, Washington, DC.

Kendrick, John W. 1961. *Productivity Trends in the United States*. Princeton, NJ: Princeton University Press.

Keulertz, Martin, and Eckart Woertz. 2016. "The Water-Energy-Food Nexus in the Middle East and North Africa." OCP Policy Center Research Paper, OCP Policy Center, Rabat, Morocco.

Kharas, Homi. 2010. "The Emerging Middle Class in Developing Countries." Working Paper No. 285, OECD Development Centre, Paris. https://www.oecd.org/dev /44457738.pdf.

Kornai, János. 1986. "The Soft Budget Constraint." *Kyklos* 39 (1): 3–30.

Kuper, Marcel, Ali Hammani, Anne Chohin, Patrice Garin, and Mohamed Saaf. 2012. "When Ground Water Takes Over: Linking 40 Years of Agricultural and Groundwater Dynamics in Large-Scale Irrigation Scheme in Morocco." *Irrigation and Drainage* 61 (Suppl. 1): 45–53.

Lipson, Rachel, Salim Benouniche, Keita Abdoulaye, and Khadija Faridi. 2014. "Public Procurement Reform in Morocco." Middle East and North Africa Knowledge and Learning Quick Notes Series 117, World Bank, Washington, DC.

Lo, Moubarack. 2016. "Relations Maroc-Afrique subsaharienne: Quel bilan pour les 15 dernières années?" OCP Policy Center Research Paper RP-16/10, OCP Policy Center, Rabat, Morocco.

McMillan, Margaret S., and Dani Rodrik. 2011. "Globalization, Structural Change and Productivity Growth." NBER Working Papers 17143, National Bureau of Economic Research, Cambridge, MA.

Ministry of Economy and Finance. 2015a. "Le secteur automobile au Maroc: Vers un meilleur positionnement dans la chaîne de valeur mondiale." Direction des Études et des Prévisions Financières. Morocco.

————. 2015b. "Relations Maroc-Afrique : l'ambition d'une nouvelle frontière." Direction des Études et des Prévisions Financières. Morocco.

————. 2015c. "Des inégalités régionales sous le prisme de l'accès aux droits humains: de la multiplicité à l'indivisibilité." Direction des Études et des Prévisions Financières. Morocco.

————. 2015d. "Rapport sur les ressources humaines." Annexe au projet de loi de finances 2015. Morocco.

————. 2015e. "Situation et perspectives de l'économie nationale: Au-delà de l'écran comptable, la transformation structurelle continue." Direction des Études et des Prévisions Financières. Morocco.

————. 2015f. "Rapport sur les dépenses fiscales." Annexe au projet de loi de finances 2015. Morocco.

————. 2016. "Rapport d'Activité 2015." Direction des Études et des Prévisions Financières. Morocco.

Ministry of Water and the Environment. 2009. "Stratégie nationale de l'eau." Morocco.

————. 2011. "Programme de protection des ressources en eaux souterraines au Maroc." Morocco.

————. 2016. "3e Communication nationale du Maroc à la Convention-Cadre des Nations Unies sur le changement climatique: Des mesures d'atténuation proposées à l'horizon 2040." Morocco.

National Observatory for Human Development (ONDH). 2013. "Évaluation des réalisations de la première phase de l'INDH (2005–2010) et de leurs effets sur les populations cibles." Morocco.

Pew Research Center. 2015. "A Global Middle Class Is More Promise than Reality." Pew Research Center, Washington, DC.

Revue Economia. 2009. "La classe moyenne, c'est qui ?" No. 9.

Rodrik, Dani. 2013. "Unconditional Convergence." NBER Working Paper 17546, National Bureau of Economic Research, Cambridge, MA.

————. 2015. "Premature Deindustrialization." NBER Working Paper 20935, National Bureau of Economic Research, Cambridge, MA.

Solow, Robert M. 1957. "Technical Change and the Aggregate Production Function." *Review of Economics and Statistics* 39 (3): 312–20.

Stiglitz, Joseph E., Amartya Sen, and Jean-Paul Fitoussi. 2009. "Rapport de la Commission sur la mesure des performances économiques et du progrès social." Paris: Éditions Odile Jacob.

Timmer, Marcel P., Gaaitzen de Vries, and Klaas de Vries. 2015. "Patterns of Structural Change in Developing Countries." In *Routledge Handbook of Industry and Development*, edited by John Weiss & Michael Tribe. New York: Routledge, 65–83.

United Nations. 2017. *World Happiness Report 2017*, edited by John Helliwell, Richard Layard, and Jeffrey Sachs. New York: United Nations.

United Nations Development Programme (UNDP). 2015. *Human Development Report 2015: Work for Human Development*. New York: UNDP.

United Nations Educational, Scientific and Cultural Organization (UNESCO). 2014. Rapport mondial de suivi sur l'EPT. "Enseigner et apprendre: Atteindre la qualité pour tous," UNESCO, Paris.

_____. 2016. *The UNESCO Institute for Statistics (UIS)*. http://www.uis.unesco.org /Pages/default.aspx.

United Nations Statistics Division (UNSTATS). 2013. "System of Environmental Accounting for Water (SEEA-Water)." Department of Economic and Social Affairs, Statistics Division. United Nations, New York.

Verme, Paolo, and Khalid El-Massnaoui. 2015. "An Evaluation of the 2014 Subsidy Reforms in Morocco and a Simulation of Further Reforms." World Bank Policy Research Working Paper 7224, World Bank, Washington, DC.

Wijnen, Marcus, Benedicte Augeard, Bradley Hiller, Christopher Ward, and Patrick Huntjens. 2012. "Managing the Invisible: Understanding and Improving Groundwater Governance." Water Papers, World Bank, Washington, DC.

World Bank. 2003. "Royaume du Maroc: Évaluation du coût de la dégradation de l'environnement." Report 25992-MOR. World Bank, Washington, DC.

———. 2006. *Where Is the Wealth of Nations?* Washington, DC: World Bank.

———. 2008. "Marchés fonciers pour la croissance économique au Maroc." Report No. 49970. Washington, DC: World Bank.

———. 2011. *The Changing Wealth of Nations*. Washington, DC: World Bank.

———. 2013. "Préparation du cadre de partenariat stratégique: Consultation sur le thème de la gouvernance et la fourniture de services, 2013." Procès-verbal. Royaume du Maroc. Washington, DC: World Bank.

———. 2016. "Royaume du Maroc: Évaluation du coût de la dégradation de l'environnement." Rapport 105633-MA. Washington, DC: World Bank.

———. 2017. *The Changing Wealth of Nations*. Washington, DC: World Bank.

CHAPTER 2

Morocco in 2040

"Productivity isn't everything, but in the long run it is almost everything. A country's ability to improve its standard of living over time depends almost entirely on its ability to raise its output per worker."

— Paul Krugman

The purpose of chapter 2 is to look ahead to 2040, that is, through to the next generation. Morocco was able to restart the engines of growth in the late 1990s after a decade of relatively disappointing economic and social performance. How can Morocco further accelerate its growth rate and maintain a high level of growth over the coming decades? As the previous chapter has shown, the search for higher growth is not a goal in and of itself but a means of achieving ambitious social objectives, improving the standard of living of the population, and making the country wealthier in a sustainable, equitable, and environmentally friendly way. This chapter therefore focuses on both the quantity and the quality of growth and the accumulation of wealth that accompanies it.

Morocco has not yet fully embarked on the development path typically associated with the "economic miracles" achieved by some countries in Southern Europe, Southeast Asia, or Central and Eastern Europe. Finding the means to achieve and maintain a higher level of inclusive economic growth that creates jobs is therefore one of the biggest political and economic challenges facing Morocco. This was underscored by the Economic, Social, and Environmental Council (CESE) in a report that indicated that "the rapid implementation and effective guidance of national policies intended to accelerate economic growth are particularly important given that Morocco faces numerous social challenges" (CESE 2013). Institutions and policies that promote economic growth generally do not just lift people out of poverty but also on average increase the incomes of the poor equiproportionally, thereby promoting shared prosperity (Dollar, Kleineberg, and Kraay 2013).

A Window of Opportunity

When looking ahead to the next generation, it is important to consider underlying structural trends already at work in society that will help to forge the Morocco of tomorrow. Moroccan society is characterized by three fundamental, potentially positive trends, that will affect the country's future: a demographic dividend, urbanization of society, and higher levels of education. The combination of these three trends has been observed in all countries that have achieved a successful economic takeoff in the past half century, both in Southern Europe (Italy, Portugal, and Spain) and in Asia (Republic of Korea; Taiwan, China). Morocco thus today appears to have all of the conditions needed to achieve its own economic and social convergence. However, these favorable conditions also entail risks: the risk of not being able to create enough jobs, the risk of not being able to generate positive agglomeration effects (which would lead to negative urban congestion effects), and the risk of not being able to offer Moroccan youth a high-quality education. If these risks are not eliminated or at least greatly mitigated by suitable public policies, Morocco could miss a unique opportunity in its history.

A Demographic Dividend

Morocco is coming to the end of its demographic transition and today benefits from a significant demographic dividend. The fertility rate has declined spectacularly over the past half century: whereas Moroccan women had seven children on average in 1960, they now have just 2.2 (see figure 2.1) (HCP 2015). This rate is at the threshold required for replacement of the population and is close to the rates observed in rich countries. It is interesting to note that this development is occurring both in urban areas (where the rate is two children per woman) and in

Figure 2.1 Morocco: Composite Fertility Index, by Place of Residence, 1962–2014
(number of children per woman)

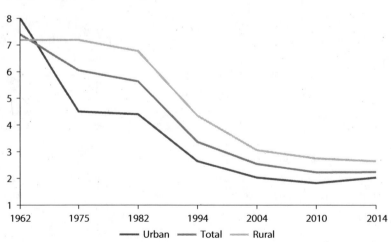

Source: High Commission for Planning 2015.

rural areas (with 2.6 children per woman). The propensity of women to have fewer children reflects profound social changes. First, although a great deal remains to be done in rural areas, the infant mortality rate has been lowered significantly, from 145 per 1,000 births in 1960 to 24 per 1,000 births in 2015. With a declining risk of losing a child, women are less likely to have large families. Second, contraceptive methods are widely available, particularly through family planning programs. Today, an estimated 67 percent of married women use contraceptive methods. Third, another profound social change is that couples are delaying marriage. In 1960, men married at age 24 years on average and women at age 17 years. In 2014, these ages have risen to 31.2 years and 25.8 years, respectively. Last, as primary education has become universal for girls, mentalities have changed and fertility has declined.

Declining fertility will lead to a moderation of Morocco's population growth and an inversion of the age pyramid. According to the 2014 census, Morocco has 33.8 million inhabitants. The rate of growth of the population was just 1.2 percent between 2004 and 2014 and is expected to continue to slow in the coming decades. Projections suggest that by 2040 the Moroccan population will reach 40 million (see figure 2.2). The additional population, on the order of 350,000 per year at present, should trend downward to 165,000 per year by 2040, or less than half the average figure observed between 1980 and 2010 (400,000 per year). As fertility has declined, the base of the age pyramid has shrunk considerably. The share of young people under the age of 15 has declined from 44 percent in 1960 to 25 percent in 2014 and will continue to decline to 18 percent by 2040. At the same time, the proportion of persons of working age (15–59 years) is increasing, having risen from 48 percent in 1960 to a peak of roughly 64 percent at present. This proportion should stay above 60 percent until 2040 before declining significantly thereafter, owing to the aging of the population.

Figure 2.2 Morocco: Total Population, 1960–2050
(millions)

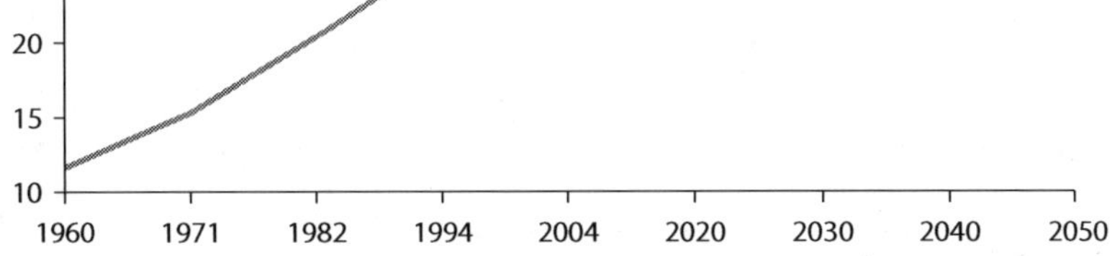

Source: High Commission for Planning 2015, based on the 2004 census.

Morocco has entered a demographic dividend period with a dependency ratio that will remain low until 2040. The life expectancy of Moroccans has increased by almost 30 years in half a century, rising from 47 years in 1960 to 75 years today. The proportion of persons older than 60 years of age will increase until they constitute 24 percent of the total population by 2050, as against 10 percent in 2010 and 7 percent in 1960. Morocco is thus currently experiencing a demographic dividend, with the size of the working-age population reaching a historic high. The dependency ratio (the ratio between the young people and the elderly and the working-age population) will remain low at around 50 percent over the next 25 years and will not begin to rise until 2040 (see figure 2.3). Over the next three decades, 550,000 young people will reach working age each year on average. This flow was 400,000 in 1980 and reached an unprecedented 640,000 in 2014. It is expected to now begin to decline, to 500,000 by 2050.

The demographic dividend significantly increases Morocco's growth potential. Several studies have shown the existence of a close link between economic growth and demographic trends. According to some economists, the demographic dividend accounts for almost one-third of the economic growth achieved by the "Asian dragons" (see figure 2.4) (Bloom, Canning, and Sevilla 2001). There are three main channels for the transmission of this effect. First, from a purely accounting standpoint, a greater proportion of working-age persons in the population increases growth potential and automatically raises per capita gross domestic product (GDP). Second, the decline in the dependency ratio eases the expenditure constraints of households and leads to a higher savings rate at the macroeconomic level, allowing for improvements in investment financing conditions. Last, the declining fertility rate is generally accompanied by greater

Figure 2.3 International Comparison of Dependency Ratios, 1950–2100
(share of those younger than 15 years of age and those older than 65 years of age in the working-age population)

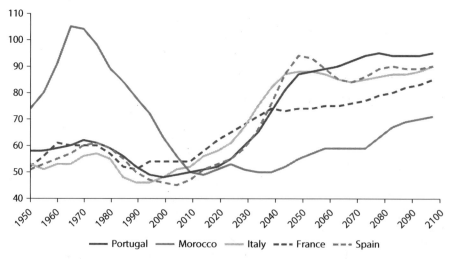

Source: World Development Indicators 2016, World Bank.

Figure 2.4 Share of Persons Ages 15–64 Years in the Total Population, 1966–2015
(percent)

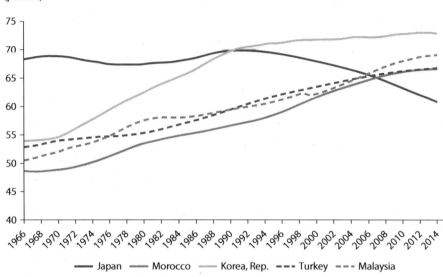

Source: World Development Indicators 2016, World Bank.

participation of women in the labor market, which further increases the employment rate and growth potential.

However, the demographic dividend will materialize only if the economy is able to generate jobs to absorb the labor supply, particularly for youth and graduates. Having a large working-age population is essential for growth, as long as that population is indeed employable and employed. Unfortunately, as underscored in the previous chapter, the employment rate is particularly low in Morocco: just 42.8 percent of the working-age population (15–65 years) has a job, with this rate falling to 38 percent in urban areas. The fact that fewer than half of young urbanites between the ages of 25 and 34 have a job is an even more worrisome phenomenon (see figure 2.5). This level of participation is low in comparison with many other countries. In most of the emerging economies, more than 70 percent of young people in this age bracket are employed (Brazil, Mexico, Poland). Even in countries that have recently suffered major economic crises, like Greece (56 percent in 2013) and Spain (63 percent in 2013), the youth employment rate is higher than in Morocco, where the economy has been comparatively more resilient.

The recent employment performance of the Moroccan economy is not encouraging. Over the past decade, the working-age population (15 years and older) has increased 1.6 percent per year on average, with trends diverging widely between urban areas (2.1 percent) and rural areas (0.8 percent). Every year, 350,000 persons are added to the working-age population (approximately 280,000 in urban areas and 70,000 in rural areas), but the job creation rate has not been sufficient to absorb these increases. At the national level, employment

Figure 2.5 Morocco: Employment Rate among Young Persons Ages 15–34 Years, by Area, Age, and Qualifications, 2015
(percent)

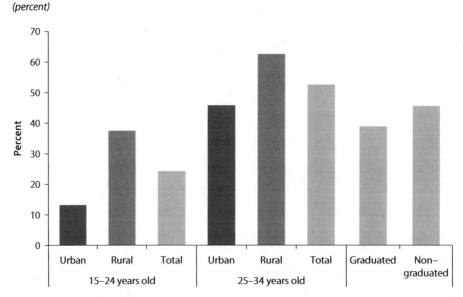

Source: High Commission for Planning.

Figure 2.6 Average Net Job Creation, 2010–14
(percentage of population of working-age individuals)

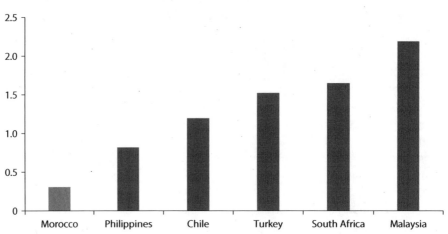

Source: ILOSTAT 2015.

has risen 1 percent per year (1.8 percent in urban areas; −0.3 percent in rural areas). Between 2010 and 2015, as the economy has slowed, the net creation of jobs in urban areas was just 61,000 positions. Relative to the size of its population, Morocco created half the jobs created by the Arab Republic of Egypt and one-third as many as those created by Malaysia (see figure 2.6).

To reach the employment rates observed in the emerging economies, Morocco must maintain a higher rate of growth—close to 5 percent on average.

In the coming years, the pressure on the labor market will tend to ease as the growth of the working-age population slows. That population will increase by just 200,000 persons per year over the next decade, as compared with 350,000 during the past decade. Alongside population change, economic growth, particularly nonagricultural GDP, is another key variable in job creation. Given productivity gains, a growth rate above 2 percent is needed to instigate job creation and a rate of at least 4 percent is needed to absorb new entrants into the labor market.

Acceleration of Urbanization

The acceleration of urbanization is another opportunity for Morocco. On the basis of the 2014 census, 60 percent of Moroccans live in urban areas today as against 29 percent in 1960, 41 percent in 1980, and 55 percent in 2004 (see figure 2.7). Over the past 10 years, urbanization has accelerated, with a 0.5 percentage point increase per year (compared with 0.4 during the previous decade). At this pace, the urbanization rate could reach 72 percent by 2040, which would bring Morocco up to the urbanization level already achieved in a number of emerging and developed countries.

Until now, rural-to-urban migration has been accompanied by a relatively slow decline in the number of farmers. Morocco has almost four million farmers today, representing 38 percent of total employment in the country. The number of farmers is declining, but at a slow rate, around 0.5 percent per year. In countries more advanced than Morocco, the exit from agriculture has taken place more rapidly, at a rate of approximately 3 percent per year (average observed in France, Italy, Portugal, and Spain, and also in the "Asian dragons," Korea and Taiwan, China). The massive reduction in the number of agricultural

Figure 2.7 Morocco: Share of Urban Population in the Total Population, 1966–2015
(percent)

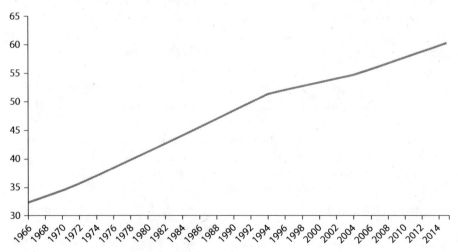

Sources: High Commission for Planning 2015; World Development Indicators 2016, World Bank.

sector workers is a general phenomenon that appears in all developed countries, without known exceptions. During its development process, Morocco will probably follow the same path, even if the pace is different. As fewer people work in agriculture, productivity will improve and family member participation, which accounts for 45 percent of agricultural employment and the contribution to production of which is relatively limited, will decline. Rural-to-urban migration and the exit from agriculture will be strongly stimulated by more widespread access to education in rural areas. International experience shows that educated young people are significantly more inclined to leave the countryside for the city. However, in the case of Morocco, this urban push would be weaker. Estimates suggest that more educated household members compared to less educated are less likely to migrate to urban areas (Bouoiyour, Miftah, and Muller 2017).

Urbanization is potentially a source of productivity gains and is closely correlated with a country's level of development. Although urbanization is often seen as a negative phenomenon because it can lead to many imbalances, academic research has shown that, on the contrary, urbanization is a formidable vector for social and economic development (Glaeser 2012). From an economic standpoint, the concentration of people in urban areas generates agglomeration effects: as cities grow larger, economies of scale and productivity rise, ideas circulate more easily, and opportunities increase. At the social level, the residents of cities generally have access to better quality and more efficient public services (for example, hospitals, schools, communications, and transportation networks).

In a globalized economy, the development of countries is now borne by the large metropolises, which have the critical mass to be competitive at the global level. Some economists, including the chief economist at the World Bank, have even advanced the view that an industrial policy with no urban policy is doomed, whereas an urban policy without an industrial policy is perfectly viable and capable of supporting catch-up growth (Romer 2015). The growth of cities is therefore expected to be accompanied by suitable urban policies if the full benefits of urbanization are to be realized. The experience of Korea is particularly enlightening in this regard (see figure 2.8). Urbanization generates both positive agglomeration effects and congestion costs that create tensions and are a source of pollution. The capacity to contain congestion costs with sound urban planning is thus essential to achieving the development potential offered by urbanization.

The last census in Morocco confirms the polarization of the population near large cities, with a trend toward urban sprawl. Seven cities concentrate 25 percent of the total population and 41 percent of the urban population. The last census shows, however, that urban growth is mainly absorbed by the cities' peripheries, leading to significant urban sprawl. For example, while the population of the greater Casablanca area has grown 1.6 percent, the population of the city of Casablanca (excluding the peripheral cities) has risen only 1 percent. Similarly, the Rabat-Salé-Kenitra region has grown 1.3 percent while

Figure 2.8 International Comparison of the Share of the Urban Population in the Total Population, 1966–2015

(percent)

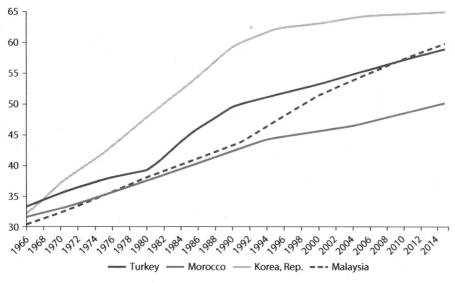

Source: World Development Indicators, World Bank.

the population of Rabat itself has declined 0.8 percent. Lastly, the population of the Marrakesh-Safi region rose 1.4 percent while the city of Marrakesh grew just 1.1 percent.

Weak urban planning and land speculation, in particular land retention, have resulted in a structural shortage of building land in large Moroccan cities, which fueled real estate price inflation. Given an essentially inelastic supply, the growth of demand in the 2000s has taken real estate prices to higher levels than indicated by economic fundamentals. The high price of real estate is a heavy burden on household budgets, fueling mortgage debt, and contributing significantly to urban sprawl. In most developed countries, the cost of housing represents three or four times the annual income of households (Demographia Housing Affordability Index). When this level is exceeded, experts consider that a real estate bubble exists. In Morocco, according to data collected from commercial banks, the cost of housing (excluding public housing) represents six to eight times households' annual income.

The steady growth of large Moroccan cities should be perceived and encouraged as an asset in global competition. Moroccan cities conceal a high growth potential, especially with respect to the land use coefficient and verticality. Even Casablanca, the largest city in Morocco with 3.3 million inhabitants, is a medium-sized city compared with the metropolises of other emerging countries (for example, Kuala Lumpur has 7 million inhabitants, Istanbul, 9 million, and Santiago, 7 million). There is room for significant improvement of urban policies in Morocco. More and more households are forced to live in the urban peripheries to benefit from more moderate real estate prices. However, these areas are generally poorly served by public transit and only 23 percent of urban households own a private car (HCP 2015). By way of comparison, in 1960 the car ownership rate for French households was 30 percent. The current pattern of urbanization thus creates significant mobility problems. Moreover, the costs of congestion risk reducing or even canceling out the positive effects of agglomeration. In 2016 after the national conference on the State's land policy, the Government established a standing ministerial committee for land policy with a view to improving land governance.[1]

Higher Education Levels

Morocco's rapid universalization of education has the potential to bear significant economic benefits in the medium term. It is estimated that the average education rate in Morocco is five years. This number of years of schooling is low in comparison with other developing countries (6.7 years in Algeria; 7.5 in Tunisia; 9.8 in Mexico; 10 in Malaysia).[2] Nevertheless, access to education has improved steadily over the past two decades, supported by the government's universal education policy. In the 1990s, just 55 percent of children between the ages of 6 and 11 were enrolled in school in Morocco. The efforts made by Morocco in the area of education increased this rate to 98 percent in 2014. Morocco has thus almost attained the Millennium Development Goal of universal access to primary education. Despite a still high absenteeism rate, the increase in school enrollment at the primary level has resulted in a significant increase in the number of students enrolled in secondary school and higher education. This has been reflected in the sharp upward trend in the number of high school graduates, which increased from 50,000 in 1990 to 90,000 in 2000 and 205,000 in 2014. Medium-term projections indicate that this trend should continue, bringing the number of high school graduates to 300,000 in 2020. At that point, 50 percent of an age cohort will be high school graduates, as compared with 30 percent today and 10 percent in 1990. The exponential growth in the number of high school graduates has spread automatically to higher education, where student populations have also exploded. On the basis of current data, it is possible to estimate that a little over one high school graduate in two obtains a higher degree. The number of young university graduates could thus increase proportionately to the number of high school graduates, reaching some 130,000 in 2020, as against roughly 100,000 today.

Improved education levels could radically transform the labor market. Morocco's lag in school enrollment has led to a poorly educated labor force. In 2013, 63 percent of working Moroccans had no diploma, not even a primary school certificate. Barely 11.4 percent of them nationally have at least a high school diploma, with a slightly higher percentage in urban areas (21 percent). Given the trends observed in school enrollment, the proportion of young graduates among workers should increase substantially in the coming decades. It could reach some 30 percent of total employment on the basis of projections. By comparison, 50 percent of workers in France today have at least a high school diploma. The increase in the level of qualification is an important economic phenomenon, since it should support the move into technology industries.

Economic development does not consist so much of producing "more" products as of producing "different" products, with greater value added and a higher technological content (Hausman, Hwang, and Rodrik 2005). This process of structural change requires a high level of human capital and competent workers trained in the use of new technologies. It is not by chance that "economic miracles" occur in countries with relatively high levels of basic education. For example, the average length of school enrolment in Korea was five years in 1960, a level not achieved by Morocco until 2010. Human capital is particularly important in an information and knowledge economy characterized by the acceleration of technical progress and the automation of production processes. Even the simplest functions now require a higher level of qualification than in the past—a phenomenon known as "skill-biased technological change" (Cohen, Piketty, and Saint-Paul 2002). The extremely rapid rise in the level of qualification of the Moroccan population constitutes a potential major asset in enabling the country to successfully move its economy into technology industries and to anchor it advantageously in global value chains.

To achieve this, as will be seen in detail in chapter 5, it is important to improve the quality of education so that students acquire genuine skills. In a recent work entitled *The Rebirth of Education: Schooling Ain't Learning,* Harvard economist Lant Pritchett emphasizes that the quantitative expansion of schooling in the developing countries has not necessarily led to an accumulation of human capital (Pritchett 2013). He notes that many developing countries have been successful in ensuring the physical presence of children in classrooms, without providing them with the basics of reading and arithmetic. Morocco is a good example of this. The universalization of education undertaken in the 1990s has been accompanied by a significant deterioration in the quality of education. In 2008, a national assessment of achievement levels conducted by the Higher Council on Education concluded that students assimilated just 30 percent of the official curriculum, irrespective of the discipline. International tests also confirm this assessment. Morocco is ranked last in the Progress in International Reading Literacy Study (PIRLS) classification, which measures reading literacy, and second to last in the Trends in International Mathematics and Science Study (TIMSS) classification, which covers mathematics. Only 21 percent of 10-year-olds master the basics of reading, as against 87 percent internationally (see figure 2.9). Education specialists considered that a lack of reading literacy at this age produces long-term irreversible effects on the cognitive development of the child and very negatively impacts adult productivity (see the section on early childhood in chapter 5). The low quality of education is transmitted from primary education to higher education, leading to a clear deterioration in the intrinsic value of diplomas. However, they do remain the best insurance against unemployment, even if the perception may sometimes be different (see box 2.1).

Figure 2.9 10-Year-Olds Able to Read a Basic Text (Grade 4)
(percent)

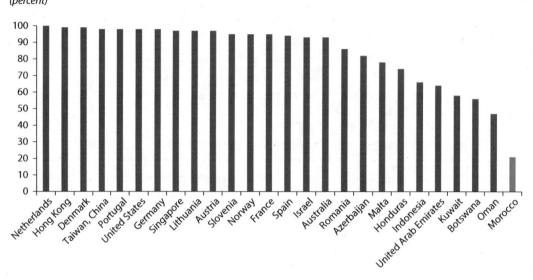

Source: UNESCO 2014.

Box 2.1 Even in Morocco, a Degree Is the Best Insurance against Unemployment

The fact that the unemployment rate for Moroccan graduates is higher than the unemployment rate for those without degrees should not lead to the conclusion that degrees exacerbate unemployment. In reality, the unemployment rate for graduates is higher because their labor force participation rate is well above those without degrees (they more actively look for work). If this bias is taken into account, the employment rate for young university graduates (56 percent) is higher than that for nongraduates (48 percent). In general, a degree improves the employability of young people. It is true, however, that employability varies significantly depending on the type of degree obtained. The employment rate is particularly high for graduates of the *grandes écoles* (specialized higher education institutions) (80 percent) and the advanced institutions of technical training (64 percent). In contrast, it is low for those with a bachelor's degree or a postgraduate degree in social sciences (43 percent).

It is also important that these higher education levels lead to greater participation of women in the labor force. One of the most visible characteristics of the Moroccan labor market is the persistently low level of female employment. In urban areas, just 14 percent of women of working age have a job, as against 60 percent of men. Even for young women between the ages of 25 and 35, this level is just 19 percent. There has been no progress in this area, despite the improvement in the level of education of women and society's greater acceptance of women's employment. International experience shows that the rate of employment of women rises steadily during the development process. In Spain, for example, just 25 percent of women worked in 1970, as against 60 percent today. In Turkey, the acceleration of growth in the 2000s was accompanied by a 10-point increase in the employment rate for women, which rose from 25 percent to 35 percent. A substantial improvement in the participation of women in the labor market thus constitutes a major challenge if the Moroccan economy is to take off (as discussed in detail in chapter 6).

Beyond the windows of opportunity that are opening in Morocco—and beyond the related challenges—lies the fundamental question of the social contract. Morocco's future lies with its youth: a more qualified, urbanized youth that is connected with the rest of the world. Moreover, the challenges presented above reflect the fact that Moroccan young people face constraints that affect their opportunities. They are aware of the risk of not finding work, as well as the risk of receiving a poor quality education and not being able to move up in society, regardless of family origin. Facing these numerous uncertainties, the youth of Morocco are plagued by a sense of hopelessness, which is primarily reflected in the desire of many of these youth to leave Morocco and try their luck abroad. According to a survey conducted by the European Training Foundation entitled "Skills Dimension of Migration," 59 percent of young Moroccans between the ages of 18 and 29 would like to leave Morocco, and a large percentage would like to do so permanently.

Morocco at a Crossroads

Morocco is today going through a remarkable period that is particularly favorable to an economic takeoff. However, the current demographic transition will not be sufficient to trigger a sustainable upturn in growth. International experience shows that sustaining strong economic growth in the long term is considerably more difficult than initiating it, and Morocco is no exception. Like many developing countries, Morocco has successfully transitioned from low-income to middle-income status, but it is struggling to move from middle-income to emerging market status.[3] To avoid the "middle-income trap" (Eichengreen, Park, and Shin 2013), Morocco will need to achieve much higher productivity and competitiveness gains than in the past and, more importantly, sustain them for two generations in a challenging international context (see box 2.2). The countries that have pulled off such "economic miracles" have generally adopted a structural change process with a number of common characteristics. While they have indeed benefited from a demographic dividend, urbanization, and higher levels of school enrollment, they have above all been able to take advantage of specific historical circumstances to facilitate structural change, technological upgrading, and economic diversification, and last, but equally important, to ensure the large accumulation of human, institutional, and social capital—a multifaceted capital asset more commonly known by the name of "intangible capital."

Box 2.2 Avoiding the "Middle-Income Trap" in a Context of Slower Growth

Avoiding the middle-income trap requires steady improvement in factor productivity. Analyses of long-term growth show that total factor productivity (TFP), that is, a country's effectiveness at utilizing its factors of production (labor and capital) and transforming intermediate goods into final output, is key to explaining economic convergence between countries (Easterly and Levine 2001). However, this convergence is difficult to sustain. On average, a person in a rich country produces in nine days what a person in a poor country produces in one year (Restuccia 2013). Economies that are successful at avoiding the middle-income trap are those that generate productivity gains, while countries that fall into this trap see their TFP stagnate or even decline. In the final analysis, a country's capacity to improve its standard of living over time depends almost entirely on its ability to increase its TFP (Krugman 1994).

As explained in the previous chapter, TFP in Morocco has scarcely changed since the 1970s. The recent acceleration of growth in the 2000s is explained primarily by a combination of factors, particularly an investment boost based primarily on large, publicly financed infrastructure projects that reached 34 percent of GDP in 2014. Without a significant improvement in TFP, Morocco risks seeing its growth slow over the medium term and falling into the "middle-income trap." To structurally increase its TFP, Morocco must increase its intangible capital so that investment and employment can achieve sustainably higher returns.

However, productivity growth has slowed worldwide, a phenomenon known as the "global productivity crisis." Data from the Conference Board 2014 database indicate that TFP growth hovered around zero for the third consecutive year, against 1 percent during the 1996–06 period and 0.5 percent during 2007–12. The decline in TFP was not limited to advanced economies; it declined in China and Sub-Saharan Africa, was barely positive in India, and was even negative in Brazil and Mexico. This slowing trend is seen in all regions, and particularly in Central Asia, Southern Europe, and Latin America (Eichengreen, Park, and Shin 2015).

Faced with numerous challenges, Morocco stands at a crossroads today. The question of Morocco's future can be presented in 2017 in terms similar to those that were used in 2004 in the analyses that marked the celebration of the 50th anniversary of the country's independence. As the report published at the time pointed out, "Morocco is facing a historic situation of major choices and major plans that lead to two fundamental but contrasting options. On one hand, the country can resolutely engage a virtuous renewal and development dynamic by seizing opportunities that present themselves and by making the reform process a permanent and structural one. On the other hand, resolving future impediments to development could be postponed to an undetermined date."[4] The idea that Morocco stands at a crossroads was also recently raised by the OCP Policy Center in a report on Morocco's growth strategy for 2025 (see box 2.3) (Agénor and El Aynaoui 2014).

Box 2.3 Morocco at a Crossroads

According to a recent report published by the OCP Policy Center entitled "Growth Strategy for 2025 in an Evolving International Environment," the Moroccan economy is at a crucial stage in its development for the following four basic reasons:

1. A new international division of labor. Changes in the international division of labor have accelerated in recent years, reflected in large part by global growth moving eastward, particularly with the emergence of China as the second largest economy in the world. The risk for Morocco is to become caught between the rapid-growing low-income countries with abundant and low-cost labor and the middle-income, larger countries capable of innovating quickly enough to move to the top of the world technology frontier.
2. A stalling of Morocco's growth strategy. While the Moroccan economy has overcome the difficulties brought about by the global financial crisis, a number of indicators clearly suggest that the growth momentum has slowed since the late 2000s: continuous growth of macroeconomic imbalances, reflected in both fiscal and balance of payments deficits; a loss of competitiveness owing to the appreciation of the real exchange rate and rising labor costs; a slowing trend growth rate; a very limited improvement in the workforce quality, which hampers the country's ability to adjust; and persistent unemployment. This overall situation could be accompanied by an erosion of economic agents' confidence in the prospects of the economy.
3. Difficulty in absorbing new arrivals in the labor market. Despite the favorable growth performance during the 2000s, the unemployment rate remains stubbornly high, particularly among youth and skilled workers. There are multiple reasons for the continuing tensions in the labor market: a growth rate that is insufficient to fully absorb the expansion of the labor force, insufficient private investment in key growth sectors, as indicated above, and institutional rigidities, including the quality of dialogue between employers and unions, high hiring and dismissal costs, and friction in the functioning of the legal framework for resolving labor disputes.
4. An outdated macroeconomic policy framework. Morocco's macroeconomic policy framework has served the country well in the past, but it must now evolve to address several issues related to the process of financial globalization and the economy's greater trade openness, which expose the country to greater volatility, with significant risk for national impact. Rising fiscal imbalances and low capacity to meet the challenges of changing economic conditions have reduced the predictability of the macroeconomic management framework and destabilized the expectations of economic agents, eroding their confidence in the future.

Three possible development scenarios for Morocco through 2040 are presented, on the basis of the evolution of the following basic macroeconomic parameters: the investment rate, the employment rate, and productivity gains. The horizon for the projections is set at 2040 to enable us to consider what Morocco might look like for the next generation (of 25 years).

Achievement of the most favorable scenario will depend primarily on the relevance of the development strategy adopted and the quality of public policies implemented.

The Unsustainable Business-as-Usual Scenario

The first projection scenario is constructed on the basis of an extrapolation of the trends observed during the period 2000–14 (see table 2.1). As explained in the previous chapter, this period was characterized by sustained growth of 4.3 percent of GDP. The main engine of growth was the accumulation of capital, with an increase in the stock of capital of 5.4 percent on average. Employment and productivity gains also contributed to this sustained growth, but to a significantly lesser extent, at about 1 percent each. Maintaining these same parameters, the trend extension of the growth achieved in the years 2000–14 would lead to a 2.5-fold increase in per capita income, which would mean a substantial improvement in the standard of living for Moroccans. Morocco would converge relatively rapidly toward the European economies, its per capita GDP and purchasing power parity (PPP) reaching 40 percent of the European level by 2040, against 22 percent today (on the basis of an assumption of per capita GDP growth of 1 percent per year for Europe).

This scenario, showing a perpetuation of the current growth model, is, however, based on an unsustainable mechanism. Given—hypothetically—that employment growth and productivity gains were to remain weak, the main source of growth would be sustained growth of the capital stock. This implies

Table 2.1 Morocco: Unsustainable Business-as-Usual Scenario, 2015–40

Scenario 1	1980–1999	2000–14	2015–29	2030–40
Exogenous variables				
Population growth rate (total)	1.9	1.0	0.8	0.5
Population growth rate (15–65 years)	2.6	1.9	0.8	0.5
GDP growth rate	3.9	4.3	4.3	4.3
Per capita GDP growth rate	2.0	3.3	3.5	3.8
TFP growth rate	−0.7	1.2	1.2	1.2
Employment growth rate	Not available	0.9	0.9	0.9
Capital stock growth rate	4.3	5.4	5.4	5.4
National savings rate	22.7	29.3	29.3	29.3
Endogenous variables				
GDP/per capita PPP (in 2011 US$, end-of-period)	4,500	7,300	12,000	17,500
GDP/per capita PPP (% Southern Europe, end-of-period)	Not available	22	30	40
Investment rate (GFCF/GDP)	24	29	41	52
Current account balance (% GDP)	−3	−2	−13	−24
Employment rate (employment/ population 15–65 years)	Not available	44.9	45.6	47.9

Note: GDP = gross domestic product; GFCF = gross fixed capital formation; PPP = purchasing power parity; TFP = total factor productivity.

that the investment rate would need to rise continually to offset the depreciation of accumulated capital. Thus, to maintain a rate of growth of capital of 5.4 percent per year during the period 2015–40, the investment rate would need to increase gradually to over 50 percent of GDP by the end of the period. However, assuming that the savings rate remained at its current relatively high level, the savings-investment imbalance would result in a rising balance of payments current account deficit to over 20 percent of GDP by the end of the period. A deficit of this magnitude is quite simply unrealistic and Morocco would face a profound balance of payments crisis well before reaching this deficit level.

This projection exercise, based on a continuation of current trends, shows the unsustainability of a growth model that draws primarily from an accumulation of capital, with limited productivity gains and job creation. Long-term strong growth is not possible in Morocco without significantly more rapid productivity gains than those observed at present. This is especially true given that the assumption that the growth of total factor productivity (TFP) will hold steady at 1.2 percent is quite optimistic. If agriculture is excluded from growth, the rate of technological change in the economy during the period 2000–15 is less than 0.5 percent. With the long-term decline of the share of agriculture in GDP, this effect will gradually disappear and overall productivity will converge with non-agricultural productivity. These are the long-term consequences of a slow and insufficient structural transformation, the main features of which were described in the previous chapter.

The Probable Slow Convergence Scenario

Without a significant acceleration in productivity gains, the most plausible scenario is slow convergence, allowing Morocco to restore its fundamentals, particularly by reestablishing a sustainable balance of payments current account deficit of around 2 percent of GDP (see table 2.2). Given the national savings rate, such an adjustment would require stabilizing investment at around 29 percent of GDP. Without a steady increase in the investment rate, the growth of the capital stock would automatically decline, as would its contribution to GDP growth. In this scenario the rate of growth of capital would decline from 5.4 percent in 2000–14 to 3 percent in 2015–29 and 2.4 percent in 2030–40. The negative impact on GDP growth would amount to more than 1 percentage point, with a trend growth rate that, while respectable, would stall at around 3 percent. With respect to employment, and to maintain the hypothesis of an unaltered contribution of employment to growth, the employment rate should increase slightly to compensate for the initial slowing of growth of the working-age population (15–65 years) during the period. The employment rate would therefore increase by 3 percentage points, from 45 percent to 48 percent. Despite a modest improvement based on favorable population growth, the outlook for employment remains unsatisfactory, leaving more than half of the working-age population unemployed. The consequences of such a scenario of slowing growth would be significant for the standard of living, poverty

Table 2.2 Morocco: Probable Slow Convergence Scenario, 2015–40

Scenario 2	1980–1999	2000–14	2015–29	2030–40
Exogenous variables				
Current account balance (% GDP)	−3	−2	−2	−2
National savings rate	22.7	29.3	29.3	29.3
Investment rate (GFCF/GDP)	24	29	29	29
Employment growth rate	Not available	0.9	0.9	0.9
TFP growth rate	−0.7	1.2	1.2	1.2
Endogenous variables				
Capital stock growth rate	4.3	5.4	3.0	2.4
GDP growth rate	3.9	4.3	3.2	2.9
Per capita GDP growth rate	2.0	3.3	2.4	2.4
GDP/per capita PPP (% Southern Europe, end-of-period)	Not available	22	28	32
Employment rate (employment/ population 15–65 years)	Not available	48.1	44.9	46.4

Note: GDP = gross domestic product; GFCF = gross fixed capital formation; PPP = purchasing power parity; TFP = total factor productivity.

reduction, and Morocco's rate of convergence with the high-income emerging economies and Southern European countries. Between 2015 and 2040, per capita GDP would increase by only 1.8 on average. By 2040, Morocco's standard of living would represent just 32 percent of that of the Southern European countries.

Macroeconomic trends in recent years can be interpreted as harbingers of this scenario. After accumulating macroeconomic imbalances in the years 2008–12, Morocco gradually restored its fundamental balances in 2013, mainly owing to fiscal adjustment, which made it possible to moderate the increase of imports, against a backdrop of plummeting oil prices. Despite the combination of several favorable internal and external factors (such as historically low interest rates), the pace of economic growth has shown a downward trend in recent years (see figure 2.10). In an unchanged growth model, an economic recovery driven by domestic demand would lead to a recurrence of macroeconomic imbalances. This scenario shows that without solid productivity gains, Morocco is essentially facing a difficult trade-off between macroeconomic imbalance and moderate growth.

Yet, international experience suggests that this scenario of flagging growth and slow convergence should come as no surprise. Economic history shows that many countries manage to ramp up their economic growth for several years, as Morocco did in the 2000s, but that in most cases these gains are generally unsustainable and growth rates end up reverting to historical trends (Hausman, Pritchet, and Rodrik 2005). The economic slowdown in recent years suggests that Morocco could be in the process of reproducing this typical scenario with, for example, GDP growth that is not estimated to exceed 1 percent in 2016 (see figure 2.10). This phenomenon of "regression to the mean" is explained by the

Figure 2.10 Morocco: GDP Growth, 1999–2006 and 2007–16
(percent)

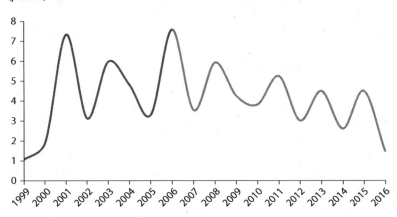

Source: High Commission for Planning 2015 (estimate) and 2016 (projection).
Note: GDP = gross domestic product.

fact that future growth is largely determined by two key factors: growth in the previous decade (countries with a history of strong growth are more likely to grow than less dynamic countries) and initial revenue levels (the poorer a country is, the larger its margin for growth) (Pritchett and Summers 2013). The application of this model to Morocco highlights the risks of economic slowdown in the coming decades, with economic growth potentially slowing gradually from 3.2 percent in the years 2015–29 to 2.9 percent in the period 2030–40.

This risk of a future slowdown of growth would, moreover, correspond to the abovementioned "middle-income trap" (Eichengreen, Park, and Shin 2013). During the development process, many countries see their rates of growth slow significantly when they reach a threshold estimated at around US$10,000. Among the countries that were in the group of middle-income economies in the 1960s, only a few have been able rise to the rank of developed countries, mainly the Southern European, Central and Eastern European, and Southeast Asian countries. However, the more a nation develops, the more difficult it is for it to maintain sustainable, strong growth. Several other countries, including Greece, Mexico, Turkey, or even South Africa, suffer from this "middle-income trap." For these countries, the stage of industrialization and development of related services has been bypassed or had petered out. These societies have become urbanized without the creation of industrial sectors or services offering significant value added, a phenomenon that American political scientist Francis Fukuyama has labeled "modernization without development" (Fukuyama 2014).

The Desirable Accelerated Economic Catch-Up Scenario

The two previous scenarios are based on the assumption that the current situation, characterized by moderate long-term TFP gains, will continue. As indicated earlier, Morocco is in an exceptional period characterized by a demographic transformation that has the potential to bring high growth. If appropriate structural reforms are introduced to seize this historic opportunity, Morocco could rebalance its growth model by scaling up its productivity gains and improving the employment rate.

Ambitious but realistic changes are simulated in the third scenario, which assumes a 2 percent increase in TFP per year (versus 1.2 percent historically). International experience shows that it is not easy to sustain such a rate of technological change in the long run. It requires a profound structural transformation of the economy and substantial efficiency gains. Yet several countries in Southern Europe (1960–80) and Southeast Asia (1970–90) have managed to achieve this fundamental change during their economic takeoff. The productivity assumption is coupled with an assumption of a rise in the employment rate of the working-age population from 45 percent in 2015 to 55 percent in 2040, driven mainly by an increase in the female employment rate, which remains very low today at around 23 percent. By way of comparison, in the developed countries and most of the emerging economies, the employment rate for those between the ages of 15 and 65 averages 65 percent. Such an increase in the employment rate would strongly stimulate the growth of overall employment, which would reach 1.6 percent between 2015 and 2030 before falling back to 1.2 percent owing to slowing population growth.

The cumulative effect of productivity gains and a higher employment rate would sustain strong average growth of around 4.5 percent per year over 25 years (see table 2.3). This growth rate would be slightly higher than the trend observed in Morocco in recent years. Yet, unlike the current growth model based on the accumulation of capital, this growth model would be based on productivity gains

Table 2.3 Morocco: Desirable Economic Convergence Scenario, 2015–40

Scenario 3	1980–1999	2000–14	2015–29	2030–40
Exogenous variables				
National savings rate	22.7	29.3	29.3	29.3
Investment rate (GFCF/GDP)	24	29	29	29
Current account balance (% GDP)	−3	−2	−2	−2
Employment/population 15–65 years (end-of-year)	Not available	45	50	55
TFP growth rate	−0.7	1.2	2.0	2.0
Endogenous variables				
GDP growth rate	3.9	4.3	4.6	4.4
Per capita GDP growth rate	2.0	3.3	3.8	3.9
Capital stock growth rate	4.3	5.4	3.6	3.6
Employment growth rate	Not available	0.9	1.6	1.2
GDP/per capita PPP (% Southern Europe, end-of-period)	Not available	22	34	46

Note: GDP = gross domestic product; GFCF = gross fixed capital formation; PPP = purchasing power parity; TFP = total factor productivity.

and job creation, which would make it perfectly viable in the long term. The rate of investment would be held steady to preserve the macroeconomic balances, which would prompt a weakening of the contribution of capital to growth, but this restrictive effect would be more than offset by the recovery of productivity and employment.

This third scenario highlights the crucial importance of productivity gains as the cornerstone of strong growth that is sustainable in the long term and thus a prerequisite for social stability in the country. Raising productivity gains by 2 percent per year for several decades is, however, a major challenge. International experience has shown that this can be accomplished, but requires that the authorities make judicious and sometimes difficult choices to successfully carry out the reforms needed to speed up the country's structural transformation. This scenario reflects the conclusions of a recent macroeconomic analysis in the context of an overlapping generations model that simulates a series of economic policies with the potential to significantly accelerate the trend growth rate of the Moroccan economy in the coming years (Agénor and El Aynaoui 2014).[5]

Changing the Development Paradigm

A sweeping change scenario, under which Morocco would embark on a structural transformation and an accelerated process of convergence in the space of a single generation, assumes that the conditions are present for making sweeping changes to the strategies and policies currently pursued. First of all, there must be a veritable collective realization that Morocco's current development model has reached its limits. As underlined in the Bank Al-Maghrib's last annual report, Morocco must begin a complete revision of its development model and promote a series of changes to the design and implementation of public policies (BAM 2016). If all stakeholders fail to come to this realization, then the current policies will not change substantially and, with the same causes producing the same effects, the country will find itself in the slow convergence scenario. Although this scenario would still be respectable, especially given the outlook of a number of other countries in the Middle East and North Africa (MENA) region, the mere continuation of current policies and reforms would not allow Morocco to quickly converge with the most developed countries over the next generation or to fully meet the aspirations of its youth.

As we have seen, the accelerated convergence scenario assumes a permanent increase in the productivity gains that would result in a doubling of the rate of convergence of Morocco with the Southern European countries in comparison with the scenario in which the pace of productivity does not increase (see figure 2.11). The development strategy and public policies should thus focus on this objective, which requires that priority be given to investment in intangible capital and the modification of the development strategy based primarily on sectoral policies.

Figure 2.11 Morocco: Per Capita GDP by 2040
(percentage of per capita GDP in Southern Europe, PPP)

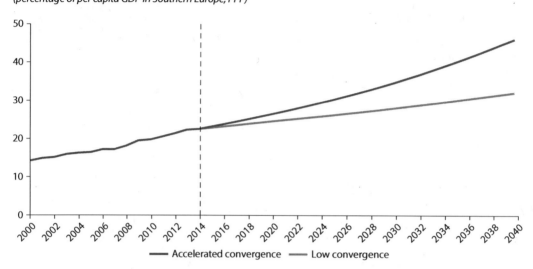

Source: World Development Indicators, World Bank.
Note: GDP = gross domestic product; PPP = purchasing power parity.

Giving Priority to Intangible Capital

As we have seen above, the additional productivity gains will not come solely from new investments in physical capital—although such investments clearly remain important and necessary—but from a greater effort to accumulate more intangible assets in the form of human, institutional, and social capital. The challenges Morocco faces in increasing TFP and developing its intangible capital in the medium term are essentially two sides of the same coin (see figure 2.12). Innovation, the adoption of new technologies, and the reallocation of the factors of production that are needed to stimulate TFP (in the neoclassical literature on growth) are directly influenced by policies designed to build human capital, institutional quality, and social capital (in the literature on the wealth of nations). Just as productivity gains correspond to "unexplained" factors of growth once the accumulation of the factors of production, that is, capital and labor, is taken into account, the accumulation of intangible capital corresponds to the "unexplained" wealth of nations once their produced capital, natural capital, and financial capital are taken into account. Productivity and intangible capital are, in both cases, "intangible" variables that reflect the quality of the institutional, human, and social environment in which the accumulation of the factors of production takes place. At the end of the day, the changes in TFP and intangible capital are largely linked and are key variables that will define Morocco's growth path and the improvements in the well-being of the population by 2040.

The speech given by His Majesty King Mohammed VI on the occasion of the 15th anniversary of his accession to the throne is the clearest signal of the

Figure 2.12 Morocco: Contribution of Productivity Gains and the Accumulation of Intangible Capital to Growth and Increased Wealth

(percentage points)

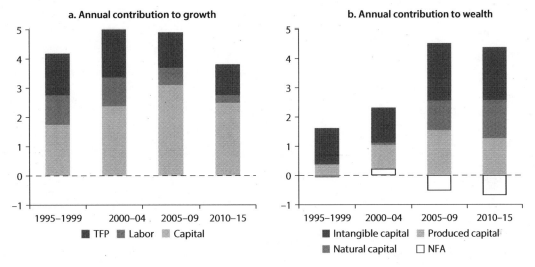

Source: World Development Indicators, World Bank.
Note: NFA = net foreign assets; TFP = total factor productivity.

resolution of the authorities to place the issue of intangible capital at the center of the discussions on Morocco's future (His Majesty the King Mohammed VI Speech 2014). On that occasion, the King stressed "the need to retain intangible capital as a fundamental criterion in the development of public policies so that all Moroccans may benefit from their country's wealth." This involves "measuring the historical and cultural capital of the entire country, along with the other characteristics that distinguish it, particularly its human and social capital, trust, stability, the quality of its institutions, inno- vation and scientific research, cultural and artistic creation, quality of life and the environment, and many other factors."

The convergence scenario assumes that Morocco is capable of significantly increasing the share of intangible capital in its total wealth. On the basis of the composition of the current wealth of the countries with which Morocco wishes to converge by 2040, it appears that Morocco would need to increase the share of intangible capital in its total capital by some 10 to 15 percentage points, depending on the scenario (see figure 2.13). The difference of five percentage points between the slow and accelerated convergence scenarios can be inter- preted as being the counterpart to the difference in productivity gains in these two scenarios.

By giving priority to intangible capital, Morocco could logically adopt a genuine, consistent, cross-cutting development strategy. Specifically, this would make it possible to benefit more from the lessons and recommendations of the many in-depth economic studies conducted on Morocco in recent years (see box 2.4). Even if these studies were not undertaken in the context of

Figure 2.13 Morocco: Share of Intangible Capital in Total Capital, 2000–40

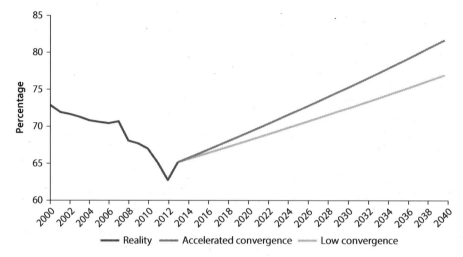

Source: World Bank 2016.

Box 2.4 Growing Consensus around Key Reforms to Strengthen Institutional and Human Capital

The previous World Bank Country Economic Memorandum for Morocco in 2006 concluded that the Moroccan economy suffered primarily from a structural transformation process that was too slow to achieve strong growth, particularly in the area of exports (World Bank 2006). The Memorandum identified four economic policy failures: (i) a rigid labor market, (ii) a tax policy that penalized the private sector, (iii) an exchange rate regime that was unsuited to the country's characteristics, and (iv) an anti-export bias in policies. It also identified three market failures: (i) information failures that resulted in the violation of property rights, (ii) coordination failures between the public and private sectors, and (iii) human resources failures. These three types of failures were significant obstacles to strong economic growth.

In 2010, the Bouabid Foundation provided a more institutional and richer perspective, supported by an analysis of the political economy (Abderrahim Bouabid Foundation 2010). The Foundation's report identified two "meta-constraints" to an economic takeoff that would enable Morocco to rise to the level of an upper-middle-income country with a high human development level in the space of a single generation:

- The political economy, characterized by an electoral system favoring ill-assorted coalitions to the detriment of coherence; an inadequate government architecture based on imitation of France and the need to distribute government positions; and a multiplicity of nongovernmental public actors with wide-ranging prerogatives that escape government and parliamentary control; and

box continues next page

Box 2.4   Growing Consensus around Key Reforms to Strengthen Institutional and Human Capital *(continued)*

- A kind of "economic illiteracy" characterized by a failure to consider the contributions of economic science (cost-benefit analyses, assessment of externalities, and opportunity costs); and insufficient consideration of the lessons of the past that would make it possible to avoid repeating the same mistakes.

In 2015, the African Development Bank, the government of Morocco, and the Millennium Challenge Corporation prepared a new assessment of growth for Morocco (AfDB 2015). The analysis of all constraints to broad inclusive growth identified two major constraints hampering faster growth generated by the private sector:

- A human capital deficit related in particular to issues of access to education and the quality of the educational system; and
- A series of microeconomic risks related to the slow-moving legal system, the distortions introduced by taxation, the difficulty in accessing land, and restrictive market regulations. In addition to these two major constraints, the growth assessment identified the existence of market weaknesses in the areas of innovation and coordination. The analysis also shed light on the need to improve access to health services and infrastructure in rural and isolated areas, and the importance of action to improve the management of scarce resources (water and energy).

In 2015, the OCP Policy Center produced a report on Morocco's growth strategy through to the year 2025 (Agénor and El Aynaoui 2015). The assessment confirmed the growing difficulties facing the Moroccan economy: a slowdown in trend growth, persistent unemployment and inadequate labor quality, a loss of competitiveness, insufficient diversification of the productive sectors and exports, an unsatisfactory macroeconomic framework, and a business environment that hinders the private sector. To promote growth and employment through to 2025, the report proposed taking action in three areas:

- Fostering a short-term boost in competitiveness by adopting a number of measures aimed at reducing production costs in labor-intensive sectors;
- Promoting private activity in the productive sectors that will enable the country to accelerate its transition to the top of the world technology frontier and compete in international markets for technology-intensive and skilled labor-intensive goods and services while improving its position in global value chains; and
- Rethinking the role that the State should play in facilitating this transition, particularly in terms of incentives for private investments, through the type of public services that would increase the productivity of private inputs in strategic activities sectors.

---

the current debate on the issue of intangible capital, they have all proposed essential reforms to improve governance, rethink the role of government, strengthen competitiveness, promote the private sector, develop human capital, and protect the environment. These are all aspects of intangible capital that will be discussed in greater detail in the following chapters.

Adjusting the Development Strategy

In addition to a new focus on public policies supporting the development of intangible capital, the current development strategy must evolve and the role of sectoral policies must be reviewed. The development paradigm in Morocco since the early 2000s has been characterized by an emphasis on "downstream" consistency through ambitious sectoral strategies supported by proactive trade, investment, and public procurement policies. In line with this paradigm, the various sectoral developments supported by the government or by public agencies (for example, agriculture, automobile industry, aeronautics, solar energy, the digital economy, tourism, and real estate) are intended to be both vectors for and examples of the country's development, which explains the emphasis on public investment and the accumulation of fixed capital over the past decade. Downstream consistency is primarily aimed at improving the coordination of sectoral policies to the extent possible, for example by avoiding "silo" implementation of such policies based on metrics, timetables, and expected outcomes that are different from one sectoral strategy to another (CESE 2014).

Despite the efforts made, sectoral policies are struggling to produce results, come up to speed, and place Morocco on a sustainably higher growth path. Morocco is clearly not the only or even the first country to be faced with limitations regarding proactive industrial policies. Many developing countries have sought to promote industrial emergence with generally disappointing—or even counterproductive—results, in several cases. From this perspective, the issue in Morocco is not very different from that currently facing Egypt (El-Haddad 2016). As in Egypt, an active industrial policy has struggled to achieve true structural transformation. The lack of productive results is not primarily related to a lack of consistency among sectoral policies (although greater consistency is always desirable). These policies are flagging because the downstream strategies do not necessarily provide solutions to the TFP challenges. In the case of the development strategy for residential property (excluding public housing), for example, the incentives and other public policies do not encourage investment in productive capital that can generate productivity (Abderrahim Bouabid Foundation 2010). Even when sectoral policies seek to address a challenge relating to a given productive sector, they can be only partial and piecemeal solutions. Given the large number and complexity of local economic problems, it would be naïve to think that the government could centrally and exogenously provide all of the necessary solutions downstream. As the Nobel Prize winner for Economics Jean Tirole notes, "Most of the time, we are not aware of phenomena with incentivizing, substituting, or transfer effects intrinsic to market functioning; we do not grasp problems in their entirety. However, policies have secondary effects that can easily render a well-intentioned policy harmful" (Tirole 2016).

In line with the new priority given to intangible capital, the development strategy should be adjusted and the institutional roots of public policies strengthened. Rather than emphasizing the completion of a development project downstream driven by a public program (additional irrigated land, a new automobile plant, another industrial or residential zone), the development strategy should rather concentrate on what influences endogenous, holistic development of the private sector "upstream" and at the outset. Although economists have difficulty developing a general theory on economic growth—let alone shared economic growth (Balakrishnan, Steinberg, and Syed 2013; Easterly and Levine 2001)—the idea that disparity in the institutional frameworks is a decisive upstream factor in explaining the disparity in the economic performance of public policies has gradually taken hold in recent decades (see box 2.5).

At the institutional level, the experience of many countries shows that the development best able to generate large economic dividends involves the promotion of an open society. The Commission on Growth and Development launched in 2006 under the joint chairmanship of the winner of the Nobel Prize for Economics Michael Spence and the World Bank to consider the conditions favorable to strong, sustainable growth analyzed the specific characteristics of the 13 economies that were able to achieve over 7 percent growth for more than 25 years since 1950.[6] It then identified the conditions for a country to attain and maintain a high level of growth. These conditions are leadership and good governance; participation in the global economy; high investment and savings levels; flexible resources, especially in terms of jobs; and a policy of inclusion designed to share the benefits of globalization, provide the very poor with access to services, and tackle gender inequalities. Many of the stylized facts brought to light

---

Box 2.5 Institutional School of Development Economics

Since the publication of the seminal book by Douglass North and Robert Thomas on the rise of the western world, it has become clear that while the production, innovation, and technological progress are immediate factors explaining productivity and economic growth, they are not the causes of growth, they *are* the growth (North and Thomas 1973).

To identify the fundamental determinants of growth upstream, the question must be asked why the accumulation of factors and innovation take place at different rates in different countries. Similarly, we must ask ourselves why countries differ in terms of governance, the quality and level of education, the quality of infrastructure, the health of the population, and other immediate factors in economic growth, such as the level of participation of women in the economy.

A consensus (Acemoglu, Johnson, and Robinson 2007; Alesina and others 2003; Frankel and Romer 1999; Gallup, Sachs, and Mellinger 1999; Glaeser and others 2004; Knack and Keefer 1997; Rodrik, Subramanian, and Trebbi 2004) is emerging that the responses to these questions are linked to history and institutional differences—with the term "institutions" being understood broadly and including, in particular, the rule of law, liberties, and trust in society—while geographic differences and other exogenous factors are often secondary.

---

by the Commission—whether in terms of rule of law and good governance, trade openness, trust, open competition, open labor markets, or female and youth participation—concern the characteristics of an open society (see box 2.6). Specifically, it is worth noting that

- Greater trade openness and transparency in all other institutional aspects of a country—whether it concerns the public or private sector—tend to create opportunities leading to better long-term results, while opaque systems of governance and regulations are prone to corruption, favoritism, and cronyism.

Box 2.6 Definition, Characteristics, and Consequences of an Open Society

According to English philosopher Karl R. Popper, an open society is defined as a society of free individuals who respect each other's rights against a backdrop of mutual protection guaranteed by the state and, through responsible and rational decision making, achieve an increasing degree of dignity and progress (Popper 1945). Thus conceived, an open society is not a utopia, according to Popper, but a form of social organization achieved empirically, which, he stresses, is in every respect superior to its authoritarian competitors, whether actual or potential.

An open society is also characterized by a flexible and tolerant system based on the rule of law and justice, freedom and personal responsibility, accountability, transparency, and freedom of information. An open society respects minorities and diverse opinions; it promotes equality of opportunity for all, without distinction of race, class, gender, religion, and other human characteristics, and fair political, legal, and economic systems; it enables everyone to participate freely and fully in civic, economic, and cultural life. In doing so, an open society tends to foster self-confidence, new ideas, and critical thinking; it tends to depersonalize trade, strengthen social ties, and build consensus on common ground; it reinforces individual merit, self-respect, and mutual respect.

On a more practical level, we can only speak of an open society if the individual or citizen is free to critically analyze the impact of the implementation of public policies, which may then be abandoned or modified in light of these criticisms. In such a society, the rights of individuals to criticize government policies should be formally protected and defended. Undesirable policies will be set aside in the same way as false scientific theories are generally rejected, and divergent views on social policy will be resolved through discussion and debate and not by force. An open society is therefore characterized by a general predisposition to critical thinking and antidogmatism, by an openness to public debate and by the subordination of authority to reason, by the abandonment of irrational taboos, by belief in scientific methods, and by faith in brotherhood among all men. This contrasts with societies that have maintained a tribal organization, where magical and rigid taboos persist, in which any change is viewed with fear and suspicion and where critical debate and the use of reason are being suppressed, where democratic, individualistic, and egalitarian principles are prohibited, and where a tendency toward economic self-sufficiency dominates (Kolakowski 1990).

box continues next page

Box 2.6 Definition, Characteristics, and Consequences of an Open Society (continued)

The reason that more open societies are more likely to generate prosperous, inclusive, and resilient economies is that openness offers opportunities and incentives to achieve superior economic and social performance. The knowledge necessary to generate prosperity cannot be the product of one individual; it must be dispersed among many. An open society creates rights and incentives that allow each individual to use his or her specific knowledge for his or her own benefit and, more importantly, for the benefit of others. This idea is, of course, the precursor idea of Adam Smith (1776) with his "invisible hand" concept: "Each individual pursuing his own interest acts inadvertently for the benefit of all and often more effectively than if he had intended to work for the common good." An open society thus protects the individual rights of everyone to choose and discover their best role in order to solve the problems of others. Adam Smith highlighted three important mechanisms that make the invisible hand so effective: the division of labor, the benefits of specialization, and the benefits of trade.

- Economies with more open and transparent domestic markets tend to promote domestic competition, economic efficiency, and structural transformation owing to the well-known phenomenon of "creative destruction" (Schumpeter 1942). These economies are less likely to be characterized by rent seeking and other types of inefficient economic rigidities.

- Economies that have open labor markets are generally more inclusive, effective, and resilient than economies with rigidly segmented labor markets based on sectors (public/private), access conditions (employees/nonemployees), or regulations in place (formal/informal sector). These economies tend to enjoy higher levels of labor market participation and lower levels of structural unemployment and exclusion, particularly for women and young people.

- In countries that are open to trade and international investment, individuals are more likely to reap the dividends of globalization, access new ideas and knowledge, and adopt new technologies and innovations, all of which are factors that contribute significantly to increasing productivity gains and economic progress.

- Socially, economies that have open education systems, managed locally and focusing on performance, offer education system providers and recipients entry and exit options. They guarantee greater latitude, autonomy, and responsibility to students, parents, teachers, and heads of educational institutions with the objective of improving the quality of education and students' performance.

- Similarly, the emancipation of women has an important economic dimension. Eliminating the obstacles that women encounter and enabling them to participate fully in the economy, on an equal footing with men, is a direct way of unleashing economic potential and improving productivity and economic and social development results.

- Last, an open society is one that is capable of easily adopting advances in other countries owing to high cultural "receptivity" (Sowell 2015). However, societies are characterized by very broad variations in receptivity, both among societies and over time within the same society. During the Middle Ages, for example, a lagging Europe had to learn from the progress made in the Arab-Muslim world, particularly in the areas of mathematics, philosophy, and astronomy, but also agriculture, architecture, and medicine. Today, the Arab nations that so desire can create the conditions for acceleration, not only of their modernization, but also of their modernity by demonstrating greater openness and receptivity.[7]

A new development paradigm based on the promotion of an open society is one possible pathway for Morocco to become the first non-oil-producing emerging country in the North Africa region. It would lead to a reorientation of public efforts toward institution building, a refocusing of government action on its sovereign functions, and the development of human and social capital. Such a paradigm is not so different from the characteristics of the "desirable Morocco" scenario already considered in 2005 in the 50th Anniversary Report (see box 2.7). Its implementation does, however, require the prior acceptance of important principles:

- The process of convergence will be complex and indirect (there are no easy direct solutions to most economic problems);
- The economic dividends will only materialize in the medium and long term (institutions and human capital cannot be built in a day);
- The results will remain largely unpredictable (it is impossible to know in advance the cumulative consequences of individual micro-decisions);
- The process likely will not be linear, but subject to the instability of economic and social life, as shown by the experiences of many other countries with their economic takeoffs (for example, consider the financial crisis suffered by a number of South Asian emerging countries in 1997–98).

In practice, such a change of paradigm would have the huge advantage of facilitating the emergence of endogenous, decentralized, and reproducible solutions to the country's economic problems by building its institutional and human capacities.

While drawing on the experiences of many other countries in promoting open societies, Morocco must guard against the risk of institutional isomorphism. Morocco must resolutely take account of the experiences of other countries around the world without falling into the trap of a kind of mimicry that all too often distorts the development process. It is true that initially the economic

---

Box 2.7 The "Desirable Morocco" Scenario Goes Back 10 Years

In 2005, the 50th Anniversary Report listed the characteristics of the "desirable Morocco" scenario for 2025 (Government of Morocco 2005). This scenario was based on a number of pillars: consolidation of the democratic process, decentralization, reduced inequality and exclusion, and harmonious insertion in globalization. The objective was a society of opportunities for all and responsibilities for every individual. The pathways put forward by this report included the following:

- A democratic Morocco, open to universal values (human rights, rule of law, freedom, gender equality, etc.), protecting its roots, valuing its cultural diversity, and sharing values of progress. This Morocco would have a more transparent government focused on the user, and a decision-making system that would give preference to the long term over the short term and planned actions over improvised actions. The development choices would be formulated jointly and would be adapted to the global ecological context. It would be a Morocco in which good governance would be deeply entrenched in the customs and practices of all of the development stakeholders: the central government, local and regional communities, political players, economic agents, and civil society.
- A decentralized Morocco in which all communities would contribute in a balanced manner to the human development process by harnessing their diversity and material potential. This decentralized Morocco would consist of regions with broad powers in the economic, cultural, and social spheres. Cities, which would be managed rationally, would be economically successful, socially inclusive, and culturally exciting. The economy of the country would nonetheless be better integrated and better anchored in a relatively balanced territorial space (city/countryside, coastal areas/interior). The country would fully integrate the rural world and take account of its economic and environmental functions and its demographic weight. Alternative energies would have been developed (nuclear, wind, solar, etc.) and the country would be exploiting its natural and mineral resources rationally.
- A responsible Morocco, involving first of all the responsibility of citizens, who would take their destiny into their own hands and would take advantage of the full range of possibilities with public-spiritedness, solidarity, and national cohesion. Citizens would be aware of the fact that their individual ambitions could also be put to the service of the collective destiny of the Moroccan nation. The responsibility of the public authorities would then come into play. They would fully assume their mandates to the citizens. In this democratic context, the government would be responsible for its successes as well as its failures. Government policies would be assumed and assessed based on their outcomes and the quality of their implementation: participation, sustainable development, and assessment. The responsible society would also be a society of solidarity: there would be solidarity among all of the individuals making it up, particularly the vulnerable—such a society would be truly inclusive.

catch-up movement is largely a process of successful imitation and adaptation of existing knowledge or know-how to local circumstances. Even for the so-called advanced countries, innovation today is less about fundamental new discoveries and more about the successful combination and development of existing ideas (*The Economist* 2015). Frequently (for example, in production, trade, and invest-ment), this imitation process is relatively simple and not at all controversial. It is aimed at providing existing, relevant solutions and practices that are adaptable to the local context. In other words, there is no need for developing countries to "reinvent the wheel." However, in the case of institutions and policies, that is, the most fundamental aspects of a country's development, the imitation process is more complex.

Many developing countries have fallen into a kind of "isomorphic mimicry," that is, the purely formal adoption of organizations or policies of third countries, without the development of real functionality and implementation capacity, which are critical (Pritchett, Woolcock, and Andrews 2010). Not only do turnkey solutions exclude any appropriation of knowledge by the country concerned, they also prove to be counterproductive and constitute what some economists call "premature load bearing." Wishful thinking in the guise of reform and unre-alistic expectations leads to stresses and demands that are far beyond the local human and institutional reality and become a further burden on already weak systems. Although it may be tempting in the short term to reform by drawing on experiences from a foreign setting—specifically France in the case of Morocco—this method seldom leads systematically to a genuine, beneficial, in-depth reform. The artificial construction of an economic modernization facade is a risk to be resisted by avoiding having recourse to idealistic laws that will be challeng-ing to implement, proactive but overly ambitious sectoral plans, or opportunistic public projects that do not respond to the immediate economic needs of the population. The risk is that there will be, as noted earlier, "modernization without development" (Fukuyama 2014).

Notes

1. The committee seeks to serve as a governmental mechanism for coordinating inter-ventions in sectors tasked with managing public and private property and ensuring a harmonized public policy in this regard.

2. Barro-Lee database.

3. The definition of an emerging market country here is an upper-middle-income coun-try with per capita GDP of between US$4,126 and US$12,735 (2016).

4. Report commissioned by His Majesty King Mohammed VI in 2006.

5. The simulations in question include increased investment in basic infrastructure, increased investment in advanced infrastructure financed by a reduction in unproduc-tive spending, education reform in the form of an education subsidy and strengthening of the curriculum, a reduction of the degree to which the minimum wage and skilled wage are indexed, a policy to promote skilled labor migration, increased foreign direct investment, and a business climate improvement policy.

6. Under the co-chairmanship of Nobel Laureate Michael Spence and former World Bank Vice President Danny Leipziger and made up of 22 politicians and business-men, this commission submitted its report after four years of work (see http://siteresources.worldbank.org/EXTPREMNET/Resources/489960-1338997241035/Growth_Commission_Final_Report.pdf).

7. The notion of modernity goes beyond mere economic modernization and denotes the emergence of individual freedom, using reason over tradition, adherence to scientific and technical values, and the secularization of society.

References

Abderrahim Bouabid Foundation. 2010. *Le Maroc a-t-il une stratégie de développement économique? Quelques éléments de réflexion pour un véritable décollage économique et social.* Cercle d'Analyse Economique de la Fondation Abderrahim Bouabid. Morocco.

Acemoglu, Daron, Simon Johnson, and James A. Robinson. 2007. "Institutions as a Fundamental Cause of Long-Run Growth." In *Handbook of Economic Growth*, Volume 1A, edited by Philippe Aghion and Steven N. Durlauf, 385–471. Amsterdam: Elsevier.

AfDB (African Development Bank). 2015. *Diagnostic de croissance du Maroc: Analyse des contraintes à une croissance large et inclusive.* https://www.afdb.org/fileadmin/uploads/afdb/Documents/Generic-Documents/Diagnostic_de_croissance_du_Maroc_%E2%80%93_Analyse_des_contraintes_%C3%A0_une_croissance_large_et_inclusive_-_version_FR.pdf.

Agénor, Pierre-Richard Karim El Aynaoui. 2014. "Politiques publiques, transformation industrielle, croissance et emploi au Maroc: Une analyse quantitative." OCP Policy Center Research Paper RP-14/03. Morocco.

———. 2015. "Maroc Stratégie de croissance à l'horizon 2025 dans un environnement international en mutation." OCP Policy Center, Rabat, Morocco.

Alesina, Alberto, Arnaud Devleeschauwer, William Easterly, Sergio Kurlat, and Romain Wacziarg. 2003. "Fractionalization." *Journal of Economic Growth* 8 (2): 155–94.

Balakrishnan, Ravi, Chad Steinberg, and Murtaza Syed. 2013. "The Elusive Quest for Inclusive Growth: Growth, Poverty, and Inequality in Asia." IMF Working Paper, International Monetary Fund, Washington, DC.

Bank Al-Maghrib (BAM). 2016. "Rapport sur l'exercice 2015." Morocco.

Bloom, D. E., David Canning, and Jaypee Sevilla. 2001. "Economic Growth and the Demographic Transition." NBER Working Paper 8685, National Bureau of Economic Research, Cambridge, MA.

Bouoiyour, Jamal, Amal Miftah, and Christophe Muller. 2017. "Maghreb Rural-Urban Migration: The Movement to Morocco's Towns." Paper 1082, Economic Research Forum, Giza, Egypt.

Cohen Daniel, Thomas Piketty, and Gilles Saint-Paul. 2002. *The Economics of Rising Inequalities.* Oxford: Oxford University Press.

Dollar David, Tatjana Kleineberg, and Aart Kraay. 2013. "Growth Still Is Good for the Poor." Policy Research Working Paper 6568, World Bank, Washington, DC.

Easterly, W., and R. Levine. 2001. "What Have We Learned from a Decade of Empirical Research on Growth? It's Not Factor Accumulation: Stylized Facts and Growth Models." *World Bank Economic Review* 15 (2): 177–219.

Economic, Social, and Environmental Council (CESE). 2013. "Rapport annuel sur la gouvernance des services publics." Morocco.

———. 2014. *Cohérence des politiques sectorielles et accords de libre-echange: Fondements stratégiques pour un développement soutenu et durable.* Morocco.

The Economist. 2015. "Time to Fix Patents: Ideas Fuel the Economy. Today's Patent Systems Are a Rotten Way of Rewarding Them." August 8.

Eichengreen, Barry, Donghyun Park, and Kwando Shin. 2013. "Growth Slowdowns Redux: New Evidence on the Middle Income Trap." NBER Working Paper 18673, National Bureau of Economic Research, Cambridge, MA.

———. 2015. "The Global Productivity Slump: Common and Country-Specific Factors." NBER Working Paper 21556, National Bureau of Economic Research, Cambridge, MA. http://www.voxeu.org/article/global-productivity-slump.

El-Haddad, Amirah. 2016. "Government Intervention with No Structural Transformation: The Challenges of Egyptian Industrial Policy in Comparative Perspective." Economic Research Forum Working Paper 1038, Economic Research Forum, Giza, Egypt.

Frankel, Jeffrey A., and David Romer. 1999. "Does Trade Cause Growth?" *American Economic Review* 89 (3): 379–99.

Fukuyama, Francis. 2014. *Political Order and Political Decay: From the Industrial Revolution to the Globalization of Democracy.* New York: Farrar, Straus and Giroux.

Fuller, Brandon, and Paul Romer. 2014. "Urbanization as Opportunity." Working Paper No. 1, Maroon Institute of Urban Management, New York University, New York.

Fund for Peace. 2016. "Fragile State Index 2016." http://fsi.fundforpeace.org/.

Gallup, John Luke, Jeffrey D. Sachs, and Andrew D. Mellinger. 1999. "Geography and Economic Development." *International Regional Science Review* 22 (2): 179–232.

Glaeser, Edward. 2012. *Triumph of the City: How Our Greatest Invention Makes Us Richer, Smarter, Greener, Healthier, and Happier.* New York: Penguin.

Glaeser, Edward, Rafael La Porta, Florencio Lopez-de-Silane, and Andrei Shleifer. 2004. "Do Institutions Cause Growth?" *Journal of Economic Growth* 9 (3): 271–303.

Government of Morocco. 2005. *Rapport Général: 50 ans de développement humain et perspectives 2025.* Rapport commandité par SM le Roi Mohammed VI à l'occasion de la célébration du cinquantenaire de l'indépendance du Maroc. Morocco.

Hausman, Ricardo, Jason Hwang, and Dani Rodrik. 2005a. "What You Export Matters." Working Paper 123, Center of International Development, Harvard University, Cambridge, MA.

Hausman, Ricardo, Lant Pritchett, and Dani Rodrik. 2005b. "Growth Accelerations." *Journal of Economic Growth* 10 (4): 303–29.

High Commission for Planning (HCP). 2015. "Recensement général de la population 2014." Morocco.

His Majesty the King Mohammed VI. 2014. Throne Speech. Morocco.

Knack, S., and P. Keefer. 1997. "Does Social Capital Have an Economic Payoff? A Cross-Country Investigation." *Quarterly Journal of Economics* 112 (4): 1251–88.

Kolakowski, Leszek. 1990. *Modernity on Endless Trial. Chicago*: University of Chicago Press.

Krugman, Paul. 1994. *The Age of Diminished Expectations.* Cambridge, MA: MIT Press.

North, C. Douglass, and Robert Paul Thomas. 1973. *The Rise of the Western World: A New Economic History*. New York: Cambridge University Press.

Popper, Karl R. 1945. *The Open Society and Its Enemies*. Princeton, NJ: Princeton University Press.

Pritchett, Lant. 2013. "The Rebirth of Education: Schooling Ain't Learning." Washington, DC: Center for Global Development.

Pritchett, Lant, and Lawrence H. Summers. 2013. "Asia-Phoria Meet Regression to the Mean." *Proceedings of the Federal Reserve Bank of San Francisco* (November): 1–35.

Pritchett Lant, Michael Woolcock, and Matt Andrews. 2010. "Capability Traps? The Mechanisms of Persistent Implementation Failure." Working Paper 234, Center for Global Development, Washington, DC.

Restuccia, D. 2013. "Factor Misallocation and Development." In *The New Palgrave Dictionary of Economics*. Online edition, edited by Steven N. Durlauf and Lawrence E. Blume. Basingstoke, UK: Palgrave Macmillan.

Rodrik, Dani, Arvind Subramanian, and Francesco Trebbi. 2004. "Institutions Rule: The Primacy of Institutions over Geography and Integration in Economic Development." *Journal of Economic Growth* 9 (2): 131–65.

Romer, Paul. 2015. "Urban Policy Drives Catch-Up Growth." Lecture at the World Bank, Washington, DC.

Schumpeter, Joseph. 1942. *Capitalism, Socialism and Democracy*. New York: Harper & Brothers.

Smith, Adam. 1977 [1776]. *An Inquiry into the Nature and Causes of the Wealth of Nations*. Chicago: University of Chicago Press.

Sowell, Thomas. 2015. *Wealth, Poverty, and Politics: An International Perspective*. New York: Basic Books.

Tirole, Jean. 2016. "Économie du Bien Commun." Paris: Presse Universitaire de France.

UNESCO. 2014. "Enseigner et apprendre: atteindre la qualité pour tous." Rapport mondial de suivi sur l'EPT. Paris, UNESCO.

World Bank. 2006. "Promouvoir la croissance et l'emploi par la diversification productive et la compétitivité." Rapport No. 32948-MOR, World Bank, Washington, DC.

PART II

Intangible Capital:
The Pathway to
Economic Emergence

"What is tangible may make a stronger visible impression but it is by no means certain that its economic effect is greater than the intangibles."
—Thomas Sowell

The accelerated economic convergence scenario outlined in the previous chapter envisages a doubling of Morocco's current rate of convergence with Southern European countries relative to the trend scenario. The average standard of living for Moroccans could thus be almost half that of Spaniards by the year 2040. This scenario could satisfy the aspirations of Moroccan youth for a decent job and rising living standards. The four groups of young people profiled in the introduction would therefore have access to new opportunities, particularly access to jobs more commensurate with their potential and ambitions. Unless the industrial and high value-added service sectors are developed, young unskilled Amine, who left the countryside for the city, will continue to do odd jobs with no prospects for the future. Without adequate additional vocational training, the doors to the job market will remain closed to Nisrine, a young low-skilled woman who lacks language proficiency. In the absence of a more rapid structural transformation of the Moroccan economy, Kawtar, a young skilled woman, will also continue to find it difficult to enter the job market owing to weak business demand for her technical skills. Last, without the development of entrepreneurship and risk taking, Réda, a young man with tremendous potential, will continue to work in the public service or within a public company or establishment instead of contributing to sharing his knowledge to improve the Moroccan economy or to promote business development.

The accelerated convergence scenario requires that strategic political economy choices be made beforehand. The preconditions to accelerate economic convergence would include putting institutions that drive growth and wealth creation back at the center of the development strategy, prioritizing investments in intangible capital, particularly education, better informing and involving all economic players in the selection and conduct of public policies, and ensuring that "the rules of the game" are changed to promote the emergence of a more open society. Morocco has significant assets and can take up real drivers for change on the political level (stability of its leadership), the institutional level (new values and principles endorsed by the 2011 constitution), and the economic level (regulatory convergence with the European Union). These drivers also form the best vectors for strengthening economic and social cohesion in Morocco.

Once these strategic choices have been made, the major pathways that can make the accelerated convergence scenario a reality must be identified. This is the goal of the second part of this book. The sustainable scale-up of total factor productivity cannot come from a single reform, however ambitious it may be. In other words, Morocco's building of its intangible capital will necessarily take a number of different forms. Considering that the proposed reforms are often institutional and difficult to quantify, the Memorandum does not provide a general equilibrium analysis of the various reforms. However, this does not detract from the importance of ensuring sound coordination of policies. For example, a partial equilibrium analysis of interactions among three subsectors only (education, social security, and the job market) shows the importance of coordinating policies to have a significant impact on employment levels: isolated interventions to improve the internal efficiency of the education system can even be counterproductive and exacerbate the unemployment problem (Marouani and Robalino 2011).

Moreover, not all the desired reforms can be implemented at the same time, despite the need to send a strong signal that sweeping change is under way. The dozen priority reform pathways proposed present the reform areas that are critical to placing the Moroccan economy on a path of greater shared prosperity. These pathways draw on the four dimensions of intangible capital discussed in the previous chapters: (i) institutional market support capital, that is, institutions that facilitate the most efficient allocation of capital and labor in the economy and facilitate Morocco's integration into the global economy; (ii) public institutional capital, working to promote the rule of law and justice, enhance the administration's effectiveness and productivity, and improve the quality of public services; (iii) human capital, which implies access for all to better education, health, and early childhood development; and (iv) social capital as the intangible asset that underlies progress in all other areas, including true gender equality and interpersonal trust in society.

Reference

Marouani, Mohammed A., and David A. Robalino. 2011. "Assessing Interactions among Education, Social Insurance, and Labor Market Policies in Morocco." *Applied Economics* 44 (24): 3149–67.

CHAPTER 3

Investing in Market Support Institutions

"With competition everyone has to try harder."

— Harold H. Greene

The scenario of economic convergence by 2040 requires an acceleration of private sector growth driven by higher productivity gains. Achieving these productivity gains will depend largely on the capacity of Moroccan society to agree on new operating rules for the market that promote more fair competition, encourage innovation and entrepreneurship, and discourage rent seeking in all economic sectors. Countries that have sustainably improved the well-being of their populations have established effective institutions in support not just of the goods and services markets but also the labor and capital markets (World Bank 2002). These institutions must accomplish three key tasks: (i) ensure transparency of information on all market conditions, (ii) define and enforce property rights and contracts, and (iii) promote economic freedom and ensure the application of the rules of competition. Effective institutions in support of the market are essential to the success of market-based solutions. Not only can they promote opportunities and facilitate structural transformation, but they can also guarantee results that are both efficient and equitable (Chauffour 2009).

Developing effective market institutions is a complex task that is closely related to public sector good governance (see chapter 4) and the promotion of a modern state, that is, a state that strictly separates public and private interests (Fukuyama 2014). Experiments conducted around the world show that there is no single valid model that fits all. The risk of "institutional isomorphism," which refers to the construction of facade institutions that merely drape a veil of modernity over outmoded practices, has already been mentioned. Moreover, an analysis of international experience reveals that efficiency in the allocation of capital and labor and in the economic integration of various countries is based largely on the quality of their market institutions, such as the quality of the measures governing competition, the relevance of the labor code to local conditions, or the rules and disciplines governing the system of foreign trade. The following three sections will therefore discuss the institutional bases that can support a more effective allocation of capital and labor and better integration of Morocco into the global economy.

Allocating Capital More Competitively

Institutions that promote and guarantee fair competition among economic agents make it possible to allocate productive resources, particularly capital, to their most efficient use. Openness and transparency create the conditions for economic freedom by placing constant pressure on businesses to provide the best possible range of products, services, and technologies at the best possible prices. Paradoxically, competition encourages businesses to innovate and adopt new technologies to reduce their costs and temporarily escape competition (Aghion and others 2001). In contrast, when businesses are successful in benefiting from specific important advantages, their competitors cannot compete fairly with them and they therefore have little incentive to innovate, weakening the economic vitality of the sector as a whole. Being incapable of innovating, the sector typically finds itself at a competitive disadvantage on the external markets and thus relies on the local protected market to survive. In an open society, competition dominates the life of businesses, whether they are focused on the domestic or external markets, to the benefit of consumers.

Fair Competition Is Key to the Efficient Allocation of Capital

Free and equitable access to the markets makes it possible to respond effectively to the demands of the population and is an essential engine of technological progress and economic growth. The main dimensions of economic freedom are generally the freedom to hold and legally acquire property, the freedom to engage in voluntary transactions (within and outside the country's borders), and the freedom to establish the terms of transactions between individuals. The institutions and policies that guarantee economic freedom can encourage stronger growth. They foster a higher return on productive efforts thanks to the protection of private property, an independent legal system, and low taxes. They also promote the emergence of a dynamic, pragmatically organized economy in which a large number of entrepreneurs may succeed or fail but where competition between all participants is fair and therefore not distorted by excessive regulation and the presence of state-owned enterprises. They facilitate rational decision making owing to a predictable and stable macroeconomic environment. As a result, they encourage the movement of goods, capital, labor, and services that favors the highest levels of satisfaction and return on investment.

Fair competition in all domains (scientific, industrial, intellectual, artistic, or sports) is generally a factor in a society's progress. For example, in the era of the Internet and information and communications technologies (ICTs), competition lies at the center of the knowledge economy, which is a growing source of wealth creation in all countries. The knowledge economy encompasses an economy's capacity to adapt existing expertise, create concepts, or produce new ideas (Jouyet and Lévy 2006). In general, innovation in one area leads to the creation of innovation clusters in other areas. The momentum thus created by the race for new ideas is a factor in the structural transformation and increasing sophistication of the economy. The organization of economies around global value chains contributes to this process of innovation and task specialization (Driouchi and Zouag 2006).

In this context, the essential role of public policy is to create a fair, predictable environment that allows players to cooperate in a secure and supportive context. Promoting innovation by establishing networks of players involves connecting public institutions (ministries, agencies, regulatory authorities, and the like) with centers of knowledge production, such as research laboratories and universities, and with the business world (including small and large companies). Through such collaborations, technologies and innovative ideas are more likely to be disseminated and influence production systems (Bouoiyour 2003). China, Finland, Japan and the Republic of Korea are examples of countries that have been successful in transitioning their economies by placing innovation at the forefront of their strategies. Their reforms took place in a context of evaluation and monitoring that have enabled them to adjust their policies proactively and improve the effectiveness of both public and private investment (World Bank and others 2013).

The establishment of free competition between market players implies that they are all subject to the same constraints—in practice as well as on paper—in terms of the legal framework and taxation, access to credit and markets, and respect of intellectual property rights. In the Middle East and North Africa, business relations are still all too often based on interpersonal relationships, and access to public procurement or large contracts is more often than not limited to a few firms or individuals with deep political connections (World Bank 2015). These privileges and connections thrive in an absence of information and transparency in the application of the rules, which discourages competition and the development of the private sector. The most well-informed market participants with access to the circles of power, whether at the national or at the local level, are able to perpetuate their vested interests. This corporatism develops to the detriment of the renewal of economic elites at an excessive cost for society that is borne by workers, by consumers, and, even unwittingly, by the entrepreneurs themselves.

Creating the conditions for fair competition is a complex challenge. Improving the conditions of competition requires resolving a number of cross-cutting problems: reducing rent-seeking behavior, ending discretionary authority in the application of regulations, improving transparency in the allocation of subsidies and other government interventions, facilitating access for all players to the economic information held by the authorities, or even involving local stakeholders in the development and assessment of public policies. Moreover, the success of an ecosystem that favors innovation depends largely on the strength of the relations between the research and business worlds, the transparency and equity of public programs, the protection of intellectual property rights, and the quality of the training and flexibility of labor (United Nations 2008).

Inefficient Allocation of Capital in Morocco

There are many reasons for the lack of competition and limited innovative capacity in Morocco. This book focuses on four main causes, as follows: a weak regulatory framework and weak authorities in the area of competition, a complex and opaque business environment, top-down sectoral strategies with mixed results, and a conservative financial system. Morocco has progressed steadily in all of these areas over the past 10 years, but the changes actually made have generally not lived up to the stated ambitions.

Still Weak Competition despite Improvements in the Legal Framework

Despite a merchant tradition and an entrepreneurial population, the competitive spirit in Morocco seems to be constrained. As seen, in spite of high levels of mainly publicly funded investment, the private sector remains relatively small and is not showing signs of significant rapid growth. The density of new businesses in comparison with the total population is certainly higher than in other countries in the region but is low in comparison with many emerging market economies (see figure 3.1). This lack of momentum in the private sector is an obstacle to the structural transformation of the economy and the productivity gains generally associated with such a transformation, and ultimately to growth and the creation of decent jobs. One of the reasons for the gap among investment, private sector development, and growth is the lack of openness of the markets, which is explained by a playing field that is often socially inequitable and economically inefficient. According to a study by the Royal Institute of Strategic Studies (IRES), "By reducing competition, protection allows for the emergence

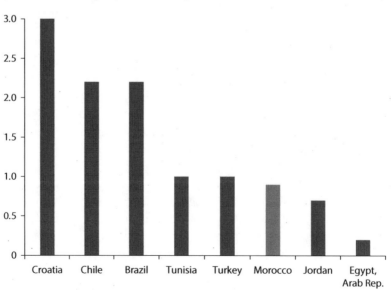

Figure 3.1 Average New Business Entry Density, 2004–09
(number of new firms per 1,000 inhabitants)

Source: Klapper and Love 2010.

of monopolistic rents. Businesses that benefit from this situation have used price increases to collect super profits rather than investing in competitiveness through quality and new techniques" (IRES 2014).

In most countries in the Middle East and North Africa region, capitalism is dominated by personal connections and privileges, which are an integral part of a complex network of economic interests that hinder the emergence of new players (World Bank 2009, 2015b). The effect is to maintain monopolies, impede the performance of the economy, and weaken the growth of productivity and job creation, as seen in Tunisia (Rijkers, Freund, and Nucifora 2014), the Arab Republic of Egypt (Diwan, Keefer, and Schiffbauer 2013), and Lebanon (Diwan and Haidar 2016). Many observers of the sociology of the Moroccan economy suggest that Morocco is not immune to this type of risk.[1] Indeed, the royal holding investment company (SNI) is present in a dozen economics sectors. A recent study estimates that almost 13 percent of a representative sample of Moroccan manufacturing companies are held by individuals connected with circles of economic influence (Saadi 2016). These businesses operate in various economic sectors and are apparently more effective than their unconnected counterparts owing, in part, to the privileges that they enjoy in terms of commercial protection, application of the rules and regulations, and access to financing. The existence of crony capitalism can also be observed through the lens of Moroccan listed companies and the role of the financial sector (Oubenal 2016). Beyond considerations of equity, the existence of connected enterprises can partially explain the slow overall structural transformation of the economy to the extent that these firms operate in sectors with low new business entry and exit rates, greater concentration, and lower than average job creation.

While some sectors have liberalized (mobile telephony, for example), this progress cannot mask the lack of real competition between economic agents in many sectors. Pricing agreements between players still exist in many sectors. In 2013, for example, the Competition Council identified a tacit pricing agreement between market participants in the dairy products sector and reported a high level of concentration. There is a lack of competition in the (fixed and mobile) broadband sector, which shows the most potential for development in the ICT sector in the coming years. The sector also suffers from incomplete and ineffective regulation as well as a lack of investment in infrastructure (World Bank 2016a). Last, the opening up of some sectors was poorly prepared, has not produced the expected outcomes, and has, in some cases, taken place to the detriment of local operators. For example, the opening of road and maritime transportation to competition between 2003 and 2006 did not have the expected impact on competitiveness and resulted in an inability of Moroccan players to respond to international competition. Nevertheless, the development of effective logistics specialists proposing a reliable and competitive supply could have a significant impact in reducing export and import costs and improving Morocco's competitiveness on the international markets. The implementation of the maritime strategy adopted in 2016 could promote the development of more effective and competitive maritime services.

The regulatory framework governing competition has been updated, but its implementation has been suspended since 2014 pending the actual appointment of the members to the new Competition Council. The Competition Council has played an active role since 2009 in the evaluation of levels of competition and identification of concentrations and illicit agreements. The Council has worked with a high level of autonomy, which has enabled it to issue some 40 opinions and conduct around 15 objective studies on the state of markets. It has thus actively participated in the propagation and dissemination of a culture of competition within the various parts of Moroccan society. The 2011 constitution and new laws adopted in 2014 have strengthened the powers of the Competition Council, making it an authority that ensures transparency and equity in economic relations and auguring well for the future. This new framework will enable the Council to investigate all issues related to competition in Morocco on its own initiative and to issue fines, injunctions, and other pecuniary penalties against any economic agents found to be in violation of the law. Businesses also have the option of referring issues directly to the Council, thus strengthening its potential effectiveness. Once its new members have been appointed, the Competition Council will be able to investigate monopolistic situations that have long adversely impacted many sectors across the country. The effectiveness of these new legal provisions will be measured by their practical application, through the demonstrated capacity of the Council to resolve competition problems in key sectors.

Despite the many reforms aimed at refocusing the government on its general interest missions, public enterprises and establishments (EEPs) continue to play a major role in the national economy. However, because of their status, modes of governance, and public financial support, they can constitute an obstacle to the opening up of many sectors. At the end of 2015, the EEP sector represented about 8 percent of gross domestic product (GDP) and almost 25 percent of the country's total investment through 212 public establishments, 44 companies in which the government had direct equity holdings, and some 442 subsidiaries and public shareholdings. Many commercial EEPs and their subsidiaries are found in key economic sectors in which the barriers to entry remain high (agriculture and marine fisheries; energy, mines, water, and the environment; infrastructure and transportation; housing, urban planning, and local and regional development). These enterprises, which often occupy monopolistic positions, are an obstacle to the emergence of new competitive and potentially innovative participants. Moreover, while for a number of years the government has endeavored to create a more competitive environment by adopting good governance rules and introducing clear and transparent regulatory mechanisms (in the area of contractual relationships, for example), the EEP sector shows signs of stalling, as reflected by shrinking investment, rising foreign currency debt levels, and the sharp increase in public transfers to the EEPs (Audit Office 2016). The cause would appear to be a lack of strategic guidance and coordination with the sectoral policies of the ministries. Despite the progress resulting from the Moroccan Code of Good Governance Practices for EEPs, their governance remains questionable, particularly as regards the makeup, administration, and operation of their governing bodies; transparency and access to information; and accountability. More critically, it is difficult to require the government and its employees to be effective in the conduct of competitive commercial affairs. This is not because they are by nature less capable than their colleagues in the private sector, but because in their role as "bureaucrats in business" they often face contradictory goals and perverse incentives (World Bank 1995).

The functioning of the economy and development of the private sector, particularly small and medium enterprises (SMEs), suffer from the lengthy payment delays between customers and suppliers, starting with the government and public enterprises. The lengthening payment delays particularly affect SMEs. According to Inforisk, between 2010 and 2014, it took an average of 279 days for SMEs to collect on claims, or the equivalent of more than nine months during which a business's sales did not enter its cash flow. The 2013 law that was aimed at reducing payment delays seems to have had little effect. According to the regulatory authorities for the insurance and capital markets, payment delays have again lengthened since 2015, reaching alarming levels, particularly for very small enterprises and certain sectors of activity. Such practices have a major impact on working capital requirements and threaten the survival of businesses. In addition, the government's delays in refunding the value-added tax (VAT) credits to businesses, particularly public enterprises, also strangle the economy. As emphasized by His Majesty King Mohammed VI, "It is also unacceptable that State agencies should refuse to pay small and medium businesses what they owe them whereas, in fact, they should be supporting and encouraging those businesses, given the important role they play in promoting development and employment."[2]

Owing to this lack of competitive momentum and respect of the regulations, SMEs are limited in their development when they should in fact be the engines of innovation. In 2016, the Global Innovation Index placed Morocco 72nd out of 128 countries (Cornell University, INSEAD, and WIPO 2016). Although Morocco leads the North African countries in this ranking and is among the 10 most successful low middle-income countries, particularly owing to its infrastructure, significant efforts must be made in the area of business sophistication to bring it into the group of emerging market countries. At the national level, the results of the Morocco Innovation Initiative are below the targets: 353 Moroccan patent applications were recorded in 2013, whereas the strategy called for 1,000 patents (OMPIC 2014). Among the applications, only 17 percent represented new and innovative products, and among Moroccan applicants, businesses represented only 10 percent of the patent applications recorded. Despite the establishment of incubation structures and dedicated programs,[3] the Morocco Innovation Initiative target of creating more than 200 innovative start-ups has also not been achieved. These results are explained in part by the weakness of the legal and operational framework protecting the intellectual property of entrepreneurs, the capital available to investors and debts to financial institutions, as well as procedural and administrative bottlenecks in the insolvency process. According to the Doing Business indicator on resolving insolvency, Morocco is ranked 131st in the world, which is average for the Middle East and North Africa region countries, but fairly far from the frontier (see figure 3.2).

Figure 3.2 Distance to Frontier for Resolving Insolvency, 2016

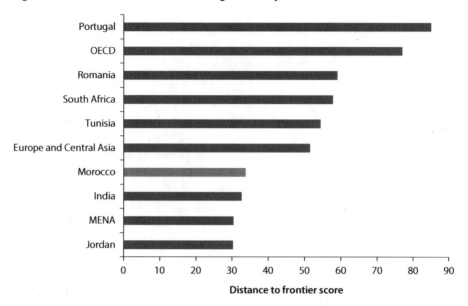

Distance to frontier score

Source: World Bank 2016c.
Note: The distance to frontier score benchmarks economies with respect to regulatory practice, showing the absolute distance to the best performance in each Doing Business indicator. An economy's distance to frontier score is indicated on a scale from 0 to 100, where 0 represents the worst performance and 100 the frontier.

Morocco has lagged behind in the development of ICTs, particularly fixed broadband, and this has stifled innovation, competitiveness, and structural transformation. The ICT sector plays an important role in the economic competitiveness of countries and its capacity to create jobs is considerable. Upstream, the ICT sector may also play an important role in political competition and the renewal of elites (Miner 2015). In Morocco the growth of this sector is losing momentum and its potential is not fully exploited (World Bank 2016a). Ten years ago Morocco was a regional leader, but today it is falling behind other comparable countries. Its broadband penetration is one of the lowest in the Middle East and North Africa region and is significantly lower than that of some Eastern European countries (see figure 3.3).

Despite efforts thus far,[4] the lag in this area is explained by a lack of competition, incomplete and ineffective regulation, and underinvestment in fixed broadband infrastructure, which is limited to the country's main urban centers and highways (World Bank 2016b). The result is an important shortfall for the government (GDP, fiscal revenues) and a persistent digital divide that creates economic and social inequalities. In Morocco, access to broadband subscriptions is too expensive for 60 percent of the population. Although this is common to other countries in the Middle East and North Africa region and other emerging market economies, the main reasons for this situation are unique to Morocco: barriers to the entry of new players who would like to deploy their own infrastructure without necessarily marketing the frequency spectrum; insufficient and unbalanced investments in fiber optics among the three operators; use of the

Figure 3.3 Fixed Broadband Penetration Rate and Mobile Broadband Penetration in Morocco and Eastern Europe

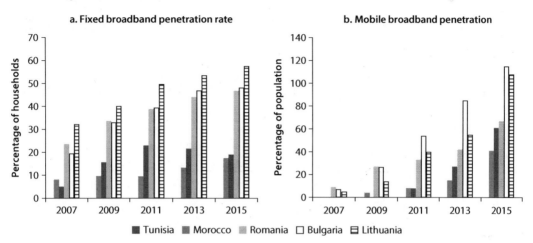

Source: TeleGeography's GlobalComms 2015, http://www.telegeography.com.
Note: For the broadband penetration rate, the international comparisons presented use end-of-year data for calendar year 2015 (i.e., December).

Universal Service Fund (Fonds de Service Universel, FSU) that is not sufficiently focused on broadband development; and ineffective regulation of broadband infrastructure (copper and fiber optics). Thus the (fixed and mobile) broadband market is consolidated around three operators, but competition does not exist in all areas of the country owing to an imbalance in the fiber optic infrastructure among the three operators.[5] Moreover, the regulations are incomplete and relatively ineffective as decisions taken by the regulator on the sharing of fixed infrastructure in the access network (particularly asymmetric digital subscriber line, ADSL) are not sufficiently applied and the regulator has made no decisions on the sharing of interurban fiber optic cables (that is, dark fiber). Moreover, access to fiber optic networks owned by alternative infrastructure operators (i.e., ONEE, ONCF) is not regulated. Last, apart from the lack of private investment by operators who have not invested massively in wired infrastructure despite their fixed next-generation network (NGN) licenses granted in 2006, the use of the FSU (contribution of 2 percent of the total sales of operators per year) has not been sufficiently focused on broadband development.

Finalization of the Digital Morocco 2020 plan provides an opportunity to establish a new model of public governance for the ICT sector, to completely overhaul the legal and regulatory framework, and to implement an ICT strategy that focuses on access to broadband and very high speed broadband, by promoting public-private partnerships for investment and shifting the use of universal service funds toward underserved areas of the country. Since the introduction of third-generation network technology (3G) in 2007 and fourth-generation technology (4G) in 2015, broadband Internet constitutes an important development potential for the ICT sector. Such development would, for example, allow Moroccan industry to position itself on technology-intensive global

---

Box 3.1 European Experience with the Liberalization of the Broadband Sector

In Lithuania, the fiber to the home (FTTH) penetration rate in 2015 was the highest in Europe[a] and most of these connections were provided by suppliers other than the historical operator.

In Bulgaria, the share of the market held by the historical operator in the fixed broadband segment is only 29 percent[b] and in Turkey 87 general authorizations were granted to wireless Internet providers.[c]

In Romania and Lithuania, policies for opening up the market have resulted in average Internet speeds higher than those in France and Italy.[d] In Morocco, the international bandwidth per Internet user is one of the lowest in the Middle East and North Africa region and is substantially lower than that in Romania, Bulgaria, or Lithuania.

a. http://www.ftthcouncil.eu/documents/PressReleases/2016/PR20160217_FTTHpanorama_luxembourg_french_Award.pdf.
b. Rood 2010.
c. World Bank 2010. Also see http://www.bix.bg/en/en_article/Bulgarian_Broadband_Market.html.
d. See http://www.speedtest.net/fr/ for Internet speed tests.

---

supply chains and move up global value chains by improving its competitiveness. To do this, Morocco must implement reforms that have been successful elsewhere (see box 3.1) to encourage the entry of new players (without limiting the number and without prohibiting them from deploying infrastructure), introduce a regulation for open, nondiscriminatory access to communications networks, and promote private investment in telecommunications.

Still Restrictive Business Climate despite Progress

Over the past 15 years, Morocco has made significant changes to its business environment and its public policies to modernize the economy and encourage efficiency and innovation. This effort has resulted in the adoption of numerous sectoral strategies, reforms of the business climate, the signing of free trade agreements, the modernization of the governance of large public enterprises, which have been converted into private corporations, and the launching of flagship projects in partnership with foreign investors. These changes have also affected the private sector, with the reform of the General Federation of Moroccan Businesses (CGEM), which is actively involved in resolving issues relating to SMEs and very small enterprises, and the emergence of new entrepreneurs wishing to become involved in matters of public interest. The National Business Environment Committee (Comité National de l'Environnement des Affaires, CNEA), chaired by the Head of Government, has brought together public and private players in a joint reform effort. The efforts made by Morocco to improve the business climate have been recognized in many international rankings, such as the World Economic Forum's Global Competitiveness Report and the World Bank's Doing Business Report (World Bank 2014a). Morocco's Doing Business ranking improved from 129th to 68th between 2010 and 2016, owing in particular to business start-up reforms (World Bank 2015).

However, the business climate is still seen by most players as too unpredictable and bureaucratic and does not inspire the confidence that economic agents
need to invest in the medium or long term. The importance of constraints such
as burdensome, slow, complex, and opaque administrative formalities and procedures is regularly confirmed in surveys of businesses. The constraints most
often mentioned by the formal sector are corruption, competition from the
informal sector, low workforce education levels, and difficulties in accessing
financing (see figure 3.4) (World Bank 2013a). For very small enterprises and
small and medium enterprises (VSEs and SMEs), these barriers can be unsur-
mountable (World Bank 2014a). Corruption is partly related to the lengthy,
complex, and opaque procedures for obtaining industrial and commercial permits at the local level, particularly owing to a legal and regulatory framework
that is not very user friendly and that often gives government departments
discretionary authority to interpret the laws and regulations. It is also related to
abuse of tax audits. Access to industrial property is difficult despite the launching of several integrated industrial platforms (P2i). Obsolete nontariff barriers
jeopardize access at a reasonable cost for international players and impede the
development of some local industries. The lack of transparency and the complexity of procedures for allocating subsidies and other forms of public support
make it a relatively inefficient system. These constraints are regularly confirmed
by CGEM barometers, which indicate that business leaders have a rather

Figure 3.4 Main Obstacles to Development Identified by Businesses
(percent)

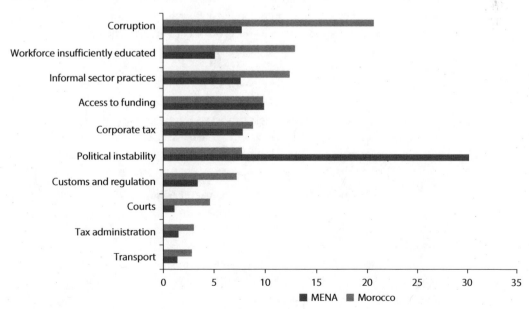

Source: World Bank 2013a.

negative view of the business climate. According to the barometer for the first quarter of 2016, only 22 percent state that the climate is favorable to business. The legal uncertainty is considered a major obstacle to growth by more than 60 percent of businesses. All in all, these various market distortions have serious adverse effects on Morocco's productivity. Based on the World Bank's Enterprise Surveys, it has been estimated that the market distortions in the manufacturing sector could explain a total factor productivity "deficit" of up to 56 percent as compared to more advanced countries that display less distortions (Chauffour and Diaz-Sanchez 2017). In other words, closing part of this deficit over the next 25 years could add significant percentage points of annual manufacturing and total GDP growth (box 3.2).

The incidence of entrenched corruption affecting businesses in Morocco is high (EBRD, EIB, and World Bank 2016). The frequency and incidence of requests for benefits or informal payments faced by Moroccan businesses in their relations with government departments and public services, in their applications for licenses and construction permits, or in import operations or tax payments, appear

---

Box 3.2 Measuring the Effects of Market Distortions in Morocco's Manufacturing Sector on Potential Total Factor Productivity

A large heterogeneity in firm-level productivity within a sector may indicate misallocation of resources across firms, with a consequent negative and sizable effect on the aggregate total factor productivity (TFP). Applying the analytical framework developed by Hsieh and Klenow (2009) to the microdata from the 2007 and 2013 World Bank's Enterprise Surveys for Morocco allows estimation of the effects of market distortions in the manufacturing sector on the level of resource misallocation in Morocco and derivation of the potential TFP gains to be expected from the (partial) removal of these distortions (Chauffour and Diaz-Sanchez 2017). Although empirical results show a reduction in the level of market distortions in the manufacturing sector in Morocco between 2007 and 2013, the overall level of distortions in 2013 remained much higher than the levels in France or the United States and somewhat higher than in some developing countries such as China and India (table B3.2.1). The manufacturing subsectors posting the largest distortions are the chemical (1.13) and food (1.06) sectors, while the textile (0.62) and machinery (0.6) sectors appeared less subject to distortions. It is estimated that the full removal of these distortions (full liberalization) would translate to around 84 percent gains in TFP. A reduction of these distortions to the level prevailing currently in advanced countries (partial liberalization) would still translate to a significant 56 percent improvement in TFP.

Table B3.2.1 Level of Market Distortion and Potential TFP Gains

Country	Morocco		United States	France	Korea, Rep.	China	India
Data year	2007	2013	1997	2005	2012	2005	1994
Level of market distortion	1.01	0.77	0.49	0.48	0.55	0.63	0.67
Potential TFP gains (%)	n.a.	83.8	42.9	n.a.	n.a.	86.6	127.5

Note: n.a.= not applicable; TFP = total factor productivity.

Figure 3.5 Incidence and Depth of Businesses' Exposure to Corruption
(percent)

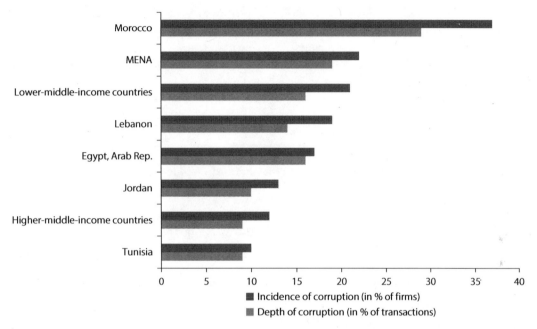

Source: World Bank Enterprise Surveys 2013 and 2014.
Note: The depth of corruption measures the frequency with which businesses are faced with requests for gifts or informal payments in six operations. The incidence of corruption measures the percentage of enterprises exposed to at least one request for a gift or informal payment.

to be significantly higher than the Middle East and North Africa region average, which itself compares unfavorably to other middle-income countries that are Morocco's competitors (see figure 3.5). While corruption involves the visible costs related to illicit payments and a poor allocation of resources, its highest cost is invisible and involves missed opportunities: the businesses that are not created, the investments that are not made, the loans that are not granted, and, ultimately, the jobs that are not created.

Sectoral Strategies with Mixed Results

In the 2000s, Morocco launched a series of sectoral strategies to correct the systemic failures or dysfunctions of many sectors and encourage investment projects. In this context, the government worked to create "positive distortions" to encourage investment, particularly in the form of tax and financial incentives, access to property and financing, and simplified administrative procedures, combined with infrastructure investment. These strategies have targeted all sectors: the Azur Plan and Vision 2020 for tourism, the Green Morocco Plan for agriculture and agribusiness, the Halieutis Plan 2020 for the fisheries industry, Morocco Export Plus for exports, the Emergence Plan (2005), the National Industrial Emergence Pact (2009–15),[6] and the new Industrial Acceleration Plan (2014–20) for industry, to mention just a few. For example, under the new

Industrial Acceleration Plan, the government commits to granting financial support of around 2 percent of GDP over 6 years. It also provides ad hoc support to attract foreign investors to large private projects that are likely to generate significant positive externalities, the most symbolic example being the Renault plant in Tangier, which aims to produce and export 400,000 vehicles per year and which benefited from favorable conditions that would be difficult to sustain financially on a larger scale (see box 3.3).

However, to date, the sectoral strategies have not led to the anticipated structural transformation of the Moroccan economy. Despite undeniable success

---

Box 3.3 Conditions for Renault's Installation in Tangier

Renault's decision to set up operations near Tangier was made in 2007. The French carmaker was seeking a new industrial site to deploy its strategy for the development of its Entry range, which was very successful on the European market. Beyond proximity to the European market and other strategic industrial considerations, Renault-Nissan's decision to locate this new plant in the Tangier area was based on the provision by the government of Morocco of international standard infrastructure and a series of direct tax, property, financial, and training incentives (Benabdejlil, Lung, and Piveteau 2016):

- "In terms of infrastructure, the Tanger-Med I deep water port located at Ksar Al Majaz, 22 kilometers from Tangier and put into service in 2007, offers an essential base for the export of automobiles. The closed-loop supply chain from the plant in Tangier is achieved by a dedicated rail link providing daily shuttles and to a lesser extent by the highway. Renault operates its own port terminal at Tanger-Med."
- "In addition to these infrastructure and logistics benefits, the fact that over 90 percent of production is aimed at the export markets enables the French manufacturer installed in the free zone to benefit from a total exemption from corporate income tax (IS) for the first five years, with a ceiling of 8.75 percent subsequently, as well as from VAT relief."
- "Investment aid was also decisive. In addition to the exceptional grant of 300 hectares of land for the construction of the plant, the Hassan II government fund subsidized the project in the form of a EUR 200 million low-interest loan to the Renault company. Three national banks have also provided EUR 105 million in financing to the project. Moreover, the Moroccan Caisse de dépôt et de gestion (CDG), which holds 49 percent of the Tangier plant equity in the amount of the EUR 240 million (51 percent, or EUR 122.4 million, contributed by Renault) paid an investment bonus of EUR 60 million while the Japanese partner Nissan has withdrawn from the project. Private Moroccan investors are involved in the amount of EUR 240 million."
- "The support of the Moroccan government has also involved personnel recruitment and training. The government has constructed and financed two training centers (Training Institute for Automotive Jobs, IFMIA) in Tangier: one alongside the Renault plant and the other in the Tangier Free Zone, where 14 of Renault's 24 suppliers are located. Two others have entered into operation in Casablanca and Kenitra in the form of public-private partnerships wholly financed by the Moroccan government. With the direct assistance for hiring, the contribution of the Moroccan government is estimated at close to EUR 150 million."

stories in various industries (automotive, aeronautics, agribusiness), the impact of the sectoral strategies remains mixed in terms of their systemic ambitions and the difficulties that most businesses continue to face. In particular, the Emergence Plan (2009–15), which aimed to create 400,000 jobs by 2015, did not have the expected outcomes. The initial modernization program had only a limited effect on the technical efficiency of the beneficiary companies (Achy and others 2010). Public initiatives launched via integrated industrial platforms (P2i) responded only partially to the problem of access to land in a manner commensurate with business needs, mainly owing to the choice of locations and prices charged.[7] One indicator is the fact that some of these industrial platforms have attracted fewer than 10 enterprises (CGEM 2014). As discussed in the previous chapter, one of the main reasons for this setback is that an industrialization strategy cannot consist simply of sectoral support policies, even if they are well coordinated, but must also be based on cross-cutting policies to create a fertile environment for all players, including those that do not yet exist and therefore cannot be heard.

In this context, the objectives of the new Industrial Acceleration Plan (2014–20) also seem very ambitious. They involve increasing the share of manufacturing value added from 14 percent of GDP in 2014 to 23 percent in 2020 and creating 500,000 net jobs in the process. The achievement of these objectives assumes that growth of the manufacturing sector, which has historically fluctuated around 2.5 percent per year, can accelerate and be maintained at 15 percent per year for six years (see figure 3.6), an unprecedented level in the recent economic history of nations.

Figure 3.6 Morocco: Objectives of the Industrial Acceleration Plan (2014–20) Compared to Historical Performance (1991–2013)

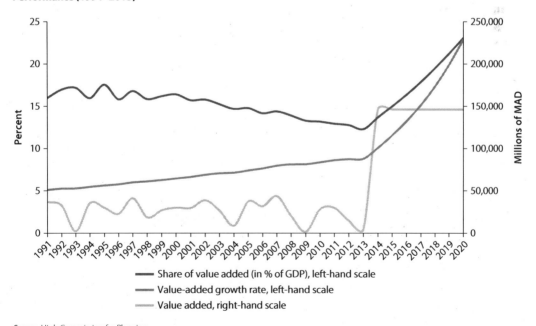

Source: High Commission for Planning.
Note: GDP = gross domestic product; MAD = Moroccan dirham.

In fact, during the first three years of the plan (2014–16), growth of the manufacturing sector remained at its historic trend level, as did the net creation of industrial jobs, which remained low. In late 2016, 43 ecosystems were launched in 12 industrial sectors[8] and close to 167,000 jobs were announced in the context of investment agreements. New support and investment incentive measures were also announced, including exemptions from the corporate income tax for 5 years for new industries, the development of at least one free zone per region, the granting of the status of free zone to large exporting industries, the granting of the status of indirect exporter to subcontractors, and the introduction of enhanced support for the most disadvantaged regions.[9] In the absence of targeting and the administrative tracking that this implies, these new incentives risk creating windfall effects and encouraging activities that do not necessarily respond to the comparative advantages of the Moroccan economy.

A major difficulty is the fact that downstream solutions in the form of case-by-case incentives cannot compensate for the cross-cutting, systemic difficulties faced by entrepreneurs upstream. Providing incentives on a case-by-case basis is generally not recommended in international best practices, which favor systems that are automatic and transparent to the extent possible. Case-by-case assessment, which is applied by the Investment Commission system, creates a number of technical risks by tasking government departments with assessing the value of projects, something that is often beyond their technical capacity, and governance risks, to the extent that the allocation criteria are not sufficiently precise. This gives government departments discretionary authority while creating a temptation for investors to influence the process. It is true that Morocco has adopted new tools to aid in decision making and promote good governance in the public incentives granted to investors,[10] but international experience generally indicates that there are long-term limitations on administrative approaches to investment. Specifically, the government often does not have the practical means to monitor businesses over time to determine whether they are continuing to meet the conditions established for the various incentives.

A Relatively Sound and Inclusive but Insufficiently Diversified Financial System

The Moroccan financial system operates relatively effectively in mobilizing national savings. Over the past 10 years, this sector has become one of the most developed and inclusive in the Middle East and North Africa. The ratio of private credit to GDP (73 percent) and the ratio of household credit to GDP (31 percent) are above the average for countries in the region. Banking, insurance, Islamic financing, and microfinance products are used by 53 percent, 41 percent, 18 percent, and 13 percent of the adult population, respectively, which places Morocco well above the Middle East and North Africa region average for financial inclusion (Zottel and others 2014). The proportion of SMEs that have contracted loans or lines of credit has doubled since 2007 (World Bank 2008, 2013a). These improvements in the accessibility of finance have been fostered by legal and regulatory reforms and improvements in the supervision structures.

For example, financial leasing and factoring have emerged as key sources of financing for businesses. A new banking law adopted in 2015 includes a legal mandate for the protection of consumers and introduces permits and supervision for new institutions: Islamic banks and nonbank providers of payment services and bank accounts.

However, the Moroccan banking system has difficulty allocating the savings collected to the most productive activities. There are many reasons for this, including objective prudential constraints related to the risk of concentration and maturity transformation and more subjective behaviors such as the reluctance and averseness of commercial banks to risk-taking. According to the Doing Business indicator on getting credit, Morocco is ranked 101st in the world and is relatively far from the frontier (see figure 3.7), particularly in comparison with other emerging market economies such as Romania, Cambodia, or Kenya. Pension funds as a source of institutional financing are reaching capacity as well: a large proportion of the civil service pension funds began to disinvest in 2014 and, despite the 2016 reform, their medium-term sustainability remains a source of concern.

Aware of these difficulties, the government has undertaken to adopt reforms to promote the diversification of financial products and mechanisms for the allocation of capital. These include improving the structure governing the financing of the capital markets, developing basic capital market infrastructure, strengthening the regulation and supervision of financial intermediaries, introducing participatory financing, or even supporting the funds dedicated to the financing of start-ups and innovative projects, particularly via the Central Guarantee Fund.

Figure 3.7   Distance to Frontier for Getting Credit, 2016

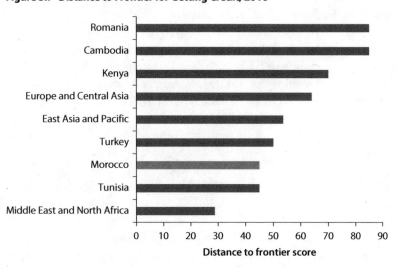

Source: World Bank 2016c.
Note: The distance to frontier score benchmarks economies with respect to regulatory practice, showing the absolute distance to the best performance in each Doing Business indicator. An economy's distance to frontier score is indicated on a scale from 0 to 100, where 0 represents the worst performance and 100 the frontier.

The government thus aims to improve the contribution of the financial system to growth over time through the diversification of the supply and greater competition.

However, these reforms have thus far had few concrete results and there is still a significant gap between the advanced development of the banking system and the development of the equity market. In June 2013, Morocco lost its status of emerging market, falling back to periphery country status, particularly owing to a lack of liquidity and capitalization and the virtual absence of new listings since the peak achieved by the market in 2008. The Casablanca Stock Exchange (CSE) suffers from a lack of new issuers, particularly large institutional issuers. Most public enterprises obtain their financing from the budget, the Caisse de dépôt et de gestion (CDG), and the banks. Family conglomerates and medium-sized enterprises, which could develop more rapidly, generally seem reluctant to share information concerning their capital and governance.

Jumpstarting the Engine of Competition and Innovation

Aware of this situation, the authorities have launched a new wave of reforms of the business climate, but these could prove disappointing in the absence of more fundamental paradigm shifts. Several reforms are steps in the right direction, such as the legal and regulatory changes concerning competition law, consumer protections, the law on public-private partnership agreements, the revision of the decree on public procurement, and a number of measures aimed at simplifying procedures for businesses (starting a business, dealing with construction permits, or paying taxes). The efforts to revise sectoral policies to promote a more inclusive approach involving the private sector and the use of more dynamic and less bureaucratic support tools are welcome. The Casablanca Finance City Authority (CFCA) project, to which a specific regulatory framework in line with international standards applies, is accompanied by wide-ranging, much-needed modernization of the banking system framework and the capital markets in general. Many public enterprises have been "corporatized," i.e., they now come under private law even though they are still owned by the government. Last, the local investment framework should be significantly altered by the establishment of local development companies (SDLs), which will make it possible to place public actions in a more flexible framework. However, these changes will not have the expected outcomes unless they are accompanied by other essential reforms that require a high-level political commitment to deal effectively with the major cross-cutting issues related to fair competition, transparency, and respect of the legal and regulatory framework. In the absence of such reforms, the above changes may prove to be counterproductive or may even jeopardize the beneficial effects of a more open and more competitive economy in the eyes of the public.

It would be in Morocco's interest to set its reforms in the framework of a strategic vision that is more strongly anchored on the principles of equity, impartiality, transparency, and a collective approach that genuinely associates all those involved in the country's economic development. Institutionally, this vision is clearly set out in the 2011 constitution. Along with the most recent phases aimed at implementing the new legal and institutional provisions of the 2011 constitution (adoption of organic laws and establishment of new authorities), Morocco must make the spirit of these constitutional changes a reality. This period of transition toward economic emergence requires an overall strategic approach that goes beyond sectoral strategies and involves the various public, semipublic, and community-based players and the various components of the private sector in a collective approach. The Economic, Social, and Environmental Council (CESE) echoed this point in its report on the consistency of the sectoral policies and the free trade agreements adopted in April 2014, in which it calls for greater consistency in the sectoral strategies through an alignment of their deadlines, territorial participation, and centralized monitoring by an interministerial monitoring committee (CESE 2014).

Implementing the Spirit of the Reforms to Strengthen Fair Competition and Combating Rent Seeking

The spirit of change toward greater competition between market players enshrined in the 2011 constitution must now be translated into actions. In the main, steps need to be taken to increase the autonomy and powers of the sectoral and nonsectoral regulatory authorities, such as the Competition Council, the Central Corruption Prevention Office (ICPC), and the regulatory authority for the financial markets, to simplify the business climate, ensure transparency in the provision of investment incentives, or reform the dispute resolution mechanisms (for example, commercial justice, arbitration, mediation). Specifically, the Competition Council provided by the 2014 law has not yet been established and the appointment of its members was still pending at the end of 2016. These appointments are crucially important in establishing the reputation of the Council on the basis of its independence and impartiality, ensuring its legitimacy and credibility in the eyes of economic players, and ensuring a "reservoir of confidence" toward the directors of the institution from the outset (El Aoufi and Hollard 2010).

The role of the various public players in the tradable and nontradable sectors needs to be reviewed to align their behavior with the principles underlying the new business framework. In the case of nontradable public services, it is important to ensure equitable access to administrative procedures, public contracts (particularly by automating and simplifying procedures), and public-private partnership contracts for all types of market players, whether they are international operators, local SMEs, or subsidiaries of large groups. The governance rules applicable to the tradable public sector should be thoroughly overhauled to prevent the participation of monopolies or quasi-monopolies (particularly public enterprises and establishments), which distort the rules of play. The privatization of public enterprises should be restarted to improve governance, competitiveness, and the quality of the services they provide and to better control costs. In the case of enterprises that will remain in the government's remit, wide-ranging reforms are also needed to strengthen their governance, redefine their strategic orientation, and structurally improve their financial position.

Discretionary practices should be eliminated to ensure a clearer, more transparent, and more equitable application of the laws and regulations to all enterprises by a competent and responsible administration. An example is the respect of payment delays between customers and suppliers and the refund of VAT credits by the government. This requires a delicate but necessary reform of government departments affecting the recruitment, training, remuneration, performance assessment, and career management of civil servants (see the section on the modernization of the government). This change also implies changes to the institutional landscape, with the emergence of new players that must be trained and professionalized. Thus, Morocco would benefit from local public authorities that have the appropriate powers and budgets, alongside competent, independent cross-cutting and sectoral regulatory agencies and from greater participation of private players who can perform a key role in respect of the principle of fair competition (for example, regulated professions, such as lawyers, notaries, accountants, arbitrators and mediators, and architects).

The public mechanisms for assessing and monitoring public policies should be enhanced. As described in chapter 2, the Moroccan authorities have limited assessment capabilities and do not yet have effective tools for assessing the impact of public policies.[11] Yet, the government must be in a position to understand the impact of its subsidies and other incentives and to make the necessary corrections when the anticipated outcomes are not achieved. Policy strategies must be flexible, proactive, and they must include an effective self-assessment capacity. Assessment bodies should be able to accurately diagnose and identify system weaknesses. The constitution adopted in 2011 also establishes (in Article 70) that Parliament is responsible for the assessment of public policies. Last, sectoral strategies should focus more on the needs of the private sector regarding the business environment. At the moment it is essentially the public sector and regional development agencies that are responsible for these strategies, which are based on the principle that the provision of infrastructure and incentives is sufficient to promote the involvement of the private sector (CESE 2014).

Improving the Business Climate and Implementing National Sectoral Strategies

Business climate reforms are politically sensitive and technically complicated. Close and efficient coordination among the various public and private players concerned is thus required. The strategic guidance and coordination of the programs and activities of the ministerial departments represent an equally complex challenge, particularly given the numerous sectoral programs and public and private participants. The success of public initiatives will therefore largely depend on the capacity of the government to coordinate, track implementation, and assess public policies at various levels: the government itself, central government departments, local governments, autonomous agencies, private sector operators, and active representatives of civil society. The establishment of an interministerial strategy monitoring committee, as recommended by CESE in its abovementioned report, represents one avenue to explore.

The public-private dialogue would benefit from involving a larger base of economic agents and including central, local, and private representatives of various sizes (large enterprises, SMEs, entrepreneurs). Public-private consultations are often seen as formalities and the recommendations of the private sector are not sufficiently taken into account in draft laws, particularly for legal or regulatory reforms. The private sector generally considers that the mechanisms for tracking and assessing reforms need to be beefed up. In this regard, the recent changes to the National Business Environment Committee (CNEA), which are aimed at strengthening its missions and resources and having it report directly to the Head of Government, are an important step toward better monitoring and evaluation of the reforms.

Using the Decentralization Under Way to Better Involve Local Participants in a Regionalized Approach to Economic Development

Government strategies and programs are still largely based on a top-down centralized sectoral strategy approach and take insufficient account of specific local characteristics and the need for social inclusion of the population. The players most active at the local level are still often decentralized representatives of central ministries and agencies, but they are still too few and constrained by financial management rules and laws, which limit their operational effectiveness and make them ill-suited to respond to the specificities of economic development. With the exception of large urban centers, the level of expertise needed to orchestrate local economic development is still weak, whether it involves encouraging entrepreneurship, providing basic business services to companies (for example, legal, accounting, management, marketing, communications), or more closely examining more complex technical issues (for example, market analysis, subsector or value chain analysis).

The regionalization under way could be used to anchor national sectoral policies in a local development approach that is more attentive to the advantages and specific needs of the regions.[12] The new regionalization model includes the principles of free administration of the new regions, cooperation, and solidarity, and makes the regions responsible for economic and social development.[13] Regional economic development and vocational training are now part of the competencies assigned to the regions. Implementation of this new institutional framework creates a number of governance challenges for the identification, financing, implementation, and guidance of development strategies and projects that must be resolved as soon as possible. This should make it possible to align all public, central, deconcentrated, and decentralized players around a sharing of clear roles and the principle of subsidiarity. It should also make it possible to better involve the private sector in a structured consultation mechanism at the regional and local levels.

Such an approach also involves reviewing the role and governance of the public establishments and enterprises that play an important role in territorial development, such as the regional development agencies, locally based public enterprises (for example, the Tanger-Med Special Agency—TMSA), and important public financing agencies (for example, CDG, Hassan II Fund), which should improve their governance and transparency to better involve local players. In general, public investment players should reform their governance and investment principles to (i) act like private investors to the extent possible by benefiting from no particular privileges and measuring their performance on the basis of transparent performance indicators; (ii) not crowd out the private sector by limiting their participation in projects that cannot be entirely financed by the private sector, in accordance with government priorities; and (iii) act like minority shareholders so as to remain subject to the requirements of the private market.

Combining the Desire for Change with a Culture Shift in Businesses

Moroccan youth definitely appear to aspire to change, but these aspirations are still held back by the slow pace of changes to social norms. A 2015 survey of high school students found that only 13.4 percent of future high school graduates wanted to enter the private sector, while 60 percent aspired to join the civil service (Ministry of National Education and HEM Business School 2015). It is vital for attitudes to change and a culture of entrepreneurship and innovation to take root in family structures if the reforms are to be sustained. Yet, the persistence of social constraints owing to the mixed and even occasionally negative views of innovation and the lack of an entrepreneurial culture is hampering the development of an innovative, vibrant, sustainable economy. A business culture based on the maintenance of an opaque patriarchal organization subsists in many businesses and constitutes an obstacle to the promotion of young generations to management functions. The same survey found that only 37 percent of high school students felt they might be interested in starting up a business, whereas over 44 percent had no opinion on the matter. The lack of turnover at the business owner level is an obstacle to the adoption of innovative concepts in companies. Businesses often are content to reproduce traditional marketing procedures and are resistant to innovation opportunities. Young entrepreneurs often face significant pressure to take over the family business or to create enterprises in the traditional sectors and are dissuaded from marketing innovative projects or launching new forms of economic activity (World Bank 2014b).

These barriers related to the difficulty in integrating younger generations are combined with a more general lack of interest in innovation and a lack of understanding of promotion mechanisms. Some 60 percent of the businesses surveyed by the Moroccan Association for Research and Development (R&D Maroc) feel that research and innovation do not provide value added. Innovation is not part of the regular activities of small businesses and most business owners believe that knowledge and know-how are not determining factors in the creation of new markets. This is explained in part by the lack of communication by public agencies on available financial incentives and benefits (United Nations 2008). Last, three-quarters of young Moroccan entrepreneurs believe that their products and services are not considered innovative by consumers and emphasize a lack of entrepreneurial culture in Morocco (World Bank 2014b). This suggests that the institutional players involved in the design and implementation of public policies on innovation should redouble their efforts to improve their credibility and effectiveness.

Given the current context, which is insufficiently receptive to innovation and the spirit of conquest, the efforts undertaken by Morocco must focus both on the psychological aspects to disseminate a culture of innovation and on the scaling up of existing initiatives to face the challenge of economic catch-up. Improving the operation and credibility of institutional players involved in the implementation of public policies is an essential factor in efficiency, particularly in the innovation sector. By ensuring the sustainability and effectiveness of its institutions, Morocco will facilitate its transition to an innovative economy, more easily position itself in global value chains, and successfully prepare to compete in the international markets (OCP Policy Center 2015). Public policies must also be scaled up in the areas of research, development, and the protection of intellectual and industrial property as the financial resources made available to players still remain limited in comparison with the challenge. Last, beyond awareness campaigns, Morocco Awards, and other support for innovative projects, Morocco could more highly value the production of intangible capital by investing in training for young people and entrepreneurs that responds more effectively to the needs of the private sector (see chapter 5).

Allocating Labor More Efficiently and Inclusively

The labor market is governed by institutions that define the interactions among employers, employees, the government, and their representative organizations such as unions, employer associations, and the national employment promotion agency. Schematically, the labor market institutions reflect the laws, policies, conventions, and practices that codify these interactions. They establish the limits on wages and benefits and working hours and conditions (via the Labor Code) and define the rules for representation and collective bargaining (collective agreements). They proscribe or prescribe particular employment policies and programs to promote a better alignment of available jobs and job seekers (for example, active labor and employment services policies). They provide social protection for employees during and between their periods of employment (unemployment insurance, continuing education). Four economic factors explain the raison d'être of these institutions: imperfect information, generally asymmetrical bargaining power between employers and employees, the risk of discrimination, and the incapacity of the market to provide an assurance that employment risks will be covered (World Bank 2014b). This section briefly analyzes the role and impact of the labor market as an economic institution before reviewing the labor market situation in Morocco. It then presents the pillars of a thorough reform of the labor market that would take better advantage of the potential of each individual and fuel the engine of Moroccan growth.

The Labor Market as an Economic Institution

The role and impact of labor market institutions, particularly the Labor Code and legislation on job protection, are often controversial.[14] The debate has intensified with globalization and technological change, which have exposed developed and developing countries to increased competition and uncertainty regarding the most appropriate institutional framework for labor market regulation (Hayter 2011). Some suggest that rigid employment protection legislation introduces distortions that lead to a two-speed labor market with workers who have protected jobs on the one hand and, on the other, excluded individuals, whether they be unemployed or employed under fixed-term, part-time, or temporary contracts. Stricter job protection legislation would have the effect of increasing long-term unemployment, making dismissals costlier, and ultimately encouraging informal recruitment (Botero and others 2004; Lafontaine and Sivadasan 2008). On the other hand, "institutionalists" argue that legislation that is insufficiently protective of employment will weaken the long-term relationship between employers and employees with damaging consequences such as underinvestment in training. Moreover, ineffective insurance mechanisms can leave workers unprotected in case of dismissal, pushing them to cut short their job-seeking efforts and accept a job that does not necessarily correspond to their qualifications. Inequality of bargaining power can give enterprises the ability to set wages lower than wages freely agreed to in more competitive conditions. The imperfections of the market and institutional weaknesses can thus affect job creation and lead to gaps between the remuneration of workers and their true social value.

International studies generally conclude that labor market employment and unemployment rules are relatively benign if they are neither too rigid nor too flexible. Over the past 10 years, access to better data and improved analysis methods have shed new light on the effects of labor market institutions on employment, not only in the industrial countries but also increasingly in the developing countries (World Bank 2014b). A recent analysis of the findings of some 150 studies on the impact of four types of labor market regulation (minimum wages, employment protection regulations, collective bargaining, and mandated benefits) suggests that in most cases the impacts of these laws and regulations is smaller than the debates would suggest (Betcherman 2012). This analysis also shows that when legislation and regulation of the labor market have a harmful effect on employment or productivity, it is generally owing to their "excesses" (in the sense of too much or too little protection). Between these extremes there is a sort of "plateau," in which the positive and negative impacts of various regulations tend to cancel each other out and where labor market institutions essentially have a redistributional impact. In most countries, labor market institutions and policies are not likely to be either a major obstacle or a solution to job growth (World Bank 2014b).

Suboptimal Allocation of Labor in Morocco
Exclusion and Unequal Opportunities
In Morocco, more than half of the working-age population (15–64 years of age) does not participate in the economic activity of the country, which makes it one of the countries with the lowest employment rates in the Middle East and North Africa, and across the globe. Low and steadily declining employment rates

Figure 3.8 Morocco: Unemployment Rate and Participation Rate, 1999–2015
(percent)

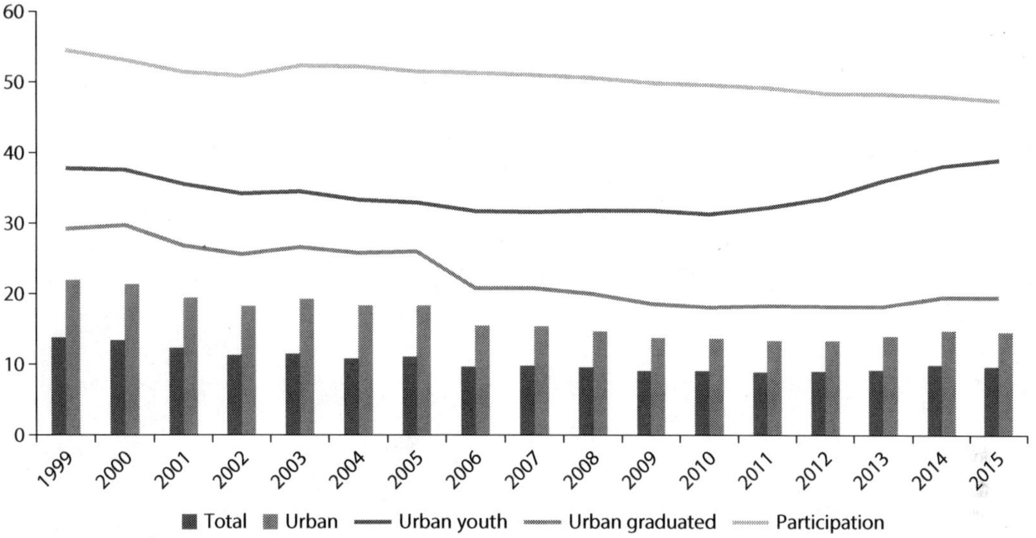

Source: High Commission for Planning.

undermine economic growth because they limit the capacity of individuals to generate economic outputs. The unemployment rate among the urban young has been increasing sharply since 2010 (see figure 3.8). As we will see in detail, the low unemployment rates in Morocco are explained by low labor market participation rates for women. Even though Morocco is perceived as a relatively liberal country in the region, it is in the last quintile of countries in the world in terms of the low labor force participation of women. For 2016, estimates indicate that there are some 2.7 million inactive youth aged 15–29 in Morocco (the vast majority of whom are young women), or almost one in three young people who is not in education, employment, or training (NEETs), either for family reasons or because they are discouraged.[15]

Beyond weak employment and participation rates, Morocco has some 1 million unemployed, most of them between the ages of 15 and 34. The level of unemployment remains high in Morocco, with a rate that fluctuates between 9 percent and 10 percent of the labor force. More specifically, the 2014 labor market survey data indicate that most unemployed are men (71 percent), between the ages of 15 and 34 (77 percent), residing in urban areas (80 percent), and with at most a high school education (79 percent). Unemployment is also long term, particularly in urban areas, where 66 percent of those who are unemployed have been unemployed for more than 12 months. It is generally considered that the high level of unemployment among young people has been one of the main driving forces behind the "Arab revolutions" since 2011 and that this massive youth unemployment continues to represent a serious threat to social stability in most countries in the region (World Bank 2013b). Young people between the ages of 15 and 29 represent approximately 30 percent of the total population of Morocco and 44 percent of the working-age population, but they have benefited little from the economic upturn in recent years.

Moreover, youth employment is mainly precarious. Most of those who have a job are in the informal sector and the quality of jobs is limited, particularly in rural areas and for women and less educated workers (see figure 3.9). Some 1.7 million young people work under precarious conditions as employees in the informal sector or are self-employed (some 88 percent of young workers do not have a contract). Most job offers do not provide social protections against risks related to employment, age, and occupational health. In 2014, according to the High Commission for Planning (HCP), some 80 percent of Moroccan workers did not contribute to social security (94 percent in rural areas and 65 percent in urban areas). Rural workers, women, and young people are disproportionately recruited for low-quality, informal, and poorly paid jobs.

The perception that access to "good" jobs is insufficiently based on merit results in a serious sense of exclusion on the part of those who are traditionally excluded, particularly young people. The labor market seems to offer several

Figure 3.9 Morocco: Composition of the Working-Age Population, 2013

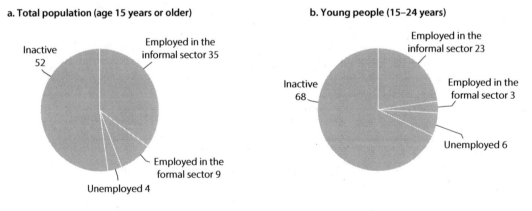

a. Total population (age 15 years or older)

Inactive 52
Employed in the informal sector 35
Employed in the formal sector 9
Unemployed 4

b. Young people (15–24 years)

Employed in the informal sector 23
Inactive 68
Employed in the formal sector 3
Unemployed 6

c. Women (age 15 years or older)

Employed in the informal sector 19
Inactive 75
Employed in the formal sector 4
Unemployed 2

Source: High Commission for Planning.

paths toward what can be called "good" jobs: protected employment (particularly in the public sector), well-paid jobs in the private sector, or well-paid self-employment.[16] When the labor market operates satisfactorily, access to good jobs results from the work effort (efforts to invest in the development of one's own human capital and job seeking) and productivity (available jobs are suited to the qualifications of candidates and their production is higher than the wage they receive). However, in Morocco some 60 percent of good jobs are held by men with higher education who are aged 35 and above and live in urban areas (World Bank 2013b). Although they represent approximately two-thirds of the working-age population, qualified young people and poorly qualified women living in urban areas hold fewer than one-third of these attractive jobs. This dispropor-tionate access to good jobs for individuals who are "integrated in the system" seems to reflect a patriarchal society in which adult men who are heads of households are those who benefit most from labor market opportunities. Moreover, inequality of access to good jobs is high in Morocco, even in compari-son with other countries in the region. Personal and family relationships remain important for those who are currently in the labor force: 28 percent of young people between the ages of 15 and 29 who are unemployed believe that this is because of favoritism in recruitment (HEM 2016). According to the 2012–14 Arab Barometer, more than 60 percent of Moroccans questioned believe that access to jobs is above all a matter of connections.

Social mobility and the ability to move from a less productive job to a more productive job are limited and take time, particularly for young people and women. Mobility across economic sectors and between the public and private sectors is very sclerotic and indicates that industrial policies and public sector reforms are lagging and need to be rethought (Verme and others 2014). The limited ability of workers to move toward high-productivity sectors and exit low-productivity sectors is also a symptom of an inefficient labor market (to the extent that human capital cannot be allocated to sectors where it could lead to higher returns). In this context, a desirable social and economic change would be for workers to be able to leave low value-added sectors and jobs more easily (particularly informal agriculture) to move toward higher value-added sectors and higher-paying jobs (particularly salaried employment in the formal sector). However, the Moroccan economy creates few new jobs. Between 2012 and 2016, just 26,400 net new jobs were created on average each year for the working-age population (15–65 years) while that population showed a net increase of 270,000 per year on average. In comparison with its population, Morocco creates half as many jobs as Egypt and a third as many as Malaysia (see figure 3.10). A matrix analysis of transitions on the labor market reveals a num-ber of trends: formal employment is a fairly stable form of employment (there is an integration effect); self-employment is on average the second most stable category of employment for a typical male worker but not for women; informal employment is often a springboard toward better jobs, but this is less the case for young people; even though unemployment tends to be long term, the typical unemployed person generally moves toward informal or self-employment.

Figure 3.10 Net Creation of Jobs, 2010–14 Average
(percentage of the working-age population)

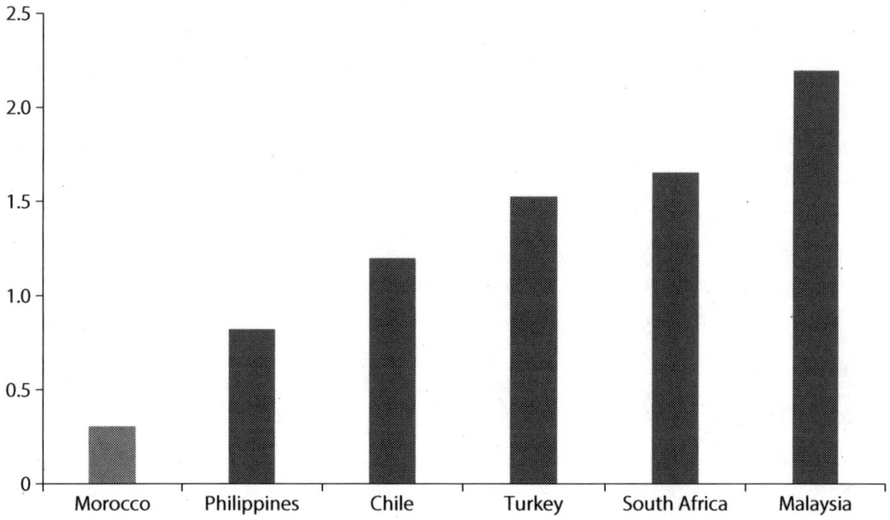

Source: ILOSTAT.

The figures also show important flows from unemployment to inactivity (sign of giving up or discouragement), particularly among young people and women.

Excessive Regulation

Morocco has adopted labor legislation that is based on the conventions and recommendations of the International Labour Organization. The 2003 Labor Code introduced significant improvements from the previous legislation: (i) it raised the minimum age for access to employment (from 12 to 15 years); (ii) it reduced the average work week from 48 hours to 44 hours; (iii) it called for a regular review of minimum wages; (iv) it improved occupational health and safety standards; (v) it promoted workplace equity (by guaranteeing equality between men and women and encouraging the employment of the disabled); and (vi) it guaranteed the right of association and collective bargaining and prohibited employers from engaging in actions against their salaried employees on the grounds of their union membership. Still, according to the HCP, the Moroccan Labor Code governs labor relations for only a minority of salaried employees on the labor market.

The negotiation, adoption, and implementation of this legislation on the basis of international conventions have, however, resulted in cumbersome and restrictive labor market regulations. According to the World Bank Doing Business indicator (2013), the Moroccan labor market is more regulated than the various regional averages around the world (see figure 3.11). Moroccan law prohibits fixed-term contracts for permanent tasks and limits their duration to 12 months, after which they cannot be renewed. Although the Moroccan law allows a certain amount of flexibility in terms of the hours worked, overtime and

Figure 3.11 Hiring and Firing Difficulties

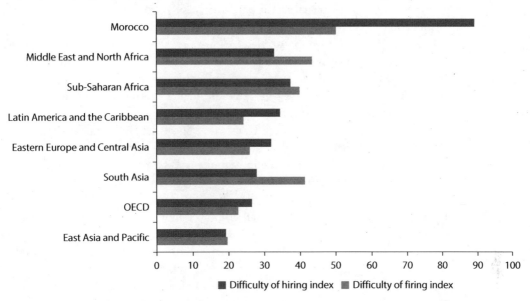

Source: World Bank 2012.

premiums for night work are expensive compared to international practices. Moroccan legislation on leave (annual leave, statutory leave, maternity/paternity leave) is more generous than that in other emerging market countries that are Morocco's competitors.

The labor regulations governing private sector terminations are restrictive in Morocco. Terminating individuals for economic reasons is prohibited. Only businesses with more than 10 employees may terminate jobs for economic, technical, or structural reasons. Reducing staff for economic reasons is subject to a prior agreement with the regional authorities. The Labor Code prohibits terminations for poor behavior (as explicitly defined in the Labor Code) or poor performance if the employer has not followed all of the legal disciplinary steps. Employers are required to help their employees adapt to any change in their position or responsibilities. The burden of proof is on the employer and the legislation is well applied, owing to the active role played by the government and unions. As a result, the number of employees terminated by medium-sized businesses is very low and almost a quarter of the businesses contacted for the Investment Climate Assessment (ICA) survey in 2008 indicated that they would have reduced their staff if redundancy conditions were less restrictive.

The minimum wage in Morocco is high compared with the average national income or the average productivity of workers. In 2015, the minimum wage in urban areas was equal to approximately 100 percent of the national per capita income or more than 50 percent of the average wage in the formal private sector, rates that were extremely high not just in the region but also in comparison with international standards, including the Organisation for Economic Co-operation and Development (OECD) countries. Such high legal minimum wages deter the creation of jobs in the formal sector, particularly for young job seekers with limited qualifications. In contrast, a lack of minimum wage laws has not prevented countries as diverse as Sweden, Switzerland, Singapore, and Denmark, to name just a few, from not only paying their employees well but also ensuring full employment and high participation rates. In Morocco, collective agreements and length-of-service bonuses can lead to wage levels that are higher than employee productivity, with the minimum wage reaching almost 80 percent of average value added per worker, or 50 percent more than in Tunisia (see figure 3.12). Overall, the high cost of labor in the formal sector contributes to a lower demand for employees on the part of employers and explains the low labor market participation rate and structural un- or underemployment.

Only a minority of Moroccan workers benefits from a social protection system. The social security system excludes self-employed individuals, farmers, and seasonal workers in the agricultural sector. Moreover, poor management and administration threaten the capacity of the system, particularly the pension system, to provide benefits on a long-term basis, even for workers who are entitled to them. All of Morocco's pension systems are financially unsustainable over the long term—some even over the short term—given the rapid increase in beneficiaries, the small number of active contributors, and the generosity of the plans. The reform of civil service pensions in 2016 should enable the Moroccan pension fund to restore financial stability for a few years. At the same time, the protection system jeopardizes the capacity of the economy to create high-quality jobs to the extent that it places a

Figure 3.12 Minimum Wage in International Comparison, 2015
(in proportion to value added per worker)

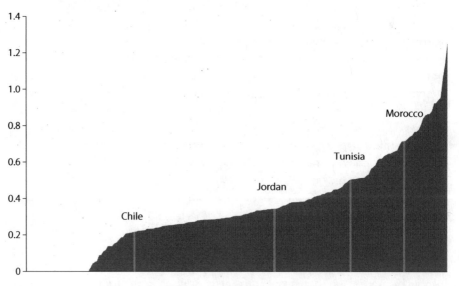

Source: World Bank 2016c (excluding Haiti, Honduras, Kenya, Mozambique, West Bank and Gaza, and Zimbabwe).
Note: The blue area represents 194 countries ranked in increasing order by their level of minimum wage to value addition per worker.

heavy tax burden on labor, reduces hiring incentives in the formal sector, and is an obstacle to worker mobility. In fact, the tax burden on labor—that is, the difference between the total cost of labor, net wages, and the value of social benefits—is an important topic in the debate on the outlook for formal jobs for young people.

Active labor market policies (ALMP) implemented by the government are struggling to produce the expected results. The agencies responsible for dealing with barriers to employment for young people with higher education and professionals, particularly the Labor Promotion and Vocational Training Office (OFPPT) and the National Agency for the Promotion of Employment and Skills (ANAPEC), have had poor results in terms of targeting and coverage and a limited response to the needs of the unemployed (World Bank 2014b). ANAPEC is currently exploring the possibility of expanding its activities to job seekers without degrees and increasing its capacity to propose intermediation services between employers and job seekers. Morocco has also developed a labor-intensive public works program as part of the National Promotion program. This public works program, which is managed by the Ministry of the Interior, aims to provide temporary jobs to un- or underemployed individuals, particularly in rural areas. Like many labor-intensive works program, National Promotion can unquestionably constitute an effective economic response. However, it does not use best practices for targeting or for the identification of labor-intensive activities, which prevents it from having a real impact, particularly in case of crises (natural disasters, drought, etc.). The government has also launched several initiatives to promote self-employment, but with limited success.

Greater labor market flexibility would make it possible to increase employment, particularly formal employment of young people and women, and to reduce unemployment while protecting wages. A modeling exercise on the effects produced by just two legislative labor market provisions—the minimum wage and payroll taxes—partially illustrates the direct impact that a liberalization of the labor market could have on employment, with the caveat that many other qualitative regulations hampering more efficient allocation of labor (particularly redundancy regulations and benefits) have not been taken into consideration in this exercise (Angel-Urdinola, Barry, and Guennouni 2016). Moreover, partial equilibrium models of this type ignore the effect on employment of higher economic growth related to a more efficient and fluid allocation of the factors of production in the economy. Nonetheless, the exercise modeling the elimination of minimum wages and payroll taxes can reveal the scope of the anticipated effects on total unemployment, youth unemployment, and female unemployment for three groups of workers (formal, informal, and self-employed) and their respective wages (see table 3.1). A labor market that is liberalized in these two areas would reduce the unemployment rate by only 2.7 percentage points and would increase the formal employment rate by 5.7 percentage points. The impact on wages would be positive for self-employed workers and those in the informal sector, but wages would decline by 4 percent for workers in the formal sector. The effects of such a deregulation would be much greater for young people and women. According to the simulations, female unemployment would

Table 3.1 Morocco: Impact of the Elimination of Minimum Wages and Payroll Taxes

	Impact on the labor force (percentage points)				Impact on wages (percentage)		
	Unemployment	Informal sector	Formal sector	Self-employed workers	Informal sector	Formal sector	Self-employed workers
Total	−2.7	−1.0	5.7	−2.1	2.0	−4.0	1.6
Women	−11.5	−2.1	14.9	−1.2	4.1	−13.1	−1.0
Young people (15–29 years)	−6.2	−1.0	8.9	−1.7	1.8	−12.1	2.3

Source: Angel-Urdinola, Barry, and Guennouni 2016.

decline 11.5 percentage points and youth unemployment, 6.2 percentage points. The participation of women and young people in the formal sector would increase considerably. In contrast, without minimum wages, the wages of young people and women in the formal sector would decline 12–13 percent. Overall, this scenario illustrates the positive potential of a liberalization of the labor market in terms of the integration of women and young people.

Developing Labor Market Institutions for the 21st Century
Morocco needs to completely reform the labor market to promote employment, particularly employment of young people and women. Although over the years it has tried to make employment the focus of public actions by developing a large number of programs to help young people into the job market[17] and promote local jobs in the context of the national employment strategy (cooperatives, small infrastructure, etc.), these measures seem to have been merely a transitional phase pending the implementation of deeper, more structural reforms. As discussed in chapter 2, given the demographic structure of Morocco's population, one of the main challenges in the coming years will be for labor markets in urban areas to absorb a sustained flow of young workers with rising education levels. The erosion of the number of agricultural jobs means that the economy will have to create productive jobs in industry and services. Moreover, Morocco has an already large public sector, representing approximately 47 percent of total formal employment, which cannot expand significantly in the coming years. Last, Morocco also faces the challenge of expanding the coverage of its social protection system to a population that is largely unprotected against the risks of unemployment and old age without penalizing the growth of the formal sector. In such a context, Morocco would benefit from adapting its labor market institutions to facilitate the convergence and structural transformation of its economy in the next 25 years.

The reforms should allow the new labor market institutions, particularly the Labor Code, to facilitate intermediation between the labor supply and demand and to significantly increase the employment rate. In the convergence scenario presented in chapter 2, the objective is to increase the employment rate from the current 45 percent to 55 percent by 2040. While the reform of the labor institutions must be combined with other reforms aimed at improving the business environment and encouraging investment, the lowering of wage costs and reform of the social protection system (particularly pension systems and unemployment insurance) could already help increase the demand for formal employment, particularly for young people and women. As soon as better unemployment insurance systems are in place, it will also be necessary to review the rules on redundancies and to reduce the current dichotomies between open-ended contracts and fixed-term contracts. Moreover, it is also important to introduce policies that actively promote the participation of women in the labor market and to consider a training system and active labor market measures that will make it more integrated and results oriented.

Easing Labor Market Regulation

By aligning its labor market legislation with international standards and practices, particularly those of competitor emerging market economies, Morocco would facilitate greater mobility of employees and encourage a more rapid structural transformation of its economy. This would involve changes to the Labor Code to introduce greater flexibility in redundancy procedures while protecting the interests of workers. Such a reform should enable employers to lay off employees for economic reasons without government authorization. It could also align bonuses for overtime, night work, and paid leave (particularly annual leave) with international standards. The regulations on redundancies should in principle be aimed at providing a sufficient advance notice and severance payments based on seniority. Such a reform should be accompanied by the establishment of an appropriate unemployment insurance system. Workers should be allowed to submit complaints in case of abusive dismissals, particularly in cases involving discrimination. Effective mechanisms should be introduced to handle these complaints rapidly and to ensure that sanctions are imposed against employers or employees found to be at fault. Moreover, the exercise of the right to strike should be better regulated in the new draft framework law currently under discussion.

As regards the various labor contracts in effect, the reform should aim to ease the constraints on the use of fixed-term contracts. Such a reform could extend the renewal periods for fixed-term contracts and ensure that such contracts offer the same types of employee benefits and protections as open-ended contracts in terms of guarantees and access to social protection programs (including access to unemployment insurance). The only difference would be that in the case of open-ended contracts, employers would have to provide sufficient advance notice in case of redundancies, while in the case of fixed-term contracts the cancellation of the contract would be automatic. The need for greater flexibility in contracting is not unique to Morocco. The same causes produce the same effects and many countries in Southern Europe with labor market institutions that are similar to those of Morocco also have troubling unemployment levels, particularly for young people. The reforms should therefore look to the countries of Northern Europe and the English-speaking countries, which have succeeded in eliminating or containing this problem.

Improving Security for Workers

Morocco could consider introducing various minimum wage schemes to attract low-productivity workers to the formal sector. The Moroccan Labor Code should offer the flexibility to contractually define different minimum wage levels for workers, depending, for example, on the sector, region, age group, and so on. Providing the possibility of aligning wage levels to productivity would make it possible to significantly increase the demand for formal employment, particularly for young people with little education in disadvantaged regions or sectors in difficulty. Moreover, the reevaluation of minimum wages should not be arbitrary and discretionary, but based on objective criteria on the changes in economic productivity and estimation of the value added of the employees concerned.

Morocco should better align social contributions paid with the benefits received and be able to clearly and explicitly finance all subsidies from general government revenues. Today, for example, workers under fixed-term contracts (whose contributions to the pension system are not fully transferable) subsidize those who are under open-ended contracts. One of the options for reducing payroll taxes and thus reducing the cost of labor and creating more formal jobs (while taking account of financial sustainability issues) would involve more directly linking individual social security contributions to the benefits received and explicitly recognizing all subsidies granted (for example, family allowances, training assistance) in the government budget. In the case of social contributions for pensions (which are currently based on a risk pooling system), the first phase would involve defining a target for the replacement rate at the statutory age of retirement to determine the required contribution rate, which would make it possible to end the current implicit subsidies.

Moreover, by separating the financing of training and family allowances from social contributions, it would be possible to create fiscal room to finance a universal unemployment insurance system. The social protection system could concentrate on covering essential risks only: illness, disability, death, old age, and unemployment. All implicit subsidies should then be financed from general taxation. For equity reasons, some people might be opposed to a shift toward financing out of general taxation on the grounds that this could lead to a regressive redistribution of revenue. This is explained by the fact that social security systems currently benefit mainly workers in the formal sector, who are, on average, in a better position than self-employed workers and employees in the informal sector. This problem could be resolved, however, if the coverage provided by social protection programs were expanded to all workers and if, for example, the minimum old age pension also applied to self-employed workers and salaried workers in the agricultural sector.

Morocco should also reform its severance payment arrangements and its system of unemployment benefits to improve the protection of workers and facilitate labor mobility. The current unemployment assistance and severance payments could be replaced by a universal unemployment insurance system offering a satisfactory replacement income rate and broader coverage and reducing distortions between the various labor markets. As in the case of pensions, the first decision would involve the level of the benefits: a replacement rate could range between 50 percent and 70 percent for 3–12 months. The contribution rate would be set accordingly, taking into account the unemployment rate in the beneficiary population. The second decision would involve the means of subsidizing benefits for workers whose contribution capacity is insufficient. As with any insurance plan, the unemployment insurance system implicitly involves a subsidy by the members of the system who are less exposed to the risk of unemployment toward those who are more exposed (Robalino and Weber 2013).

Improving the Effectiveness of ALMP

One of the basic active labor market policy reforms would be first to outsource employment and training services under performance-based contracts. As discussed above, the existing ALMP and training regimes in Morocco are primarily guided by the public sector. This model tends to limit coordination with the private sector, which often results in employment assistance and training programs that do not respond to the needs of businesses. Public structures, particularly ANAPEC and OFPPT, should develop and expand their services through public-private partnerships involving private sector employers (for example, to develop training and apprenticeship programs) and associations, to better target the populations concerned and provide specific employment assistance services (particularly focusing on the labor market, coaching, information on existing programs, and general skills). Training providers would be remunerated on the basis of various outcomes, specifically on the basis of their performance in the placement of job seekers under fixed-term or open-ended contracts.

Second, ALMP could be developed to include the unskilled population, depending on demand and private sector needs. By 2040, significant demand for new jobs for medium-skilled technicians and those without secondary school diplomas should be expected, particularly in key high-growth sectors such as tourism, logistics, the automobile industry, trade, ICTs, business services, and construction. Moreover, recent studies (including the assessment of the Education for Employment (E4E) initiative by the International Finance Corporation [IFC] in 2014) indicate that labor demand and the growth of employment in Morocco could be higher if employers were able to fill positions that are currently vacant owing to a lack of candidates with the required qualifications. Future employment assistance programs should also integrate the needs of medium-skilled young people who are seeking jobs.

Third, ALMP should promote the integration of programs through the establishment of one-stop shops at the local level. There are many employment assistance and training programs but their coordination is limited and random at the local level. Moreover, existing programs do not follow a systematic approach in terms of registering, contacting, or providing information to potential beneficiaries. To fill these gaps, the government should study the possibility of setting up local one-stop shops, where beneficiaries, particularly young people, could register, obtain information, and receive guidance on the available range of services (public and private). Specifically, several networks of structures at the local level are currently underutilized (including approximately 1,500 centers dedicated to young people and women that fall under the Ministry of Youth and Sports). They could serve as points of entry for job seekers, particularly young people and women. These centers could be managed by local associations, which would be responsible for registering beneficiaries and providing them with a series of basic services (profiling, consulting, basic skills training, and referral to other employment assistance and training services).

Fourth, it is important to develop a performance-based monitoring and evaluation framework to improve the governance, effectiveness, and efficiency of ANAPEC's labor market policies. ANAPEC should establish a clear governance structure, quality assurance mechanisms, and a monitoring and evaluation strategy based on performance and not just on outputs to increase the effectiveness and efficiency of its programs and improve the use of public resources. The recently created National Employment Observatory could play a role in such evaluations. Rigorous impact studies are essential to demonstrate what is working, to develop capacities at the regional level, and more broadly to improve the definition of policies. Moreover, it is essential that impact studies be conducted for new experimental programs before they are taken to the national level, to make the necessary adjustments in program design and thus avoid developing inefficient and ineffective programs.

Integrating Morocco More Closely with the International Economy

Like the market institutions that promote an efficient allocation of capital and labor, the institutions that govern a country's foreign trade are intangible assets that can be used to increase productivity. The benefits of specialization and division of labor at the international level include greater economic efficiency, more rapid structural transformation, and rising incomes. At the societal level, free trade is not just a means of stimulating economic growth, creating jobs, and reducing poverty; it is also a way of promoting individual liberties, bringing people together in a peaceful dialogue that is beneficial to all, and advancing peace and stability. This section first analyzes the link between economic integration and productivity and then assesses the situation in Morocco in terms of openness and integration and proposes ways to accelerate the integration process and promote the country's assets in world trade.

The Link between Economic Integration and Productivity

Globalization offers all countries, but particularly emerging market economies, many opportunities to use the international markets to promote their own economic efficiency. It allows countries to benefit from know-how and technologies that have been developed throughout the world to improve production processes, whether this involves the use of machines, intermediate goods, services, foreign direct investment (FDI), or individuals. Economic integration has proven to be a particularly effective strategy in support of the kind of rapid economic catch-up that Morocco is attempting. High-performing countries, that is, the dozen or so countries that have had annual growth of 7 percent or more for at least 25 years since 1950, have all used globalization to increase their productivity through trade, FDI, and economic integration (Commission on Growth and Development 2008). All have used this approach and have endeavored to secure the maximum benefit from the global economy, not to expand the frontiers of technology, but to adopt existing technology and know-how, which is a much more manageable task. These high-growth countries have benefited from economic integration in two ways: they have imported ideas, technology, and know-how from the rest of the world, and they have exploited global demand, which has provided a deep, elastic market for their goods and services. As the Commission on Growth and Development (2008) puts it very simply, "they imported what the rest of the world knew, and exported what it wanted."

Apart from trade in goods and services, the liberalization of the capital account is another important step in eliminating the distortions that are an obstacle to a more efficient integration into global markets. When the preconditions are there, the convertibility of national currencies improves the distribution of (domestic and foreign) capital and constitutes a source of efficiency and productivity. It facilitates the development of the marketable sector, access to foreign savings, including FDI and portfolio investments, and the development of the financial system. It promotes greater discipline in the management of macroeconomic policies and is a powerful sign of confidence for economic partners and foreign investors.

The link among trade, investment, and services lies at the heart of world trade today and the structure of global production has been changed as a result (Baldwin 2011). The emergence of production networks, global value chains, and trade in "tasks" (and not just finished or intermediate goods or services) characterizes this new environment and changes the qualifications and skills needed to access employment. Trade in services, particularly services to businesses, has become a dynamic component of trade while at the same time being a source of diversification of exports for many developing countries. Participating in global value chains requires significant skills on the part of economic agents, particularly a good logistic capacity and trade financing (Chauffour and Malouche 2011).

The impact of global value chains on domestic economies constitutes an important channel of transmission for increasing national productivity. Many emerging countries have benefited from globalization. For example, Turkey was able to accelerate its economic growth until recently and create more than three million new jobs since it opened up to the global markets and entered the process of regulatory convergence with the European Union in the mid-2000s. A recent analysis of global value chains in Turkey shows that supplying companies that are wholly owned by foreigners significantly increases the productivity of local Turkish companies (Taglioni and Santoni 2015). Nevertheless, the impact is even greater if the productivity gap between domestic and foreign investors is relatively small. This suggests that this gap can be reduced by policies promoting domestic competition and aiming to increase the average productivity of local businesses. In this context, trade policies that discriminate against foreign producers are even more doomed to failure than in the past.

One consequence of the emergence of global value chains is that the trade and investment policy agenda is increasingly moving beyond the scope of trade ministries to include many domestic policies and legislation. When a process of economic openness is not accompanied by reforms promoting competition and transparency on the domestic market, often its only effect is to displace rent seeking rather than to reduce it. The "new" international trade agenda targets the harmonization of policies and a process of convergence between the main trading partners (Chauffour and Maur 2011). For many emerging countries, the agenda has therefore evolved toward the implementation of comprehensive national reforms aimed at promoting competitiveness, raising production standards, liberalizing services, modernizing regulatory systems, promoting labor mobility, protecting intellectual property, improving governance, encouraging transparency and the rule of law, and, over time, developing common values and standards. In these countries, economic integration has been at the heart of a credible development strategy aimed at accelerating economic growth driven by productivity.

Integration Policies and Results in Morocco
International Trade

The opening of the Moroccan economy to international trade over the past decade has been opportune. Tariff and nontariff barriers have been lowered and international trade procedures have been simplified. Modern trade infrastructure has been developed for all types of transport (such as the Tanger-Med port) and the country has been fully updating its customs regulations and its transportation and trade logistics. Morocco has also developed its economic and trade relations by concluding preferential trade agreements with the European Union, the United States, and Turkey. Following this external liberalization, the trade openness rate increased from 53 percent of GDP in 1990 to 73 percent in 2015, thus catching up with levels observed in the emerging countries or economies similar in size. The liberalization of trade is estimated to have had the general effect of increasing the well-being of households by reducing consumer prices for agricultural goods and manufactured products and increasing wages (Cherkaoui, Khellaf, and Nihou 2011).

At the same time, Morocco has adjusted its trade legislation, including three main regulations: (i) economic regulations that directly concern market decisions such as price setting, competition, and entry into or exit from the market; (ii) social regulations that are of public interest such as health, safety, the environment, and social cohesion; and (iii) administrative regulations such as paper forms and administrative formalities by which governments collect information and intervene in individual economic decisions. Morocco also adopted laws defending commerce and international trade that are aligned with the policies of the World Trade Organization, to provide Morocco with trade protection mechanisms (antidumping, protection clauses, and trade remedies) and mechanisms protecting national production, particularly new industries, using measures applied at the frontier in the form of tariffs, quantitative restrictions, and tariff quotas, as well as government assistance measures.

Figure 3.13 Morocco's Share in World Trade, 1980–2013
(index 100 in 1980)

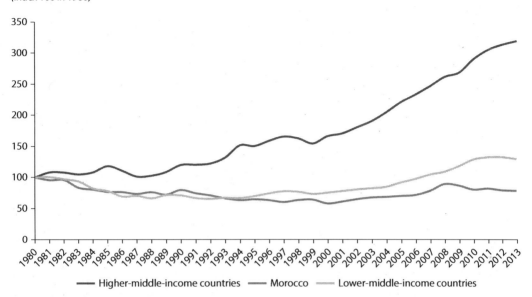

Source: World Development Indicators, World Bank.

Despite these efforts, Morocco's share in international trade has tended to decline since the early 1980s, while most of its competitors have seen their shares increase (see figure 3.13). Morocco is finding it difficult to increase the level of sophistication and leverage the value of its exported products. Close to 70 percent of Moroccan consumers find "made in Morocco" products to be of average quality compared to the foreign competition (CGEM 2014). Morocco has lagged in comparison with many similar countries in terms of the share of its intermediate high-tech exports. The emergence of "new" industries (automobile, aeronautics, and electronics) is certainly encouraging to the extent that these sectors occupy a more central position in the global production space and are thus a potential source of higher revenues than traditional exports. However, Morocco's commitment in these emerging sectors is rather limited and the international competition is stiff. Morocco's trade performance is slowed by high production factor costs owing to protected service sectors and rigid domestic prices, and by a fixed exchange rate system and a skills and qualifications mismatch. A recent analysis of the price competitiveness of the Moroccan exportable supply suggests that on the whole Morocco is less competitive on prices than the most successful comparable countries: the export price differential between Moroccan products and the most competitive rival products can range from 10 percent to almost 100 percent depending on the products and sectors in question (CGEM 2014). To date, Morocco has been able to penetrate only a small portion of potential markets.

One of the explanations for Morocco's difficulties in benefiting more from the development of international trade lies in the delays and costs related to merchandise export and import logistics. According to the Doing Business indicator that measures distance to the frontier in terms of the accumulation of delays and costs (excluding customs duties) associated with three categories of procedures (documentary compliance, border compliance, and domestic transport), Morocco scores better than other countries in the Middle East and North Africa, but not as well as its main competitors, particularly Central and Eastern Europe (see figure 3.14). Morocco was ranked 86th out of a total of 160 countries in 2016 on the Logistic Performance Index, falling 24 places from its average ranking during the period 2007–14 (World Bank 2016b). Morocco ranks well for the quality of its infrastructure but loses in this classification owing to weaknesses and dysfunctions in foreign trade services. In fact, Morocco is ranked 124th in the provision of customs services (it was ranked 73rd from 2007 to 2014) and is ranked 122nd in terms of the ability to track and trace consignments.[18]

The lack of diversification of exports toward more sophisticated products can be partially explained by exporters' risk aversion, given the current state of market incentives. Moroccan export enterprises are often old and small. A recent study using databases on customs transactions at the firm level reveals that Moroccan firms have adopted a relatively conservative export growth strategy (Jaud and Dovis 2014). Moroccan exporters have successfully established stable trade relations and the development of these relations has taken precedence over experimenting with new markets and new products. On average, during the period 1998–2014, the growth of exports was essentially led by the intensive

Figure 3.14 Distance to Frontier for Trading across Borders, 2016

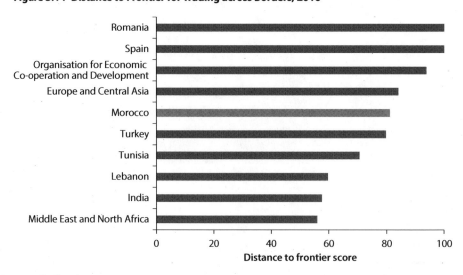

Source: World Bank 2016c.
Note: The distance to frontier score benchmarks economies with respect to regulatory practice, showing the absolute distance to the best performance in each Doing Business indicator. An economy's distance to frontier score is indicated on a scale from 0 to 100, where 0 represents the worst performance and 100 the frontier.

margin, that is, the intensification of sales of existing export products on existing export markets (Ministry of Economy and Finance 2016). The renewal of the export base in terms of the entry and exit of firms is also limited and the export survival rate is low. A network of ecosystems based on integrated industrial products is certainly beginning to emerge around the development of phosphate mining, the agri-food industry, the automobile industry, electronics, aeronautics, and Morocco's other new global business lines. A reconfiguration of the structure of exports, particularly to benefit the automobile industry, is under way (see figure 3.15), but with limited local value added. National firms are less able to supply global value chains than the local subsidiaries of multinationals. In Morocco, the share of local inputs supplying multinational corporations is among the lowest of a group of similar countries.

Although Morocco has begun to develop service industries, their potential is largely untapped. The export of services from Morocco had risen significantly until the 2008 global financial crisis. Morocco was the front-runner among the Maghreb countries in successfully liberalizing air transport thanks to an audacious agreement signed with the European Union in December 2006 to open its airspace. It thus clearly indicated its commitment to liberalizing and its intention to benefit from liberalization. The number of tourist arrivals from around the world more than doubled between 2000 and 2010, barely missing the target of 10 million arrivals in 2010 ("Vision 2010"). The export of other services accelerated significantly, reflecting Morocco's willingness to take market shares in business process outsourcing and the information and communications technology market, targeting Francophone customers. However, despite these developments,

Figure 3.15 Morocco: Structure of Exports, 2007–15
(percent)

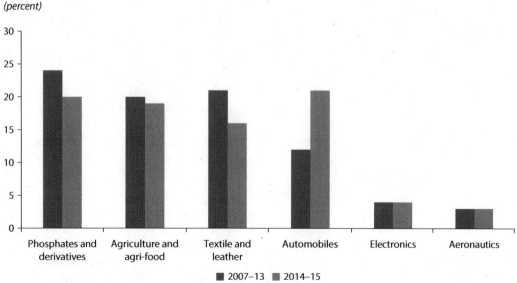

Source: Foreign Exchange Office, Morocco.

the share of services in value added has stagnated during the past decade, reflecting the fact that Morocco has specialized in relatively unsophisticated service areas. In many global value chains, the value added resides in localized intangible activities either upstream of the chain (preproduction activities such as basic and applied R&D, design, and marketing), or downstream of the value chain (postproduction activities such as marketing, publicity and trademark management, specialized logistics, and after-sales service). In comparison, there is little knowledge creation in the middle of the value chain, where standardized production and services are located (Cattaneo and others 2013; Taglioni and Winkler 2016).

In the area of trade facilitation, economic agents, exporters, and importers face serious challenges relating to the distribution chain. Despite real progress in customs management and the efficiency of the ports and air transport, trade logistics are not an advantage for Morocco compared to some of its major competitors such as Tunisia and Turkey. Data in the Logistics Performance Index established by the World Bank, which is based on the perceptions of freight forwarders, suggest that the areas in which Morocco is lagging are logistics, timeliness, and tracking and tracing systems, all areas that are affected by the inefficiency of the domestic portion of the value chain. The main constraint identified in Morocco resides in the dual nature of the domestic transport sector, which is shared between a small number of effective transporters that meet international standards and numerous small operators providing low-quality, fragmented services. This duality prevents the emergence of modern land transport groups that can effectively respond to the needs of shippers. Port taxes are relatively high in Morocco, for both containers and trucks. The lack of competition among ferry services also contributes to the high cost of crossing the Strait of Gibraltar compared to other maritime passages. It remains to be seen whether the entry into operation of a new Moroccan company providing a connection with Spain in 2016 will result in greater competition.

The limited penetration of Moroccan exports, both goods and services, underscores the country's significant competitiveness problems. These problems relate not only to the quality of products and the infrastructure and trade logistics that are necessary to bring products to their potential purchasers, but also to innovation, higher education, training, and technological maturity (see figure 3.16). They are also exacerbated by a fixed exchange regime and capital controls that protect the nontradables sector and constitute a significant obstacle to price competitiveness, product diversification, and Morocco's regional and global integration. In many cases, the lack of an adequate economic environment creates the impression that globalization has not led to the desired changes but has, on the contrary, helped to weaken some sectors and fostered the informal economy.

Foreign Investment

Morocco has substantially improved the investment conditions for foreign investors. Globally Morocco is ranked relatively well in terms of FDI regulation. Morocco's Investment Charter, which dates back to 1995, provides a nondiscriminatory framework for Moroccan and foreign investors. Foreign investment is allowed in

Figure 3.16 Morocco: Global Competitiveness Index

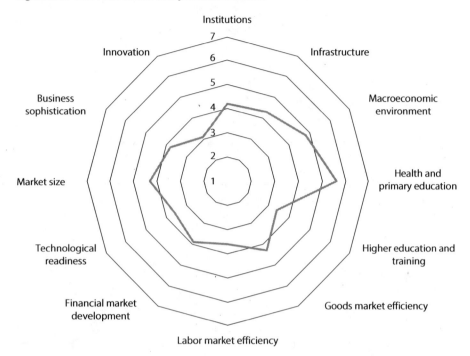

Source: Global Competitiveness Report 2015–2016, World Economic Forum.
Note: Index scores are based on a scale from 1 (worst) to 7 (best).

almost all sectors, with foreign investors even benefiting from more flexible foreign currency controls. Morocco has pursued a proactive FDI policy to attract foreign companies in sectors identified as having potential for development and support for the country's economic growth. The Moroccan Investment Promotion Agency (AMDI) and several Regional Investment Centers (CRIs) have been created to minimize and accelerate administrative procedures and increase FDI flows.[19]

Owing to this improvement in the institutional framework for investment, FDI entries have increased significantly and have become the most important source of foreign financing. The contribution of FDI as a share of GDP increased strongly from the late 1990s until the 2008 global financial crisis, although the starting point was relatively low. Since 2008, annual FDI flows have ranged around 2.5 percent of GDP. However, owing to its concentration in the mining and real estate sectors, FDI has not generated all of the expected benefits for domestic production and employment. To the extent that the manufacturing sector accounts for a small fraction of all FDI flows to Morocco, there is room to develop FDI in this sector in the future in support of the creation of manufacturing jobs.

Based on the present exchange, trade, and investment regimes, an analysis of Morocco's current location in the product space suggests that Morocco is moving its exports relatively slowly toward higher technology and higher value-added

Figure 3.17 Morocco: Position in the Product Space, 2010

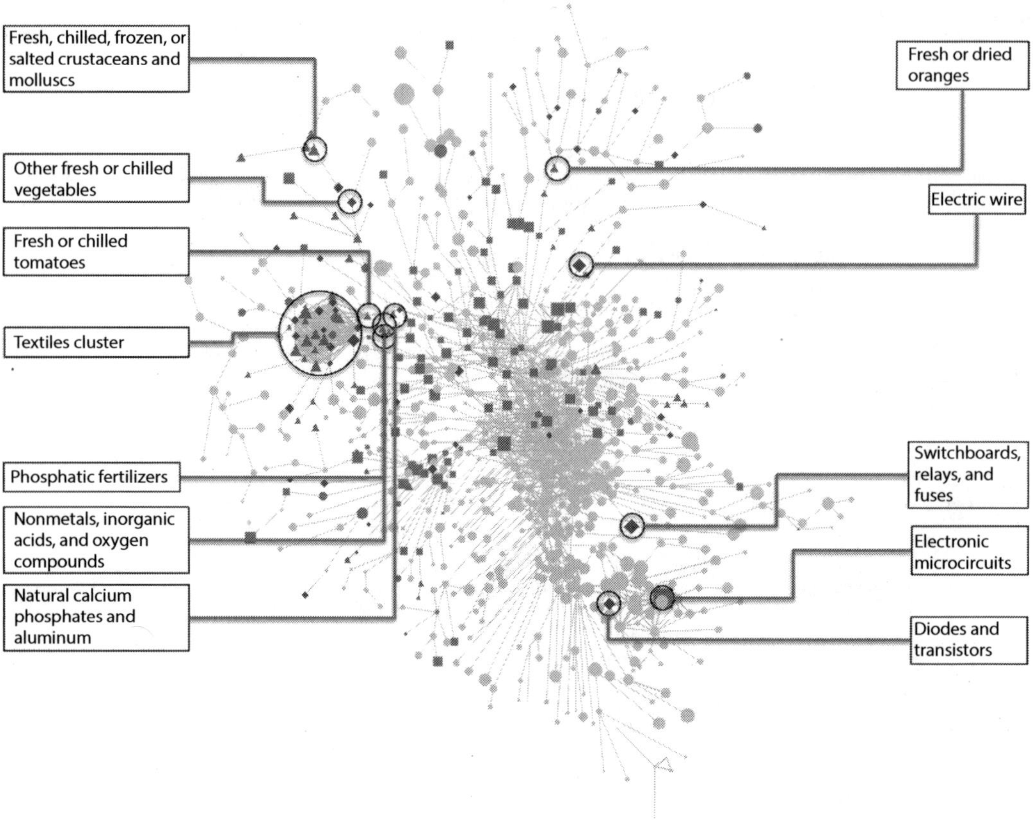

Fresh, chilled, frozen, or salted crustaceans and molluscs

Other fresh or chilled vegetables

Fresh or chilled tomatoes

Textiles cluster

Phosphatic fertilizers

Nonmetals, inorganic acids, and oxygen compounds

Natural calcium phosphates and aluminum

Fresh or dried oranges

Electric wire

Switchboards, relays, and fuses

Electronic microcircuits

Diodes and transistors

Source: Osorio Rodarte and Lofgren 2015.

products (see figure 3.17). The current map positions the various products exported by Morocco between 1980 and 2010 and shows that classic export products (shown in red) and emerging exports (shown in blue) are located around the periphery of the global product space (in gray). This means that the underlying characteristics of these products are not easily transferable to other more sophisticated products and offer limited diversification potential. For example, in the case of Morocco's natural resources, rapid growth of phosphate fertilizers and their derivatives can be expected. In contrast, given their position on the periphery of primary international trade, the diversification possibilities are limited. However, products that are marginally exported (shown in green) are closer to the center of global trade and thus have a higher diversification potential. Structural changes in the exportable supply are already being reflected in a more sophisticated range of exported products and better positioning, not only of low-cost, low-technology goods, but also in terms of qualitative competition (Ministry of Economy and Finance 2015). Morocco is developing capacities to export these products in the context of "new industries" (automobile, aeronautics), but these capacities must improve to move to the next level.

The lessons from other emerging countries that have previously trodden this industrial path suggest the importance of sectoral reforms. It is increasingly acknowledged that policies that favor a country's overall capacity to increase its productivity and quality and move toward more sophisticated tasks are more important than the identification of sectors that promote growth and diversification (Lederman and Maloney 2012). In other words, interventions that are aimed at diversifying economies seem to work only if they are accompanied by policies that diversify assets (both tangible and intangible). The correlation between diversified asset portfolios and greater economic efficiency is higher than the correlation between diversified products and economic efficiency (Gill and others 2014). This suggests that the most important pending item on Morocco's reform agenda could well be the most difficult: strengthening the institutional structures that are invisible but whose weakness is likely to hold back the country's prosperity.

Deriving the Full Benefits from Globalization through Competitiveness

Morocco has undertaken large-scale changes to integrate in the world economy, but it has not yet derived the full benefit of its political stability, its proximity to Europe, and its relative attractiveness for investment to make this integration a decisive competitive advantage that will enable it to achieve rapid, inclusive catch-up growth. A key aspect of Morocco's success in increasing its productivity is its capacity to increase exports of goods and services. This means that the tradable goods sector must develop and contribute more to growth and to this end it is essential that the economy's "anti-export bias" be reduced (World Bank 2006). There are many reasons for this bias: (i) an exchange system that favors the non-tradable goods sector (as opposed to sectors open to international competition) and that tends to weaken Morocco's price competitiveness on other markets, (ii) a trade regime and trade policies that are overly protective of national producers against international competition and that encourage them to supply the domestic market rather than the global markets, and (iii) an investment regime and domestic regulatory framework that increase the costs of inputs and reduce Morocco's competitiveness. It is important to emphasize that the lack of economic integration is both the cause and the consequence of this "anti-export bias": without more sustained domestic competition, the economy has not turned toward innovation, efficiency, and modernization and is at a disadvantage on the international markets; in the absence of greater participation in international trade, domestic companies are not exposed to foreign knowledge and know-how and are little pressed by competition or encouraged to modernize and optimize. These issues are discussed in the following sections.

Easing the Exchange Arrangements and Controls

Morocco should consider adopting more flexible exchange arrangements to improve the likelihood of sustainable higher growth led by productivity and exports. When the conditions are there in terms of macroeconomic stability, fiscal consolidation, a sound banking system, or a sufficient level of international reserves, the transition to a more flexible exchange regime would enable the dirham to find its equilibrium price on a sustainable basis. As the relative price between the sector comprising tradable goods exposed to international competition and the protected nontradable goods sector, the exchange rate is a key price in any economy. All other things being equal, an overvaluation of the exchange rate encourages economic agents to invest in the generally unproductive nontradable goods sector (for example, real estate). In contrast, an undervaluation of the exchange rate promotes investment in more productive sectors exposed to international competition. Thus, over the long term, the real effective exchange rate is potentially a powerful economic and integration policy instrument. Many emerging countries, particularly in Asia, have based their development strategies on productivity-rich growth driven by competitive prices for their basket of exports (see figure 3.18). More recently, a number of Morocco's foreign competitors have not hesitated to use the exchange instrument. For example, the dirham has appreciated approximately 100 percent in relation to the Brazilian real and the South African rand since 2012 and 50 percent in relation to the Turkish pound since 2013. A recent study of firm-level data in Egypt, Jordan, and other countries in the Middle East and North Africa shows that a depreciation of the real effective exchange rate favors the development of exports in these countries both on the intensive margin (exports of existing products on existing markets) and at the extensive margin (exports of new products or to new markets) (Elbadawi and Zaki 2016). The free determination of the dirham exchange rate would, moreover, be a means of leaving the economic policy dimension of exchange rate fluctuations to the market.

At the same time, Morocco should continue to make its exchange controls more flexible to ensure the full convertibility of the dirham. This will require the elimination of the main controls still in place for the purchase of foreign exchange, which impede the development of national and foreign firms and limit

Figure 3.18 Real Effective Exchange Rates, 1988–2015
(index 100 in 1988)

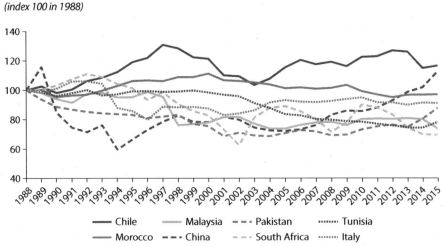

Source: WDI, World Bank.

the economic freedom of Moroccans to convert their dirham assets. Total convertibility of capital transactions would enable residents and nonresidents to use their resources freely for international transactions. It would pave the way for a more efficient allocation of savings and would increase the attractiveness of Morocco in the eyes of investors and global trade operators. For example, the current limit on the prepayment of imports is a de facto obstacle. It can be an issue, for example, for American exporters who require a 100 percent advance payment to finance their sales or who prefer contracts in which letters of credit are not mandatory for doing business.

The transition to a flexible exchange regime and convertibility of the dirham would also have the advantage of making monetary policy fully autonomous to influence real activity on the basis of various (internal and external) shocks that constantly affect the economy. The "impossible trinity" states that a national economy cannot simultaneously achieve the following three objectives: a fixed foreign exchange rate, an independent monetary policy (the ability to set short-term interest rates), and the free movement of capital (Mundell 1960). In a context of increasing external openness, emerging countries must generally choose between a fixed exchange rate and an independent monetary policy. The Bank Al-Maghrib has in recent years begun considering the appropriateness of gradually transitioning to greater exchange flexibility and a so-called inflation targeting system that would enable it to better anchor expectations and increase its contribution to economic development (Bank Al-Maghrib 2016). With all of the prerequisites for a soft transition being present, it should now be possible to turn this discussion into action (IMF 2016a, 2016b).

Improving the Trade Regime and Trade Facilitation Policies

Morocco would benefit from renewing its efforts to lower trade barriers. Morocco's export performance seems to be weakened by its import regime. The difference in export unit values between firms that both import and export and firms that export only is large and, most importantly, has been increasing over time. This suggests that better access to intermediate inputs subsequently boosts the growth of firms' exports and the diversification and quality of products (Bussolo and Cruz 2015). For businesses that are not located in free zones or involved in global value chains with the support of their buyers, identifying reliable suppliers that can provide them with intermediate products can be a challenge. The most direct way that Morocco can support manufacturing exports, reduce real effective protection, and limit trade diversion would be to build on the success of the 2008–12 plan by launching a new medium-term plan aimed at reducing and consolidating the most-favored nation tariffs.

At 25 percent, maximum most-favored nation tariffs on goods are still relatively high, particularly in comparison with the zero duty applied to preferential trade partners under the free trade agreements signed with the European Union, the United States, and other countries. High duties on intermediate products tend to be an obstacle to the productivity of firms and the growth of Moroccan exports (Jaud and Freund 2015). This results from the fact that, generally speaking, a tax on imports ends up becoming a tax on exports. Moreover, Morocco's tariff structure acts as an escalator, to the extent that import duties on raw materials are lower than those on semi-processed goods, which are in turn lower than those on finished goods. Tariff escalation is particularly pronounced in the textile and clothing and leather and footwear sectors. In these sectors, producers for the domestic market have access to inputs taxed at low rates while being protected behind significant export barriers for their finished products. The degree of real effective protection is thus often higher than the level of duties on finished products suggests.

There is still a significant gap between preferential tariffs and most-favored nation tariffs (applied to imports from the rest of the world), which tends to divert trade. Morocco has opened its domestic market selectively, since only countries that are preferential partners can sell their products on the Moroccan markets at low or zero import tariffs, while exporters from third countries face high most-favored nation tariffs. This asymmetry can push trade flows from exporters in more efficient third countries toward less efficient partner producer countries, resulting in a loss of tariff revenues without the economy benefiting from lower purchase prices.

Reviewing the nontariff measures is another important priority if Morocco is to benefit further from the advantages of economic integration. Morocco should streamline its nontariff measures and related procedures in terms of time and cost. Morocco has considered the possibility of establishing a public-private committee to reevaluate existing nontariff measures and the regulatory process that allows for the creation of new such measures. Some policy reforms have been identified, but specific changes have not been made. In the absence of transparency, nontariff measures tend to be used somewhat discretionarily and result in bureaucratic border procedures, particularly with non–European Union member partners. Morocco should also reduce its use of trade defense mechanisms (antidumping clauses and measures) intended to protect its domestic production (for example, steel, paper, PVC materials, wood, and insulin).

Given that the level of duties collected on agricultural imports amounted to more than 300 percent for some products and given the tariff quotas applied, there is an immense potential to liberalize Morocco's agricultural trade. Morocco should gradually open its agricultural markets because agriculture constitutes one of the engines of its economy. An agricultural strategy should offer better opportunities for the heads of small and large operations to transform the agrifood sector into a stable source of growth, competitiveness, and general economic development in rural areas. Protection of agricultural trade is an ineffective poverty reduction tool. Vulnerable households should be assisted using targeted social safety nets. Decoupled payments are one way of reducing the distortionary effects of policies in support of agriculture while still helping farmers. At present, Morocco offers its farmers guaranteed prices for food and industrial crops and a large range of subsidies on the purchase of inputs. Price support for essential goods and energy subsidies (for pumps) is also widespread. The policy objectives are to improve food security and reduce urban drift. However, this price support system and nonspecific subsidies are not aimed at the poor. Moreover, they have a significant budget cost, rewarding low-value crops and encouraging excessive use of water.

The facilitation of trade and regional connectivity is an incomplete but essential agenda item for Morocco. One of Morocco's comparative advantages is its geography, which means that the quality of its ports, land transport, and trade logistics are key to its competitiveness. Moroccan exporters cannot successfully exploit their proximity to the European Union market unless their transport transaction costs are lower than those of their competitors. The existence of functional links along the supply chain has become even more important owing to changing deadlines, which target just-in-time deliveries, and trade partners' increasing demands in terms of delays, reliability, and, delivery quality. The high cost of transport, logistics, and communications has been identified as one of the factors that penalizes transportation in Morocco and, more broadly, the region (CGEM 2014). Priority measures in this area would aim to improve the quality of all import-export services at the port (clarification of procedures and improvement of processing delays, particularly customs clearance of goods).

Improving the Foreign Investment Regime

Although Morocco has opened most sectors of its economy to foreign investment, clear legal restrictions remain in many sectors, particularly the services sector. Morocco would benefit from gradually removing the remaining restrictions on foreign equity participation in all sectors, with the exception of a list of sectors with strong monopoly powers, based on the national treatment principle. Thus, foreign control is limited to a maximum of 49 percent in domestic and international transport enterprises. In the oil and gas sector, the National Hydrocarbons and Mining Office maintains a mandatory 25 percent share in all operating licenses or permits. Moreover, Morocco should endeavor to standardize the rules for domestic and foreign investors by privatizing companies in the trade sector and eliminating restrictions such as licensing conditions and other regulatory constraints.

Conversely, it is also very important to ensure that the incentives used to attract foreign investors do not prevent local integration. This involves ensuring that firms belonging to foreigners do not have preferred access in certain areas such as import taxes, customs concessions, or duty refunds. Similarly, reserving special economic zones for foreign companies can create supply barriers for domestic companies. It is true that incentives for foreign investors or other international purchasers are primarily intended to create positive spillover effects, but these incentives should be based, if not on specific outcomes in terms of effects (which are difficult to measure), at least on the commitment of foreign investors or other international purchasers to favor such effects. For example, incentives could be created to encourage foreign investors to work with local universities, research institutes, and training institutes. Specifically, this would involve research funds, counterpart grant programs, or tax incentives for R&D in Morocco, internships, retraining programs, and the development of joint training and study programs.

It is also important to ensure that legal provisions concerning local content are clearly defined and appropriately applied. The objective should be enhancement of the local content rather than control by the country. However, legal provisions can operate successfully only if the domestic supply dimension allows the supplier to be competitive; otherwise, these regulations tend to weaken the competitiveness of investors, which has a negative impact on all outcomes. In all cases, it can be counterproductive and difficult to implement strict local content targets. On the other hand, it is essential to reduce the information asymmetry by facilitating information sharing on the needs of foreign investors and capacities of local suppliers and on skills requirements. Rather than setting rigid local content constraints, the objective should be to favor the collaborative development of flexible co-localization plans enabling investors to make their own proposals to promote beneficial impacts for the local economy.

Morocco would benefit from introducing a more consistent policy to improve land management and protect property rights. This would enable it to lower the risks and promote a better use of the opportunities of FDI in real estate. Improving access to information on land and its availability for economic activities while taking measures to sharply reduce transaction delays, would significantly increase Morocco's attractiveness in the eyes of foreign investors. Property purchases by foreign private investors have been limited over the years.

Negotiating an Ambitious Deep and Comprehensive Free Trade Agreement with the European Union

A deep and comprehensive free trade agreement with the European Union and the necessary upgrading of Morocco's rules and regulations in many sectors could be key strategic objectives for the country. This would enable Morocco to better position itself in global competition, including through its insertion in European global value chains, thereby helping to significantly increase total factor productivity. Deep economic integration with the European Union would require the promotion of freedom of circulation of goods, services, capital, and labor. Morocco could currently benefit from the promotion of greater regulatory convergence of rules and standards and other cross-border regulations that are related to competition policy, public tenders, and other aspects of the regulatory environment that concern the improvement of trade and FDI. Regionalization with the European Union and, to some extent, with Sub-Saharan Africa could constitute a springboard toward global integration and improvement of Morocco's competitiveness, which are the ultimate goals.

Frank measures aimed at integration and competition in the services sectors and the facilitation of trade could improve the productivity and accelerate the structural transformation of the Moroccan economy. The lack of sophistication and modernization of Moroccan services underscores the lack of openness and competition that are necessary to enhance them. Morocco has introduced liberalization measures in a relatively limited number of subsectors under the General Agreement on Trade in Services, and logistics services, which are essential for trade development, are not included. Morocco has opened up significantly only in the areas of trade in financial services, telecommunications, and electronic commerce under the bilateral free trade agreement concluded with the United States. Increased openness of services would help to produce significant economic results owing to competition, FDI, and vertical spillover effects in the areas of knowledge and market development. The liberalization of services would also positively impact industrial productivity, the competitiveness of exports of manufactured goods, and even the competitiveness of other services through their secondary effects. Efficient port and maritime services are essential to export goods such as textile products competitively. Similarly, attracting more tourists depends in particular on the cost of air transport. The capacity to participate in the outsourcing of business processes and to export services based on ICTs depends on telecommunications services. The positive effects of the liberalization of trade in services on productivity in downstream industries would be even greater if it were accompanied by an improvement in the quality of the institutions governing foreign trade, particularly the foreign investment regime (Beverelli, Hoekman, and Fiorini 2016).

It will be essential to take account of the economic policy dimension of a deep and comprehensive economic integration strategy. In Morocco, public opinion generally considers that the process of opening up initiated by governments over the past decade has not necessarily produced the expected outcomes. Past attempts that have aimed to strengthen the private sector through privatization and the liberalization of markets have not had all the expected benefits, particularly when the advantages have been captured by connected persons. External liberalization has not always been accompanied by the domestic reforms that are necessary to improve governance, increase transparency, and create a level playing field so that workers and consumers can also reap the benefits. As elsewhere, there is a coalition of protectionist interests in Morocco that would like to maintain the status quo and it knows how to make itself heard. It exerts pressure on the government to slow the process of economic integration and the structural transformation that must accompany it. Rather than favoring the development of an independent and autonomous private sector, some past reforms have tended to strengthen existing protection networks (Malik and Awadallah 2011).

To avoid the errors of the past, account must be taken of the fact that the Moroccan people need to understand what "there is for them" in a policy of deep and comprehensive integration with the European Union. Public opinion trends seem to be favorable. According to the 2012–14 Arab Barometer, 60 percent of those questioned believe that Morocco would benefit from opening up further to the rest of the world, but if this is to be successful, the population must own the integration process and its general objective. It must be informed of the changes relating to global trade and the FDI environment and must clearly see the improvements in terms of infrastructure, trade, and investment. Moroccans need to further access economic opportunities for themselves and their children and to be shown that the reforms are producing results. Last, they need convincing proof that all social groups benefit from the process and will continue to do so over the long term. This refers to the need for an informed public discussion on the impact of economic integration on the Moroccan economy. What economic integration means is making the economy more efficient and more competitive, which should result in economic growth and higher, more sustained incomes. According to the ECORYS study (ECORYS 2013) conducted on behalf of the European Commission, the deep and comprehensive free trade agreement could in the long term result in a 1.6 percent increase in Morocco's GDP, a wage increase of between 1.5 percent and 1.9 percent depending on assumptions, and a 15 percent increase in exports, leading to a relative improvement in the trade balance. However, some industrial sectors, such as the leather industry or services sector, particularly professional services, could suffer from the increased competition and see their output decline. Establishing public mechanisms to help those that are penalized by the shocks produced by trade (or technological innovation) is the best means of taking account of the potentially negative secondary effects of transformational reforms and ensuring their longevity.

Notes

1. Since the time of political science professor John Waterbury's works on this subject (1975), a vast, primarily sociological literature has documented the historical formation of the Moroccan elites (Leveau 1985; Catusse 2008; Benhaddou 2009; Bencheikh 2013).

2. Speech delivered by His Majesty King Mohammed VI at the opening of the 1st Session of the 1st Legislative Year of the 10th Legislature (November 2016).

3. Significant budgetary resources have been allocated by the Moroccan public authorities to maintain and accelerate the various works and programs launched to achieve the objectives of the Morocco Innovation Initiative. These include the establishment of a Cluster Support Fund to stimulate innovation and R&D in the industry and technology sectors; the launching of a program for the establishment of "innovation complexes" in partnership with Moroccan universities; building of the capacity of the Technical Industrial Centers (CTI) as technical structures for the development and dissemination of industrial expertise in the respective areas of activity; establishment of a development center dedicated to advanced technologies such as nanotechnologies, microelectronics, and biotechnologies; and the establishment of programs for the financing of business innovation (small and medium enterprises and very small enterprises/start-ups).

4. Particularly the granting of new generation fixed licenses in 2006, the publication of various regulatory decisions on infrastructure sharing, the preparation of a national broadband plan through 2022 by the National Telecommunications Regulation Agency (ANRT) in 2012, the launching of 4G in 2015, and the launching of a consultation by the ANRT in 2016 to cover the financing of broadband in rural areas by the Universal Service Fund (FSU).

5. Maroc Télécom has a fiber optic backbone measuring almost 25,000 km as against just 5,000 km for Méditel and 6,000 km for WANA. On the asymmetric digital subscriber line (ADSL) market (fixed broadband), which was limited to around 1.1 million lines in 2015, Maroc Télécom holds 99.97 percent of the market (as against 0.03 percent for WANA) in 2015 (National Communications Regulation Agency 2016).

6. The National Industrial Emergence Pact consists of 10 pillars: offshoring, automobiles, aeronautics, electronics, textiles, leather, SME competitiveness, investment climate,

training, and industrial zones. It sent strong signals to the automobile and aeronautics sectors, which have benefited from significant foreign investment in recent years.

7. In a report on the Moroccan Investment Development Agency (2015), the Audit Office calculated the occupancy rate of the P2i's: in 2011, just 10 out of the 21 companies converted were located on these platforms; in 2012, the number was 12 out of 24. The attractiveness rate of the P2i's is thus 50 percent.

8. Automobiles, aeronautics, industrial vehicles and trucks, textiles, chemicals and parachemicals, leather, pharmaceuticals, metallurgical and mechanical industries, construction materials industry and offshoring, plastics, and phosphates.

9. In 2016, a new investment reform plan was launched, focusing on six main areas: recalibration of the Investment Charter and redefinition of its content, adoption of new support and investment incentive measures, restructuring of the investment promotion agencies, creation of general directorates dedicated to industry and trade, and the overhaul of the digital strategy.

10. Specifically, the introduction of cost-benefit analyses for investments submitted to the Investment Committee and respect of strict selection procedures for Industrial Acceleration Plan (PAI) investment files in the context of the Industrial Development and Investment Fund (preparation of comprehensive investment files, assessment of files by third parties, assessment report, etc.).

11. For example, in assessing the Digital Morocco 2013 strategy, the Audit Office (2014) noted that a number of indicators had not yet been tracked with sufficient rigor and that most of the objectives set by the strategy had not been achieved.

12. Organic Law No. 111-14 on the regions (published in the Official Bulletin of July 7, 2015) is based on the 2011 constitution, which calls for decentralization and establishes advanced regionalization based on an integrated system of regional governance in Morocco.

13. Article 136 of the constitution and Article 4 of Organic Law No. 111-14.

14. Employment protection legislation comprises the rules governing recruitment and dismissal and defining the degree of job security.

15. World Bank calculations using HCP data for 2009 extrapolated to 2015.

16. *Protected* is defined as benefiting from social protection; *well-paid* is defined as leading to a wage higher than two-thirds of the average wage or as leading to independent living in a house and being part of the upper quintiles of the population.

17. These include (i) the Idmaj program (2006), which is aimed at enabling young job seekers to have their first experience in a business; (ii) the Taehil program (2006), which is aimed at improving the employability of job seekers through the acquisition of professional skills for identified or potential jobs; (iii) the self-employment program, which is aimed at creating very small enterprises; and (iv) the Tahfiz program, which is aimed at promoting employment by introducing incentives for businesses and associations in the context of permanent employment contracts.

18. The record seizure of 40 metric tons of cannabis at Algésiras in 2015 may have weakened the Tanger-Med control chain's reputation for reliability.

19. In 2016, in the context of the implementation of the Industrial Acceleration Plan (PAI), AMDI, Morocco Export, and the Office of Trade Fairs and Exhibitions (OFEC) were grouped together in a new agency called the Moroccan Investment and Export Development Agency (AMDIE) and placed under the supervision of the Ministry of Industry, Trade, Investment, and the Digital Economy.

References

Achy, Lahcen, Samy Bennaceur, Adel Ben Youssef, and Samir Ghazouani. 2010. "Restructuring and Efficiency in the Manufacturing Sector: A Firm-Level Approach Applied to Morocco." Economic Research Forum Working Paper 565, Economic Research Forum, Giza, Egypt.

Aghion, Philippe, Christopher Harris, Peter Howitt, and John Vickers. 2001. "Competition, Imitation and Growth with Step-by-Step Innovation." *Review of Economic Studies* 68 (3): 467–92.

Angel-Urdinola, Diego, Abdoul Gadiry Barry, and Jamal Guennouni. 2016. "Are Minimum Wages and Payroll Taxes a Constraint to the Creation of Formal Jobs in Morocco?" World Bank Economic Policy Research Paper 78080, World Bank, Washington, DC.

Audit Office (Cour des comptes). 2014. Assessment of "Digital Morocco 2013" Strategy. Rabat, Morocco.

———. 2016. *Rapport sur le secteur des établissements et entreprises publics au Maroc: Ancrage stratégique et gouvernance*. Rabat: Morocco.

Baldwin, Richard. 2011. "Trade and Industrialisation after Globalisation's 2nd Unbundling: How Building and Joining a Supply Chain Are Different and Why It Matters." NBER Working Paper 17716, National Bureau of Economic Research, Cambridge, MA.

Bank Al-Maghrib (BAM). 2016. *Rapport sur l'exercice 2015*. Rabat, Morocco: Bank Al-Maghrib.

Benabdejlil, Nadia, Yannick Lung, and Alain Piveteau. 2016. *L'émergence d'un pôle automobile à Tanger (Maroc)*. Bordeaux, France: Cahiers du GREThA, n°2016-04.

Bencheikh, Souleiman. 2013. *Le dilemme du Roi ou la monarchie marocaine à l'épreuve*. Paris: Casa Express Éditions Rabat.

Benhaddou, Ali. 2009. *Les élites du Royaume: Enquête sur l'organisation du pouvoir au Maroc*. Paris: Édition Riveneuve.

Betcherman, Gordon. 2012. "Labor Market Institutions: A Review of the Literature." Policy Research Working Paper 6276, World Bank, Washington, DC.

Beverelli, Cosimo, Bernard Hoekman, and Matteo Fiorini. 2016. "Services Trade Policy and Manufacturing Productivity: The Role of Institutions." Economic Research Forum Working Paper 1012, Economic Research Forum, Giza, Egypt.

Botero, Juan C., Simeon Djankov, Rafel La Porta, Florencio Lopez-de-Silanes, and Andrei Shleifer. 2004. "The Regulation of Labor." *Quarterly Journal of Economics* 119 (4): 1339–82.

Bouoiyour, Jamal. 2003. "Système national d'innovation marocain." *Critique Économique* 9.

Bussolo, Maurizio, and Marcio Cruz. 2015. "Does Input Tariff Reduction Impact Firms' Exports in the Presence of Import Tariff Exemption Regimes?" World Bank Policy Research Working Paper 7231. World Bank, Washington, DC.

Cattaneo, O., G. Gereffi, S. Miroudot, and D. Taglioni. 2013. "Joining, Upgrading and Being Competitive in Global Value Chains: A Strategic Framework." World Bank Policy Research Working Paper 6406, World Bank, Washington, DC.

Catusse, Myriam. 2008. *Le temps des entrepreneurs: Politique et transformations du capitalisme au Maroc*. Paris: Maisonneuve et Larose.

Chauffour, Jean-Pierre. 2009. *The Power of Freedom: Unifying Human Rights and Development*. Washington, DC: Cato Institute.

Chauffour, Jean-Pierre, and José L. Diaz-Sanchez. 2017. *Product and Factor Market Distortions: The Case of the Manufacturing Sector in Morocco.* Washington, DC: World Bank.

Chauffour, Jean-Pierre, and Mariem Malouche. 2011. *Trade Finance during the Great Trade Collapse.* Washington, DC: World Bank.

Chauffour, Jean-Pierre, and Jean-Christophe Maur. 2011. *Preferential Trade Agreement Policies for Development: A Handbook.* Washington, DC: World Bank.

Cherkaoui, Mouna, Ayache Khellaf, and Abdelaziz Nihou. 2011. "The Price Effect of Tariff Liberalization in Morocco: Measuring the Impact on Household Welfare." Economic Research Forum Working Paper 637, Economic Research Forum, Giza, Egypt.

Commission on Growth and Development. 2008. *The Growth Report Strategies for Sustained Growth and Inclusive Development.* Washington, DC: World Bank.

Cornell University, INSEAD, and WIPO. 2016. *The Global Innovation Index 2016: Winning with Global Innovation, Ithaca, Fontainebleau, and Geneva.*

Diwan, Ishac, and Jamal Ibrahim Haidar. 2016. "Do Political Connections Reduce Job Creation? Evidence from Lebanon." Economic Research Forum Working Paper 1054, Economic Research Forum, Giza, Egypt.

Diwan, Ishac, Philip Keefer, and Marc Schiffbauer. 2013. "The Effect of Cronyism on Private Sector Growth in Egypt." Femise. http://www.femise.org/wp-content/uploads/2015/10/Diwan.pdf.

Driouchi, Ahmed, and Nada Zouag. 2006. *Prospective Maroc 2030, éléments pour le renforcement de l'insertion du Maroc dans l'économie de la connaissance.* Rapport pour le compte du HCP. Morocco.

EBRD, EIB, and World Bank. 2016. "What's Holding Back the Private Sector in MENA?" Washington, DC: World Bank: Lessons from the Enterprise Survey.

Economic, Social and Environmental Council (CESE). 2014. *Cohérence des politiques sectorielles et accords de libre-échange: Fondements stratégiques pour un développement soutenu et durable.* Auto-saisine no. 16, 2014. Rabat, Morocco.

ECORYS. 2013. "Trade Sustainability Impact Assessment in Support of Negotiations of a DCFTA between the EU and Morocco." http://trade.ec.europa.eu/doclib/docs/2013/november/tradoc_151926.pdf.

El Aoufi, Noureddine, and Michel Hollard. 2010. *Fondements d'une pragmatique de la concurrence au Maroc—Note d'orientation.* Rabat, Morocco: Conseil de la Concurrence.

Elbadawi, Ibrahim, and Chahir Zaki. 2016. "Does Exchange Rate Undervaluation Matter for Exports and Trade Margins? Evidence from Firm-Level Data." Economic Research Forum Working Paper 1004, Economic Research Forum, Giza, Egypt.

Fukuyama, Francis. 2014. *Political Order and Political Decay: From the Industrial Revolution to the Globalization of Democracy.* New York: Farrar, Straus & Giroux.

General Confederation of Moroccan Companies (CGEM). 2014. *Étude sur les leviers de la compétitivité des entreprises marocaines.* Casablanca, Morocco.

Gill, Indermit S., Ivailo Izvorski, Willem van Eeghen, and Donato De Rosa. 2014. *Diversified Development: Making the Most of Natural Resources in Eurasia.* Washington, DC: World Bank.

Hayter, S. ed. 2011. *Le rôle de la négociation collective dans l'économie mondiale: Négocier pour la justice sociale.* Geneva, Switzerland: International Labour Organization.

HEM. 2016. *La jeunesse au Maroc: Marginalités, informalités et adaptations*. Casablanca, Morocco: HEM Business School.

Hsieh, Chang-Tai, and Peter J. Klenow. 2009. "Misallocation and Manufacturing TFP in China and India." *Quarterly Journal of Economics* 124 (4): 1403–48.

International Monetary Fund (IMF). 2016a. *2015 Article IV Consultation*. IMF Country Report 16/35. Washington, DC: IMF.

———. 2016b. "Morocco—Request for an Arrangement under the Precautionary and Liquidity Line and Cancellation of the Current Arrangement." EBS/16/66. IMF, Washington, DC.

Jaud, Mélise, and Marion Dovis. 2014. "Standards Harmonization as Export Promotion." Forum for Research and Empirical International Trade Working Paper 748, International Monetary Fund, Washington, DC.

Jaud, Mélise, and Caroline Freund. 2015. "Champions Wanted: Promoting Exports in the Middle East and North Africa." Working Paper No. 95681, World Bank, Washington, DC.

Jouyet, Jean-Pierre, and Maurice Lévy. 2006. *Rapport de commission: L'économie de l'immatériel, la croissance de demain*. Ministry of Economy, Finances and Industry. Paris, France.

Klapper, Leora, and Inessa Love. 2010. "The Impact of the Financial Crisis on New Firm Creation." World Bank Policy Research Working Paper 5444, World Bank, Washington, DC.

Lafontaine, Francine, and Jagadeesh Sivadasan. 2008. "Do Labor Market Rigidities Have Microeconomic Effects? Evidence from within the Firm (May 1, 2008)." Ross School of Business Paper 1069, University of Michigan, Ann Arbor.

Lederman, Daniel, and William F. Maloney. 2012. "Does What You Export Matter? In Search of Empirical Guidance for Industrial Policies." Latin America Development Forum, World Bank, Washington, DC. https://openknowledge.worldbank.org/handle /10986/9371.

Leveau, Rémy. 1985. *Le fellah marocain défenseur du trône*. Paris: Presses de Sciences Po.

Malik, Adeel, and Bassem Awadallah. 2011. "The Economics of the Arab Spring." Working Paper 2011-23, Center of the Study of African Economies, Oxford, England.

Miner, Luke. 2015. "The Unintended Consequences of Internet Diffusion: Evidence from Malaysia." *Journal of Public Economics* 132 (December): 66–78.

Ministry of Economy and Finance. 2015. *Compétitivité hors prix des exportations marocaines: Esquisse de la qualité des produits des secteurs phares*. Direction des Études et des Prévisions Financières. Rabat, Morocco.

———. 2016. *Décomposition de la compétitivité structurelle du Maroc: Marges intensives et extensives de nos exportations*. Direction des Études et des Prévisions Financières. Rabat, Morocco.

Ministry of National Education and HEM Business School. 2015. *Enquête nationale socioéducative réalisée par le groupe "L'Étudiant marocain."* Rabat, Morocco.

Moroccan Intellectual Property Office (OMPIC). 2014. *Rapport d'activité 2014*. Casablanca, Morocco.

Mundell, Robert. 1960. "A Theory of Optimum Currency Areas." *American Economic Review* 51 (4): 657–65.

National Communications Regulation Agency (ANRT). 2016. *Tableau de bord du marché de l'internet*. Morocco.

OCP Policy Center. 2015. "Stratégie de croissance à l'horizon 2025 dans un environnement international en mutation." OCP Policy Center, Rabat, Morocco.

Osorio Rodarte, Israel, and Hans Lofgren. 2015. "A Product Space Perspective on Structural Change in Morocco." World Bank Policy Research Working Paper 7438. World Bank, Washington, DC.

Oubenal, Mohammed. 2016. "Crony Interlockers and the Centrality of Banks: The Network of Moroccan Listed Companies." Economic Research Forum Working Paper 1066, World Bank, Washington, DC.

Rijkers, Bob, Caroline Freund, and Antonio Nucifora. 2014. "All in the Family: State Capture in Tunisia." Policy Research Working Paper 6810, World Bank, Washington, DC.

Robalino, David A., and Michael Weber. 2013. "Designing and Implementing Unemployment Benefit Systems in Middle and Low Income Countries: Beyond Risk-Pooling vs. savings." *IZA Journal of Labor Policy* 2: 12.

Rood, Hendrik. 2010, Very High Speed Broadband Deployment in Europe: The Netherlands and Bulgaria Compared. TPRC 2010. Rood, Hendrik, Very High Speed Broadband Deployment in Europe: The Netherlands and Bulgaria Compared (August 15, 2010). TPRC 2010. Available at SSRN: https://ssrn.com/abstract=1989172.

Royal Institute for Strategic Studies (IRES). 2014. *Industrialisation et compétitivité globale du Maroc* (p. 15). Rabat, Morocco.

Saadi, Mohammed Saïd. 2016. "Moroccan Cronyism: Facts, Mechanisms and Impact." Economic Research Forum Working Paper 1063, World Bank, Washington, DC.

Taglioni, Daria, and Gianluca Santoni. 2015. "Networks and Structural Integration in Global Value Chains." In *The Age of Global Value Chains*, edited by Amador and di Mauro. London, Center for Economic and Policy Research, 68–84.

Taglioni, Daria, and Deborah Winkler. 2016. *Making Global Value Chains Work for Development*. Washington, DC: World Bank.

United Nations. 2008. Examen de la politique de l'investissement du Maroc. Conférence des Nations Unies sur le commerce et le développement.

Verme, Paolo, Abdoul Gadiry Barry, Jamal Guennouni, and Mohammed Taamouti. 2014. "Labor Mobility, Economic Shocks, and Jobless Growth: Evidence from Panel Data in Morocco." Policy Research Working Paper 6795, World Bank, Washington, DC.

Waterbury, John. 1975. *Le commandeur des croyants: La monarchie marocaine et son élite*. Paris: PUF.

World Bank. 1995. "Bureaucrats in Business: The Economics and Politics of Government Ownership." World Bank Policy Research Report, World Bank, Washington, DC.

———. 2002. *World Development Report 2002: Building Institutions for Markets*. Washington, DC: World Bank.

———. 2006. *Mémorandum économique pays Maroc 2006*. Washington, DC: World Bank.

———. 2008, 2013. Enquêtes de la Banque mondiale auprès des entreprises [World Bank Enterprise Surveys]. Washington, DC: World Bank.

———. 2009. *From Privilege to Competition: Unlocking the Private-Led Growth in the Middle East and North Africa*. MENA Development Report. Washington, DC: World Bank.

———. 2010. *Socio-economic Assessment of Broadband Development in Egypt*. Washington, DC: World Bank.

————. 2012. *Doing Business 2013: Smarter Regulations for Small and Medium-Size Enterprises.* Washington, D.C.: World Bank.

————. 2013a. *Enterprise Surveys, Morocco Country Profile 2013.* Washington, DC: World Bank.

————. 2013b. "Jobs for Shared Prosperity: Time for Action in the Middle East and North Africa." Working Paper 72469. World Bank, Washington, DC.

————. 2014a. *Doing Business 2015: Going Beyond Efficiency—Morocco.* Washington, DC: World Bank.

————. 2014b. *Financing Innovation in Morocco: Challenges and Solutions to Accelerate Growth.* Washington, DC: World Bank.

————. 2015. *Emplois ou privilèges, libérer le potentiel de création d'emplois au Moyen-Orient et en Afrique du Nord.* MENA Development Report. Washington, DC: World Bank.

————. 2016a. *Le haut débit: Plate-forme de l'économie digitale et enjeu critique pour le développement du Maroc.* Note pour le Ministère de l'industrie, du commerce, de l'investissement et de l'économie numérique.

————. 2016b. *Connecting to Compete 2016: Trade Logistics in the Global Economy.* The Logistics Performance Index and Its Indicators. Washington, DC: World Bank.

————. 2016c. *Ease of Doing Business 2017.* Washington, DC: World Bank.

World Bank, European Investment Bank, CMI, and IESCO. 2013. "Transforming Arab Economies: Travelling the Knowledge and Innovation Road," World Bank, Washington, DC.

World Economic Forum. 2015. "The Global Competitiveness Report 2015-2016." Geneva.

Zottel, Siegfried, Claudia Ruiz Ortega, Douglas Randall, and Sarah Yan Xu. 2014. "Enhancing Financial Capability and Inclusion in Morocco: A Demand-Side Assessment." World Bank, Washington, DC.

CHAPTER 4

Investing in Institutions and Public Services

"Our country faces significant challenges if we are to achieve our ambitions, leaving little room for hesitation and passivity in the conduct of public policy."
—Abdellatif Jouahri

In addition to market institutions, quality public institutions and services are essential in accelerating private sector growth. Although the accelerated economic convergence scenario for Morocco through 2040 primarily involves using market solutions to develop the private sector, this does not mean that the market can by itself provide all of the solutions to the country's development problems. Public institutions and services have an important complementary role to play. There are three aspects to this role. First, the State must promote and guarantee the rule of law and justice for all. The rule of law and its application are basic components of a nation's institutional capital. When a country's legal system is unable to guarantee the protection of persons and the right to property or ensure the enforcement of contracts and settlement of disputes in a manner accepted by all parties, the openness of society and smooth commercial relations are at jeopardy. As far back as 1776, Adam Smith noted that "commerce and manufactures … can seldom flourish in any State in which there is not a certain degree of confidence in the justice of government" (Smith 1776). Second, the rule of law and justice must be guaranteed at a reasonable cost by a modern and effective administration. In other words, the government administration must also contribute to the growth of the country's productivity by increasing its own productivity, particularly that of the civil service. Third, just as the institutions in support of the market contribute to the steady improvement of goods and services offered to consumers by the private sector, State governance must ensure the increasing quality of public goods and services supplied to citizens. Each of these three essential functions of public institutions and services—respect for the rule of law, management of the civil service, and public service governance—is discussed in the following sections from the point of view of its contribution to economic development, its status in Morocco, and the outlook for reform and modernization.

Strengthening the Rule of Law and Justice

The rule of law is recognized as a basic component of a nation's institutional capital. Beyond the multiplicity of definitions of this term, the rule of law is based on a few general principles such as the generality, publicity, nonretroactivity, clarity, noncontradiction, constancy, and congruence of the law. To this can be added the independence of the judiciary, judicial review, and access to justice. By virtue of these principles, a nation is governed by the law and all of its members are equally subject to its legal codes and procedures. The rule of law protects persons, goods, and contracts. It is measured by the degree of compliance of the legal system with the standards specifically formulated. It ensures and guarantees a strict separation of public and private interests in order to prevent any culture of favoritism, privilege, or special interests at the expense of the population. The absence of the rule of law promotes corruption, patronage, and a poor allocation of economic resources and can even result in violence in the settlement of conflicts and threaten the social peace.

Morocco's new constitution strengthens the rights of citizens to participate in and monitor public affairs. The first consideration in enabling citizens to effectively exercise their rights is access to information. The right to access public information is an essential right under the 2011 constitution. The legislation being prepared should be in keeping with the spirit of the constitution and be implemented in such a way as to strengthen the transparency and accountability of the government and the public sector in practice and to support informed citizen engagement in public affairs. Beyond its intrinsic value, greater access to information represents a potentially important source of growth and employment. A growing body of literature suggests that the wealth of information and data produced by the public sector has a market value that can lead to substantial economic profits. Consequently, improved and seamless access to information in the public sector (for example, laws and regulations, public contracts, economic and social statistics, or data on education) can save businesses significant expenditure and reduce risks. In some sectors, the reuse and combination of public information and data can also lead to important dynamic gains in the form of the development of new products, services, and processes. To fully benefit from these advantages, Morocco should develop a sound legal and institutional framework to guarantee the new constitutional law and its effective implementation.

The Rule of Law and Economic Development

Well-functioning legal institutions and a government subject to the rule of law are generally considered essential conditions for economic development. Since the time of Adam Smith we have known that economic activity cannot develop "in any state which does not enjoy a regular administration of justice"

(Smith 1776). If individuals and businesses lack the confidence that contracts will be enforced and that the fruits of their productive labor will be protected, their incentive to engage in a productive activity and invest will be seriously eroded. In contrast, legal systems that provide solid protection for investors promote the development of sophisticated financial markets, increase the ability of economies to bear risk, and encourage entrepreneurship and economic growth by spreading risk over a multitude of investors.

The power of legal and judicial reforms to spur economic development is supported by a growing body of research. The capacity of national legal institutions to protect property rights, reduce transaction costs, and prevent coercion can be decisive in determining whether economic development takes place. According to the Economic Freedom of the World Index, which measures the consistency of a nation's legal structure in terms of the rule of law, unbiased enforcement of contracts, independence of the judiciary, and protection of property rights, all countries with sound legal systems on average perform much better economically than countries with weak legal systems. The conclusion, corroborated by numerous studies, indicates that the more the rule of law is respected, the richer a country grows over the long term (Knack and Keefer 1995; Kaufmann and Kraay 2002; Butkiewicz and Yanikkaya 2006). A major explanatory factor is that without a legal system capable of enforcing contracts and protecting property rights, trade will occur mostly among mutually trusting parties and cover only a relatively small geographic or market area. The gains from what Douglass North, winner of the Nobel Prize for Economics, called "depersonalized exchange," that is, trade between parties that do not know each other and will probably never meet, then go unrealized (North 1990).

The impact of the rule of law on economic development depends both on the real content of the law and on its application, particularly through an independent and effective judicial administration. Poor governance and corruption can make the codified law ineffective and harm development. An independent, effective judiciary that is free of corruption thus plays a central role in the promotion of the rule of law and development of society. Objective measures of the independence of the judiciary that look only at de jure factors such as the judicial system or the force of judicial decisions under the law are not necessarily associated with long-term growth (Glaeser and Shleifer 2001). In contrast, the de facto independence of the judiciary can positively influence the growth of per capita real gross domestic product (GDP) (Feld and Voigt 2003). This finding confirms the risk of "institutional isomorphism" (Di Maggio and Powell 1983). Thus, in the current debate on the law and development, the question is not whether legal reform is feasible or whether it can promote development, but determining what types of legal reforms would be most appropriate in the local context (Davis and Trebilcock 2008).

Judicial reforms that aim to introduce the rule of law and ensure that it is respected must be part of broader efforts aimed at making legal systems more democratic and more favorable to the free operation of the markets. Beyond measures aimed at strengthening the power and independence of the judiciary, facilitating access to dispute resolution mechanisms, accelerating trials, and professionalizing judges and the bar, judicial reforms should encompass other reforms that are equally important for the development of the market. These include the drafting or revision of commercial codes, bankruptcy laws, and laws on corporations. This comprehensive approach should also involve the overhaul of the regulatory bodies and the training of justice officials in the drafting of legislation favorable to private investment.

Ensuring that the rule of law is respected and guaranteeing the protection of persons, property, and contracts is necessary both in principle and for economic efficiency. Looking at the protection of persons, the civil conflicts currently raging in a number of countries in the Middle East and North Africa perfectly illustrate the harmful impact of insecurity and violence against persons on economic growth. Restoring "law and order" and controlling crime are thus important preconditions for any other social and economic objectives. Moreover, in the case of the protection of goods, it is generally acknowledged that the stronger the protection of property rights, the greater the incentive to work, save, and invest and the more effective the operation of the economy. Peruvian economist Hernando De Soto is renowned for having stated that the main constraint preventing many countries around the world from profiting from capitalism is the incapacity to transform existing assets, particularly those held by the poor, into productive capital (De Soto 2000). Sounder property rights considerably increase the incentive to accumulate physical and human capital. Rules guaranteeing the enforcement of contracts improve the predictability of development projects, reduce the cost of trade, favor transactions, and can open the path to competition and more egalitarian participation in commerce for all. In particular, impartial, low-cost enforcement procedures for contracts provide the necessary incentive for the conclusion of complex trade agreements, thus facilitating trade and economic growth.

A recent examination of commercial law in the Middle East and North Africa indicates that the main commercial laws—the laws on corporations, commercial leases or sales, collateral, and insolvency and bankruptcy—do not sufficiently protect persons, property, and contracts (World Bank 2014a). Commercial law in the region does not offer market operators the necessary degree of certainty and predictability owing to the persistence of certain prohibitive, overly rigid, or out-of-date rules and the lack of clarity of legal provisions, which are often too vague to provide appropriate guidance to market operators and judges.

Inconsistent Reforms of the Rule of Law in Morocco

In recent years, the government of Morocco has undertaken several reforms to strengthen the rule of law, particularly the fundamental rights of citizens via the 2011 constitution and the adoption of a Justice System Reform Charter. The new constitution introduced a number of new political and social rights in the area of "fundamental rights and freedoms" (the right to life and security of the person, the right to physical and moral integrity and the respect of privacy, the presumption of innocence and the right to a fair trial and legal aid, access to information, the right to health care, the right to social protection and decent housing, and the right to issue petitions). At the same time, the Justice System Reform Charter (the Charter) lists ambitious general objectives for the reform of the justice sector, particularly to improve the guarantees for due process and the right not to be subject to inhumane treatment (prisoner conditions, protection of the rights of suspects, legal aid, alternatives to incarceration). Moreover, the institutional framework intended to supervise the protection of fundamental human rights has also been strengthened with the expansion of the mandate of the National Human Rights Council to enable it to intervene more actively in the prevention of human rights violations, including the protection of persons and goods, and to regularly publish reports on human rights.

Despite these general reforms, the rule of law and judicial system in Morocco still face clear challenges (World Bank 2014b). According to the Rule of Law Index (World Justice Project 2016), the main weaknesses relate to criminal justice (particularly the lack of independence of the judiciary), fundamental rights (particularly the right to privacy), and corruption (particularly in the judicial system) (see figure 4.1). A major reform launched in 2002 focused on the revision of the Family Code and the Code of Criminal Procedure, the creation of specialized commercial and administrative courts, and the modernization of the courts. These reforms are under way, but various international studies and evaluations have shown that the judicial authority still suffers from a poor reputation in the eyes of the general public (inefficiency, lack of independence, and corruption). According to the 2012–14 Arab Barometer, fewer than one-quarter of Moroccans questioned consider their judicial system to be effective, while in Jordan or Kuwait, for example, more than three-quarters of those questioned have favorable views of their justice system. In Transparency International's Corruption Perceptions Index (2016), Morocco has regressed and is now ranked 90th, outperformed by several countries in Sub-Saharan Africa and the Middle East and North Africa. The commercial courts, created more recently, performed slightly better, as indicated by surveys of businesses on the enforcement of contracts for the Doing Business Index (2017). The main dysfunctions identified as obstacles to the rule of law in Morocco and the establishment of a modern state—in the sense of a strict separation of private and public interests—are related less to the laws than to the institutions and individuals responsible for their application, a topic that will be discussed further in chapter 6 on Morocco's social capital. The momentum of the justice reform thus needs to be reestablished. According to the Bank Al-Maghrib's 2016 Annual Report, this is a fundamental task in terms of both human and social rights and also for the improvement of the business climate, investment, and entrepreneurship. The completion of this project in a reasonable period of time will change the negative perception of justice held by investors and the general public (Bank Al-Maghrib 2016).

Figure 4.1 Rule of Law Index for Morocco, the Middle East and North Africa Region, and Lower-Middle-Income Countries

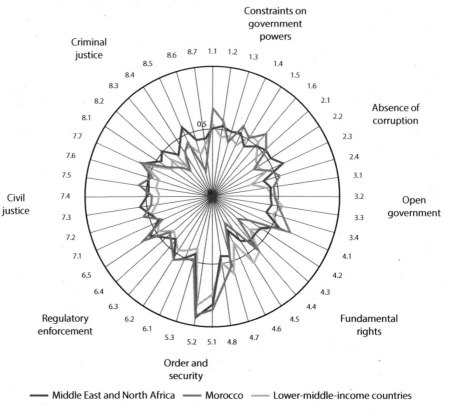

Source: World Justice Project, Rule of Law Index, 2016.
Note: Each number around the circle represents an indicator.

Protection of Persons

By improving its judicial system, particularly in terms of procedural justice (right to life and the protection of persons) and criminal justice (impartiality and anticorruption), Morocco would ensure more effective legal protection and better security of persons (see figure 4.2). As shown by existing specialized documentation,[1] Morocco's scores are relatively low in the areas of protection of physical integrity and security of persons, although Morocco has taken important measures to end the most flagrant human rights violations.

Overall, Morocco's performance is poorer than that of other middle-income countries (lower or upper) in terms of the right to life and security of the person (World Justice Project 2016). Morocco does not have sufficient safeguards against torture, the existing guarantees often being insufficiently respected and investigations of allegations of torture rarely being completed. Moreover, officials (judges and prosecutors) responsible for preventing torture and other abusive treatment and sanctioning those responsible are often hesitant to act and

Figure 4.2 Legal Protection and Security of the Person, 2008–12

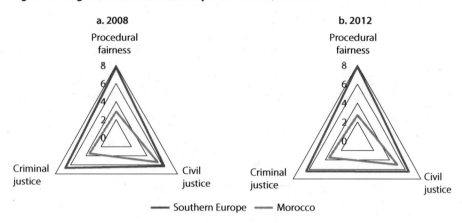

Source: The Human Freedom Index 2015: A Global Measurement of Personal, Civil, and Economic Freedom.

there are no mechanisms for collecting credible evidence on abusive treatment or effective reparations for the victims of torture and abusive treatment in Morocco. Morocco also ranks lower than other middle-income countries regarding protection against arbitrary arrest and detention, and the control of abusive police practices seems ineffective and information on sanctions very limited. Last, in the area of legal aid, legislation guaranteeing access to a lawyer during the detention period and the assignment of counsel by the courts for the poorest prisoners is not systematically respected. Although Morocco records low levels of the violent crimes that would justify pretrial detention, such detentions often extend beyond the legal limits (which can sometimes mean that prisoners receive shorter sentences than their period of incarceration) and judges remain reluctant to use substitute penalties, which further aggravates the problem of prolonged detention.

Protection of Property

The protection of goods also remains a challenge for Morocco and constitutes an obstacle to investment. Morocco is ranked higher than the average among countries in the Middle East and North Africa in terms of the protection of general property rights,[2] but remains below the ranking of many competitor countries. According to the 2017 Doing Business indicator on transferring property, Morocco was ranked 87th (out of 189 countries) in 2016 and is outperformed by a number of emerging countries (see figure 4.3). Land insecurity and poor performance of the property market are major obstacles to investment and industrial productivity. More than 40 percent of Moroccan businesses consider access to industrial property to be a major or severe constraint on their development, as against fewer than 10 percent in Turkey (World Bank 2009). The legislative framework governing the land tenure system is fragmented (customary systems, Islamic laws, French-based legislation),

Figure 4.3 Distance to Frontier for Transferring Property, 2016

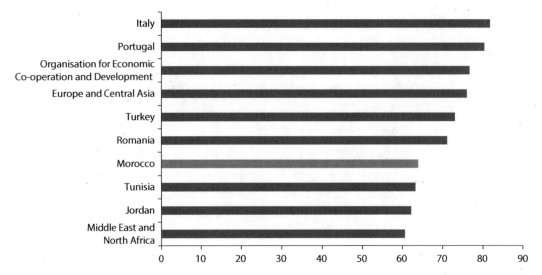

Source: World Bank 2017a.
Note: The distance to frontier score benchmarks economies with respect to regulatory practice, showing the absolute distance to the best performance in each Doing Business indicator. An economy's distance to frontier score is indicated on a scale from 0 to 100, where 0 represents the worst performance and 100 the frontier.

out of date, and ineffective (most property transactions are informal, contributing to a real insecurity of property titles), expropriation practices are opaque, and the registration of property rights is complicated and costly (World Bank 2008). In addition, the current legal context does not favor land ownership by women and Morocco is ranked at the bottom of the lower-middle-income countries in terms of the percentage of farms headed by women (see chapter 6).

Protection of Contracts

Morocco's performance is also very mixed in the area of contract enforcement: processing times are good on the whole, but the number and cost of procedures are not, reflecting an enormous variation in terms of the effectiveness of the commercial courts. Despite the reforms undertaken (modernization of the commercial courts, creation of the position of enforcement judge to supervise the enforcement of contracts), Morocco is ranked 57th in the 2017 Doing Business Index in terms of its capacity to enforce contracts, as measured by the number of judicial procedures, the related costs, and the time required. Although Morocco is comparable to many middle-income countries and other countries in the Middle East and North Africa, its performance in this area is again below that of a number of competitor countries such as Turkey or Romania (see figure 4.4). Moreover, although Morocco has invested massively in its commercial courts, this has not yet been reflected in an improved performance of these courts over time.

Figure 4.4 Distance to Frontier for Contract Enforcement, 2016

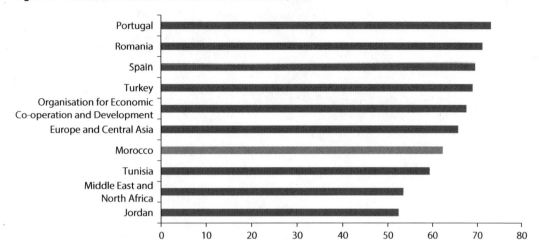

Source: World Bank 2017a.
Note: The distance to frontier score benchmarks economies with respect to regulatory practice, showing the absolute distance to the best performance in each Doing Business indicator. An economy's distance to frontier score is indicated on a scale from 0 to 100, where 0 represents the worst performance and 100 the frontier.

A breakdown of Morocco's performance in the area of contract enforcement shows that it recorded good results for processing times and poor results for the number of judicial procedures and their cost. For the latter measure, Morocco is ranked second to last with 40 procedures, ahead of Algeria, which has 45 procedures. The performance of the Moroccan commercial courts also varies considerably from one city to another. It would benefit Morocco to examine the sectors and geographic areas where performance is best to understand the reasons why some courts or procedures are more effective than others.

Investing in the Rule of Law and Justice

Effective implementation of the new rights provided by the constitution and the Justice System Reform Charter would be an important step forward in strengthening the rule of law. Additional provisions will be necessary to ensure that the new laws are in keeping with the spirit of the constitution and that they are accompanied by appropriate implementing provisions. For example, according to many Moroccan nongovernmental organizations (NGOs), the draft law on access to information approved by Parliament does not seem to be in keeping with the spirit of the constitution in terms of expanding the scope of data accessible to citizens. The list of exceptions could make this right—which is essential to good governance and accountability—meaningless.[3] Moreover, Morocco should adopt a strategy aimed at ensuring that all ancillary legislation will enter into effect within a reasonable period of time. Without such a legislative framework, it will be difficult to apply the laws, with judges and other public officials benefiting from significant discretionary authority, particularly in providing services related to the protection of persons and goods.

Sequencing and prioritization would make the commitment to implement the new provisions provided by the Charter more credible. In particular, the Justice System Reform Charter would benefit from a comprehensive monitoring and evaluation framework to assess implementation and guide the new reforms.

Improving the Security of Persons

The principle of the security of persons is guaranteed by the 2011 constitution. The effective consolidation of this principle through measures protecting from, providing recourse against, and monitoring abusive practices would send a positive signal regarding the country's commitment to this constitutional principle. Safeguard measures against the torture and abusive treatment of prisoners should be enhanced and implemented effectively, particularly through increased control and monitoring by the Ministry of Justice and Liberties of the application of its instructions and the publication of the information collected, and also by notifying families of detentions, respecting the rights of prisoners, and providing effective and, if appropriate, free legal aid. In addition, the recourse mechanisms offered to the victims of torture and abusive treatment should be enhanced (access to medical, psychiatric, and forensic expertise, for example) to facilitate their compensation under equitable conditions. Better monitoring of arbitrary arrests and detentions and an increased role for civil society organizations and families would also help to prevent the persistence of such acts.

Strengthening the legal aid system and better controlling recourse to pretrial detention (and using alternatives) would help to better guarantee equality of access to justice. Without waiting for the completion of the legislative reform projects concerning legal aid, the existing mechanisms for the provision of legal aid could be improved, particularly to guarantee respect of the right to free access to a lawyer, including using additional budgetary resources. Moreover, precise criteria should define the circumstances justifying pretrial detention. The Ministry of Justice and Liberties should better monitor the respect of legal deadlines. Moreover, alternatives to pretrial detention could be developed and implemented (more systematic release of persons accused of minor offenses pending their trial).

Strengthening the rule of law requires the implementation of major reforms in governance and justice, particularly to increase the security of persons. Morocco should strengthen the transparency of the activities of officials, particularly in the arrest and detention of citizens, and land administration practices. To this end, key performance indicators and standards should be introduced, for example, as well as data collection standards (including user satisfaction) to increase effectiveness and accountability and better guarantee equality of treatment by the courts. The political landscape still lacks a comprehensive strategy on land administration that responds to the specific challenges faced in Morocco, that is, access to land, land protection, and effective management of public and private lands.

Improving the Protection of Property

Because the status quo may hinder investment and development opportunities, the protection of property must be improved to ensure that the principles of equity and equality are respected. This involves making the system of land governance, particularly the land tenure regime (divided into the official land tenure regime based on official registration and the traditional, customary regime), more predictable. The legislative framework could be clarified through the adoption of a single comprehensive property law. Moreover, simplification measures and tax measures should be taken to ensure that land transactions are increasingly recorded in the land registry and the government could ensure that a system combining formal and informal dispute resolution mechanisms is genuinely accessible to all citizens to better guarantee the security of property rights. The opaqueness of the current expropriation regime also calls for measures to clarify the compensation criteria and processes, as well as the publication of relevant reliable data that will allow for better monitoring of the administrative use of public lands. To support changes to the status quo in terms of equality of access to land for women and men, the government should try new approaches to make the property rights of women more secure (see chapter 6).

Improving the Enforcement of Contracts

Last, an in-depth review of enforcement procedures and processes should help to improve and standardize the performance of the courts in the enforcement of contracts, which is another important factor in promoting economic activity. An in-depth review should identify the bottlenecks along the enforcement process (timetable, costs, and procedural steps), include a detailed survey of users, and thus help to overcome practical and procedural obstacles to the provision and effective enforcement of services throughout the national territory.

Modernizing the Civil Service

Twenty years ago, in its report "The State in a Changing World," the World Bank emphasized the importance of a competent and effective civil service in supporting development and reducing poverty (World Bank 1997). The state does indeed play an important economic role in all societies. A large portion of the national product is devoted to public consumption, public investment, and public transfers to households. The civil service is responsible for increasingly complex activities; it must guarantee the rule of law and effectively perform the state's sovereign and redistributional functions. By facilitating the operations of the markets, public institutions play an indirect but essential role in increasing productivity and ensuring the development of the private sector. This section focuses on ways in which the civil service can, through its operations and its own modernization, directly help to increase Morocco's productivity.

Modernization of the State and the Productivity of Nations

A functional civil service can contribute directly to productivity gains and the well-being of the population. Civil services have a democratic and ethical function; they should serve society and the law, protect the population, and function in a sustainable manner (Demmke and Moilanen 2010). In many respects, the quality of the life of citizens depends on an effective civil service. Max Weber is among the precursors who emphasized the fundamental role played by the bureaucracy (defined as a form of administrative organization with specific structural characteristics) to supplement market institutions and promote both economic growth and well-being (Weber 1922). According to Weber, a civil service can be more effective than other forms of bureaucratic organization and directly contribute more to development as long as it is organized around the following principles: meritocracy in recruitment and predictability and transparency in the criteria for advancement and promotion. Many empirical studies have confirmed the relations between a more or less "Weberian" state and economic growth (Evans and Rauch 1999). The World Bank's recent World Development Report confirms the importance of the role played by a competent bureaucracy in the economic and social progress of nations, a competent bureaucracy constituting, together with the rule of law (as indicated above) and the accountability of governments, one of the three fundamental conditions of a modern and effective state (World Bank 2017b).

The efficiency and effectiveness of the civil service depend largely on the mobilization of the talents of public sector officials and recognition of their skills. The quality of human resources management (HRM) largely determines the performance of the civil service. Historically, government employees were considered the servants of a sovereign authority and in exchange for their loyalty, neutrality, and impartiality received better and more stable employment conditions than those in the rest of society (OECD 2008). Beginning in the 19th century, many of the countries that are today developed applied this approach to construct relatively effective, modern professional bureaucracies. During the 20th century, a number of emerging countries were also successful in transforming weak, often corrupt, and patronage-based public services into more meritocratic and transparent institutions. These new administrative systems were based in part on the principle that meritocracy and a long career made it possible to build an esprit de corps and guaranteed the commitment of each to serve the collective objectives. This esprit de corps was largely based on intangible factors: social recognition, government officials' understanding of their missions, a shared identity among colleagues, and so forth (Akerlof and Kranton 2010). The armed forces are emblematic of this intangible esprit de corps: commitment and giving of oneself to serve one's country, a heightened sense of responsibility and duty, and a limitless solidarity in the service of an honorable mission. An individual heroic act is recognized by a medal and not a bonus.

However, in recent decades, traditional civil services have often encountered serious difficulties in adapting to the changing role of the state. They have tended to be risk averse, to inhibit innovation, and to impede the adaptation of employees' qualifications and skills to a changing environment, particularly in the provision of services that meet the new needs of users. In many countries, the esprit de corps that is supposed to improve the performance, effectiveness, and accountability of civil servants has tended to be undermined, gradually replaced by failing civil services characterized by their incapacity to attract and retain skills, and overstaffed, unproductive civil services with demotivated officials who seem more concerned with serving themselves than serving their fellow citizens. This situation feeds a widespread perception in the general public that civil servants exist in a privileged, protected environment that is disconnected from the economic reality of the world around them.

Throughout the world, the changing role of the state requires a change in the design of public services and the civil service. In particular, statutory employment conditions defined centrally are considered in many countries to be an obstacle to the development of effective administrations focusing on service to the citizen. Improving the quality of personnel management, particularly making civil servants more accountable and motivating them, lies at the heart of the essential changes needed to increase productivity in the civil service and improve the quality of services provided. International experience shows that countries generally implement the same major reforms to improve the quality of their personnel management: decentralization of HRM responsibilities and increased empowerment of managers, greater flexibility in recruitment and career development policies, a stronger focus on individual and organizational performance management, and a general trend toward de-bureaucratization (Demmke and Moilanen 2010). According to the OECD, the modernization of civil services generally involves six transitions, all of which are essential: (i) toward decentralized systems of working conditions, (ii) toward nonstatutory and contractual systems, (iii) toward job and competency systems rather than career systems, (iv) toward delegated management systems, (v) toward systems of remuneration aligned with private sector practices, and (vi) toward common and nonspecific pension plans. These transitions take place in the context of a change of paradigm concerning the functioning of the administration, which moves from a so-called command and control version toward a performance-based managerial paradigm (OECD 2011).

In recent decades, a number of OECD countries have reformed the public employment framework, particularly by aligning it with general labor laws. In New Zealand, the special civil service status was abolished in the 1990s through an alignment with private sector rules. The Scandinavian countries, Switzerland, and other European countries maintain the civil servant status for very specific groups of public sector employees, such as judges, the police, and other employees responsible for sovereign functions of the state (Demmke and Moilanen 2010). Many emerging countries, such as Singapore, Mexico, and the Republic of Korea, have followed their example, gradually replacing lifelong jobs in the civil service with private contract positions (excluding positions related to sovereignty).

Making such changes is a delicate task given the many advantages acquired by civil servants and their generally strong union representation. International experience seems to indicate that it is essential that these reforms be implemented gradually in a context of sound, strategic workforce planning (OECD 2011). A review of successful experiences in the modernization of the civil service also clearly underscores the need to involve civil servants upstream in the development of new policies, to propose innovative solutions making it possible to manage staff reductions or redeployments as best as possible, and to consider each civil servant as a potential asset and not as a cost to be eliminated. As also shown by the experience of a number of countries, reduction and reassignment measures should not be isolated, but, on the contrary, should take place in the context of broader reforms. Recruitment freezes are the most detrimental approach to downsizing because they are indiscriminate and abrupt and limit the ability of organizations to restructure and rescale. In contrast, demographic changes and financial pressures often provide the conditions for effective reform of administrations to ensure appropriate staffing levels and skills.

Incomplete Civil Service Reforms in Morocco

In 2002, Morocco embarked on a program of state reform intended to increase the productivity and efficiency of its civil service and to adapt it to better suit its essential missions.[4] At the heart of this civil service reform program was the modernization of the HRM system, particularly using tools to assess skills and performance. New transparent performance assessment procedures were introduced for civil servants. The institutional framework for training of public officials was strengthened to facilitate their upgrading and adaptation to the new requirements and missions of the civil service. In keeping with the 2011 constitution, the General Civil Service Regulations (SGFP) were further aligned with the principles of merit, transparency, and equality of opportunity, particularly via the new performance-based terms and conditions for promotion and the more widespread use of competition as the main method of recruitment. The current regulations prohibit the holding of multiple posts concurrently and double-dipping, and make the redeployment of civil servants an HRM tool. They authorize the recruitment of officials under fixed-term contracts and for defined missions and tasks.

Despite these efforts, the General Civil Service Regulations in Morocco remain insufficient to respond to the needs of modern HRM (Ministry of the Civil Service and Modernization of Administration 2013). The changes made to the SGFP do not replace a genuine overhaul of the regulations, which remains necessary to allow the civil service to evolve in line with changes in Moroccan society. The SGFP, which dates back to 1958 and which, supplemented by a multitude of individual laws, still governs the civil service, does not facilitate the use of modern performance-based management instruments or the effective mobilization of human resources that would enable the state to fully play its new role of regulator and facilitator. The civil service continues to operate on the basis of notions of status and seniority, whereas the concepts of position and performance should be the operating principles of a modern administration. In the current context, remuneration does not compensate for performance, whether individual or collective. Seniority remains the main criterion for promotion and the remuneration structure is rigid and sometimes even inequitable. Gaps in the recruitment strategy, the existence of barriers to staff mobility in the public sector and between it and the local and regional governments, and the poor supervision and regulation of the civil service impede the introduction of a more effective and efficient HRM system. In addition, the provisions of the SGFP on disciplinary procedures have proven to be ineffective or impossible to implement. Many ministerial departments that suffer from disciplinary problems, particularly absenteeism or ghost workers, are powerless to deal with these challenges, which threaten the quality and continuity of public services. Last, as summed up by His Majesty King Mohammed VI in his address to Parliament, "State agencies are suffering from several shortcomings, including weak performance and issues relating to the quality of the services provided to citizens. They also suffer from an inflated workforce and from the lack of competence and absence of a sense of responsibility among many employees."[5]

In Morocco, the reform of the civil service has also aimed to control operating costs, particularly the wage bill. To this end, two key measures were adopted: an early retirement program (which affected almost 40,000 civil servants in the mid-2000s) and a policy to control staffing levels through the simple replacement of retirements each year. These measures were essentially aimed at controlling staffing levels in the civil service. However, starting in 2009, pay increases and large-scale recruitments to deal with the effects of the international economic crisis and then to calm the social climate eroded the progress that had been made and reversed the downward trend of the wage bill. As a result, the relatively strict recruitment policy in place since the mid-1990s, which involved recruiting some 7,000 new civil servants each year (corresponding to the number of departures), was abandoned. Since 2008, between 13,000 and 26,200 new civil servants have been recruited each year (see figure 4.5). During the period 2006–14, the number of recruitments net of retirements totaled 87,730, almost 2.3 times the number of early retirements in 2005. The only possible justification for increasing public employment should be the provision of high-quality public services, as it is clear that creating civil service positions does not create jobs (Tirole 2016). In 2015 Morocco had some 585,500 civil servants in the central government, in addition to 180,000 officials in the local governments and almost 350,000 in the security services and armed forces.

In Morocco, the cost of operating the civil service is high, particularly in comparison with the services provided. On average, civil service wages are twice as high as private sector wages. They are almost triple the guaranteed minimum wage in the private sector and more than three times per capita gross domestic product (GDP). In 2015, the central government wage bill represented 10.6 percent of GDP (and close to 14 percent including local civil

Figure 4.5 Morocco: Central Government Staffing Levels, 2003–15

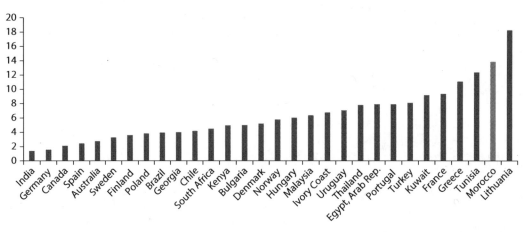

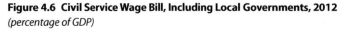

■ Recruitments ▨ Retirement ▨ Net recruitements ── Headcount

Source: Ministry of Economy and Finance.

Figure 4.6 Civil Service Wage Bill, Including Local Governments, 2012
(percentage of GDP)

Source: World Development Indicators, World Bank.
Note: GDP = gross domestic product.

servants) and 40 percent of the government budget, making Morocco one of the countries with the highest total wage bill among competitor emerging countries (see figure 4.6). At the same time, as explained in greater detail later, various studies conducted by the Economic, Social, and Environmental Council (CESE), the Audit Office, and the National Anticorruption Office (INPC) underscore the dissatisfaction of users with the quality of public services.

Such a high wage bill tends to burden public finances, reinforce spending rigidities, and reduce the government's latitude to reallocate this expenditure to priority programs, particularly social programs. The implementation of the provisions of the new Budget Framework Law (LOLF) in early 2016 could resolve this problem by placing a ceiling on the overall wage bill, if greater latitude is given to the various ministries to manage their personnel appropriations autonomously.

Developing a More Productive Civil Service

The Moroccan experience over the past two decades confirms that, as elsewhere in the world, modernizing the civil service is a delicate task and the results are often frustrating. In addition to the difficulty in designing a reform suited to the country's problems, there is the problem of difficult implementation through administrative structures that do not necessarily have the required motivation or performance capacity. As underscored by His Majesty King Mohammed VI, "The efficiency of State agencies is a yardstick of a nation's progress, and until the citizen's relationship with them improves, Morocco will continue to be classified as a Third World country, or even Fourth or Fifth World country."[6] The recommendations proposed in this section are part of the "advanced regionalization" process and the implementation of the provisions of the 2011 constitution. They are first of all aimed at consolidating the reforms under way by introducing notions of performance and results in the management of human resources to make the civil service more efficient. Broader recommendations concern delegated services, the digitalization of public services, and the sharing of services and propose the opening of a national dialogue on the role and missions of the civil servant in the 21st century.

Successfully Implementing Decentralization and Deconcentration

Advanced regionalization has arrived at just the right time to attempt to correct the institutional and central, regional, and local governance imperfections and to establish the authority, means, and mechanisms to establish a better balance in the distribution of powers among the central government, the regions, and the local authorities. For this to happen, Morocco must embark upon a systemic decentralization and deconcentration process by organizing a gradual genuine transfer of decision-making powers with the deployment of the appropriate skills for assuming governance at the local level, and the corresponding resources and means to the appropriate local and regional levels. The process will need to be particularly careful and diligent to avoid deconcentration resulting in the multiplication of deconcentrated departments, a pure and simple duplication of central government organization charts, or the development of a regional bureaucracy without any real decision-making authority or adequate means for action. While the advanced regionalization proposal constitutes a significant opportunity for local democracy and inclusive local and regional development, particularly with a view to the emergence of regional economic centers, its success requires a careful approach to avoid redundancies in decision-making centers and ensure a rational use of resources. International experience shows that if it is poorly planned, it can become a financial black hole (Bank Al-Maghrib 2016).

Modernizing the Civil Service

Modernizing the civil service requires a complete overhaul of the civil service regulations. International experience shows that a modern civil service can reconcile the notions of status and career and useful public employment. First, the regulations must be revised to recognize the position as the central component of the HRM and promotion process. In this new regulatory framework, all recruitment should aim to fill vacant positions responding to clearly defined needs. The overhaul of the civil service regulations should also facilitate the establishment of a modern HRM system through the systematic use of benchmarks for the positions and skills sought. It should also allow for deconcentrated management of human resources.

Combating absenteeism should be a priority, as it is an obstacle to the accessibility and quality of public services while representing a significant financial cost for the country. Weak institutions supplying public goods, particularly education and health, are obstacles to economic development in many countries (Chaudhury and others 2006). The Moroccan civil service continues to suffer from absenteeism despite measures taken to enhance control over absences and efforts to apply disciplinary actions. The circular issued by the Head of Government in 2012 calls upon the civil service to strictly apply the legal provisions concerning absence from work and asks the supervisors directly concerned to assume their responsibility for dealing with unjustified absences, particularly by regularly monitoring absences and preparing the relevant reports. A website has also been set up to track absenteeism. It is important that the new civil service regulations simplify the provisions regarding the disciplinary regime to allow for their systematic application in a framework of greater transparency and accountability.

Second, performance management of civil servants should be results based. A rigorous, accurate, and impartial results-based system of annual performance assessment for civil servants should lie at the heart of the HRM process. The assessments should take place at all levels of the administrative hierarchy. Their aim should be to qualitatively assess the achievement of the results approved by the staff member at the beginning of the assessment cycle. The assessment should be designed and perceived as a process of dialogue and constructive appreciation that recognizes strengths and good practices and potentially identifies opportunities for improvement to overcome any insufficient results identified. To enhance the credibility of the system, the results of assessments should constitute basic criteria for any advancement, promotion, or appointment to supervisory positions.

The current performance assessment and management system does not effectively handle good or poor performance by civil servants. To improve performance management, the civil service should implement a unified and transparent performance framework that can identify and classify the various levels of performance rigorously and equitably. The related assessment system should make it possible to identify high-performing officials and those performing poorly. The latter should benefit from individual monitoring and performance improvement plans. This means that all managers should be given responsibility for implementing the performance framework and be accountable for their staff's performance quality and attendance through their own performance objectives.

Third, a reform of civil service remuneration should improve its effectiveness. If Morocco's civil service is to recruit, retain, and compensate the necessary skills for more efficient public services, the country should introduce a new system of remuneration for its officials that is motivating, consistent, and transparent and compensates for the effort and degree of complexity of the job performed. The current remuneration system could be replaced by a modern regime that takes account of equity and operating cost control requirements. This new system, which would be simplified, unified, consistent, and equitable, should help to improve staff motivation. In addition, making the remuneration system more flexible should make it possible to respond more effectively and equitably to pressures for wage increases in the context of collective agreements.

Fourth, strengthening human capital within the civil service through a coherent and effective continuing training policy would benefit the Moroccan government. A training policy to update skills on an ongoing basis is today essential to improve the effectiveness and efficiency of the civil service and thus the quality of public policies and services. The civil servant training policy should be based on a regularly updated assessment of skills leading to the design of training plans for all members of the civil service. To strengthen regionalization, which assigns more tasks to the local and regional governments and increases the possibilities for delegations of services to the private sector, more civil servants will need to acquire skills in the design, management, and monitoring of contracts and projects. Their participation in training programs should flow from individual annual training proposals discussed with each civil servant, particularly in the context of the annual performance assessment. Active, positively assessed participation in training programs should constitute one of the criteria for promotion or appointment to supervisory positions.

Reducing Operating Costs

Morocco should seek to reduce the operating cost of its civil service to improve its efficiency. Making the Moroccan civil service more efficient requires two types of actions. First, it will not be possible to control the wage bill without effective career and position management in order to avoid recourse to non-regulatory measures for exceptional promotions and wage increases associated with job reclassifications. These exceptional promotions and wage increases, which were negotiated in the context of the social dialogue, have been expensive. It also appears necessary to rigorously implement the Budget Framework Law (LOLF), which aims to cap personnel appropriations. The line ministries should be allowed to manage their remuneration appropriations and their budget accounting. This is necessary to make managers accountable and also to make program management meaningful: currently, ministry program budgets exclude remuneration, which can represent more than 90 percent of their recurring costs (in the case of the National Education ministry, for example). The transfer of responsibility for the management of personnel appropriations to the line ministries should, however, be accompanied by the requirement that they respect a sectoral system of capped appropriations to ensure consistency between HRM actions and macroeconomic fiscal constraints. Moreover, it is essential that the government maintain the discipline that it established in controlling recruitment in order to stabilize civil service staffing levels, that is, creating only the number of budget items needed for the effective operation of the government.

Envisaging a Civil Service 2.0 to Create a More Modern, Productive, and Ultimately More Strategic Civil Service

Beyond these reforms, which have been partially undertaken, more ambitious reforms should aim to transform the civil service into a more productive organization. Greater encouragement should be given to innovation in the provision of services and increased use of information and communications technologies (ICTs), particularly by continuing its program for the automation of citizen and business services, to ensure more rapid, more transparent, and more efficient services.[7]

The Moroccan civil service must also become more efficient and more strategic. In this context, recourse to delegated services in partnership with the private sector could be expanded to all departments when it allows for better quality of service at a lower cost for taxpayers. A number of delegated services (relating to the distribution of water and electricity, public transport, sanitation, and hygiene) do not seem to have achieved the expected outcomes, probably owing to weaknesses in the design of the specifications (in terms of the quality of the public service or investment expected) and in the monitoring and evaluation system (CESE 2015). The capacity of the officials responsible for preparation of the specifications for delegated services and for their operational monitoring should be improved by upgrading competencies in the area of management of delegated projects, particularly at the local level.

Recourse to shared services should become the rule. Experiments conducted in a number of countries show that some cross-cutting services can be shared between ministerial departments through the creation of specialized units that provide these services to all departments. These solutions help improve the effectiveness of the provision of services (owing to a concentration of know-how and expertise) and reduce operating costs. Such shared services can initially include legal services, internal auditing, project management and programming expertise, and commercial procurement competencies. In the long term, shared services should gradually be expanded to become the norm, which would lead to small ministerial departments eliminating the internal units providing such services.

Last, broader strategic national discussions should be held in a transparent and open manner on the very notion of the civil service in the 21st century.

As indicated earlier, in many countries, including emerging countries that are Morocco's competitors, specific rules guaranteeing civil servants a privileged status and, in particular, a job for life have been abolished or relaxed for most positions (van der Meer, Raadschelders, and Toonen 2015). These changes have not taken place on the same scale and at the same speed as in a country such as France, which continues to inspire Morocco's institutional changes. However, Morocco should today look beyond France and other Southern European countries for inspiration from the reforms implemented by reforming countries around the world.[8] Such reforms have generally required a change in mentality and a return to core principles in terms of the role of the state: the notion of civil servants "in the service of the state" has been replaced by the notion of civil servants "in the service of the citizen," a new paradigm that seems more suited to the general public interest (Koenig 2015). Thus, the modernization of the Moroccan civil service could contribute directly to increasing the productivity and well-being of the population.

Improving Public Service Governance

After the rule of law and modernization of the civil service, good governance in public services constitutes the third essential pillar for strengthening public institutions. The capacity of governments to effectively manage public resources so as to provide high-quality public services and goods accessible to all at the lowest possible cost is an essential dimension of public sector governance. By *governance*, we mean "the manner in which public officials and institutions acquire and exercise the authority to provide public goods and services, including the delivery of basic services, infrastructure, and a sound investment climate."[9] Although the dividing line between a public good and a private good is sometimes tenuous, a public good is understood to mean a good the consumption or, more generally, use of which by one individual does not formally prevent its use by other individuals, in contrast with a private good, which can be used exclusively at a given point in time by one individual only. In the case of public goods, we speak of goods or services the use of which is nonrivalrous and nonexclusive. The provision of public goods and services is generally the responsibility of the state. Indeed, without public intervention, the production of public goods and services tends to be suboptimal, with each individual looking for a level or quality of public goods or services that is higher than that produced spontaneously in equilibrium.

Economic Importance of Good Governance

The provision of high-quality public goods and services is an essential condition for the development of the private sector and expansion of the middle class. The economic importance of public service governance relates to the fact that the cost of poor governance is high in terms of lost growth opportunities, inequality, and poverty. Thus, a particularly high-profile aspect of poor governance such as corruption is strongly and negatively correlated on average with per capita wealth.

As many empirical works have shown, corruption affects economic performance as it impacts both the volume and the composition of government revenue and expenditure. On the expenditure side, the misappropriation of resources allocated to the development of human capital, institutional capital, or social capital in favor of less productive, sustainable development activities jeopardizes growth. Similarly, if we look at the business environment, poorly established and poorly enforced property rights can lead to lower investment, which affects the accumulation of capital. The cost of corruption does not consist only or even primarily of visible misappropriated resources. The main cost is invisible: businesses that are not created, investments that are not made, loans that are not granted, or jobs that are not created owing to corruption.

Although the debate on the meaning of the causality link between the quality of institutions and economic development is ongoing, it is nonetheless clear that this link exists and that the quality of institutions constitutes a lever on which policy makers can directly act. Access for all to high-quality basic public services helps to promote opportunities for all, favors equity, and contributes to the development of the middle class (Bluhm and Szirmai 2011). Along with transfers, subsidies, and redistributions via the fiscal and tax policies, public services constitute a lever that allows the state to combat poverty and inequality by giving each individual the possibility to exploit his or her opportunities. The economic literature is rich in examples of low, medium, or high-income countries that have acted on the supply of services to promote access by the most disadvantaged populations, thereby helping to increase productivity, growth, and the revenues needed to improve services and thus creating a virtuous circle of opportunities. There is increasing evidence that improving access to public services for all and reducing inequality of opportunities, particularly those linked to the development of human capital among the very young, do not only constitute means of increasing justice and building more just societies, but also of achieving the aspirations of each individual within a society of shared prosperity.

Beyond the purely economic interests, good governance of public services positively affects the morale of the population and thus contributes to a country's social capital. Several studies conducted in the OECD countries and the Middle East and North Africa on the sense of happiness of the population underscore the importance of the quality of public services and the confidence of the citizens (Fereidouni, Najdi, and Amiri 2013; Helliwell and others 2014). When institutions are of high quality and accessible to all in a transparent way, they contribute not only to economic performance but also to the collective well-being, confidence, and public spirit and thus to the social capital (as discussed in chapter 6). The importance placed by the citizens on the way in which public services are organized highlights the need to involve the populations and communities concerned in their design, organization, and monitoring and the importance of the principle of accountability at the heart of public service governance.

Users have a clear role to play in improving public service governance and strengthening the accountability of the state. As shown in the World Bank's 2004

World Development Report, the level of expenditure on public services is not an essential and sufficient condition to guarantee the quality of those services (World Bank 2004). This report and numerous papers since have confirmed the importance of taking systematic account of institutional accountability in the provision of services and as a key aspect of their good governance. Accountability means that the actions and decisions taken by public authorities are subject to monitoring to ensure that the posted objectives correspond to the communities' needs and that these objectives are achieved. Today it is understood that good governance in public services must look at the quality of the services rendered rather than merely focusing on the inputs or importing models that are not well suited to the local context and problems (Di Maggio and Powell 1983). Figure 4.7 shows the supervisory and accountability relations between the three players in the accountability framework: public institutions, users, and service providers and managers. The route of accountability is "long" when it implies strengthening institutions as a precondition for improving services. The route is "short" when recipients of public services can directly exercise their supervisory authority over service providers.

Whatever the route of accountability chosen, improving public service governance requires placing the user at the center of the system as its beneficiary and regulator. Strengthening accountability to improve public service governance also implies taking account of all the incentives and values governing the relations between all public service players and potentially improving them. Aside from the fact that it is important to understand the motivations of service providers to improve public services, it is also important to note that the choice of incentives is based on other more important factors such as the standards, values, or cultural codes governing societies, which must be taken into account to ensure the success of reforms (World Bank 2015b).

Figure 4.7 The Long and Short Routes of Accountability

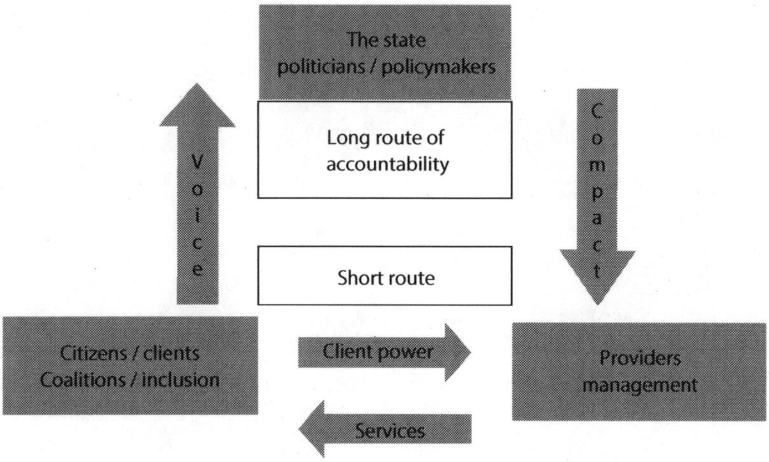

Source: World Bank 2004.

Challenges of Good Public Service Governance in Morocco

Many international governance indicators emphasize Morocco's uneven performance in comparison with other low and middle-income countries. According to these indicators, Morocco's performance is relatively good or satisfactory in comparison with countries in the region or all middle-income countries in three areas: organization of markets, performance of supreme audit institutions, and ease of registering property (figure 4.8). However, Morocco does less well in comparison with the same countries in terms of the independence of justice, control and transparency of the budget, efforts to combat corruption, and the use of bribes in the private sector. Its performance is also deteriorating in the areas of political participation, freedom of the press, and the three indicators related to governance and the private sector (ease of starting a business, ease of registering a property, and bribes).

An in-depth assessment of public service governance conducted by the CESE underscored the high degree of dissatisfaction of Moroccans and the scope of the reforms to be undertaken. In early 2011, CESE took up the subject of public service governance. The findings published in 2013 are detailed and conclusive: they indicate that a very large proportion of Moroccans is dissatisfied with public services and that the services are provided to them as though they were a favor and not a right (figure 4.9) (CESE 2013).

The CESE report analyzed the numerous failings of the system in detail and indicated avenues for a comprehensive reform that has, in part, inspired the reforms undertaken since that time. The CESE assessment emphasizes that the

Figure 4.8 Governance Indicators, 2014

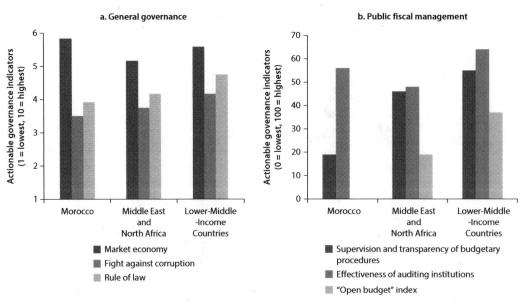

Source: Actionable Governance Indicators, World Bank.

Figure 4.9 Morocco: Perception of Public Service Governance

"Your general opinion of public services is..."

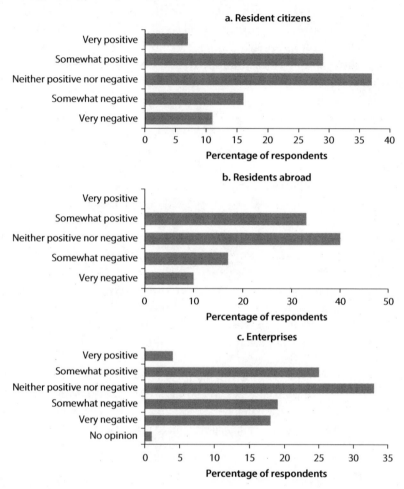

a. Resident citizens

b. Residents abroad

c. Enterprises

Source: CESE 2013.
Note: Survey represents a sample of 1,339 resident citizens and 203 citizens living abroad.

failures of the system relate more to a problem of governance, particularly the weakness of the relationship between the government and the user, than to a problem of resources. Logically, the proposed reform is concerned with improving transparency and information, improving access, strengthening participation and accountability, and improving efficiency. Thanks to this report and the discussions that followed, a growing awareness has emerged of the importance of improving the quality of public services, particularly the governance on which that quality is based. This awareness was also influenced by the complaints made by citizens themselves during the 2011 spring demonstrations and is reflected in a strong desire to participate in the management of public affairs, which was confirmed in a nano-survey of Internet users conducted by the World Bank in 2014.[10] In a context that shows not only the country's patent weaknesses in supplying public services but also the population's growing dissatisfaction with the situation, the authorities have undertaken a series of reforms involving four essential challenges for improving the quality of public services: accessibility and quality, equality and universality, information and transparency, and evaluation and accountability. However, the status quo in each of these four areas remains unsatisfactory on the whole.

On the basis of the available data, the supply of and access to public services have improved overall in recent years in Morocco owing to targeted reforms undertaken in specific sectors, but these improvements are mainly seen in homogeneous basic services, that is, those with identical or similar characteristics and modalities, such as infrastructure (access to drinking water, development of the road and highway network, and access to electricity), and for which administrative regulatory procedures are relatively simple. In contrast, more complex services that affect human development still face challenges in terms of accessibility and quality owing to information asymmetry and the persistence of some discretionary practices. According to the 2012–14 Arab Barometer, more than 80 percent of Moroccans questioned consider government institutions and agencies to be corrupt and almost 30 percent believe that this situation is getting worse. This is particularly the case in the health sector, which remains fragmented between various management organizations and is directly impacted by the problem of illicit payments.

Equality of access to services is still hampered by numerous obstacles. Several reports underscore the persistence of strong regional and local inequalities (Ministry of Economy and Finance 2015) and strong economic and social inequalities. For example, universal access to care is impeded by the high out-of-pocket payments of around 54 percent required of households and the inequality of the distribution of care, with some 50 percent of doctors located along the Rabat-Casablanca corridor (World Bank 2012). Moreover, in some regions, issues of access to information, illiteracy, and other barriers related to the slow pace of attitude changes constitute serious obstacles to equality of access to services, such as in the judicial sphere, where some women hesitate or have difficulty in recognizing their new rights (with the new family tribunals, for example). Last, absenteeism in some public services such as education or health is harmful to equality of access for all Moroccans, particularly those in rural areas.

The lack of access to information remains a serious constraint and contributes to inefficiencies, as shown by Morocco's scorecard in Global Integrity's 2017 transparency indicators[11] or in the 2016 World Justice Project Rule of Law Index survey. Access to information and transparency are essential levers in combating corruption (which the Moroccan Minister of Communications estimated cost some 1.5 percent of GDP per year in 2012), while surveys conducted by Transparency International (2016) show the extent of the problem in Morocco. The lack of transparency of public services also impedes the development of businesses in the private sector. The lack of transparency in the awarding of public contracts (which total some 17 percent of GDP per year) has been the subject of numerous official reports by the Audit Office and the Competition Council. The lack of transparency and supervision also relates to the management of public spending, particularly procedures for the allocation of budget resources, the nomenclature and criteria governing these allocations, or the monitoring, evaluation, and surveillance of budget execution.[12]

The culture of evaluation and accountability could be strengthened in Morocco. This is particularly true in the area of public policies and the budget programs that finance them. The performance-based budget reform set out in the new Budget Framework Law (LOLF) adopted in April 2015 aims to correct these weaknesses and create a more transparent framework that is more propitious to the monitoring and evaluation of public service performance. However, this reform is still in its early stages. Its ownership by all the players concerned, its effective implementation, and its extension to the entire public sector are all essential stages if its full benefit is to be achieved. Some sectors, such as health, suffer from a fragmentation of players and the lack of an integrated management information system. Occasionally, when performance control has been introduced, it is not applied under conditions that promote genuine accountability.[13] A burdensome bureaucracy and centralized administrative management also do not favor greater autonomy, empowerment, and accountability of the players most closely interacting with the user-beneficiaries (such as, for example, in national education). Despite some timid reforms, users hesitate to lodge complaints and it is unlikely that their complaints will be addressed. The surveys of individuals and businesses conducted by CESE on this topic highlight a wide range of serious problems: nonexistent mechanisms, the belief that this is pointless, fear of reprisals, and the like (CESE 2013).

The situation could be improved if two significant structural obstacles could be removed: the design and implementation of the reforms and the social standards and ways of thinking that influence behavior.

- The aforementioned deficiencies affecting citizens in their dealings with public institutions and administrations confirm the social norms that place personal connections above the public interest (World Bank 2015a). This contributes to a vicious circle in which accountability remains an abstract principle, resulting in a weakening of the provision of services. This situation is certainly not something that cannot be changed: creating a virtuous performance circle is possible. To do this, the structural obstacles to change and the reasons why the positive actions taken by Morocco have not yet given results must be considered. The design and implementation of the reforms face a number of obstacles: the temptation to institutional isomorphism that has led Morocco to reproduce exogenous schemes without taking sufficient account of the local context and capacities (Abderrahim Bouabid Foundation 2010); the lack of a comprehensive, cross-cutting vision of the state and the systematic guidance of the reforms, which remain fragmented and inconsistent (CESE 2013); the weak capacity to evaluate and monitor and the lack of follow-up of recommendations for improving public service governance; the growing complexity in terms of the number of participants, which jeopardizes the route of accountability for users; deficiencies in the training of public officials and the lack of effective incentives for improving the provision of public services; the failure to implement decisions (only 15 percent of all decisions handed down in civil proceedings are registered for enforcement purposes); and the persistence of corruption, despite the establishment of a central anticorruption agency, which explain Moroccans' mistrust of their institutions. The law establishing a requirement to provide the grounds for administrative decisions is not systematically applied.

- The reform efforts run up against the problem of insufficient consideration of the social norms and modes of thinking that influence behavior. Considering these aspects would make it possible to understand why some situations change very little or not at all (informality, lack of participation, and lack of accountability) and to devise actions more likely to have a real leverage effect (empowerment, competition, user monitoring). Incorporating all human and institutional factors in the analysis of governance issues should make it possible to break the vicious circle of poor performance (users have little confidence in their institutions and are discouraged from making their voices heard) and define a strong, coordinated overall approach that is solidly anchored in the new standards, new institutions, and institutions more favorable to a genuine culture of accountability.

Investing in Better Public Service Governance

The national institutional context, the global context, and Morocco's partnerships have never been so favorable to improving public service governance, but Morocco must find its own way to change the paradigm. The user must be placed at the center of the provision of public services. Morocco should not import preconceived solutions but rather identify the levers of reform based on the experience of other countries and its adaptation to the Moroccan context, with a view primarily to establishing a culture of accountability and performance at all levels of the service delivery chain. The accountability framework (long and short routes) defined by the World Bank in 2004 can serve as a conceptual framework. It should be expanded through an in-depth shared analysis of the challenges and constraints facing Morocco and be based on the lessons learned by various countries and a sharing of experience within communities of practice while adapting it to the Moroccan context.

While looking to the 2011 constitutional provisions as a basis, Morocco should seek to activate four levers of reform that are essential if the user is to be placed at the center of the provision of public services: (i) giving the user a voice, (ii) informing and reporting, (iii) simplifying and bringing decision making closer to the user, and (iv) testing and assessing new approaches.

Giving the User a Voice

Giving the user a voice is today encouraged by the 2011 constitution, which promotes an institutional overhaul and new rules of play (long route) and calls for several new mechanisms providing an increased role for the user (short route); but Morocco has lagged in these areas. Several of the 21 organic laws resulting from the 2011 constitution should improve public service governance by strengthening the voice and participation of citizens in the development and implementation of public services and policies. These reforms are on the government's agenda, but difficult trade-offs, the complexity of the subject, and Morocco's limited experience with an inclusive dialogue and participation have resulted in delays from the proposed timetable (adoption of all organic laws by the end of the 2016 parliamentary term). Morocco should look to new opportunities for dialogue and the sharing of experience to avoid wasting too much time. Several tools are available to Morocco for the role that the citizen can play directly with the service provider (short route) and should be examined in accordance with the spirit of the constitution and on the basis of practices in other countries. This is the case, for example, with the right of petition and legislative motion, which can under certain circumstances bring out new ideas; or public consultations, such as the one Morocco undertook in the health sector to clarify the areas of reform (Ministry of Health 2012).

Informing and Reporting

Informing and reporting also constitute a lever that is as important as it is sensitive for Morocco, given the country's limited experience in this area. However, Morocco's 2011 constitution and several of the reforms under way are opportunities that will allow the country to improve transparency and reporting along both the long route and the short route of accountability. The constitution introduces a right to information held by the public sector for all Moroccans as long as this is not harmful to the legitimate interests of individuals and the State. A law on access to information has been submitted to Parliament. The effective implementation of such a policy is an essential lever for improving the management and quality of public services, as seen in Mexico and India. It will guarantee equal access to information for all citizens and for businesses and strongly reduce the possibility for discretionary acts, injustice, and corruption. The implementation of this cross-cutting law will require the adoption of several complementary measures and an awareness and support campaign with civil society to enable it to fully benefit from it.

Information and accountability should be based on the development of new technologies and digital administration. In the context of its Digital Morocco 2013 strategy, Morocco undertook to develop the use of new ICTs. The government could draw lessons from the difficulties encountered in implementing the strategy and adopt realistic objectives with priority given to the digitalization of data and e-government. Capitalizing on the Digital Morocco 2013 assessment, the new Digital Morocco 2020 strategy, launched in July 2016, provides an opportunity to accelerate the digital transformation of the country by reducing the digital gap by 50 percent, bringing 50 percent of administrative procedures online, and ensuring an Internet connection for 20 percent of Moroccan small and medium enterprises (SMEs). Moreover, beyond issues of networks and organization, the content of information systems should also be reviewed to ensure that it becomes more relevant and useful in improving public service governance. Realistic and measurable monitoring indicators targeting essential aspects of the supply of public services (for example, absenteeism rate and wait times) could be adopted to regularly inform the revision of public policies.

The performance-based budget reform should be accompanied by complementary reforms to increase its effectiveness. The implementation under way of the performance-based budget reform, which is aimed at enhancing the transparency and efficiency of public spending, is promising if it is accompanied by a civil service reform and incentives for a genuine asymmetrical distribution of appropriations, which is essential to promote a new culture of performance and accountability. Other levers are available to Morocco to promote a genuine culture of accountability in public service. These include the development and implementation of a public service charter (provided in Article 157 of the constitution) based on the national experience in certain sectors (education, judicial reform) and on that of countries seeking genuine consistency and greater effectiveness (for example, Malawi), or the adoption of scorecards providing users with the ability to evaluate services and encourage their improvement. The implementation of such scorecards could run up against Morocco's still limited experience with the spontaneous participation of the population in the management of basic services, but it is important to note that these arrangements have developed successfully in a number of countries from the point of view of both the users and the service providers.

Simplifying and Bringing Decision Making Closer to the User

Simplifying and bringing decision making closer to the user should help improve the relevance and efficiency of the service provided. The 2011 constitution called for significant advances in terms of decentralization and paved the way for a new phase of administrative modernization, enhanced competencies, and delegation of authority, as well as the improvement of governance, accountability, and the participation of citizens in public policies. The effective implementation of the new constitutional provisions requires adequate technical, budgetary, financial, and statistical support and the mobilization of all players concerned (public and private) through a national program in support of decentralization and tripartite (state-region-commune) contracting. Improving public service governance at the commune level is particularly urgent because it is the level closest to the user and given the weaknesses identified by CESE.

Reconciling Moroccans with their social services and restoring their confidence in institutions involve simplifying procedures and access to services.[14] Administrative simplification requires changes to the laws and implementing regulations and the establishment of information technology (IT) systems that can digitize or reorganize working processes and methods. These essential measures take time. An initial phase could thus be to increase the standardization of procedures for both individuals and businesses by creating complete and all-inclusive forms as a number of the developed countries did in the 1970s and 1980s and ensuring that the entire Moroccan population effectively has equal access. Simplified relations between businesses and the government should also be instituted to reduce the vagueness of the rules, which leads to corruption. Many developed countries have ensured the standardization of procedures by developing national public forms, the readability, quality, and validity of which are certified by a central agency (the Office of Management and Budget in the United States or CERFA in France). The experiments under way in Morocco should be analyzed to determine the possibility of expanding this action to all administrative procedures and services. Further, priority should be given to the interconnection between government departments and the establishment of one-stop shops for individuals and businesses.

Testing and Evaluating New Approaches

Experimentation and evaluation should enable Morocco, like many other countries, to test new approaches—especially when they run up against ingrained habits and special interest groups—and to better understand the psychological motivations of users and service providers. Some reforms, particularly those aimed at introducing competition in sectors where there is serious information asymmetry and strong control by certain players or at recognizing an increased role for the private sector among public service providers, should be undertaken in the form of duly evaluated and discussed experiments. National education could be the first candidate for such testing and evaluation. Moreover, the failure of some reforms (the creation of support services for women in rural areas proved more theoretical than actionable, for example) indicates the importance of pragmatic approaches and the use of various measuring tools, resulting in a more easily shared and understood assessment, which will, in turn, facilitate the definition and application of new measures. The conceptual voluntarism and lip service of the past in reforming some of Morocco's public policies should be replaced by a more modest and pragmatic interactive approach based on the notion of continuous learning, a better understanding of behavior, experimentation with innovative and alternative solutions, and the successful and regular use of evaluations. These are all essential aspects of the empowerment and participation of all public service players in restoring the confidence of Moroccans in their institutions and thus the realization of their opportunities, which are essential for higher growth and improved well-being.

Notes

1. See, for example, the report of the U.S. Department of State (2016); the work of the United Nations Working Group on Arbitrary Detention (2014); the United Nations Special Report on Torture (2013); articles in the international press, such as the *New York Times* (2015); and various documents of Moroccan specialized government

agencies, such as the National Human Rights Council (CNDH); and nongovernmental agencies, particularly the Moroccan Human Rights Association (AMDH) and the Moroccan Human Rights Defense League (LMDDH).

2. Recognition of the diversity of the land tenure system, delays and costs involved in the transfer of property, particularly the reliability of infrastructure, transparency of information, geographic coverage, and resolution of land disputes.

3. The list of exceptions indicated in the text adopted in a plenary session of the House of Representatives in July 2016 goes well beyond the secrecy normally covering topics such as state security, national defense, or even personal data, to include data on the country's monetary, economic, and financial policy, the deliberations of the Council of Ministers and the government, the details of administrative investigations and inquiries, judicial procedures (except with the agreement of the competent authorities), etc.

4. Documents of the Public Administration Reform Development Policy Programs (PARAPs), World Bank (2010).

5. Speech delivered by His Majesty King Mohammed VI at the opening of the 1st Session of the 1st Legislative Year of the 10th Legislature (November 2016).

6. Speech delivered by His Majesty King Mohammed VI at the opening of the 1st Session of the 1st Legislative Year of the 10th Legislature (November 2016).

7. The flagship e-services established by Morocco include e-filing and e-payment of the corporate tax, income tax, and value-added tax; online payment of the special annual tax on automobiles; online publication and tracking of calls for tenders, publication of senior positions and high-level positions in the public sector; automation of public procurement; online ordering of court records; and online electoral registration.

8. For example, Sweden reduced the number of civil servants from 400,000 to 250,000 by using private contracts, reserving civil service positions for sovereign or strategic ministries, and delegating operational matters to about 100 specialized agencies with autonomy in their recruitment and remuneration decisions.

9. Definition proposed in the strategy for strengthening the World Bank Group engagement on governance and anticorruption adopted by the World Bank Board of Executive Directors in March 2007.

10. A nano-survey is an innovative technology that extends a brief survey to a random sampling of Internet users. See: https://finances.worldbank.org/dataset/Morocco -Citizen-Engagement-Nano-Survey-Response-Ma/kfvm-naym/data.

11. Morocco's scorecard by Global Integrity regarding access to information is "weak," 26 out of 100 in the 2017 report.

12. See, for example, the public expenditure reviews conducted by the World Bank in the education, health, and justice sectors.

13. World Bank Health Expenditure Tracking Survey.

14. Morocco implemented a program to simplify procedures in 2013. This program, which was implemented by MFPMA, simplified 112 procedures (57 involving citizens and 55 involving businesses).

References

Abderrahim Bouabid Foundation. 2010. *Le Maroc a-t-il une stratégie de développement économique?* Cercle d'Analyse Économique de la Fondation Abderrahim Bouabid. Morocco.

Akerlof, George A., and Rachel E. Kranton. 2010. *Identity Economics*. Princeton, NJ: Princeton University Press.

Bank Al-Maghrib (BAM). 2016. *Rapport sur l'exercice 2015*. Rabat, Morocco: Bank Al-Maghrib.

Bluhm, Richard, and Adam Szirmai. 2011. "Institutions, Inequality and Growth: A Review of the Institutional Determinants of Growth and Inequality." UNICEF Innocenti Research Center Working Paper 2011-02, UNICEF, New York.

Butkiewicz, James L., and Halit Yanikkaya. 2006. "Institutional Quality and Economic Growth: Maintenance of the Rule of Law or Democratic Institutions, or Both?" *Economic Modelling* 23 (4): 648–61.

Chaudhury, Nazmul, Jeffrey Hammer, Michael Kremer, Karthik Muralidharan, and F. Halsey Rogers. 2006. "Missing in Action: Teacher and Health Worker Absence in Development Countries." *Journal of Economic Perspectives* 20 (1): 91–116.

Davis, Kevin E., and Michael Trebilcock. 2008. "The Relationship between Law and Development: Optimists versus Skeptics." New York University Law and Economics Working Papers, New York University, New York.

Demmke, Christoph, and Timo Moilanen. 2010. *Civil Services in the EU of 27: Reform Outcomes and the Future of the Civil Service*. Frankfurt: Peter Lang.

De Soto, Hernando. 2000. *The Mystery of Capital: Why Capitalism Triumphs in the West and Fails Everywhere Else*. New York: Basic Books.

Di Maggio, Paul J., and Walter W. Powell. 1983. "The Iron Cage Revisited: Institutional Isomorphism and Collective Rationality in Organizational Fields." *American Sociological Review* 48 (2): 147–60.

Economic, Social and Environmental Council (CESE). 2013. "Rapport Annuel sur la gouvernance des services publics." Morocco.

———. 2015. *Pré-rapport sur la gestion déléguée*. Morocco.

Evans, Peter, and James E. Rauch. 1999. "Bureaucracy and Growth: A Cross-National Analysis of the Effects of 'Weberian' State Structures on Economic Growth." *American Sociological Review* 64 (5): 748–65.

Feld, Lars, and Stefan Voigt. 2003. "Economic Growth and Judicial Independence: Cross-Country Evidence Using a New Set of Indicators." *European Journal of Political Economy* 19: 497–527.

Fereidouni, Hassan Gholipour, Youhanna Najdi, and Reza Ekhtiari Amiri. 2013: "Do Governance Factors Matter for Happiness in the MENA Region?" *International Journal of Social Economics* 40 (12): 1028–40.

Glaeser, Edward, and Andrei Shleifer. 2001. "Legal Origins." *Quarterly Journal of Economics* 107 (4): 1193–29.

Helliwell, J. F., Haifang Huang, Shawn Grover, and Shun Wang. 2014. "Good Governance and National Well-Being: What Are the Linkages?" OECD Working Papers on Public Governance 25, OECD, Paris.

Kaufmann, Daniel, and Aart Kraay. 2002. "Growth without Governance." World Bank Policy Research Working Paper 2928, World Bank, Washington, DC.

Knack, S., and P. Keefer. 1995. "Institutions and Economic Performance: Cross-Country Tests Using Alternative Institutional Measures." *Economics & Politics* 7: 207–27.

Koenig, Gaspard. 2015. *Le révolutionnaire, l'expert et le geek*. Paris: Plon.

Ministry of Economy and Finance. 2015. *Des inégalités régionales sous le prisme de l'accès aux droits humains: De la multiplicité à l'indivisibilité.* Direction des Études et des Prévisions Financières, Morocco.

Ministry of Health. 2012. Rapport global de la consultation publique "Intidarat Assiha," Attentes en matière de santé. Morocco.

Ministry of the Civil Service and Modernization of Administration. 2013. *Rapport général relatif au Colloque national sur la refonte globale du statut général de la fonction publique, Skhirat 21 juin 2013.* Morocco.

New York Times. 2015. "Muzzling Dissent in Morocco." *The Opinion Pages.* October 18.

North, Douglass. 1990. *Institutions, Institutional Change and Economic Performance.* Cambridge, UK: Cambridge University Press.

Organisation for Economic Co-operation and Development (OECD). 2008. "Towards Employment Conditions in Central Governments that Are Closer to General Employment Rules." In *The State of the Public Services.* Paris: OECD Publishing.

———. 2011. *Public Servants as Partners of Growth.* Paris: OECD Publishing.

Smith, Adam. 1776. "An Inquiry into the Nature and Causes of the Wealth of Nations." Chicago: Encyclopedia Britannica, 1952.

Tirole, Jean. 2016. *Économie du bien commun.* Paris: Presses universitaires de France.

Transparency International. 2016. Global Corruption Barometer. People and Corruption: Middle East & North Africa Survey 2016. Berlin, Germany.

U.S. Department of State. 2016. *Country Reports on Human Rights Practices for 2015.* Washington, DC: Bureau of Democracy, Human Rights and Labor.

United Nations. 2013. Report of the Special Rapporteur on torture and other cruel, inhuman or degrading treatment or punishment, Juan E. Mendez. Human Rights Council 22nd session. A/HRC/22/53/Add.4.

———. 2014. Report of the Working Group on Arbitrary Detention. Mission to Morocco. Human Rights Council 27th session. A/HRC/27/48/Add.

van der Meer, Frits M., Jos C. N. Raadschelders, and Theo A. J. Toonen. 2015. *Comparative Civil Service Systems in the 21st Century.* Basingstoke, UK: Palgrave Macmillan.

Vásquez, Ian, and Tanja Porcnik. 2015. "The Human Freedom Index: A Global Measurement of Personal, Civil, and Economic Freedom." Cato Institute, Washington, DC.

Weber, Max. 1922. *Economy and Society.* Berkeley: University of California Press.

World Bank. 1997. *World Development Report: The State in a Changing World.* Washington, DC: World Bank.

———. 2004. *World Development Report: Making Services Work for the Poor.* Washington, DC: World Bank.

———. 2008. *Maroc—Marchés fonciers pour la croissance économique au Maroc (Vol. 1 of 5): Héritage et structures foncières au Maroc, (31 mai 2008).* Washington, DC: World Bank.

———. 2009. *From Privilege to Competition: Unlocking Private-Led Growth in the Middle East and North Africa.* MENA Development Report. Washington, DC: World Bank.

———. 2010. "Fourth Public Administration Reform Development Policy Loan." Report No. 51064-MA. Washington, DC: World Bank.

———. 2012. *Health Public Expenditure Review.* Washington, DC: World Bank.

———. 2014a. *Moderniser le droit commercial dans la région MENA: Traitement des questions régionales à travers les priorités courantes.* Washington, DC: World Bank.

————. 2014b. *Maroc: Revue du secteur de la justice*. Washington, DC: World Bank.

————. 2015a. *Trust, Voice and Incentives: Learning from Public Service Delivery in the MENA Region*. Washington, DC: World Bank.

————. 2015b. *World Development Report: Mind, Society and Behavior*. Washington, DC: World Bank.

————. 2017a. *Doing Business 2017*. Washington, DC: World Bank.

————. 2017b. *World Development Report: Governance and the Law*. Washington, DC: World Bank.

World Justice Project. 2016. *Rule of Law Index*. Washington, DC: World Justice Project.

CHAPTER 5

Investing in Human Capital

"In the long run, your human capital is your main base of competition. Your leading indicator of where you're going to be 20 years from now is how well you're doing in your education system."

— Bill Gates

Human capital is essential both for personal well-being and the wealth of nations. As the philosopher Jean Bodin (1576) has observed, "there is no wealth nor strength but in men." Human capital encompasses the body of knowledge, qualifications, skills and individual characteristics that foster the creation of personal, social and economic well-being. "Human capital is an intangible good that can help advance or sustain productivity, innovation and employability" (OECD 1988, 2001). Some kind of investment is required for the building of capital. The theory of human capital posits that individuals can improve their productivity or the future productivity of their children by making voluntary investment choices, particularly in education and health.[1] The income gaps between countries could then be explained by the fact that individuals in different societies make different investment choices, which then generate a variety of outcomes in terms of productivity. In the case of Morocco, the shifting of investments toward intangible capital, particularly human capital, is one of the conditions for the country's accelerated convergence with Southern European countries by 2040. The application of human capital theory opens the way for a range of investments in major sectors such as education, health and early childhood development (ECD). This chapter seeks to analyze the contribution of each of these areas to the strengthening of human capital and development and, thereafter, to take stock of the progress made by Morocco and outline reform pathways that would allow the country to further develop all the talents of all Moroccans.

Placing Education at the Heart of Development

According to Klaus Schwab, founder of the World Economic Forum, "talent, not capital, will be the key factor linking innovation, competitiveness and growth in the 21st century."[2] At the global level, more than one third of employers indicate that they find it difficult to source the skills they seek and almost one half believe that the shortage of talent has a negative impact on gross sales. Yet talent is not only innate. It can also be stimulated or acquired. Awakening and honing talent is, to a great extent, the responsibility of the school system.

The pathways through which the educational system contributes to the economic development of a country are multiple and quite easily identifiable from both a theoretical and empirical point of view. For an emerging country such as Morocco, economic convergence requires that existing knowledge be adapted to the local context. Morocco does not need to "reinvent the wheel." As Morocco is relatively far removed from the technology frontier, the country can—as other countries have done before—expect to attain a higher level of total factor productivity. In this way, it can look forward to sustainably accelerated growth by adapting the technologies as well as the production and management methods that have proven their worth elsewhere. Now, in order to make the process of economic catching-up a success, the country must be in a position to rely on sound human capital, characterized in particular by a population that harnesses the teaching and basic knowledge imparted at the primary and secondary education levels.

Enhancing the level of functional studies is equivalent to increasing the labor force, or in other words, to increasing productive efficiency at constant technology. The increase in efficiency helps to offset the automatic reduction in the return on physical capital and, consequently, to sustain long-term growth. Without continuous improvements in the level of education, a country will only be able to maintain positive long-term growth by saving and continuously accumulating more physical capital. Of course, it is impossible to accumulate capital beyond a certain threshold. As we have seen, with an investment rate exceeding 30 percent of GDP, Morocco is among the countries with the highest investment rates in the world. In order to accelerate or even maintain its rate of economic growth, Morocco cannot bank on further significant increases in its investment rate. To maintain positive long-term growth—let alone increase economic growth and rapidly narrow the gap with Southern European countries—Morocco has no choice but to increase its productivity and therefore the educational level of its population.

Improving the educational level of the population cannot be achieved by merely increasing the budgets of the Ministry of Education or by stepping up existing policies without modifying them. Indeed, many developing countries have adopted education policies that are centralized, bureaucratic and elitist, favoring higher education over lower levels. Such policies have tended to inhibit growth by eschewing development opportunities. In their report on growth and education, the economists Phillipe Aghion and Elie Cohen note that the excessive emphasis placed by some Latin American countries such as Brazil and Mexico on higher education and the pursuit of advanced research, to the detriment of primary and secondary education, has undermined growth in these countries. According to Aghion and Cohen, this choice perhaps goes some way to explain the reasons that some Latin American countries have registered lower growth levels than countries of Southeast Asia, where the educational system is organized on much less elitist principles (Aghion and Cohen 2004). For this reason, the adaptability of the educational system and the quality of education are at the heart of the debate on human capital and central to a country's propensity to innovate and catch up economically.

The Economics of Quality Education
Education Is Widely Available, But of Poor Quality

In the 1990s, Morocco began a process of making education more generally available, potentially paving the way for significant economic benefits in the medium term. Although Morocco introduced general access to education later than other developing countries, it set about to implement the concept at a rate that was unheard of at the time. As a result, net enrolment at the primary level grew from 55 percent in 1990 to 98.8 percent in 2014. Morocco recorded remarkable progress in terms of equity and parity in access to education and achieved the Millennium Development Goal of universal primary education before the 2015 deadline.

Nevertheless, despite the progress made in quantitative enrolment, the Moroccan education system continues to lag considerably in terms of performance. Around 10 million Moroccans (almost one third of the population) are illiterate. While illiteracy has receded over the past 20 years, it is still high, particularly in rural areas (where 40 percent of the population still resides). In 2014, the illiteracy rate for women in rural areas was roughly twice as high as in the cities, and also double the rate for men (see figure 5.1). Notwithstanding the 14-percentage point improvement over 2004, the illiteracy rate for rural women was still 60.4 percent in 2014 (HCP 2015).

Figure 5.1 Morocco: Percentage Change of the Illiteracy Rate among the Population Ages 10 Years and Older, 1994–2014

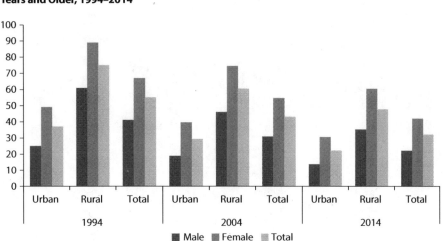

Source: High Commission for Planning 2015.

Morocco 2040 · http://dx.doi.org/10.1596/978-1-4648-1066-4

The generalization of school enrolment, using a purely quantitative approach, has not necessarily led to an accumulation of human capital (National Agency for the Fight against Illiteracy 2015). In a recent study entitled "Schooling Ain't Learning," the economist Lant Pritchett underlines the fact that quite a few developing countries manage to ensure the physical presence of children in school, without necessarily imparting basic reading and numeracy. Morocco is one such country. The results of the 2011 Progress in International Reading Literacy Study (PIRLS) and Trends in International Mathematics and Science Study (TIMSS) international tests indicate that Moroccan pupils of the fourth year of primary school placed last in reading (with a score of 310) and second-to-last in mathematics, in a survey of 50 developed and developing countries (see figure 5.2). Looking at the PIRLS survey together with other regional surveys on the African Continent (UNESCO 2014), it appears that the reading level of Moroccan students is consistent with the average for Sub-Saharan African countries and even below the level for Zambia, Kenya and Cameroon.

Education specialists conclude that failure to master reading at the primary level produces irreversible effects on the cognitive development of students throughout their school life and has a negative effect on their productivity as adults. The setbacks accumulated at the primary level increase the likelihood of failure at the secondary level and at university, and are to blame for the significant downgrading of the intrinsic value of the degrees. A study conducted by the faculty of sciences of Rabat has concluded that 70 percent of a sample of 3,000 high school graduates had barely achieved an elementary level in French, even though French is the principal language of instruction at university![3] It will take quite an effort to overcome the historical *littératie restreinte* (limited literacy) of Moroccan society (see box 5.1) (Janjar 2016).

Figure 5.2 Reading Level of Students at Age 10 Years (Grade 4)

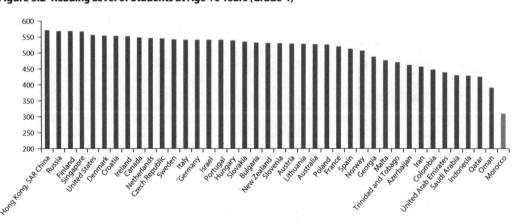

Source: UNESCO 2014.

Box 5.1 Origins of "Limited Literacy" in Moroccan Society, Extracts from Janjar, 2016

"When the German printer Johannes Gutenberg developed the movable type printing technique in 1450, he would have been in no doubt that such an invention would go on to change the world. Among other things, an unusual method of communication between the governed and those governing would be introduced in the West, whereby communication would, from that point onwards, be based on the dissemination of knowledge, rational criticism of the authorities, the free circulation of written texts and the challenge to the monopoly on the written word, which until then had been exercised by a small number of clerics. Fifty years later, Europe would witness the circulation across the continent of over twenty million volumes. As a result of the widespread use of printing presses, the promotion of literacy among the people and access to written works, the process of internalizing the ideals of The Enlightenment through reading had become irreversible across the length and breadth of Europe.

Historians have pondered why printing was not introduced in Morocco until 1865, considered late even in relation to other countries of the region. In addition, it appeared at the time that printing was not part of a well-defined project of cultural modernization or education reform. The catalog of some 500 titles printed between 1865 and the introduction of the protectorate in 1912 show that, with the exception of a text by Euclid, almost all the published works were in the form of manuals that had been in use at Al Quarouiyine for over two centuries, traditional hagiographic texts, or prestigious editions of the Quran and popular religious literature. Unlike in countries such as Lebanon, the Arab Republic of Egypt and Turkey, where printing presses were used as a tool to promote cultural modernization, the advent of printing in Morocco was viewed as an instrument for the maintenance of traditions by other means. For this reason, printing was not accompanied by cultural innovations or by the widespread dissemination of written works in Moroccan society.

The daunting cultural legacy of the pre-colonial period, together with the time lost in education between the years 1970–90 and the failure to introduce a cultural modernization policy mean that Moroccan society now finds itself in the era of the digital revolution in the context of "limited literacy." After a half century of university instruction, 90 percent of Moroccan publications focus on literature, law and religion. In other words, the fields of knowledge in vogue at the dawn of the 21st century are practically the same as those put forward by the traditional Moroccan clerics on the eve of the introduction of the Franco-Spanish protectorate. Following the end of the colonial period and the Arabization of instruction, the intellectual tradition has reclaimed its rightful place by progressively reactivating the fields of local knowledge as well as of the cognitive universe. In the global "cognitive market" that has been ushered in by the advent and development of information and communications technologies, the winners will, above all, be those countries that have seen fit to imbue their young people with the essential prerequisites for operating in such a market: education for critical thinking and for developing independent minds, scientific culture, logical reasoning and access to the great literary and artistic works of humanity.

box continues next page

Box 5.1 Origins of "Limited Literacy" in Moroccan Society, Extracts from Janjar (2016) *(continued)*

In the absence of such educational and cultural training, the widespread application of digital content may cause users who are cognitively impaired to fall back on tradition and the familiar. Of all the revolutions over the past two centuries, the digital revolution will undoubtedly prove to be the most global in scope, to the extent that it permeates every dimension of human activity, and particularly, the dimension that will magnify to the greatest extent the effects of the great cultural exchange ushered in by rationale writting."

Source: Janjar 2016.

A Dynamic of Decline and Growing Inequality…

In addition to the problems associated with low levels of education, Morocco must also contend with constantly deteriorating results. Successive surveys point to a decline in the quality of education, with a continuous drop in the results obtained by students across all the subjects evaluated (see figure 5.3). At first glance, one might be tempted to believe that the drop in students' performance levels is an inevitable consequence of making education more generally available. However, the correlation between the generalization of education and declining performances is not validated in international experience. Many developing countries have managed to post improved results in international surveys, even while making education widely accessible. This has been the case particularly in Brazil, Colombia, Mexico, Peru and Turkey. Morocco is one of the only countries to experience such a constant and broad-based decline in the quality of education, even though the responsible authorities have sought to introduce numerous corrective measures in the context of a number of national plans.

An analysis of the results of the PIRLS and TIMSS surveys reveals that the level of educational inequality is extremely high in Morocco in comparison with other sample countries. Students whose results placed them in the top 10 percent obtain scores 2.5 times higher than the bottom 10 percent. These learning gaps are far more pronounced than the global average of 1.5. Morocco has the most unequal educational system of the countries surveyed, with scores that are significantly lower than the four closest States in the classification, namely Oman, Qatar, The United Arab Emirates and Saudi Arabia. The polarization of the education system is a reflection of what can be described as the "educational divide" in Moroccan society. Instead of promoting social mobility, the school system tends to perpetuate the social inequalities that are based on the socioeconomic background of the parents. The general mistrust of the national education system is driving up demand for enrolment in private schools.[4] Consequently, young Moroccans increasingly live in parallel educational worlds that are delimited by the financial capacity of their family.

The continuous decline in the quality of public schools is a source of concern for a country such as Morocco that aspires to emerge economically. Indeed, in the majority of countries that have experienced rapid development, based on

Figure 5.3 Morocco: Progression of the Score under TIMSS and PIRLS

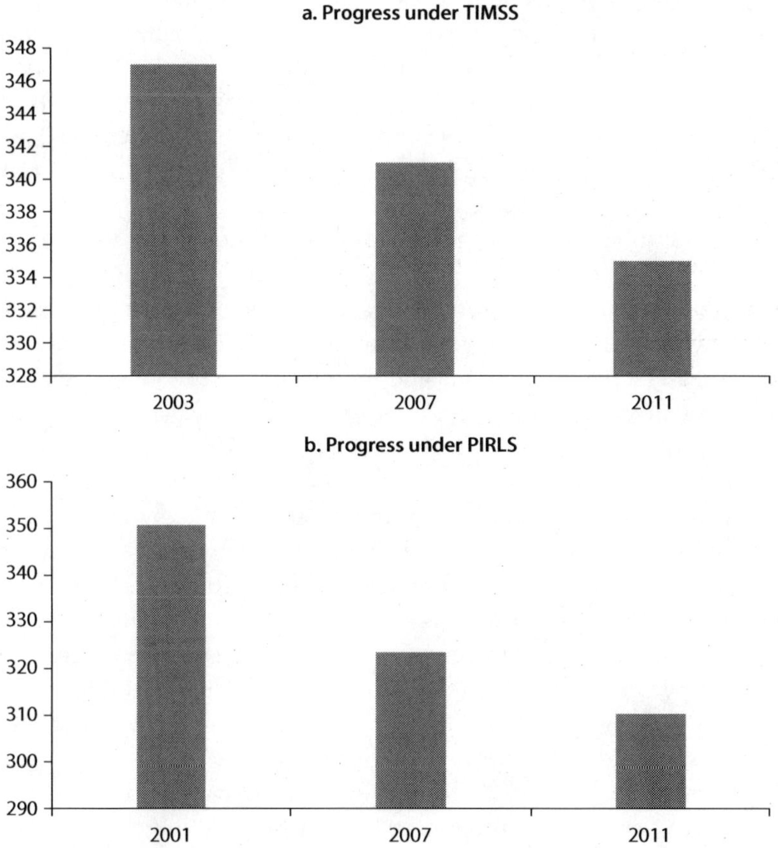

a. Progress under TIMSS

b. Progress under PIRLS

Source: a. TIMSS; b. PIRLS.
Note: PIRLS = Progress in International Reading Literacy Study; TIMSS = Trends in International Mathematics and Science Study.

high-level human capital, primary education is predominantly public or publicly financed and is the cornerstone of the national educational pact. While it is true that the private sector also plays an important role, this applies in the main at the secondary and university levels. In Finland, Korea, Singapore, and Taiwan, China, which top the Program for International Student Assessment (PISA) rating, the public sector accounts for almost 100 percent of the school population at the primary level. International experience has shown that there is a strong correlation between the performance of the educational system and the degree of educational equity. The most effective way of raising the general level of education is to ensure that disadvantaged populations have access to quality education.

...with Significant Economic Consequences
The poor quality of education and the extent of the inequalities in the school system weigh heavily on Morocco's economic and social development.

After leaving school and even university, students, including those who successfully completed their education, face a high risk of unemployment. The unemployment rate for young graduates (baccalaureate or higher) is 59 percent among 15–24 year-olds and 30 percent among 25–35 year-olds. Contrary to the experience normally associated with the rest of the world, the rate of unemployment among young non-graduates is lower than for graduates (10 percent and 20 percent, respectively). In Morocco, possession of a qualification triples the risk of being unemployed. This is due in part to the poor performance and slow structural transformation of the Moroccan economy. But it is also symptomatic of the real problem of failing to ensure that the training imparted is in line with the needs of the labor market, a fact borne out in surveys conducted with employers.[5] The very delicate issue of the high rate of unemployment among young graduates could become more acute in the years ahead, as the cohorts that emerge from the generalization of educational access arrive on the job market, with an even lower level of achievement than the current unemployed graduates.

In view of the opportunity to capture a demographic dividend, the country should move quickly and decisively to bring about a veritable "educational miracle," by gradually narrowing the performance gap between Moroccan students and students in other emerging countries. Morocco should make it a strategic objective to come to terms with its educational inequalities by offering quality education to all students, including the most disadvantaged. A medium- to long-term scenario is envisaged for the attainment of this ambitious target for the educational sector. Indeed, an analysis of the international tests conducted over the past two decades (PISA, TIMSS, PIRLS) shows that the countries that had the most success in educational reform (for example, Brazil, Chile, Peru, Poland and Turkey) tend to improve their scores at an average rate of four points per year. Assuming that Morocco is able to generate a similar rate of improvement to that of the most successful nations, it would take the country some 30 years to match the current educational level of emerging countries such as Turkey (as the gap to be closed exceeds 100 points).

The inevitable time lag between the introduction of reforms and the achievement of results underlines the urgency for Morocco to begin immediately the process of large-scale transformation. As indicated by the Governor of Bank Al-Maghrib, "the failure of the many reform initiatives calls for the introduction of shock therapy where all stakeholders should understand that beyond vested interests, it is the future [of Morocco] that is at stake" (Bank Al-Maghrib 2015). International experience shows that large-scale educational reform can start to produce the first significant social and economic benefits some four to five years after rollout.

Causes of Low-Quality Education in Morocco

The factors underlying the poor quality of education in Morocco are multidimensional. These factors are also present in several other countries: lack of infrastructure, overcrowded classrooms, program overload, pedagogical methods based on rote learning, inadequate training of teachers, lack of quality control and performance incentives, excessive centralization, low parental involvement, particularly fathers, and so on. In view of this litany of problems and in order not to dilute the reform initiatives, it is vital to identify the major shortcomings in education and to come up with solutions for improving performance within the system that would maximize the impact on the educational level of students. A recent International Monetary Fund (IMF) study has suggested that the main determinants of the ineffectiveness of the Moroccan educational system are corruption and lack of ethics, misuse of public funds, training of teachers and the relative salaries of teachers (IMF 2016). The IMF estimates that, even at the current level of public expenditures per student, Morocco's test scores could improve by around 50 points if it were to improve budgetary management (better allocation of public expenditure and a reduction in the misuse of public funds), reinforce teacher incentives with better training and care and improve the quality of institutions and governance.

The combined findings from research and field studies point to three categories of major constraints among a large number of potential problems: quality of education, governance of the educational system as a whole, and the influence of the social environment. These constraints are unique in that they are "interdependent" in nature. If not treated at the root, all other reforms are at risk of becoming ineffective. Moreover, analyses show that the big issues that regularly polarize the debate in Morocco, relating primarily to program content and linguistic discontinuity (classical Arabic upon entering primary school, French at university), are really lesser problems. Indeed, if system practitioners were more skilled and motivated and if students had the benefit of a favorable learning environment, the content of the programs and the linguistic discontinuity would not present insurmountable obstacles to the realization of quality education.

Educational Quality

Experts in the field of education agree that the performance of the educational system can only be as good as the quality of the teachers. There is a strong empirical correlation between the academic skills of teachers and the educational achievements of pupils (Hanushek, Piopiunik, and Wiederhold 2014). The numerous shortcomings in the skills level of the Moroccan teaching corps are largely to blame for the weakness of the quality of education. At the international level, the top-performing educational systems recruit their teachers (including primary school teachers) from among the top third of tertiary level graduates: among the top 5 percent of graduates in Korea; 10 percent in Finland; and 30 percent in Hong Kong SAR, China and Singapore. The selection process in these countries is rigorous. It is based not only on academic qualifications but also on psychological and behavioral profiles. Teachers undergo full basic training and have access to coaching throughout their first years of work. They also benefit from a career-long program of professional development. New recruits are not permanently appointed to their posts until they complete a probationary period during which their skills are duly evaluated. The teaching profession enjoys high social status and the remuneration is sufficient to attract the best talents.

The way the Moroccan education system functions is not consistent with best practices observed abroad, starting with the recruitment of teachers. A decision to enter the teaching profession is often made by default, rather than vocation, and usually after other options have been exhausted. This is particularly so for unemployed graduates, some of whom have managed to take advantage of automatic entry into the profession (*Idmajmoubachir*). The method for selecting teachers improved with the introduction in 2012 of a competitive examination for access to Regional Centers for the Teaching and Training Professions (CRMEF). Nevertheless, despite the stringent selection criteria of the competition (success rate of less than 10 percent), the majority of those admitted to the CRMEF have shortcomings that require remedial action to bring them up to speed in their core subjects. Because of its low social status, the teaching profession cannot attract the best talents. This is compounded by the fact that the working environment for teachers and the assignments in various locations are often seen as forbidding. Many of the teachers that participated in the field surveys reported that they were relatively dissatisfied with their jobs and felt undervalued by society.

In addition to weaknesses in the selection process, the gaps in basic training and the lack of continuing education contribute to the skills deficit of the teaching corps. All teacher training should cover at least the academic discipline (subjects to be taught), profession (pedagogy, teaching methods and practices) and classroom practice. The performance level of pupils is determined principally by the capacity of teachers to utilize effective pedagogical methods, such as lesson planning, sequencing of learning, continuous checking of learning outcomes, explanation of difficulties encountered, early intervention for children in difficulty and the like (Hattie 2009). Bearing in mind that the basic university training for trainee teachers in Morocco is not up to par, a large part of the CRMEF training year is dedicated to bridging the academic gaps. This has the knock-on effect of further reducing the time reserved for pedagogical training and practice, two elements that are essential in teacher training. Despite lacking practical experience, the new teachers are automatically assigned to schoolrooms without any prior period of internship or mentorship from more experienced teachers. There is no real probationary period, at the end of which candidates who fail to meet the required standards would be weeded out. The majority of teachers encountered in the survey had not participated in a single training program over the previous ten years. In this scenario, educators have no real chance to improve their teaching practice or adopt more effective pedagogical methods. Whenever the government has introduced new pedagogical initiatives, as was the case recently in relation to the pedagogy of integration, the impact on the ground has been limited owing to insufficient training, lack of take-up upstream and scant participation by teachers.

Governance in the Education System

The recruitment and training of high-level teachers is not enough to guarantee quality education. In order to be efficient, the educational system must also be properly governed. The field survey showed that Moroccan teachers are largely demotivated and, in many cases, have lost faith in their profession. It is true that there are still teachers who are enthusiastic and fully committed to the performance of their educational duties. However, they often end up feeling discouraged because of a lack of support from the other stakeholders in the educational system. This sense of discouragement is reflected in a number of behavioral patterns that are detrimental to student learning, particularly absenteeism, inefficient time management in the classroom, lack of pedagogical effort to overcome learning difficulties, indifference and resignation in relation to students in difficulty, reduced frequency of assessments as tools to alleviate the burden of remedial action, lack of communication with parents, recourse to verbal and physical abuse (still frequently used according to testimonials collected from students), commoditization of grades (through additional tutoring) and the like. The absence of performance incentives is the main reason teachers are discouraged. The result is a high degree of inefficiency in public expenditure on education (see figure 5.4) (IMF 2016).

This climate of complacency is exacerbated by the lack of a system of evaluation, whether for formative assessments for students or summative appraisals of the educational system.[6] The evaluation mechanisms in place do not facilitate the early detection of learning difficulties or academic failure, thereby making it difficult for the teacher or school to put in place remedial or catch-up strategies. As is the case for students, teacher assessments also leave a lot to be desired. It appears that the system of educational supervision

Figure 5.4 Average Inefficiency in Public Expenditure on Education, 2003–11

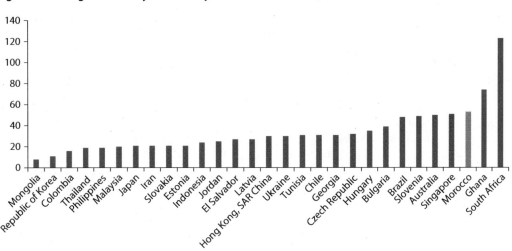

Source: International Monetary Fund 2016, calculated using the TIMSS results for mathematics and sciences.
Note: TIMSS = Trends in International Mathematics and Science Study.

can no longer fulfill its primary function of monitoring and improving the quality of education. The system for career advancement is not adequate to promote teachers based on their performance. The heads of educational institutions are tasked exclusively with administrative functions and assume no pedagogical or managerial responsibilities.

Over and above the lack of performance incentives, the loss of motivation affecting teachers has deeper roots, notably a general sense of resignation. The view that national education produces predominantly mediocre students is firmly held and taken as a fait accompli. The world's top performing educational systems are founded on the notion that all students can achieve success and excellence, regardless of their socioeconomic status. The sense of resignation is borne out by the fact that following the publication of the country's international test results, there was no outcry in the country and broad corrective action was not taken. In Germany, for example, the publication in 2001 of the first PISA survey exposed the learning gaps of German students. This "PISA shock," as it has come to be called, was a turning point in that it triggered action on many levels and spurred an unprecedented wave of innovations and reforms. The experience at the international level holds a fundamental lesson for Morocco: in order to build an effective education system, one must never lose sight of the goal of pushing all students toward success, regardless of their social origin.

Influence of the Social Environment

One of the most substantive findings from the educational research conducted is that the socio-economic origin of students is a key determinant of their academic results. Social origin influences the education of students in multiple ways. First, and most strikingly, children from disadvantaged households live in material conditions that are not conducive to self-fulfillment or cognitive development, including conditions relating to health, transportation, accommodation and family stability. Although some efforts have been made recently to address the situation, such as the Tayssir program or the operation to distribute one million school bags, the provisions in place to protect vulnerable children continue to be woefully inadequate. For example, public schools hardly provide free school transportation for disadvantaged children (barely 2,000 beneficiaries were identified in Morocco). The provision of health services at schools is also deficient. For example, much more needs to be done in the area of monitoring and correcting visual disorders, as their detection and treatment can play a decisive role in the success of children.

In addition, disadvantaged children operate in an unfavorable cultural context. They are not sufficiently exposed to foreign languages (particularly French), do not take part in artistic or sporting extracurricular activities, and have no books at home. The parents, and particularly mothers for the most part, are often illiterate and, therefore, not in a position to help their young children in their school studies and homework. All these factors serve to widen the already broad gap between poor and privileged children in terms of their ability to learn and think, as well as in relation to their mastery of languages, general knowledge and curiosity. It also affects deeper psychological dimensions such as confidence and self-esteem. The adverse effects that these socioeconomic handicaps have on academic success are compounded by the fact that they are shared by a large proportion of students in the same class. The aversion to social diversity in Morocco's public schools creates "peer effects" with negative repercussions among children in difficulty (discipline, motivation and emulation). A student from a family of modest means attending a school where the majority of children are disadvantaged will hardly find role models in the immediate environment who can inspire and nurture his or her ambitions.

In addition to the issues of social determinants, the Moroccan educational system has failed to guarantee equity in education. International experience shows that it is possible to make education more generally available in a poor country while simultaneously improving its quality and reducing inequalities. This is the case, for example, of Vietnam, whose per capita GDP is lower than Morocco's, yet is ranked more highly in the PISA classification than many rich OECD countries (OECD 2011). The same applies to Turkey and Mexico, both of which have set out recently to make access to education more generally available. Over the past 10 years, these two countries have recorded remarkable improvements in their average scores, while still managing to substantially reduce educational inequality. Morocco has not been able to match this performance because the process of educational generalization that it has undertaken has not been accompanied by appropriate measures to promote equity, such as making preschool widely available, placing emphasis on the acquisition of basic knowledge (numeracy, reading, writing), rolling out more robust support mechanisms for students in difficulty, promoting extracurricular activities, allocating additional resources and assigning experienced teachers to low performing schools, and the like. Moroccan schools do not endear themselves to their students. Almost one third of those who ended their studies prematurely attributed this decision to not liking school (see figure 5.5). International experience demonstrates that it is technically possible, even for developing countries, to offer quality education to all children, provided that this objective is adopted as a national priority.

Transforming Moroccan Schools

There is broad agreement on the need to radically reform education in Morocco. In his 2015 Throne Speech, His Majesty King Mohammed VI noted that "educational reform is integral to development. It is the key for promoting openness and social advancement, guaranteeing that individuals and society as a whole are protected from the scourges of ignorance and poverty as well as from the demons of extremism and ostracism." He appealed for "substantial reforms to be introduced in this vital sector, so as to rebuild the Moroccan educational system and place it in a position to fulfill its rightful mission in relation to education and development." Referring to the approach to be adopted for the reforms, the

Figure 5.5 Morocco: Reasons for Dropping Out of School among Children Ages 6–17 Years

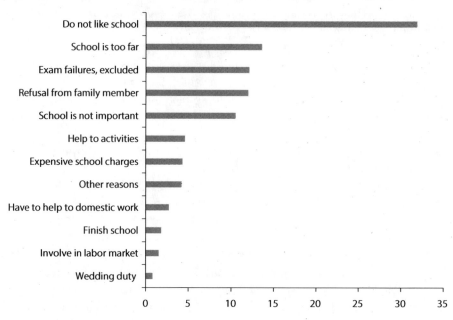

Source: ONDH 2015, report on the initial findings of the household panel survey.

King suggested that the country needed to "identify an overall strategic vision," "demonstrate seriousness and realism, and engage with Moroccans openly and frankly," and finally, "lay aside all selfishness and political maneuvering that would jeopardize the future of the younger generations." Thereafter, the Higher Council on Education, Training and Scientific Research (CSEFRS) proposed a strategic vision for reform (2015–2030) toward education with equity, quality and upliftment.

The vision of the authorities to achieve tangible progress will not be realized unless Morocco focuses on eliminating the major constraints to the provision of quality education, as opposed to concentrating on a significant number of objectives and drivers that may or may not be realistic. Any attempt at educational reform that fails to deal unequivocally with these stumbling blocks will not lead to real transformations in educational quality or learning inequalities. The process of change should also take account, in a realistic manner, of certain exogenous constraints. Educational reform is therefore a complex undertaking. It must balance ambition with realism, while advancing the following four priorities: (a) modernization of the educational ecosystem, (b) adoption of new public education governance, (c) promotion of alternative educational choices, and (d) utilization of information and telecommunications technologies. The success of such reforms will depend on the adoption of a new results-based social contract for education.

Taken together, these priorities could become the "shock therapy" needed to radically transform the quality of Moroccan education, by creating the conditions for a veritable "education miracle." The term "education miracle" is used to refer to a substantial improvement in the average learning outcomes of Moroccan students, as reflected in particular by an improvement in students' international test scores of around 1 standard deviation, in a relatively short period of time. This would allow Morocco to exceed the 400-point mark and move closer to the academic level of the other emerging countries.[7] The reference framework for the key lines of action proposed here are informed by the values of good public policy governance (transparency, accountability and performance) and the principles of openness and inclusiveness in the provision of educational services.

Modernizing the Educational Ecosystem

This educational ecosystem includes both teaching (curriculums, teaching methods, academic support) and the key operatives of the system, namely the teachers. First, the curriculums—comprising the programs, pedagogical methods, assessment methods, academic pace and teaching materials—are integral to the modernization of the educational system. The reform of curriculums as part of the process of educational renewal must be based on certain universal founding principles. The educational ecosystem must, therefore, transmit the values of merit (no gain without sacrifice), progress (personal ownership of society's objectives for progress), liberty (rejection of oppression, opinion censorship, and respect for intellectual tolerance), altruism (solidarity, respect for gender and minorities), reflection (discovery on one's own, expression of critical views), initiative, professionalism and responsibility. It is recognized that the inclusion of these values is prescribed in the CSEFRS strategic vision. However, these values should not only be upheld in official instructions, mission statements of institutions or school manuals, but should also be applied in the day-to-day activities of the stakeholders of the system, starting with the teachers and education managers.

The issue of pedagogical engineering is of equal importance and as such, the desired competencies should be reflected in the design of the teaching and evaluation programs and methods. This is a complex task that must be based first and foremost on a results-oriented approach (what the students should know and the knowledge that students have acquired) rather than be input-driven (what should be taught). In terms of knowledge and cognitive skills, students should be able to recognize letters and words, calculate rapidly, discern shapes and patterns, and generally acquire the competencies measured in IQ tests (Hart and Risley 1995). Schools should also provide an appropriate framework for students to develop know-how and adopt attitudes that are associated with non-cognitive competencies, such as curiosity, self-control, sociability, persistence, the ability to postpone gratification, follow a plan and instructions and other psychological traits (Tough 2012). The proposal to introduce balanced education in its cognitive and non-cognitive dimensions does not necessarily mean that specific subjects or lessons should be added. For example, it is often the case that merely increasing the number of hours of instruction is neither sufficient nor necessary to improve the teaching of a language. Unfortunately, there are too many instances where pedagogical reforms end up expanding the number and complexity of programs without achieving the expected outcomes in terms of students' learning. Rather than increasing the number of subjects, what is required is to employ different teaching methods. New developments in the science of pedagogical methods should be harnessed to ensure that basic skills (particularly writing, reading, comprehension of basic texts and simple oral expression) are well and truly acquired by young Moroccans. Otherwise, the development of aptitudes, critical sense and civic skills will be compromised, and the building of meaningful social capital will be made even more difficult (see chapter 6).

Morocco should seek by consensus to introduce into its programs of higher and vocational education a number of values that are essential for promoting the occupational integration of young Moroccans. The following three values appear to be particularly important in the Moroccan context: (a) entrepreneurial spirit, not only in terms of preparing students to form companies, but also because it is associated more broadly with the qualities of resourcefulness and responsibility on the job and within the enterprise; (b) professionalism, that is, the requirement and appetite for a job well done; and, (c) the stimulation of creativity and innovation. Instead of merely testing their know-how or their capacity to understand techniques and regurgitate them, curriculums should also facilitate an assessment of the extent to which the intern or student has acquired the capacity to become productive and efficient in his or her future assignment. The curriculums should also systematically and explicitly promote ways for students to find professional employment, including in its most demanding manifestations such as engagement in the private sector and self-employment through very small enterprises (VSEs) or income-generating activities. This will also require a new results-oriented pedagogical approach and the diversification of training options (apprenticeship, work-study, other forms of public/private partnership) and the involvement of potential private sector employers in the design and evaluation of training programs.

An effective strategy of academic support for students in difficulty could help Morocco to significantly enhance the internal efficiency of its educational system and to progress rapidly in international classifications. This strategy could draw on the Finnish remedial system, considered one of the world's best. Its success is attributed mainly to the highly developed mechanisms at the primary level to fight against academic failure. It involves the early diagnosis of learning gaps in order to prevent them from accumulating later on. This tool for remedial action is the corollary of the policy that seeks to contain the repetition rate, which in Finland is as low as two percent. In the case of Morocco, a "students-in-difficulty support group" comprising teachers at similar levels of the educational cycle could be established in each school. This group would be tasked with the early detection of students experiencing difficulty learning, with special emphasis on analyzing the results obtained from standard tests.

Improving the Selection and Training of Teachers

Candidates in the new rounds of teacher recruitment should be required to have the necessary training, skills and motivation. Over the next five years, almost one third of the 125,000 teachers employed at public primary schools will retire. Unless far-reaching reforms are adopted, the automatic renewal of the cadre of teachers could lead to an even greater deterioration in quality, as experienced teachers are replaced by young, less well-trained colleagues. Indeed, the renewal of the teaching corps could be viewed as an opportunity to improve the quality of the recruitment and training processes. A replenishment process could be managed by upgrading skills and putting in place provisions for continuing education as well as by recruiting young, well-trained teachers who are creative and highly proficient in the use of information and communications technologies (ICTs). While the recent reforms in teacher training have facilitated the introduction of a competitive and transparent recruitment process, the problems associated with the recruitment pool and the gaps in basic university training remain. The young candidates admitted to the CRMEF continue to be drawn predominantly from the pool of university graduates seeking the security of public sector employment. These candidates are often poorly prepared and without any particular vocation for teaching. These issues cannot be resolved exclusively by the Ministry of Education. They require the involvement of several institutional stakeholders and, in particular, very close collaboration between the Ministry of Higher Education and the Ministry of Administrative Modernization. Unfortunately, such a degree of collaboration has been lacking.

Putting in place coaching mechanisms for teachers could become another powerful tool for increasing the effectiveness of pedagogical practice in classrooms. Morocco could draw on the ongoing experience of the city of Shanghai in this area. With a population of 23 million inhabitants, Shanghai placed first in the 2009 and 2012 PISA classifications, ahead of all OECD countries. Shanghai's success is based primarily on a unique system of professional teacher development. In the same way, the implementation of a coaching system in Morocco would complement the system of continuing education and help to bridge the gaps in the preparation of Moroccan teachers. In this regard, the pilot project conducted by the Ministry should be encouraged and provided with the necessary support to be successfully rolled out in the Kingdom.

Adopting New Public School Governance

The experience of education reforms in many emerging countries proves that expanding the number of classes, recruiting teachers and increasing budgets in a defective system is counter-productive. A purely quantitative and superficial approach will serve only to maintain the performance curve at a low level. In order to significantly reverse this trend, decisive measures to improve the education supply are necessary. Such measures should be focused on providing better service to students and enhancing the organization and operation of the system so as to make it more effective, more transparent and more efficient.

This will require the following steps: (a) a review of the powers and responsibilities of all stakeholders in the educational system with a view to improving its organization and enhancing its responsiveness to the needs of students, (b) more frequent and better assessment of learning outcomes so as to make stakeholders more accountable and promote quality, and (c) greater participation by parents in initiatives to improve the quality of the system, in collaboration with school institutions.

In order to ensure that the school regains its place as the central focus of the system, it is necessary first of all to radically reform the framework in which public schools operate, particularly the way the relevant ministries are organized, the powers of the central and regional bodies that manage education (academies, delegations, schools), the methods for allocating budgetary expenditure in education and even the powers of the local communities in relation to schools. The current remit of the various bodies that govern school education is not adequate to allow schools to discharge their primary role as guarantors of teaching quality. The decisions taken by the central agencies or by a regional delegation do not necessarily help to improve the quality of service provided to students at the various institutions. By contrast, strengthening the decision-making powers of schools should increase the likelihood that students will be successful in their studies, provided that the necessary human, organizational and technical resources are made available. Some countries have adopted the School-Based Management Concept (SBM).[8] While there have been some challenges in implementing this concept, the countries that have managed to do so have seen significant improvements in outcomes by putting in place a management framework that is closer to the ground, more responsive and better suited to the specific needs of students. The implementation of the SBM required strong action to transfer certain powers and responsibilities from the center to the field, that is, in the direction of school management bodies, namely, the director and assistant directors of institutions, and the schools' management boards and educational councils.

The autonomy of schools should be considerably strengthened and school directors should be accountable for the quality and effectiveness of the teaching imparted at their institutions. Priority must be assigned to granting greater autonomy to schools (World Bank 2015). This applies to the planning and management of budgets, recruitment of staff and evaluation of teachers and students. The remit of school directors should be expanded to include responsibility for certain decisions that need not remain in the purview of the delegations or academies. At the same time, the system for appointing directors should be democratic and transparent and should be overseen by a commission comprising parents, local stakeholders and heads of companies that collaborate with the schools concerned. In this way, the process of promotion and appointment of school personnel could serve to more effectively support the performance targets set by the institution.

To complete the new arrangement for the distribution of tasks between the Ministry of National Education and the stakeholders that collaborate with it in the management of schools, the currently very weak role played by local communities must be strengthened through a process of negotiations. Based on the goal of administrative decentralization set forth in the 2011 constitution, reform of the educational system should make it possible for locally elected bodies to be granted responsibility for the construction and maintenance of institutions, as is the case in many developed and emerging countries. The remit of the Ministry of Education should be focused on and redirected toward the essential functions of the educational system and the management of the teaching and administrative staff.

At this juncture, the reform of Morocco's public school governance cannot proceed without a review of the status of teachers. It is true that this is a sensitive issue that each government approaches with much caution. This notwithstanding, the public-sector establishment regulations of the Regional Academy of Education and Training (AREF) and the wider powers granted to new regions make it possible to amend the staff regulations for teachers to increase flexibility. Based on the new AREF statute, teacher evaluations must be effective and transparent, and must be used as a tool to determine career advancement. Mechanisms to encourage innovation and performance should also be introduced.

Regardless of the educational system (public, private or mixed), the objective measurement of the acquisition of knowledge and skills by students is an essential tool for improving the performance of the system as well as for responding to parents' need for information on the performance of the educational system. There is no system in place in Morocco for evaluating and providing objective and regular information on the scholastic progress of students. The paucity of information currently available is largely to blame for the lack of accountability of stakeholders and the failure to respond to the continuous decline in the quality of teaching. The implementation of a robust national system for evaluating learning is therefore essential to the reform of the Moroccan educational system. The new ICTs could be utilized to measure learning outcomes and individual knowledge-building of students on an ongoing basis.

The institutionalization of students' evaluations would have the effect of making all stakeholders accountable (particularly supervisory staff and teachers) and encouraging performance. The publication through the appropriate media of the results obtained by schools would provide information to families on the quality of their children's schools and would constitute a strong performance incentive for directors, members of school boards, teachers and other education personnel. The provision of information to parents is a necessary first step for enhancing their involvement and for developing a culture of accountability within the educational system. In Morocco's case, the reports collected in the course of the field survey indicate that, in general, parents' associations are not adequately fulfilling their role and are, in fact, deficient in many ways. As a result, parents, particularly those from disadvantaged areas, are very poorly informed about school operations, the academic progress of their children and the steps that they could take to help them succeed. After all, it is possible to sensitize parents and particularly fathers, to the fact that education is a worthwhile investment for their children.[9]

Developing Alternative Educational Options

Improving the ecosystem and governance of Moroccan public education must be complemented by broader actions to encourage performance and account-ability. The measures proposed above should allow Morocco to improve the quality of the system and the service provided to students. However, the imple-mentation of these measures is neither simple nor quick. Above all, they must go hand in hand with another equally essential reform, namely the promotion, in conjunction with the reform of the traditional public system, of alternative educational options. This is entirely consistent with the mission to guarantee quality education to all Moroccan children, while enhancing freedom of choice and innovation.

Offering families the widest possible choice in education is a powerful tool for stimulating better quality education in Morocco. The freedom to choose would offer at least three advantages: it would facilitate the mobilization of additional resources for the educational system as a whole, not only from fami-lies, but also from investors and other private actors; it would provide a wider range of education solutions that would help to contain the costs borne by the public system and even to reduce them, while guaranteeing better use of the resources expended; finally, freedom of choice will promote competition and transparency, good governance and innovation, whether in relation to manage-ment of schools, choice of pedagogical methods, or the utilization of new technologies. Of course, the proposal to develop alternative educational solu-tions would not be viable if the selection process is based on the financial standing of families, as this would have the effect of excluding low and middle-income populations. Morocco could therefore embark on a new path that would entail looking anew at the school map and encouraging educational innovation, while safeguarding the role played by the school as a defender of social cohesion. A number of different approaches have been tried around the world over the past few decades (charter schools, education-vouchers, sectar-ian schools, home-schooling), with generally positive academic results, not only among students attending alternative schools, but also among students in the surrounding public schools.

Promoting "21st Century Skills"

In order to reap the benefits of the current digital revolution, schools must by all means inculcate in students the skills necessary to thrive in tomorrow's economy: collaboration, communication, social and cultural skills, civic respon-sibility, and, of course, mastery of ICTs. Experience has shown that using ICTs in the field of education can strongly support school transformation and contrib-ute to the attainment of several objectives, including (a) improving the manage-ment of educational institutions; (b) enabling out-of-school children to gain access to some form of education; (c) providing teachers with additional oppor-tunities to access training in educational best practices; (d) promoting another form of student learning by way of specialized interactive programs adapted to the academic level of each student; and (e) increasing the frequency of student evaluations so as to better identify gaps. Furthermore, it appears that the controlled use of multimedia tools (radio, DVD, CD and other media) helps to boost student motivation. The experience of countries as diverse as Indonesia, Nepal and Mali shows how ICTs can be utilized to improve the management and governance of institutions, support the training of teachers and the education of students, and enhance school education. More generally, enhancing connectivity and ICT usage in the education sector helps to improve the proficiency of the workforce and to promote a greater level of responsiveness to the needs of the private sector, which will, in the medium term, boost employment and economic growth.

Provided that they are well thought out and effectively applied, ICTs hold great promise for improving education in Morocco. Morocco's 2013 digital strategy aimed to expand the use of ICTs in public education through a number of major programs.[10] Nevertheless, the development of ICTs should be seen as complementing and at times underpinning the other in-depth reforms referred to above. In some circumstances, the introduction of ICTs can help address training issues and teacher absenteeism, support learning evaluations and enrich program content, reduce the school dropout rate, narrow sociocultural gaps between students and limit the perpetuation of inequalities. In view of the challenges and potential opportunities associated with the use of ICTs, their introduction into the school system should be done in the context of an overall national strategy. Such a strategy should not be based exclusively on technical or technological considerations but should include an investment and equipment installation program for schools, proper training for teaching staff, and the production of suitable qualitative content and methods that will facilitate the introduction of this new tool for supporting educational programs and improving educational outcomes in all areas, including basic learning.

Investing in Health for Improved Well-Being

Investing in health—as in education—implies a cost. However, investing in health today can help to improve an individual's future productivity. Promoting better health for the population can be an investment in a type of capital (Schultz 1960; Becker 1962). There is widely acknowledged empirical evidence that improvements in health conditions contribute to growth and the economic development of nations. However, while a country's GDP reflects the benefits of improved economic productivity, it cannot reflect all of the intangible and intrinsic value of better health, or in other words, the value of health as an end in itself. In 2013, the Lancet Commission on investment in health demonstrated with empirical evidence a factor that was already widely and intuitively acknowledged: the value of improved living conditions and life expectancy for men and women goes well beyond the direct causal link to economic growth. The "total revenue from the return on investment in health would far exceed the utilitarian value as measured by GDP" (The Lancet 2013).

General Health and Economic Health

Human health and economic development are intricately intertwined and it is reasonable to suppose that this causal relationship works both ways. Healthy individuals are more apt to learn, be productive and invest in their own human capital—and that of their children—because they can expect to live longer and see a long-term return on their investment. In return, economic growth supplies resources that can lead to improved health. High-income countries (or individuals) can afford to spend more on their health, whether in terms of nutrition and hygiene, prevention and treatment or medical equipment and infrastructure. The chart below summarizes the various ways in which improvement in health leads to an increase in per capita GDP (see figure 5.6).

Improvements in the health and nutrition of children and adults can have multiple positive impacts on the revenue of households and the nation, because of their effect on cognitive capacity, education, fertility, participation in the labor market, and individual productivity. Improving overall health in a country can have additional positive effects on human behavior. It can develop the drive to innovate or to make use of available innovations, where such innovations enhance the value of work. While estimates of the measure of real positive effects of health on economic development may vary, a reasonable calculation based on the existing literature suggests that health accounts for a 20 percent to 30 percent variation in revenue among countries. This disparity may be explained by three main effects: (a) the effect of health on human capital in terms of productivity and training, (b) the effect of health on demographics and fertility, and (c) the effect of health on savings and investment. Longer life expectancy due to better

Figure 5.6 The Links between Health and per Capita GDP

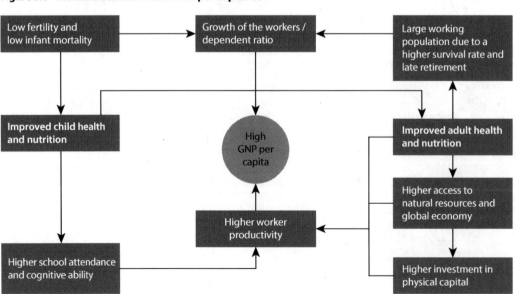

Source: Lancet 2013.

health and a long-term return on investment in human capital lead to greater incentives to save and invest.

The economic benefits of health are also measured in terms of wealth and additional years of life. While many micro- and macroeconomic studies assess the impact of improved health on economic productivity and GDP, they fail to take into account the intrinsic value that people attribute to their personal health or the significant investments that they are prepared to make to improve their living and working conditions. The phrase "health is money" is common to many cultures, and not just in the figurative sense. The Millennium Survey carried out for the United Nations Millennium Summit, showed that good health was the number one desire of men and women throughout the world. The fear of illness and premature death has made the fight against disease one of the main priorities of every society and has led to the inclusion of the right to health as a fundamental human right in international law. This same concern is voiced in surveys among Moroccan households that list health, employment and the education of their children among their main concerns (HCP 2012).

The estimated "total income" of a country, over and above GDP, provides a more accurate and complete picture of the value of investing in health. A "total income" approach links the growth of national revenue to the value that people attribute to longer life as measured in additional years of life (AYL) (see box 5.2). This approach exemplifies the way in which people will forego the possibility of

---

Box 5.2 Measuring "Total Income"

Imagine two countries with identical per capita GDP, but with starkly different situations as far as health is concerned. The population of country A lives longer and enjoys better health than the population of country B. If per capita GDP is the sole measure used to determine wealth, this approach does not take account of the monetary value of country A's superior performance. The lower risk of mortality in country A will not be considered when calculating the national revenue. Whenever one attempts to calculate changes in the levels of well-being of a population, the fact that reduced levels of mortality cannot be taken into account constitutes a major omission. "Total income accounting" takes care of this oversight.

Source: The Lancet 2013.

---

more income, certain pleasures or comforts for the sake of increasing their life expectancy. By using a "total income" approach, it is estimated that between 2000 and 2011, almost a quarter of the growth in total revenue of developing countries was due to benefits derived from AYL.

Beyond GDP and total income (which takes account of the AYL), quality of life is an important intangible capital but one that is difficult to measure. The economic cost of ill-health goes beyond the direct and indirect expenses associated with medical care (consultation, hospitalization, drugs, transport, etc.) and opportunity costs (loss of productivity and income). It includes the intangible costs resulting from an illness, such as distress, anxiety, pain and in general, the loss of well-being and decline in the quality of life experienced by the patient and his or her loved ones. In order to determine the number of years lived with a diminished quality of life, the Disability Adjusted Life Years (DALY) is a measure for quantifying the burden of disease by measuring life expectancy in good health; that is, by deducting from the overall life expectancy the number of years of life "lost" as a result of ill health, disability, or early death.

Status Report on Morocco's Health
A Mixed Overall Performance

Since its independence, Morocco has seen significant improvements in health outcomes. Over the past 50 years, infant-child and maternal mortality have registered a marked decline while life expectancy at birth has increased. Infant mortality fell from 145 per 1,000 live births in 1960 to 63 in 1990 and 24 in 2015, while infant-child mortality dropped from 240 per 1,000 live births in 1960 to 80 in 1990 and 28 in 2015. Maternal mortality declined from 317 per 100,000 live births in 1990 to 121 in 2010, while life expectancy at birth rose from 48 years in 1960 to 75 years in 2015 (World Bank WDI). As is the case for other countries within the region, these results are partly attributable to the demographic transition underway in Morocco. The country is also experiencing a transition in terms of a reduction in the number of communicable diseases and an increase in non-communicable diseases (NCDs). While there has been a reduction in overall mortality rates, the share of NCDs and accidents in the morbidity burden has increased. At the same time, urbanization has expanded, lifestyles have evolved and there has been a decrease in the prevalence of communicable diseases. The burden of morbidity in Morocco clearly shows the prevalence of NCDs (diabetes, hypertension, etc.) (see figure 5.7).

Despite some progress, health outcomes in Morocco do not measure up to the results in other countries with similar levels of socioeconomic development. Ratios of maternal and infant-child mortality are still very high and well above the level of comparable countries within the region (see figures 5.8 and 5.9). These mixed results are due in particular to healthcare delivery that is inadequate, unequally distributed and insufficient to satisfy demand.

Figure 5.7 Morocco: Morbidity Burden, 2013

Morocco, both sexes, all ages, 2013, DALYs

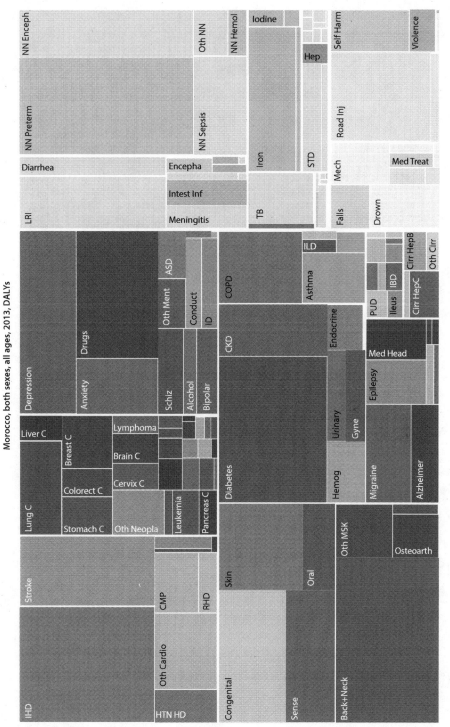

Source: Global Health Data Exchange. http://ghdx.healthdata.org/global-burden-disease-study-2010-gbd-2010-data-downloads.

Figure 5.8 Maternal Mortality Ratio: International Comparison
(number of deaths per 100,000 births)

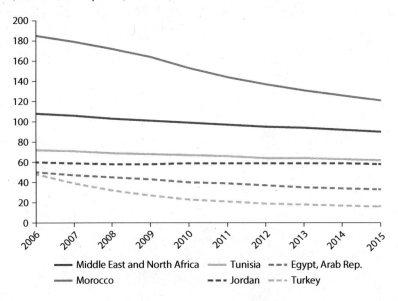

Figure 5.9 Infant-Child Mortality Ratio: International Comparison
(number of deaths per 1,000 births)

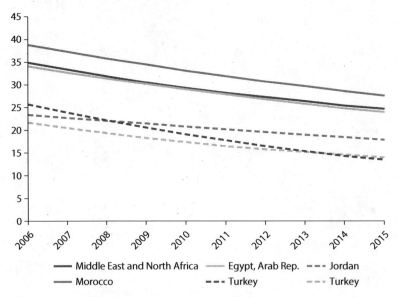

Source: World Development Indicators, World Bank.
Note: For the sake of comparison, international databases are used here. The data may differ slightly from national data.

Inadequate and Precarious Healthcare Supply

According to the WHO (2012), Morocco is one of 57 countries whose supply of health services is inadequate. The ratio of doctors or nurses per 10,000 inhabitants does not meet international standards and remains below critical thresholds. The ratio of doctors per 10,000 inhabitants is 6.2 in Morocco, whereas Algeria, Tunisia, Libya and Spain register ratios of 12.1, 11.9, 19 and 37.1, respectively. The ratio of paramedics is 8.9, close to that of Mauritania, (6.7), but far behind the numbers for Algeria, Tunisia, Libya and Spain (with 19.5, 32.8, 68 and 51.6, respectively). The number of hospital beds per 10,000 inhabitants is 11, which is low compared to Algeria, Tunisia, Libya and Spain (with 17, 21, 31 and 32, respectively). With regard to mental health, Morocco has less than one bed per 10,000 inhabitants, as against an international average of 4.4 beds. Moreover, the health system is beset by operational problems such as absenteeism, dual practice and training that is ill-adapted to actual needs.

Regarding the overall supply of health services and the allocation of public funds, primary healthcare has traditionally been underserved in comparison to hospital care, especially at the tertiary level. In 2010, hospitals received 60 percent of funds invested while only 5 percent was allocated for primary healthcare. More specifically, the five university hospitals (*Centres Hospitaliers Universitaires*) accounted for 19 percent of the total budget of the Ministry of Health. Between 2005 and 2010, their allocations increased by a multiple of 2.25, whereas the overall budget of the Ministry of Health grew by a multiple of only 1.7. The tradition of according greater importance to tertiary facilities, to the detriment of primary and preventive health services, tests the long-term financial sustainability of the sector, especially at a time of epidemiological transition, and when the system is burdened by the increase of costly chronic diseases. Furthermore, there is a level of disconnect between outpatient and hospital care, thus making follow-up of patients difficult and generating unnecessary costs.

Disparities have been observed among regions in terms of the supply of healthcare, especially in the allocation of resources and deployment of health personnel. While the public sector continues to provide most essential services, the private sector is fast developing health services, albeit in an unregulated and poorly organized manner.[11] Access to essential health services is limited, especially in rural areas, as reflected in the low number of medical consultations registered in these areas. In terms of access to healthcare, Morocco suffers more than the other countries of the region from glaring inequalities among its regions, as well as between rural and urban areas and between rich and poor populations (see figure 5.10). Human resources in the health sector are unevenly distributed, especially at the primary healthcare level. While it is acknowledged that Morocco's health system is faced with a shortage of human resources, there is also consensus that human resources are unequally distributed throughout the country. The number of health professionals is not proportionate to the needs of the population, especially in rural areas. In Morocco, the average number of people to one doctor is 2,107, with the ratio increasing to double that number in the Taza al Hoceima Tounate region (4,201), while in the Greater Casablanca area,

Figure 5.10 Number of Assisted Births, by Region and Income Level
(percent)

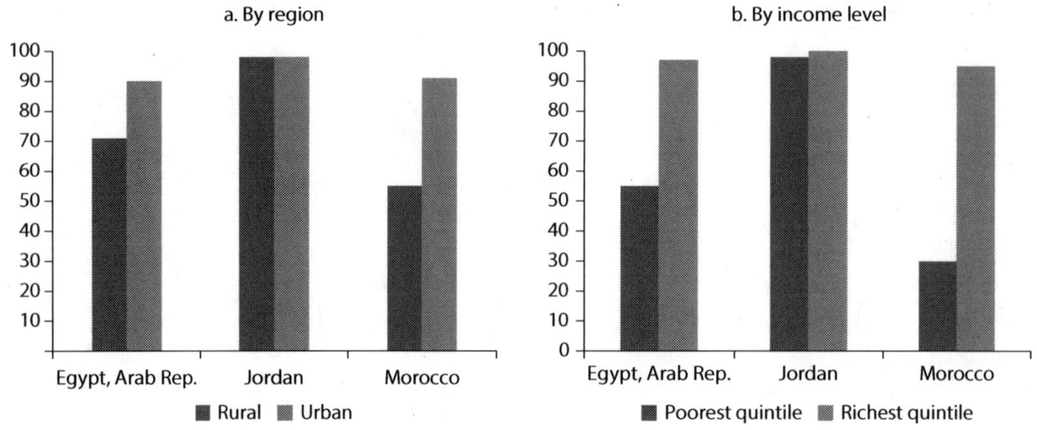

a. By region

b. By income level

Source: World Bank 2012.

the ratio is half that number. Furthermore, the number of inhabitants per nurse also varies widely between regions, from 2,147 inhabitants to one nurse in Greater Casablanca to 571 in the Laâyoune-Boujdour-Saguía El Hamra region. The training of medical and paramedical staff has not evolved to adapt to the changing needs of the population, while access to continuing training is limited and its impact has not been assessed. There is a high level of absenteeism among healthcare professionals and the Ministry of Health has very limited scope for developing and implementing strategies for retaining health professionals and actively managing their careers.

The supply of healthcare is also affected by problems of governance. These problems include the high degree of centralization of the healthcare system, the lack of intersectoral collaboration and the absence of coordination and synergy of public policies, the limited involvement of users, local authorities and communities in the preparation and implementation of health programs, as well as the practice of informal payment. These governance issues have been documented in many official and unofficial reports, such as reports of the CESE, the Audit Office, Bodies of the Central Authority for the Prevention of Corruption, or Transparency International. For the past few years, the improvement of governance has been one of the priorities[12] of the Ministry of Health. However, to date, it has not managed to make any significant changes to the situation.

An Unmet Demand for Healthcare

It is also estimated that a quarter of Moroccans do not seek medical care when they are ill. This figure rises to a third of the population in rural areas. Furthermore, only a half of women in rural areas give birth with the help of qualified medical professionals, whereas the rate is 92 percent for women in urban areas. In addition to being a function of the remoteness of rural health centers, these figures also reflect the effects that differences in education and standards of living between urban and rural populations have on decisions taken in relation to delivery (Ministry of Health 2011). Overall, the annual per capita demand for medical consultation is 0.6 (compared to an average of 6.6 in OECD countries in 2011) and the poorest people account for only 13 percent of users of primary healthcare facilities and 11 percent of patients in hospitals. Approximately 90 percent of maternal deaths in Morocco could be avoided. Emergency obstetric and neonatal care is given in less than 30 percent of cases of complicated births (Ministry of Health 2012). Similarly, pneumonia, diarrhea and malaria were the cause of 43 percent of deaths of children under the age of 5, while a third of child deaths were caused by malnutrition.

Medical coverage is spotty, and the number of Moroccans currently benefiting from such coverage is limited. Apart from medical coverage provided by the ESSPs (primary health care institutions), which is accessible to all, the proportion of the population covered by a pooled funding mechanism remains limited. The *Régime d'Assistance Médicale* (Medical Assistance Plan for Financially the Underprivileged RAMED) waives the total cost of hospitalization for poor and vulnerable populations. At end-2015, approximately 3.4 million households or almost 9 million persons had been deemed eligible for RAMED. The mandatory health insurance (AMO), which should in principle cover the rest of the wage-earning population, was created in 2005 and included about 8 million beneficiaries in 2013. The first medical insurance plan intended for craftsmen, traders and members of the liberal professions, Inaya, suffered from deficiencies in the coverage selected, resulting in a very low take-up rate. Optimistic estimates place the total population of Morocco currently benefiting from this type of coverage at just 60 percent. This is partly explained by the large proportion of the population in informal employment, the low level of membership among employers and wage earners in the agricultural sector and the very limited coverage of independent workers who are not poor.

The share of direct payments by households consequently remains very high. In Morocco, public health expenditure for a population of 33 million inhabitants is less than US$2 billion per year. While the State budgetary allocation for health has doubled since 2007 to reach 5.7 percent of the budget as stipulated in the 2016 Budget Law, it is still well below levels observed in other comparable countries. The share of mutualized expenditure in total health expenditure is less than 35 percent, whereas the average for surrounding developing countries of the MENA region is 50 percent. As a consequence of limited medical coverage, households are left to shoulder huge costs for health services, thus resulting in limited total public expenditure for health and an inadequate and inequitable health system, as observed above.

In light of the unmet demand for public services in the health sector, the expectations of the population for effective reforms to be implemented are growing. These expectations pertain particularly to improved access, quality and distribution of health services. Indeed, despite recent initiatives undertaken by the authorities to extend health coverage and improve governance of the system and the quality of care, efforts to provide funding for and organize most health services continue to be fragmented. This is indicative of the overlapping of roles and responsibilities between service providers and those who pay for these services and the consequent inequity of access to healthcare. Furthermore, the low level and poor distribution of public expenditure for healthcare (in the absence of an effective integrated information system) result in the inefficient allocation and use of public funds and high private costs to the user. Correcting the prevailing inequalities and inefficiency is a matter of social justice. Furthermore, a radical reorganization of the system could yield significant economic gains at the individual level—by increasing productivity and reducing the charges to be borne by the user—as well as at the level of citizens in general, by enhancing their well-being, their confidence in the future and their capacity to enrich the human capital that Morocco needs in order to spur its growth and prosperity.

Investing in Health Capital

International experience shows that health reforms depend on the political context, the institutional framework and the design and scope of proposed reforms (Donaldson 1994). The approach to health issues cannot be restricted to technical choices about planning relating to infrastructure, equipment and services, the setting of priorities for the allocation of resources or personnel management, even though all of these issues of governance do contribute to the overall efficiency of the system. As a starting point, matters of health reflect society's political choices first and foremost. Two new international trends have emerged: first, there is expansion of the concept of the rights of the patient and the medical responsibilities of health professionals, and then there is also the strengthening of the link between the accountability of healthcare providers and the outcome of their efforts. The concept of universal health coverage,[13] which is increasingly taken into account in legislation or mentioned in national constitutions, is included in the form of patients' rights and the quality of the health system. These laws are intended to build a "health democracy," improve the quality of the health system and better prevent and offset health risks. In the same way that the efficient distribution of the factors of production (capital and labor) depends on the quality of market support institutions, the performance of the health system depends to a large extent on the quality of the institutions that govern it.

Necessary Intervention by the State

The health sector is unlike other sectors of the economy. While the Memorandum mainly advocates market solutions for the efficient allocation of resources, this chapter on health could also prescribe market-based solutions for resolving the problems of the health system. Similar to other sectors, the supply and quality of health services should be able to evolve and adapt to demand, which in turn should develop in keeping with the price and quality of the health services supplied. Why shouldn't the market and free competition without distortions be as successful in terms of access, price and quality of service as other service sectors, such as mobile telephony, for example? While these arguments do have merit, it is nonetheless true that health cannot be marketed in the same way as cellular phones. This is so because, while it is socially acceptable that the market may not satisfy everyone's desire for a smartphone (or even a roof over their heads), it is not socially acceptable that market forces should preclude life. Life and death are not just ordinary commodities, and for this reason, public sector intervention in the health sector is justified (Krugman 2009). Musgrove names nine criteria that justify public sector intervention in the health system. These criteria pertain to questions of economic efficiency (public goods, externalities, catastrophic cost and efficiency cost), ethical reasons (poverty, horizontal and vertical equity and duty to assist), as well as issues of political economy (mainly linked to the demands of the population) (Musgrove 1999).

It would appear that all the criteria that justify State intervention apply in the case of Morocco. Specifically, Morocco's health indicators are characterized by glaring disparities between rural and urban areas and between socioeconomic groups (notably, concerning health status and access—see above). The improvement of the health of the population and the reduction of disparities can only generate significant positive externalities. There is also strong public demand for accessible healthcare for all, due to the expectations created by the inclusion of the right to health in the Constitution and the development of RAMED.

The Strategy of Regulatory Authorities

The Moroccan Constitution of 2011 explicitly recognizes that the people of Morocco have "a right to healthcare." Specifically, Article 31 stipulates that "the State, the public establishments and the local and regional governments work for the mobilization of all the means available to facilitate the equal access of all citizens to conditions that permit their enjoyment of the right to healthcare, to social protection, medical coverage and to the mutual or organized, joint and several liability of the State." On the basis of *Intidarat*, an innovative national consultation on health issues, in July 2013 Morocco organized a second national conference on health (the first one was held in 1959), to seek consensus on the nature and extent of the problems in the health sector and to organize future reforms. The conference drew on a Royal Letter issuing a call to action, as well as on a strategy for the health sector covering the period 2012–16 and the White Paper for the health sector.

These national commitments have recently been bolstered by commitments made at the international level. Universal health coverage is the third of the Sustainable Development Goals (SDGs) adopted in September 2015 by Morocco and other United Nations member States. It is defined as the enjoyment by all members of the population of quality basic healthcare, in accordance with their needs and without catastrophic financial implications, i.e., without a significant fall in the living standards of patients or without them falling into poverty as a result of health expenditure.

Extending Medical Coverage

The extension of health coverage (or mutualized funding) is at the core of the projected reform of the health sector in Morocco. Extended medical coverage is an essential component of the access for all to basic healthcare, in accordance with their needs and without catastrophic financial consequences; in other words, without a drastic decline in the patients' living standards or without them falling into poverty as a result of the illness. A number of considerations must be taken into account when measuring and extending medical coverage. Medical coverage may revolve around three axes (see figure 5.11). These are (1) population (what is the proportion of the population that benefits from healthcare paid for with collective funds?); (2) essential health-related goods and services (what proportion of essential health goods and services are paid for with collective funds?); (3) the cost of health-related goods and services (what percentage of the costs is paid for with collective funds?). The progression toward universal health coverage requires the extension of medical coverage along these three axes. Owing to the fact that resources are typically limited, it is impossible to cover 100 percent of the costs of essential health goods and services for the entire population. There should therefore be an ongoing process of negotiation and the resulting agreements should be based on the health needs of the population and the expectations of stakeholders. The extension of medical coverage presupposes an increase in the resources allocated to health and/or an improvement in the unit costs of health goods and services.

The extension of medical coverage requires an adjustment in the supply of healthcare. Generalized mutual health insurance is necessary to ensure access for all to quality basic healthcare. However, this is in itself not sufficient. Public health policymakers should also give consideration to the availability and quality of health-related goods and services: healthcare institutions, the equipment in these establishments, the availability of skilled human resources, essential drugs and quality control. The implementation of universal health coverage often involves making investments in the health sector in order to improve and increase the supply of public healthcare, but also to integrate the supply of independent care/private care (and in turn, to better regulate it).

Figure 5.11 Diagram Showing Medical Coverage in Morocco

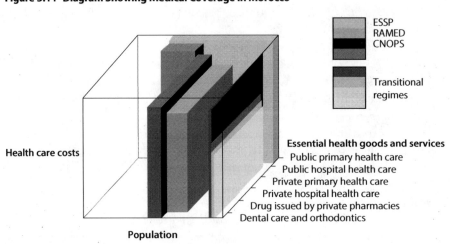

The first step toward extending medical coverage in Morocco would be the adoption by the various stakeholders of a coherent overall vision. Such a strategic vision would take account of all the modalities for coverage that currently exist (public and private insurance and State expenditure on health), the various types of care (ambulatory care, hospitalization in public and private hospitals) and all categories of the population (salaried workers, those working in independent and liberal professions, the poor and vulnerable). An interministerial steering committee for health coverage reform and an interministerial technical committee have recently been formed and report directly to the Head of Government. Such an institutional arrangement should invest these committees with authority and visibility and facilitate the necessary interministerial collaboration for developing a common and coherent approach to the extension of health coverage. In order to achieve this common, coherent vision, consultations must be held with other stakeholders, notably civil society (and especially the patients), health providers (including private ones) and private insurers. Since the end-users of health services are still under-represented, a preliminary stage could involve associations of patients suffering from a specific pathology, together with consumers' associations, while awaiting a more consolidated representation of the users of the health services in Morocco.

The harmonization of current and future systems is another important aspect. In order to achieve this objective, one should determine a basket of essential health services/universal healthcare, taking account not only of the needs and expectations of the population (studies on demand—both met and unmet—as well as health delivery costs at different levels and sectors are essential), but also existing constraints, including financial difficulties. This requires in particular that plans including RAMED, intended for non-salaried workers, should in time, cover the basic healthcare currently provided by the private sector. The rates of coverage/copayment[14] and the rates of contribution[15] would also need to be harmonized. At the same time, efforts must be made to extend coverage to new sectors of the population. The existing compulsory health coverage for salaried workers should therefore be extended to independent and self-employed workers in the formal sector. With respect to persons working in the informal sector, it seems particularly necessary to strengthen the capacities of both the institutions charged with monitoring the medical coverage of salaried workers, and those of the labor inspectors. It is also necessary to expand the RAMED eligibility criteria.

Improving Allocative Efficiency
In order to achieve universal health coverage and strengthen its human capital, Morocco should invest more in health. Budgetary allocations must evolve in accordance with real needs, of which relatively little is known, due to the lack of information on the heath of the population or the access of citizens to health services. Furthermore, budgetary allocations must be earmarked on the basis of activity/number of patients treated, or the population in general, and not made to adhere to the health expenditure of previous years, which themselves have

no bearing on the actual budgetary activities or population numbers. In the years 2000–10, some attempts were made to improve allocative efficiency by contracting services in hospitals and in the regions. However, these efforts were largely unsuccessful. In collaboration with the Health Ministry, the Ministry of Economy and Finance has begun to prepare a medium-term expenditure framework, which includes budgetary allocations for the Ministry of Health for the 2014–16 period.

Specific investment in health institutions, including those that provide primary healthcare, is an absolute necessity. There are complex inequalities in terms of the health of the population and access to healthcare services, which reflect the financial constraints on the demand side and geographical and administrative imbalances on the supply side. These shortcomings are indicative of a lack of human and material resources in ESSPs or of effective, targeted programs. In order to reduce such inequalities, the Government should adopt a two-tier strategy. First, it should try to understand the risk factors and diseases to which the poor living in rural areas are exposed and second, to adopt a health map that will inform all investment decisions. In addition, there should be a quantitative and qualitative strengthening of human resources in the health sector. Human resource training capacity is currently very limited and Morocco must explore innovative solutions if it wishes to quickly bridge the gap (for example, by reducing the time periods for training, redefining the roles of medical and paramedical staff, etc.).

In a bid to improve the efficiency of public expenditure on health, the Government recently undertook an ambitious budgetary reform with the development of a program-based budgeting system. The Ministry of Health is part of a second wave of ministries that have been called upon to carry out performance-based budgeting, involving the structuring of its budget and the use of a multiannual, program-based format, as well as the preparation of a performance plan (with objectives and indicators). The aim is to achieve greater transparency and accountability in the use of public funds, while gaining greater flexibility in management and ensuring enhanced performance all along the service delivery chain. The aim of budgetary reform is to strengthen the link between the budgeting function and the strategic priorities and to increase the transparency of budgetary allocation through the use of a budgetary program structure as well as targets and performance indicators.[16]

Prioritizing Prevention and Primary Healthcare

Prevention is an indirect means of freeing up budgetary resources in the medium term. When health services are regularly adjusted to adapt to health priorities (such as the prevention, detection and treatment of diabetes, hypertension, cardiovascular diseases and breast, cervical and uterine cancers), savings may be made on curative treatment and the freed-up resources reinvested. Morocco is in the middle of a period of demographic and epidemiological transition, a process leading to an increase in chronic illnesses, thus generating significant costs. Today, NCDs are already the leading causes of death in Morocco, accounting for 75 percent of the total number of deaths. Diabetes is the main cause of morbidity (followed by complications in premature babies and isch-emic heart disease). In view of worldwide trends, an increase in the rate of NCDs in the future is highly probable.

To improve the prevention, detection and treatment of NCDs, it is imperative that primary healthcare and the referral system be strengthened. A recent World Bank study has shown that more than half (54 percent) of patients treated in hospital in Morocco had direct recourse to treatment without prior referral (World Bank 2012). The promotion of the use of primary healthcare services can be most effective in containing the prevalence of NCDs, while also representing considerable savings.

The extension of ambulatory services is another source of budgetary efficiency and a means of improving health delivery, especially for people who are margin-alized or living in remote communities. Several countries have successfully devel-oped mobile health teams to improve the delivery of health services in rural and isolated areas. For example, integrated mobile teams have been set up in Burundi; these were originally established to support the family planning services and fight against gender-related violence among populations in transition. The services were subsequently extended to include antenatal care, the prevention and treat-ment of malaria, the promotion of proper nutrition, the consumption of clean water, as well as vaccination campaigns and sanitation services (USAID 2012). Preliminary observations have revealed that the integrated mobile teams are able to reach a large number of male patients, a task that had proved difficult for the non-mobile health services. The use of mobile health teams shows great potential in terms of long-term viability, as their activities are now integrated into the work plans of the relevant health districts and are subject to monthly scheduling in each district. Currently available data suggest that mobile teams are effective and very useful in reaching large populations in transition that have limited access to health services. In Nigeria, it has been shown that the mobile health team devel-oped in the region of Abuja has also been successful in providing primary health services in rural, isolated areas (United Nations 2013).

Strengthening Governance in the Health System

The current system of governance in Morocco's health sector does not provide the necessary incentives to promote greater efficiency and proper management of resources, or ensure improved access and quality of health care. International experience suggests that the design of the system should be oriented toward patient-centered service delivery, rather than on bureaucratic requirements. Specifically, this presupposes: (a) the consolidation of the health financing sys-tem; (b) the organizational reform of the Ministry of Health; (c) increased accountability of stakeholders; (d) greater motivation of health professionals and (e) more modern information systems.

The extension of medical coverage will necessitate major reforms in terms of governance of the system and financing of health care. First, while medical cover-age is generally mixed (a combination of funding from the State budget, social security contributions and insurance premiums), this diversity of coverage should be part of a coherent framework and there should be coordination among the various funding modalities. Second, it is important to limit health coverage fragmentation, as this leads not only to disparities and inequity, but also to inefficiency. The administrative costs of medical coverage are subject to economies of scale. In other words, a well-integrated institutional structure, backed by an efficient information system, helps to reduce the cost of managing health coverage. Third, it is advisable to have a rational distribution of functions within the health system; specifically, a separation of the functions of financial management and health delivery, in order to optimize collective resources. The separation of these functions can help to prevent situations whereby management institutions try to induce their policyholders to use the health services that they offer, to the detriment of more efficient external sources. The separation of functions also makes it possible for the body in charge of managing and regulating the health system (usually the Health Ministry) to carry out its work effectively. The Health Ministry often tends to neglect its core functions when it is also required to provide health services and ensure financial management. A management body (whether new or existing) could therefore be entrusted with the management of RAMED's resources. The Ministry of Health could, for its part, outsource the management of its health institutions or make them self-sufficient, so that it may focus on its basic functions of supervision and regulation. With such enhanced powers, the Ministry of Health could perform the crucial functions of regulating and monitoring the quality and quantity of healthcare delivery (whether public or private, and including drugs and health products), providing oversight, presiding over multiparty negotiations and promoting better health. All of these functions would help to increase the efficiency of health coverage.

Ideally, the institutional reorganization of the health sector should be carried out in parallel with an organizational reform of the Health Ministry (notably, the deconcentration of its functions). The technical audit conducted in 2004 with a view to decentralizing the Health Ministry found that while the centralized structure established in 1994 to resolve the major health problems had indeed been effective, it was no longer relevant and was hampering governance of the sector, for the following reasons: (a) the centralized structure is essentially hierarchical but fragmented, thereby hampering integration at the central level and coordination with the lower levels of administration in the Ministry of Health; (b) the separation of ambulatory healthcare from hospital care prevents the emergence of a genuine first line of care, the continuity of treatment and effective guidance of patients; (c) the current structure has no mechanism or administrative unit in place for such essential services as regulation of the private sector, setting of standards, delivering licenses, sub-contracting and conducting technical audits; and (d) the current institutional framework does not allow for the separation of the functions of financing/purchase and delivery of services.

The governance issues besetting the health sector compromise accountability to the public and jeopardize equality of access to health services. First, in Morocco, there is no generalized system for monitoring and regulating healthcare providers, and more specifically the quality of the care they provide. Second, the rule of law and discipline should become more firmly entrenched within health institutions, making them accountable to the population and tackling corruption. For this, strong leadership is required. In other words, chief medical officers that are dynamic, energetic and visionary are needed. There should also be a team spirit, an "esprit de corps" that is inspired by the sense of a common mission and a commitment to collaborative action and a willingness to act in concert with the local and regional offices of the Ministry of Health. Third, practices of proven effectiveness, such as the Quality Competition, should be rolled out across the system. Fourth, in health, as in other public services, there must be greater accountability on the part of all stakeholders if governance is to be improved. This requires the creation of a comprehensive system of grievance management.[17]

In order to obtain better results, it is important to ensure that health workers are competent and motivated. It is a proven fact that financial incentives can have positive effects on the productivity of workers, as well as the quality of services rendered, through a more rigorous adherence to professional standards and greater attention to satisfying users' needs. Incentives can also serve to lessen rates of absenteeism. In 2011, representatives of health worker organizations accepted in principle the introduction of financial incentives. This creates a conducive environment for the introduction of performance-based incentives, although the details must be worked out and approved by all stakeholders, including the Ministry of Economy and Finance. It has also been demonstrated that financial incentives can only have a short-lived effect on worker motivation if they are not complemented by more intangible benefits, such as possibilities for continuing education and attractive career prospects, effective supervision, a competent management team and a transparent and fair process of evaluation that rewards performance. It is also an acknowledged fact that motivation alone cannot guarantee improved performance. Other more tangible elements, such as improvements in infrastructure and access to equipment, medication and modern communication technologies, together with organizational arrangements and procedures that enhance efficiency, such as deconcentrated decision-making and teamwork, are equally important.

The effective and efficient operation of a modern health system requires the development of an integrated health management and information system (HMIS). In recent years, Morocco has developed a system of data collection in some areas (for example, for pharmacovigilance and a number of vertical programs such as maternal and infant health), as well as the blueprint for the development of an HMIS. However, the blueprint was never implemented and the HMIS remains a largely fragmented, compartmentalized and paper-based system. Each unit collects its own, often duplicative data, leaving health delivery services with a heavy burden of reporting. There is little centralized data integration and scant information that may be helpful for health institutions in taking decisions on medical or administrative matters. National statistics are published with a two-year delay and policymakers do not have the benefit of timely, verified, reliable and complete data. There is no interoperability between the information systems of the main insurers, while the private sector is not party to the information system managed by the Ministry of Health. The lack of data in turn contributes to the absence of transparency and accountability in the sector, as citizens have little or no opportunity for questioning the access, quality and responsiveness of the health system. Furthermore, the lack of data complicates the task of the Government in assessing the effectiveness of ongoing or planned reforms aimed at reducing inequalities and improving the quality of services in the health sector.

The creation of a computerized HMIS system would be a priority for improving the performance of the health sector in Morocco (Kyu and Michelman 1990). This is a priority that has been acknowledged by the Moroccan authorities and showcased in the White Paper, as well as in the 2012–16 sectoral strategy. With regard to technological solutions, the authorities should be guided by the experiences of many countries in designing the system on the basis of the following elements: reporting, institutional management, patient management (patients' electronic records), a referral system, quality assessment, data analysis at the provincial, regional and central levels and reporting systems, as well as the central data repository (Chetley 2006). Apart from technological solutions, the successful implementation of the system will depend to a large extent on factors of governance and behavior, notably the involvement, sensitization and empowerment of stakeholders, but also the building of human capacity and the inclusion of social and cultural considerations, as well as financial and budgetary constraints.

Prioritizing Early Childhood as the Foundation of Human Capital

Attention to ECD is the foundation on which to generate the best returns on human capital investment. Investments made in early childhood, particularly by parents and communities providing care and giving of their time, is essential not only for the protection of the rights of children and for reducing different forms of exclusion, determinism and social inequalities, but also for increasing a country's economic efficiency, productivity and wealth accumulation in the long term.

The Economic Dimension of Investing in ECD

The period of early childhood is crucial for the future development of an individual. The period of early childhood is marked by a number of crucial and rapid changes that influence the development of young children at a time when they are particularly receptive to their environment. Whatever the life circumstances of young children, be they peaceful or troubled, their living conditions will have lasting repercussions on their physical, cognitive, social and emotional development. Their performance in school, their health as adults and their on-the-job productivity will, to a large extent, depend on the quality of investments in early childhood. The protection and support received during early childhood play a decisive role in the fight against social exclusion, as poverty and inequalities in adult life often stem from the inequalities experienced in the early formative years.

In view of the fact that living conditions during early childhood play a decisive role in later development, investments made during this period can generate far greater economic returns than actions taken at a later stage (see figure 5.12). The deficiencies accumulated during early childhood in terms of security, affection, awareness and stimulation are more difficult, costlier and often harder to overcome later in life. Investing in the healthy development of young children is therefore invaluable in many ways: it is a means for guaranteeing the health, success and well-being of individuals over the long term, while contributing to the reduction of inequalities.

Early Childhood Protection and Education in Morocco

It is difficult to evaluate with precision the status of ECD in Morocco, owing to a lack of information. Some elements can be measured with greater accuracy than others, depending on the frequency of available data (for example, data on mortality). Other elements, such as the extent of cognitive and non-cognitive development or parental involvement with their children are also extremely important but much more difficult to assess. This section will examine the state of ECD in Morocco in terms of health and survival of young children, nutrition, role of parents, learning at an early age and the fight against inequalities.[18]

The progress made in providing healthcare during early childhood has led to a reduction in infant mortality. The number of deaths in the first year of life declined from 38 to 27 per 1,000 births between 2003 and 2012. As indicated

Figure 5.12 Rate of Return on Investment in Human Capital, by Age

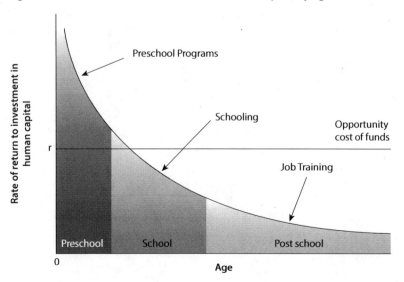

Source: Carneiro and Heckman 2003.

in the previous chapter, this rate of infant mortality remains high and significantly above the average for the MENA region (24 deaths per 1,000 births). The majority of children from the poorest families and rural areas are still not receiving the necessary levels of protection and education. The provision of postnatal care is particularly unsatisfactory. In 2011, only 22 percent of births received postnatal care. It is clear that additional investments in this type of care would yield significant returns in terms of good health and young child survival, as the majority of neonatal deaths are preventable.

There are serious weaknesses in Morocco's immunization program and treatment of infant diseases. Children from the poorest households and from rural areas, in particular, are significantly less likely to benefit from immunization coverage. This increases the risk of epidemics, diseases, health and developmental problems, and death. The rates of immunization coverage have even shown a slight downward trend over the past 10 years, as they were higher in 2003 (around 90 percent) than in 2011 (87 percent). In view of the very high returns from investments in vaccinations, increasing the rate of immunization coverage to contain the outbreak of epidemics appears to be a priority.

Despite significant progress, a large number of Moroccan children, particularly those in rural areas, continue to suffer from malnutrition. In 2011, 15 percent of children suffered from delayed growth at the national level (down from 23 percent in 2003). The figure was in excess of 20 percent for rural areas. These children are also at higher risk of being underweight (4.3 percent) or emaciated (3 percent). Children suffering from delayed growth are more likely to be affected by cognitive deficits, serious health problems, lower productivity, and lower income levels as adults. Micronutrient and vitamin deficiencies are another threat to the healthy development of children: in 2006, only 20 percent of Moroccan children lived in households in which adequately iodized salt was consumed. Furthermore, certain types of care provided by parents are also determinants of the health and nutrition of young children, particularly breastfeeding and treatment of diarrhea. In Morocco, only 28 percent of children are breastfed exclusively up to the age of six months. Proper hygiene, particularly through access to potable water and sanitation and certain daily practices such as hand-washing, also plays a fundamental role in the prevention of diseases and the improvement of nutrition. Notwithstanding the considerable increase in access to water and sanitation services, fewer than 40 percent of rural households are connected to the water supply network (running water in dwelling) and fewer than 3 percent have access to a public sanitation network (HCP 2015).

Parental stimulation and nurturing are not commonly practiced, even though they are essential factors for the physical, social, emotional and cognitive development of children. Such forms of behavior should be practiced as soon as possible after birth. Although behavioral evaluations in this area are rare, the available data suggest that Morocco is falling short and that there have been no notable improvements over time. The percentage of Moroccan children participating in developmental activities is estimated to have fallen from

48 percent in 2006 to 34 percent in 2011. This rate is lower than that recorded by Iraq (58 percent) and Tunisia (71 percent) and slightly higher than The Republic of Yemen (33 percent). This finding could be due in part to the limited involvement of fathers in the education of their children: only 58 percent of Moroccan fathers participate in at least one activity with their children. Furthermore, with reading and play being essential to their development, only 21 percent of young children live in households with at least three books, and 34 percent have no toys in the home.

Violent discipline is an additional obstacle to the healthy development of children. Violent discipline refers not only to physical and corporal punishment of varying degrees of intensity, but also to forms of psychological aggression, such as addressing children by shouting, screaming and yelling. Violent discipline is a violation of the rights of children and does severe harm to their physical, emotional, social and cognitive development. In Morocco, no less than 90 percent of young children experienced some form of violence over the preceding month. In a survey of 50 developing countries, Morocco was found to have the 11th highest rate of violent discipline (El-Kogali and Krafft 2015).

Early childhood education is a launching pad for the social, emotional and cognitive development of children and is fundamental to their preparation for schooling. There have been instances in the past of Morocco registering relatively high rates of preschool enrolment (peak of 65 percent of children enrolled in preschool in 1998), owing essentially to the so-called traditional sector (Kouttab, M'sid). More recently, however, these rates have tended to stagnate or decrease slightly, particularly for young boys. Children may be enrolled in formal nursery schools up to two years before the primary level and also have access to other forms of preschool education, such as crèches and daycare. Nevertheless, the information available in Morocco is not sufficient to evaluate the rate of access to such institutions or their quality.

In addition, Moroccan children are faced with deep-seated inequalities from a very young age. These disparities are particularly distressing as, even before they can walk, Moroccan children are already following very different tracks that will define them for the rest of their lives. These inequalities are caused as much by unequal access to public services as by the sociocultural levels and extent of investment by families in their children. As a result, although salt iodization is a compulsory requirement under law throughout Morocco, it has been observed that a child from the Tensift region has only a three percent chance of growing up in a home where sufficiently iodized salt is used, as compared to 25 percent for a child from the Center-North region (see figure 5.13).

Investing in Early Childhood

Although largely intangible and invisible, the serious shortcomings and inequalities that mark ECD in Morocco are a major challenge to the country's economic and social development. Whether in relation to human rights, equal opportunity or even economic efficiency, it is critical to ensure that all Moroccan children can

Figure 5.13 Morocco: Percentage of Children Consuming Adequately Iodized Salt, by Region

(percent)

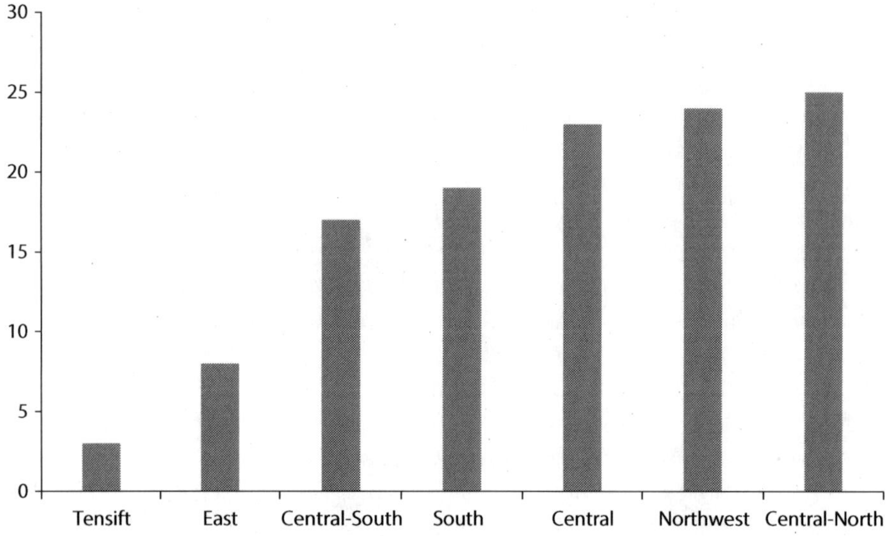

Source: El-Kogali and Krafft 2015, adapted from ENIMSJ 2006/2007.

benefit from better protection and care during early childhood. This will require action in terms of public information, coordination of State programs, quality investments and parental responsibility.

Launching Public Awareness and Information Campaigns

Even where parents have the best interest of their children at heart and have the necessary resources, they sometimes cannot access information to help them make better choices for their children. A survey of Moroccan parents has revealed that they often hold erroneous perceptions of ECD (Zellman, Karam, and Perlman 2014a and 2014b). Indeed, although sensory development begins during the prenatal period, brain development linked to language reaches its highest point before the end of the first year, and brain development linked to higher cognitive functions is at its peak at the age of three. Moroccan parents think that sensory and brain development begin later and that their impact on development occurs only after the child is older. Only 15 percent of parents surveyed correctly identified the pre-natal period as marking the beginning of brain development. In addition, only 8 percent of parents understood correctly that their own impact on the brain development of their children began during the prenatal period (see figure 5.14).

Following the birth of a child, it is vital that the parents be better informed about ideal nutritional practices (e.g., breastfeeding, introduction of complementary feeding and treatment of diarrhea, etc.) and issues of health and general hygiene. The implementation of systematic information campaigns could go a long way toward raising the awareness of parents on the importance of paying closer

Figure 5.14 Morocco: Parents' Knowledge of Early Childhood Development
(percent)

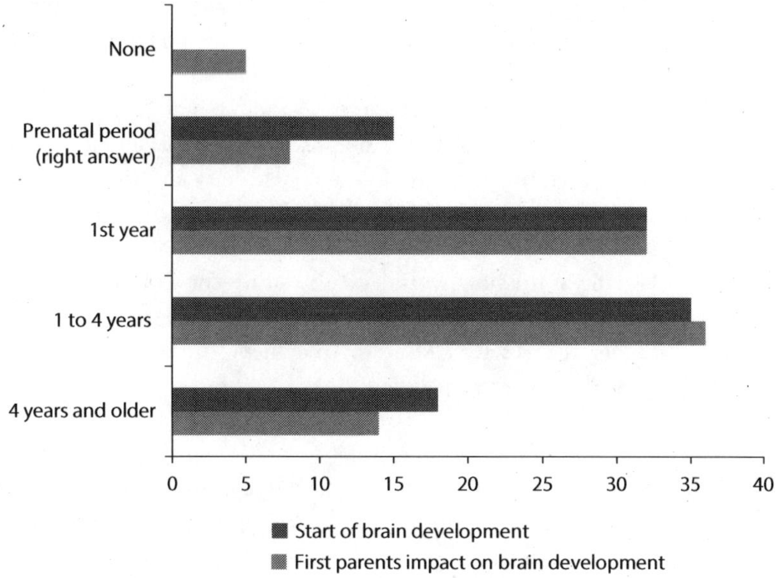

■ Start of brain development
■ First parents impact on brain development

Source: Adapted from Zellman, Karam, and Perlman 2014.

attention to infants. Such information campaigns could help parents to improve their nutritional practices and correct certain inappropriate behaviors that are often carried out with the best intentions. For example, a recent study in Jordan found that parents were introducing food supplements too early, in the belief that this practice would stimulate their children's growth (Obeidat, Salameh, Tayem, Mutair, and Gawasmeh 2014). Morocco is also at risk in this regard, underlining the need for in-depth surveys to evaluate the prevalence of this phenomenon.

The awareness campaigns and messages to families and communities would have a more meaningful impact if they were packaged as public health issues. For example, after conducting surveys on the knowledge, attitude and practices of its population, the archipelago of the Maldives implemented a program identifying about a dozen key messages on ECD that were then disseminated across all media channels (for example, the role of play and various daily practices that promote children's learning) (Naudeau, Kataoka, Valeri, Neuman, and Elder 2011). Using the same approach, Morocco could easily identify the information gaps within communities and families and provide the necessary advice to address these shortcomings and change behaviors and, in so doing, help families to better support the development and growth of their children. For example, greater understanding of the virtues of positive discipline would help parents, teachers and educators to consider a range of tools and methods, neither too lenient nor too punitive, for promoting self-discipline, a sense of responsibility, autonomy, love of learning and mutual respect among children (Nelsen 1981).

Better Coordination of Public Programs and Policies

In assigning priority to early childhood care, one of the major challenges to be faced is the fact that this is a crosscutting issue: there is a degree of fragmentation among the various organizations, programs and policies concerned with early childhood management in Morocco. There is no single body responsible for coordinating early childhood programs. The responsibilities and programs are dispersed among various ministries. Some of these responsibilities and programs also involve the not inconsiderable participation of civil society and the private sector, as well as actions by communities and families. Morocco would do well to identify a single organization—either a Ministry or a high-level interministerial coordinating council—whose mission would be to define the country's vision and objectives for early childhood protection and support (with clearly defined indicators and targets), formulate a strategy to achieve these objectives and put in place arrangements to measure progress.

Investing in Quality Preschooling

In view of the proven importance of the first few years of life for the development of a child, and in light of the evidence that early interventions produce enhanced outcomes, it would be appropriate to assign a higher degree of priority to public investments in early childhood as opposed to investments in the later stages of development. Public investments in this sector could also play an essential role in the promotion of equality and human rights. For example, it is widely recognized that the development of public preschool education is the most effective way of reducing inequalities and social determinism. Early childhood support programs can help to reduce the gaps between rich and poor from the moment children enter school. By increasing investments in this sector, Morocco could mitigate the market shortcomings that result in a shortage in the number of preschool places provided by the private sector and, in so doing, reap some significant benefits.

Notwithstanding the foregoing, the fact that public intervention is fully justified does not mean that the State should be the only or even the principal service provider. Private health institutions can also offer vaccinations on a paying basis or subsidized by the State. The principal role of the State should be to ensure coverage of the entire country regardless of the situation of the children or the modalities and means used. Substantial savings in public sector expenditure can be achieved in certain cases, for example, by organizing "children's health days" on a regular basis or launching nationwide vaccination campaigns. In other cases, the private sector may prove to be the most efficient service provider.

In order to optimize the impact of public interventions in the area of early childhood, it is essential to develop both a qualitative and quantitative approach. Improving the quality of children's services can be a daunting task, but it can also be an opportunity to mobilize existing resources. Public authorities are well placed to ensure the quality of interventions by enacting appropriate norms. For example, in preparing an integrated preschool education strategy, the establishment of norms and programs by the Ministry is an important factor for guaranteeing the quality, usefulness and relevance of investments in pre-school education. The Ministry of Health could also take similar steps to establish quality standards for pre- and postnatal care protocols and for utilizing children's healthcare consultations to advance early childhood protection initiatives, such as screening for malnutrition among pregnant women and disseminating messages on infant development.

Involving Parents and Bringing Them on Board

No public program or initiative can substitute for the full and informed engagement of parents in their children's education. With minimal training and with the benefit of the appropriate messages, parents can dedicate the same amount of time and effort to their role as educators as they do at present while having an even more significant impact on their children's development. Communities can also play a major role by providing information and messages on early childhood and by inviting families to make behavioral changes. The Jordanian program "Improving the Role of Parents" is a good example of using information to mobilize parents. While acknowledging that parents cannot know everything about child development, the program seeks to sensitize them to a variety of topics, including, notably, the role of fathers. Morocco could consider adopting this interesting model as a tool for improving parenting skills and for more effectively mobilizing their efforts to promote their children's development.

Notes

1. The activities that influence future monetary income, whether monetary or non-monetary, are determined by the nature of investments in human capital. The many forms of such investments include schooling, on-the-job training, medical care, migration and searching for information about prices and incomes. Gary Becker, *Human Capital*, N.Y, 1964

2. Quotation from Klaus Schwab on the occasion of the publication of the 2015 Human Capital Index by the World Economic Forum. See World Economic Forum portal.

3. Throughout their schooling, these students have nonetheless undergone over 2,000 hours of French instruction (eight hours per week in primary school, four hours at the lower secondary level and two hours at the upper secondary level). According to the experts, a basic level can be attained after only 200 to 300 hours of regular classes.

4. In 2000, the private sector accounted for only 4.7 percent of Morocco's school population, versus 13.6 percent in 2013. Today, that figure is more than 20 percent for urban areas.

5. A 2008 World Bank study on the investment climate revealed that around 31 percent of countries surveyed pointed to lack of adequate skills among the labor force as one of the major constraints to doing business in Morocco.

6. Formative evaluation takes place during a process of learning or training and is designed to allow pupils and students to become aware of their achievements and

difficulties, and to discover on their own how to move forward. Summative evaluation is conducted at the end of a period of learning or training and measures the achievements of the pupil or student, particularly when moving from one educational cycle to the other.

7. In 2011, Morocco's TIMSS scores ranged between 264 and 376, depending on the subjects and levels.

8. The *school-based management* system has gained widespread acceptance as a mechanism for managing the educational system. It aims to grant more autonomy and management powers to schools. Countries such as Canada, USA, Australia and Israel have been using this system for many years.

9. Although not tied to school attendance, the Tayssir program is presented as an educational support initiative. It involves the transfer of cash to fathers of school age children in poor rural communities. An evaluation of the program has shown that sensitizing fathers to the fact that investing in their children's education is a worthwhile proposition has had the effect of significantly increasing school enrolment (Benhassine and others 2014).

10. The Genie Program was extended to 2017 to equip 1206 junior high schools and 233 high schools with internet-ready multimedia classrooms. The Lawhati Program, launched in 2015, aims to equip students and teachers in institutions of higher learning and interns in vocational training establishments with "2 in 1 tablets" at preferential rates. The Injaz Program, which has been subsidized since 2011 and is now in its sixth edition, has made it possible for 106,000 students to have computers.

11. Approximately 50 percent of all private sector doctors are based along the Rabat-Casablanca axis (Ministry of Health 2009).

12. Specifically, through the holding of the second national conference on the subject, under the distinguished patronage of the King of Morocco on July 1, 2013 in Marrakesh

13. Universal health coverage is defined as the situation wherein all members of the population have access to the healthcare they need without having to incur financial difficulties.

14. Copayments may vary according to treatment, medical condition or income level of the patient, but should not vary from one treatment regime to the next.

15. Contributions may be proportional or progressive. In any event, the poor must be exempted from making contributions.

16. The first wave of Ministries to undertake this reform included the Ministry of Economy and Finance, the Ministry of National Education (with the recent addition of vocational training to the portfolio), and the Ministry of Agriculture, Water and Forest.

17. To this end, at the beginning of 2016, the Ministry of Health officially launched a dual platform; a web portal (www.chikayasanté.ma) and a telephone contact unit accessible through a specially assigned number (allochikayate). A pool of officers was specially appointed to handle grievances with all central and decentralized stakeholders of the Health Ministry, that have received a complaint about the way in which their health units interacted with users, suppliers and other providers or partners.

18. Unless indicated otherwise, data are sourced from El-Kogali and Krafft (2015) and El-Kogali and others (2016).

References

Aghion, Philippe, and Élie Cohen. 2004. "Éducation et croissance." Rapport pour le Conseil d'analyse économique, La Documentation française, Paris.

Arrow, Kenneth J. 1963. "Uncertainty and the Welfare Economics of Medical Care." *American Economic Review* LIII (5).

Bank Al-Maghrib (BAM). 2015. *Rapport annuel 2014*. Morocco.

Becker, Gary S. 1962. "Investment in Human Capital: A Theoretical Analysis." *Journal of Political Economy* 70 (5): 9–49.

Benhassine, Najy, Florencia Devoto, Esther Duflo, Pascaline Dupas, and Victor Pouliquen. 2014. "Turning a Shove into a Nudge? A 'Labeled Cash Transfer' for Education in Morocco." http://web.stanford.edu/~pdupas/Morocco_Tayssir_LCT.pdf.

Bodin, Jean. 1576. Les six livres de la République. Edition de Paris (1583).

Carneiro, P, and J. J. Heckman. 2003. "Human Capital Policy" *In Inequality in America: What Role for Human Capital Policies?*, edited by J. J. Heckman, A. B. Krueger, and B. Friedman, 77–237. Cambridge, MA: MIT Press.

Chetley, A. 2006. "Improving Health, Connecting People: The Role of ICT in the Health Sectors of Developing Countries." Framework Paper, InfoDev.

Donaldson, Dayl. 1994. "Health Sector Reform in Africa: Lessons Learned." Department of Population and International Health Harvard School of Public Health, Boston, MA.

El-Kogali, Safaa, and Caroline Krafft. 2015. *Expanding Opportunities for the Next Generation: Early Childhood Development in the Middle East and North Africa.* Washington, DC: World Bank.

El-Kogali, Safaa, Caroline Krafft, Touhami Abdelkhalek, Mohammed Benkassmi, Monica Chavez, Lucy Bassett, and Fouzia Ejjanoui. 2016. "Inequality of Opportunity in Early Childhood Development in Morocco over Time." Policy Research Working Paper 7670, World Bank, Washington, DC.

Hanushek, Eric A., Marc Piopiunik, and Simon Wiederhold. 2014. "The Value of Smarter Teachers: International Evidence on Teacher Cognitive Skills and Student Performance." NBER Working Paper 20727, National Bureau of Economic Research, Cambridge, MA.

Hart, Betty and Todd R. Risley. 1995. *Meaningful Differences in the Everyday Experience of Young American Children*. Baltimore, MD: Brookes.

High Commission for Planning (HCP). 2012. *Enquête sur le bien-être des ménages*. Morocco

———. 2015. *Recensement général de la population (RGPH) 2014*. Morocco.

Hattie, John. 2009. *Visible Learning: A Synthesis of Over 800 Meta-Analyses Relating to Achievement*. New York, NY: Routledge.

International Monetary Fund (IMF). 2016. *Selected Issues-Efficiency of Public Spending on Education in Morocco*. IMF Country Report 16/36, International Monetary Fund, Washington, DC.

Janjar, Mohammed-Sghir. 2016. "La place des livres dans une société à faible littératie." Dans *Le tissu de nos singularités: vivre ensemble au Maroc*. Presse de l'Université citoyenne. Fondation HEM Casablanca.

Klarman, H. A. 1965. "The Case for Public Intervention in Financing Health and Medical Services." *Medical Care* 3: 59–62.

Krugman, Paul. 2009. "Why Markets Can't Cure Healthcare?" *New York Times* Opinion page, July 25.

Kyu, Kim K., and E. Michelman. 1990. "An Examination of Factors for the Strategic Use of Information Systems in the Healthcare Industry." *MIS Quarterly* 14 (2): 201–15.

Ministry of Health. 2009. Comptes nationaux de la santé. Ministry of Health, Rabat, Morocco.

———. 2011. *Enquête nationale sur la population et la santé familiale (ENPSF)*. Morocco.

———. 2012. *État de santé de la population marocaine*. Morocco.

Musgrove, Philip. 1999. "Public Spending on Health Care: How Are Different Criteria Related?" *Health Policy* 47: 207–23.

Naudeau, S.; N. Kataoka, A. Valerio, M. J. Neuman, and L. K. Elder. 2011. *Investing in Young Children: An Early Childhood Development Guide for Policy Dialogue and Project Preparation*. Washington, DC: World Bank.

National Observatory for Human Development (ONDH) 2015. Report on the initial findings of the 2012 Household Panel Survey.

Nelsen, Jane. 1981. *Positive Discipline*. Fair Oaks, CA: Sunrise Press.

Obeidat, M., G. Salameh, A. Tayem, R. Mutair, and Y. Gawasmeh. 2014. "Feeding Practices in the North of Jordan." *Journal of the Royal Medical Services* 21 (1): 11–16.

Organisation for Economic Co-operation and Development (OECD). 1998. *Human Capital Investment. An international Comparison* OECD publishing

———. 2001. *The Well-being of Nations. The Role of Human and Social Capital* OECD publishing.

———. 2011. *Program for International Student assessment (PISA)*.

Schultz, Theodore W. 1960. "Capital Formation by Education." *Journal of Political Economy* 68 (6): 571–83.

The Lancet. 2013. "Global health 2035: a world converging within a generation." Prepared by a Commission of The Lancet on investment in health, an international multidisciplinary group of 25 commissioners chaired by Lawrence H. Summers and co-chaired by Dean Jamison.

Tough, Paul. 2012. *How Children Succeed: Grit, Curiosity and the Hidden Power of Character*. First Mariner Books edition.

UNESCO. 2014. Global education monitoring report. Teaching and learning: Achieving quality for all.

United Nations. 2013. "United Nations Public Service Awards Winners." Fact Sheet, p. 6.

USAID and Pathfinder International. 2012. *Introducing Integrated Mobile Teams to Burundi: Technical Update*.

World Bank. 2012. *Health Public Expenditure Review*. Washington, DC: World Bank

———. 2014. "Morocco Improved Access to Water and Sanitation Services Output-Based Aid Project." OBA Lessons Learned, note 4, Washington, DC.: World Bank.

———. 2015. *Morocco—School Autonomy and Accountability. Systems Approach for Better Education Results (SABER) Country Report: School Autonomy and Accountability*. Washington, DC: World Bank.

Zellman, G. L., R. Karam, and M. Perlman. 2014a. "How Moroccan Mothers and Fathers View Child Development and Their Role in Their Children's Education." *International Journal of Early Years Education* 22 (2): 197–209.

———. 2014b. "Predicting Child Development Knowledge and Engagement of Moroccan Parents." *Near and Middle Eastern Journal of Research in Education* 1 (5).

CHAPTER 6

Investing in Social Capital

"A society's endowment of social capital is critical to understanding its industrial structure, and hence its place in the global capitalist division of labor."
— Francis Fukuyama

Whereas institutional capital is based on the relationship between individuals and the state and human capital mainly lies within individuals themselves, social capital refers to the capital derived from the relationship between individuals within society. Social capital is deemed to be "social" because it refers to the set of collective norms among specific groups of people who have regular interactions as part of their daily lives. Moreover, it is a "capital" since it contributes to economic activity and the productive potential of individuals, businesses, and companies (Putnam 1993; Fukuyama 1995). Depending on the type of discipline (anthropological, sociological, economic, or political science), the term "social capital" may cover many concepts: collective identity, common values, shared ideals, cultural norms, mentalities, interpersonal trust, the sense of civic duty, civic engagement, the influence of networks, the rules that allow individuals to engage in collective action in a coherent manner, or the degree of harmony and collective empathy (Coleman 1988; Portes 1998; Putnam 2000; OECD 2001). Nobel Prize winner for Economics George Akerlof has noted that "in every social context, people have a notion of who they are, which is associated with beliefs about how they and others are supposed to behave. These notions play important roles in how economies work" (Akerlof and Kranton 2010). These beliefs have a bearing on the way in which fundamental individual freedoms and their attendant rules and responsibilities impact social relations—to allow each person to think freely, to question dogma, immutable truths, and other commonly held assumptions, to develop their ability to criticize and be self-critical, and to build the world of tomorrow.

This last chapter of the Memorandum will examine social capital and its development in Morocco. Although of all the intangible assets social capital is the most intangible and therefore the most elusive to grasp and measure, social capital nonetheless determines the effectiveness of all the other types of capital discussed thus far (produced, institutional, or human capital) and hence the process of wealth creation in general. For American political scientist Francis Fukuyama, by focusing the debate on the respective merits of industrial policy and the unfettered operation of markets, the literature on economic competitiveness overlooks an essential factor in the emergence of a modern economy: it is the weight of social virtues in society (Fukuyama 1995). These views are consistent with those of Max Weber, for whom honesty, reliability, the spirit of cooperation, and a sense of duty toward others are all social virtues that allow for the development of more individual virtues such as a work ethic, thriftiness, the ability to behave rationally, the capacity to innovate, and the willingness to take risks (Weber 1905). It would appear, therefore, that economic development is primarily linked to the development of a type of social capital that makes it possible for businesses, associations, and other groupings within society to organize themselves to produce an endogenous and holistic development.[1]

Contribution of Social Capital to Development

Social capital—or the set of norms and networks that facilitate collective action—exerts positive, concrete effects on economic life. First, when there is trust among individuals, the business climate is more favorable. By contrast, with a limited level of trust within society, people are disinclined to engage in exchanges and collaborate as they would have done in other circumstances. This generates additional costs for those persons who do collaborate. Second, when the social networks within a society are numerous and interlinked, whether within private enterprise or through the supply of collective goods, it becomes easier for individuals to act as part of the group. Third, when all members of society can fully exploit their potential and contribute to economic and social life, regardless of their gender, their religion, or any other defining factor, society as a whole derives economic benefit. Last, social capital is important for economic life in that it prevents various types of destructive conflicts among sectors of the population, such as riots, political instability, or disruptions to public order that may seriously stymie investment and growth. All in all, social capital is a key element in enhancing the effectiveness of a country's political and economic institutions. Extensive studies conducted in various regions and in a number of countries have shown that there is a close and significant link between social capital and economic growth, whether at the regional level, or within or among countries (Putnam, Leonardi, and Nanetti 1993; Helliwell and Putnam 1995; Keefer and Knack 1997).

Empirical studies in the field of institutional economic theory have shown that a country's sustained economic growth is contingent on the level of its social infrastructure; that is, the norms, past experiences, and collective expectations accumulated over time, which help to support capital accumulation (Hall and Jones 1999). Formal institutions (for example, courts that ensure the protection of property rights and rigorously apply the rule of law), as well as informal institutions (such as interpersonal trust within the society, social cohesion, and voluntary engagement), would seem to be the only stable determining factors to ensure long-term, sustainable capital accumulation; in other words, leading to long-term economic growth (North 1990). Numerous econometric studies have empirically substantiated their theory on the relationship between social institutions and economic growth (Helliwell and Putnam 1995; Zak and Knack 1998; Beugelsdijk, de Groot, and van Schaik 2004). One should note, however, that in the absence of usable data, application of the institutional approach has generally focused more on the role of formal institutions of governance (Acemoglu, Johnson, and Robinson 2001) at the expense of informal institutions, whose role in economic development is just as important (Landes 1998).

For example, the economists Philip Keefer and Stephen Knack used indicators from the World Values Survey to demonstrate how social capital—calculated using measures for interpersonal trust, norms of civic involvement, and the role of networks—plays an important part in economic performance (Keefer and Knack 1997). Societies that are characterized by a high level of cooperation and interpersonal trust not only tend to innovate more and to accumulate physical capital, they are also more likely to enjoy higher returns from their accumulated human capital.[2] The role of networks, on the other hand, is more ambiguous and more subject to debate, as the negative effects of some forms of associational life (for example, mafia-type associations) appear to counteract the positive effects of other associations and networks within society. In line with these studies, this concluding chapter of the Memorandum seeks to examine the economic advantages that Morocco could gain by increasing its social capital.

As seen in chapter 1 on Morocco's economy in 2016, the main factor determining the wealth gap between high-income countries and developing countries is the level of accumulation of intangible capital. Within this intangible capital, the level of accumulation of social capital is the main factor to be considered when determining its direct or indirect influence on the accumulation of human and institutional capital. While developing countries do have a lower level of human and institutional capital than high-income countries, differences in levels of education and governance cannot be the main factor accounting for the development gap between wealthy and less wealthy countries. There is another factor shared in varying degrees by all developing countries that would seem to help explain the gap. In empirical studies, country-specific effects linked to geography, history, culture, and other more "permanent" aspects of a society seem to account for the gaps in development between countries, once differences in education and governance have been taken into account (World Bank 2011). These effects may reflect a country's unrealized potential human and institutional capital owing to unfavorable societal characteristics. A low level of social capital is essentially an opportunity cost, a shortfall with respect to investments made in all other areas.

While social capital may not be a variable that is easily modified, it can be strengthened through public policies in at least two areas: achieving gender equality and enhancing the quality of interpersonal relations. Since it is the fruit of history, geography, and culture, social capital is not very malleable. Unlike in the case of citizen mobilization, it is not possible to mandate generalized trust among citizens, no more than one can mandate how people should interact, live, or work together. Public policies therefore have a limited margin of influence, especially since, by definition, social capital has more to do with interpersonal relations than with the relationship of the citizen with the State. However, this chapter will focus on two of the many aspects of social capital, which have a direct bearing on possibilities for improving productivity in Morocco and which can be addressed by the public authorities with significant concomitant benefits: gender equality and interpersonal trust. In the sections below, the significance and status of gender equality and interpersonal trust in Morocco will be successively analyzed before formulating specific proposals regarding these two areas, followed by more general recommendations for strengthening social capital with a view to enhancing the country's economic development.

Achieving Gender Equality

The relationship between men and women and the status of women within society are among the most visible and important manifestations of a nation's social capital. The notion of gender pertains to the social architecture that accords cultural meaning to sexual identity, thus tending to determine the entire gamut of choices and possibilities available to men and women, respectively. The lack of opportunities and economic freedoms that prevent women and girls from realizing their potential has very significant economic consequences not only for themselves, but for their families and, by extension, the society as a whole. Gender-based discrimination hampers the development and the building of social capital. It undermines trust between the sexes, distorts relationships within the family, limits social networks, and weakens social capital as well as society's ability to work toward common objectives (Picciotto 1998).

Throughout the world, equal participation and autonomy for women have traditionally come up against many obstacles. Women and girls are still deprived of fundamental freedoms and must contend with grave inequalities. In extreme cases, they are subjected to physical aggression; they are not allowed to go to school or leave their homes, own property, or open a bank account. For the most part, women and girls own less real and movable property, cultivate smaller and less productive plots of land, work in less productive sectors, and face discriminatory laws and rules that restrict their freedom of choice. Overwhelmingly, they perform unpaid household tasks, for which they are often penalized in terms of income and retirement benefits. The root causes of this situation often lie beyond the traditional economic analyses to touch on the degree of openness of societies, their sociocultural characteristics, and types of morality and religion (see box 6.1). Rather, it is the transposition of these characteristics into everyday life that explains the reasons behind persistent discrimination and occupational segregation, despite the effects of competitive market forces (Akerlof and Kranton 2010).

It must be emphasized that equality between men and women is important in itself and requires no utilitarian justification. As Amartya Sen (Sen 1999)

Box 6.1 Morality and Religion in an Open Society

The contemporary roots of the concept of the open society, popularized by Karl R. Popper (1943), may be found in the works of Henri Bergson and his principle of "creative evolution." This principle adopts a philosophical approach, which seeks simultaneously to acknowledge the continuity of life for all living beings—as creative beings—and the principle of discontinuity, which implies the evolutionary nature of creation, which he calls "*élan vital*," or "life force." (Bergson 1932)

For Bergson, the concept of life brings together two opposing forces, giving rise to two types of morality and religion: the closed morality associated with a static religion and an open morality whose religion is dynamic. On the one hand, a closed morality and static religion are concerned with maintaining social cohesion. Certain species have been conceived by nature in such a way that the individual members to which they belong cannot exist independently. They are fragile and, as such, need the support of the community (Bergson uses the image of bees to illustrate this). On the other hand, there is open morality, whose religion is dynamic and concerned with progress and creativity and not so much with inclusion as with social cohesion. Bergson describes this as an "open" morality, since it is all-inclusive and aims at achieving peace. It seeks to achieve an "open society" (Lawlor and Moulard Leonard 2013).

Far from being a purely Western idea, one of the sources of the open society may be found in the works of the great Maghrébin thinker and philosopher Ibn Khaldoun (1332–1406). Several centuries before the Encyclopedists and the philosophy of the Enlightenment in 18th century Europe, Ibn Khaldoun, in his Muqaddima or Prolegomenes (the three-volume preface of his Universal History), drew a fundamental distinction between two complementary but discrete ways of thinking. It is the difference between natural science (or humanities) with its rational discourse, with man as a rational, thinking being, and the traditional (or religious science), the discourse of faith founded on revealed texts (Goumeziane 2006). For Khaldoun, "the first category brings together the philosophical sciences, which are acquired naturally by man through the process of reflection. In this way, he succeeds in understanding objects, problems, arguments and methods. He grasps the difference between truth and falsehood by exercising the speculative and investigative faculties that are inherent to the thinking being. The second category includes the traditional and institutional sciences. Here, everything is contingent on information supplied by the authorities of a given religious law. Reason has no place in this system, except for interweaving some problematic details into the general principles" (quote in Goumeziane 2006, pp. 169–70).

explains, development is a process whereby freedoms for all are developed. Furthermore, in the same way that development means less poverty and better access to justice, it also implies a narrowing of the prosperity gap between men and women. At the international level, the Convention on the Elimination of All Forms of Discrimination Against Women (CEDAW) acknowledges that the empowerment of women and gender equality are, in themselves, development goals. Increased autonomy and freedom of choice for women are indispensable for rolling back inequality between the sexes and contributing to the emergence of an open and inclusive society.

Gender equality is also advantageous from an economic standpoint. Greater gender equality can improve a nation's productivity, enhance development outcomes for future generations, and render institutions more representative. These objectives are at the very heart of Morocco's 2040 accelerated convergence scenario presented in chapter 2. As noted in the 2012 World Development Report (World Bank 2012), gender equality is smart economics. It leads to economic efficiency and helps to improve development outcomes in three ways. First, by effectively removing the barriers that prevent women from enjoying the same access as men to education, economic opportunities, and the factors of production, significant productivity gains can be generated in a competitive and globalized world. Second, improving the relative and absolute status of women leads to many other development benefits, including enhanced early childhood protection and development. As noted above, the trust capital of each individual is rooted in the early development of the child and especially in the mother-child relationship (Picciotto 1998). Third, creating a level playing field for the participation of men and women, so that they may enjoy equal opportunities for an active social and political life, take their own decisions, and shape policies can, over time, lead to more representative and inclusive institutions and political choices. This, in turn, will engender more sustainable development. The removal of discriminatory factors that hamper women, by improving their status and leveling the playing field, could help not only to improve the well-being of women, but also that of men and children and could bring about more inclusive economic development (World Bank 2012).

The Present Status of Gender Parity in Morocco

Over the past decade, Morocco's legal system has undergone significant reforms to improve and guarantee gender equality. Morocco today has one of the most liberal and progressive legal systems in the Middle East and North Africa. The 2011 constitution guarantees the equality of all Moroccan citizens and obliges public agencies to promote the freedom and equal access of all citizens to enjoy their political, economic, social, cultural, and environmental rights. With strong support from women's rights organizations, the *Moudawana* (Family Code) was revised in 2004 to extend the rights of women in such areas as guardianship, marriage, and access to divorce. Gender equality is at the heart of many legal provisions, including the 2003 Labor Code and the Nationality Law of 2008. The introduction in 2009 of a quota in local elections and measures taken following the adoption of the 2011 constitution have helped to enhance the level of representation by women.[3] In 2011, Morocco formally withdrew its reservations concerning the CEDAW and adopted the law approving the optional protocol in 2015. Moroccan women consequently enjoy greater freedom than in the past to travel, have access to jobs and education, and negotiate the terms of their marriage and divorce. In some cases, institutions have been set up to provide support in implementing these reforms. In this connection, the Family Support Fund was created and the system of family courts improved. An Authority to Ensure Parity and Combat All Forms of Discrimination (APALD) should soon be established, in accordance with the constitution.

Despite achievements on the legal front, Moroccan women still face great inequality and discrimination, particularly on the economic and political fronts. According to the latest Global Gender Gap Index supplied by the World Economic Forum (2016), Morocco ranks 137th out of 144 countries in economic participation, progress in education, and health and political empowerment of women (see figure 6.1). According to the index, Morocco's overall performance has been relatively stable since 2006, with some improvements in access to education and political enfranchisement, but also shows a deterioration in terms of economic inequality. The effective implementation of new legislation favoring gender equality is being hampered by a lack of support from certain sectors, a situation that is indicative of the complex mix of customs, norms, and values within the society (Chaara 2012).

Over the past 10 years, Moroccan women have benefited from the significant progress made in terms of social and human development. The implementation of public policies and programs through the Government Equality Plan (2012–16) and the use of gender responsive budgeting have helped to promote gender equality (see box 6.2). While the gaps in school enrolment between boys and girls have been partially narrowed, the disparities between the two sexes relating to learning achievements continue to be felt. Furthermore, the gender gap in reading has shown a continuous upward trend over the course of the various PIRLS surveys (Ibourk 2016). Women have also benefited from greater access to health services, a fact that is underscored by the improvement in

Figure 6.1 Global Gender Gap Index in 144 Countries
(1 = perfect equality)

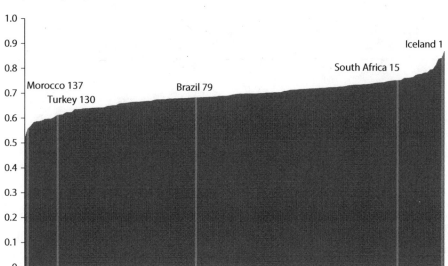

Source: World Economic Forum 2016.

Morocco 2040 • http://dx.doi.org/10.1596/978-1-4648-1066-4

Box 6.2 Government Equality Plan and Gender Responsive Budgeting

The Government Equality Plan (PGE). Building on the adoption in 2006 of the "National Strategy for gender equity and equality through the mainstreaming of gender into development policies and programs" as well as the incentives that have been in place since 2007 to encourage gender mainstreaming into sectoral policies and programs, the PGE is the framework that brings together the various initiatives implemented to mainstream women's rights into public policies and development programs. The PGE sets out 26 objectives to be achieved through 132 actions, with a view to promoting greater equality on the basis of (a) Institutionalization and dissemination of the principles of equity and equality and the establishment of the baselines for parity; (b) the fight against all forms of discrimination and violence against women; (c) the upgrading of the system of education and training on the basis of equity and equality; (d) strengthening of equitable and equal access to health; (e) the development of basic infrastructure to improve the living conditions of women and young girls; (f) social and economic empowerment of women; (g) equal and equitable access to decision-making positions at the administrative, political, and economic levels; and (h) the equalization of opportunity between the sexes on the job market.

Gender Responsive Budgeting (GRB). GRB is an approach to budgeting that seeks to encourage the formulation of budgetary and fiscal policies with built-in mechanisms for measuring the extent to which human rights are upheld in the implementation of public policies and for improving gender equality outcomes. Since its launch in 2002, the process of GRB has helped Morocco to reallocate existing resources in support of gender equality. The introduction of the performance-based budget reform process in 2002 and the adoption in 2015 of the Budget Framework Law have institutionalized the gender dimension within the programs of ministerial departments as well as in their monitoring and evaluation processes.

In its last report on the status of women's rights in the world, UN Women cited Morocco as an example in the region, commending the country's progress under the PGE and the GRB approach, and underlining the vital role played by associations that defend women's rights. UN women also indicated that much more needs to be done to bring all national laws into line with the international human rights instruments to which Morocco is signatory.

---

certain indicators, such as those relating to reproductive health. The fertility rate among Moroccan teens is now lower than the average for middle-income countries, having fallen to 32 births (per 1,000 women between the ages of 15–19) in 2014. Disaggregated data from the gender inequality index show that there is almost equal treatment of men and women in relation to education and health (see figure 6.2).

Nevertheless, Morocco is marked by sharp inequalities between the sexes in the areas of economics and politics. Women's freedom to manage their own time, income, and what they consume as well as to take decisions within the household, the extended family, or in the wider society remains limited and inferior to that of men. Although the 2011 constitution affirms in Article 19 that "men and women enjoy equal rights and liberties," it places conditions on the exercise of

Figure 6.2 Morocco: Factors Contributing to Gender Inequality
(1 = perfect equality)

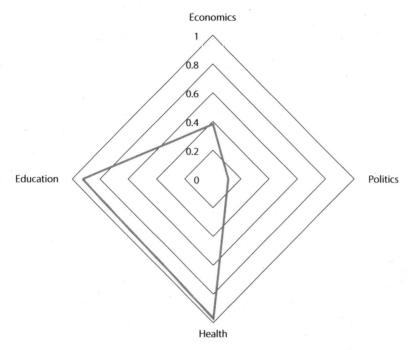

Source: World Economic Forum 2016.

this liberty by referring to the need for "respect for the immutable values of the Kingdom and its laws." This is a reference to inequalities based on religious matters and which are considered permanent as they stem from "immutable values" and therefore from the realm of the sacred (Lamrabet 2016). In reality, such inequalities in the exercise of free choice are reflected in the lack of equal opportunities and outcomes. Women's access to certain basic resources and essential economic assets remains unequal. For example, even though encouraging initiatives have been undertaken,[4] gender discrimination in relation to access to formal credit limits the possibilities for women to be self-employed or engage in entrepreneurship. In 2012 only 27 percent of women held an account with a formal financial institution. Furthermore, gender equality before the law is not necessarily replicated in practice, owing to weaknesses in the provision of public services and the delays in the implementation of legislation, particularly where new provisions conflict with social and cultural norms. The following sections will briefly examine the economic and de jure inequalities faced by Moroccan women as well as the inequalities they face in the application of the law.

Economic Inequalities between the Sexes

The inequalities between men and women are particularly striking on the job market. Less than one in four working age women (23.6 percent in 2016) is engaged in the job market, placing Morocco above the regional average for the Middle East and North Africa (21.8 percent), but among the 20 percent of countries with the lowest level of participation by women in the labor force (see figure 6.3). In addition to lagging far behind other countries with a similar income level, the share of women participating in the workforce is trending downward owing to structural factors. This applies, in particular, to women of 25 years of age (average age of marriage) or older, living in urban areas. In reality, the gap between urban and rural areas remains wide. The urban labor force participation rate of women in 2016 was 16.6 percent (versus 66.3 percent for men), while the corresponding rate for rural areas was 34.9 percent (versus 77.9 percent for men). The higher rate of participation by women in rural areas should not necessarily be regarded as positive, as this is often driven by need and poverty. Economic growth in Morocco is characterized not only by a low level of labor intensity, but is concentrated in sectors that traditionally employ few women. The result is that demand for female workers is low, particularly among urban women with secondary education. And when men and women compete for the rare available jobs, the men are generally given priority owing to preferences of employers and households (Verme, Gadiry, and Guennouni 2014). According to the IMF, the cost associated with the gender gap in terms of participation of women in the labor market and their access to entrepreneurship is estimated at 46 percent of per capita income, in comparison to a situation where women would have the same level of participation in the labor market and opportunities for entrepreneurship as men (IMF 2017).

Figure 6.3 Rate of Participation by Women in the Labor Force, 2014
(percentage of the female population ages 15 years and older)

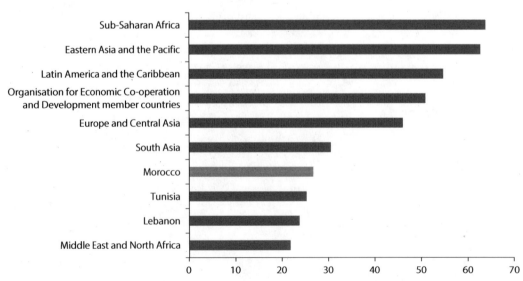

Source: World Development Indicators, World Bank.

Nonetheless, outside the labor market, as in many other countries, women carry out the clear majority of household tasks. If there is one basic economic resource over which women have no control, it is their time. According to an HCP survey, the time spent by men on their professional activity is four times more than that spent by women, while men devote seven times less time than women in household work (see figure 6.4). The division of labor according to gender therefore places the man-woman ratio within the classic scenario of the man as the breadwinner and the woman as the homemaker. While it is true that men are open to the idea of women working more outside the home, they expect women to continue at the same time to perform the customary domestic duties (Serajuddin and Verme 2012). For their part, women indicate a readiness to perform more household tasks than men, while continuing to aspire to work outside the household. These responses reflect the strong gender-related bias held by both men and women in relation to labor force participation.

In addition, once employed, women are on average more likely to be exposed to job insecurity, informal work, and lower remuneration. When all the relevant factors are considered, including education, experience, and recruitment bias (World Bank 2015), the wage gap between men and women may be as high as 77 percent. It appears that the wage gap between the sexes is even more pronounced in the upper bands of the salary range; and company data indicate that the "glass ceiling" effect could well become more entrenched over time (Nordman and Wolff 2007). These differences are due to the phenomenon of gender discrimination and they continue to exist because the view that men and women are confined to certain types of employment is deeply ingrained. Such differences in treatment are a major obstacle for women, particularly those who have pursued studies, to rejoin the workforce. They also have negative repercussions for the economy in general, in terms of productivity and growth,

Figure 6.4 Morocco: Inequality between Men and Women with Respect to Workload

(percentage of the female population 15 years of age and older)

Source: HCP 2012: National Survey on time use in Morocco 2011/2012.

since they distort market incentives to efficiently allocate talent toward the most productive uses.

The traditional explanations for the deep-rooted tendencies affecting the participation of women in the labor market are not sufficient to account for all the results observed in Morocco. The fall in the fertility rate and the rise in the educational level of women who participate in the labor force (two factors that are closely correlated) appear to explain to a great degree the growth trend in terms of labor force participation (acting as a pull factor). By contrast, other factors that would be expected to promote the increased participation of women—particularly economic factors—appear not to play a significant role. The relative stagnation in the rate of women's participation in the labor market can be attributed to the slow rate of structural transformation of the economy and the limited growth in sectors that in other countries support jobs for women, particularly manufacturing and services (Marotta, Prettitore, and Verme 2015). Another factor may be linked to "culture" and social norms, which, together with the lack of facilities catering to the needs of children, might help explain why women appear to leave the job market near marriage age. Indeed, invariably, marriage reduces the probability of women participating in the workforce, a fact that applies to both urban and rural areas.

In Morocco, most women are not free to decide on their own whether or not they wish to work: for most women, it is the family, particularly the men, who decide (World Bank 2015). Decision making in the home is a decisive factor for understanding the low level of participation of women in the workplace in Morocco. Data from the 2010 survey of households and youth in Morocco indicate that only one-third of Moroccan women between the ages of 15 and 49 years take their own decisions about their employment. Other family members, notably husbands and brothers, influence the decision of women to work. It is not unusual for women to be prevented from seeking work outside the home because of the views of family members: 19 percent of women who are unemployed and not seeking remunerated employment indicated that the reason they were not looking for work was the opposition of their husband or brother(s). According to the 2012–14 Arab Barometer survey, more than one-third of men interviewed (versus 13 percent of women) hold the view that a married woman should not work outside the home.

Gender inequalities on the job market also show up in relation to professional mobility. In Morocco, men and women have very different experiences of transitioning between jobs, with women having far fewer opportunities than men in almost all aspects of labor mobility (Verme, Gadiry Barry, and Guennouni 2014). The reallocation of work across economic sectors and between the public and private sectors does not benefit women. Women are as mobile as and sometimes more mobile than men, but their mobility is restricted to a transition between agriculture and joblessness. Moving from informal to formal employment is more restrictive for women than men. In addition, when it comes to reacting to economic shocks and structural transformations, the labor market has tended to treat men and women in an asymmetrical manner. It appears that women in rural areas, in particular, are playing the role of economic "shock absorbers." When the economy is doing well, rural women are active on the job market in good numbers, but when the economy sputters, they are the first, and often the only ones to be excluded from the market.

In the same way, the process of structural transformation of the economy does not benefit men and women equally. If the relative changes in the share of employment by sector are disaggregated by gender, it emerges quite starkly that the reallocation of jobs between sectors for jobs held by men and women is inversely related. While men tend to leave low-productivity sectors—such as agriculture—for more productive areas, women tend to remain for the most part stuck in low productivity sectors: agriculture, small services, and textiles (despite a relatively significant presence in the manufacturing industry, the services sector, and general administration). In fact, their rate of participation in agriculture increased between 2000 and 2011, moving from 36 percent to more than 41 percent of employment in the sector. In 2011, more than 60 percent of active women worked in agriculture. In Morocco, women are disproportionately more vulnerable as a result of the weak structural transformation of the economy toward greater value-added manufacturing industries and services.

De jure Gender Inequalities

Notwithstanding the important reforms mentioned above, discrimination between men and women continues to exist in law. Such discriminatory practices relate, for the most part, to matters of the family and personal life, and include the legal restrictions affecting women's access to economic assets, particularly inheritance, social security benefits, and matrimonial assets; marriage to non-Muslims; and the unequal rights of men and women in relation to divorce petitions and transmission of citizenship to a foreign spouse.

The rules governing inheritance and matrimonial property, together with the restrictive social norms, prevent women from exercising greater control over property. From a social standpoint, it is perceived as less acceptable for a woman to purchase land in certain areas, owing essentially to the notion that men should be the head of the household and that single women should not live on their own. More often than not, various provisions of the Family Code relating to the apportionment of inherited land tend to award a smaller parcel to women than men, particularly in the case of brothers and sisters. Inheritance of land is an important mechanism for wealth transmission, particularly in rural areas. Although the government of Morocco does not currently produce data on land ownership among women,[5] there is enough information to suggest that this remains weak, particularly in relation to agricultural land. For example, according to the Food and Agriculture Organization (FAO), women control approximately 4 percent of agricultural lands, a percentage that is well below that of other low- or -middle-income countries. There is no formal, legal restriction against the purchase, sale, or registration of land by women acting individually, and married couples may choose to register land jointly. But the available data, albeit partial, indicate that land ownership among women remains low.

Family benefits payable through the social security system to employees who are married and have children are paid out to men only. The retirement age is the same for men and women in the private and public sectors. Nevertheless, public sector employees may proceed on early retirement after 31 years of service for men and 18 for women. Individuals who contribute over a given period to the National Social Security Fund are entitled to a family allowance per child. If both spouses are covered by the National Social Security Fund and make their contributions, the family allowances are paid out to the husbands only. In the event of divorce, the payments are made to the individual having physical custody of the child. Nevertheless, a divorced woman, unlike her male counterpart, will face certain administrative obstacles when seeking to obtain a card from the Medical Assistance Scheme (RAMED), even if she is the sole provider of the family, as it is assumed that the head of the family must be a man. When one partner dies, the widower may benefit unconditionally and for life from his spouse's pension, while the widow loses this entitlement if she remarries.

The prevailing matrimonial regime for the separation of property is disadvantageous to women because of their low rate of participation in the labor market and their limited control over economic assets, in comparison to men. In the event of divorce, each partner reclaims the property registered in his or her name. When one spouse dies, the property registered in the name of the deceased is subject to the inheritance regime. Strengthening the built-in provisions of the Family Code (2004) relating to the introduction of a common property regime, whereby property acquired during the marriage is owned jointly by both parties, would offer several advantages to Moroccan women. Indeed, such a regime would give recognition to the equal contribution of both spouses to the maintenance of the home and would be consistent with the Family Code amendment, which recognizes both partners as household heads. In addition, it would provide security for spouses who work outside the formal sector, such as those who undertake unremunerated work linked to the maintenance of the home. Strengthening these provisions would therefore benefit the very high number of married women (around 75 percent) who work outside Morocco's formal labor market.

Notwithstanding the legal equality of spouses as heads of families, men are still legally responsible for the financial maintenance of families. This tends to skew social norms in their favor. For example, a woman loses her right to maintenance payments if she refuses to reside in the matrimonial home. In the event of divorce, women are entitled to maintenance payments during "*iddah*" only, a period that lasts around four months. Support is therefore guaranteed for only a relatively short period of time, affecting, in particular, women who have no significant assets to fall back on. The strict timelines prescribed by "*iddah*" preclude the possibility of extending the period during which maintenance payments may be disbursed to take account of the particular situation of vulnerable women, including the poor.

As far as family law and individual rights are concerned, women may enter into marriage under the same conditions as men. However, in the large majority of cases, marriage acts are signed on behalf of women by male guardians. Women are now legally entitled to sign their own marriage acts, although they rarely exercise this prerogative. Around 20 percent of women signed their own marriage acts in 2011, a figure that has remained constant since 2007 (Ministry of Justice and Liberties, Family Court Statistics 2011; HCP 2012). This situation may be explained by the conservative nature of social norms and results from the perception that the signing of the marriage act by men forms part of the marriage ceremony. There is also pressure from judges who insist that the marriage act be signed by male guardians. Furthermore, several other gender discrimination practices persist: Muslim women can marry only Muslim men, while a Muslim man can marry a non-Muslim woman from a monolithic religion; men retain the right to polygamy, even though the introduction of stricter regulations has led to a reduction in the number of polygamous marriages to around 0.3 percent of new marriages in 2015, according to statistics from the Ministry of Justice and Liberties (2011).

Unlike men, Moroccan women cannot easily transmit nationality to their non-Moroccan spouse. Foreign spouses of Moroccan men are automatically entitled to Moroccan citizenship. However, women must undertake complex administrative procedures in order to transmit nationality to their foreign spouse. This is an exceptionally burdensome requirement, which will, if not carried through to completion, make it quite difficult for the foreign spouses of Moroccan women to reside and find work in Morocco and enjoy access to public services.

The number of marriages contracted by young Moroccan girls who are legally minors remains high, even though the minimum marriage age was raised and despite the fact that judicial controls that apply to early marriage were made obligatory. One of the amendments to the Family Code was to raise the minimum marriage age of girls from 15 to 18 years of age, placing them on the same legal footing as boys in this regard. However, there is an exception to this rule. Boys and girls under the age of 18 can enter into marriage with the approval of a judge. If the goal of this reform was to reduce the number of early marriages, it must be noted that the number of marriages involving female minors grew by 15 percent between 2007 and 2010, totaling over 44,000, or more than 10 percent of all marriages performed (HCP 2012). However, according to statistics from the Ministry of Justice and Liberties for 2015, it would appear that this percentage has stabilized. This is due to the fact that the need for judicial approval does not seem to favor the appropriate control of the legitimacy of the marriage of minors. In fact, the rate of approved applications grew from 89 percent in 2007 to 92 percent in 2010. Young girls who married while still under age are exposed to additional risks, particularly domestic violence.

Women must complete certain procedures in order to obtain a *livret de famille* (family record book), a document required in certain administrative procedures and for access to some public services. The *livret de famille* is issued to individuals with a family and is used to guarantee the legal identity and status of the person, such as marital status. It is drawn up at the time of marriage and the original document is produced in the husband's name and handed over to him. A woman (wife, divorcee, or widow) must request a certified copy by completing an administrative procedure. The *livret de famille* must be presented when carrying out various everyday administrative tasks, such as obtaining an identity card, passport, or driver's license, accessing certain social services and legal aid, proving identity for job purposes, opening a bank account, inheriting property, registering a company, and enrolling a child at school. The practice of automatically handing over the *livret de famille* to the husband and then requiring women to go through various bureaucratic procedures to obtain this book is not consistent with the principle enshrined in the reformed 2004 Family Code recognizing husbands and wives as equals in the household. Furthermore, the current system is burdensome for women, requiring them to dedicate time and resources to wade through the numerous administrative processes.

The 2004 Family Code reforms have significantly improved women's access to divorce, but some discriminatory practices remain. The most significant effect of the Family Code reforms relating to divorce was to give women the possibility to institute divorce proceedings without having to provide certain reasons relating to the husband. Under the reformed code, women now have the right to request a divorce by mutual consent, provided that both parties are in agreement and that insurmountable differences are cited. Divorce proceedings may also be initiated by either the husband or the wife in the form of a unilateral divorce. The fact that conditions for divorce apply equally to men and women is significant, as women are more likely than men to request a divorce. Nevertheless, men can still unilaterally repudiate their wives before a judge. Women are not entitled to exercise a similar right unless it was provided for in the marriage contract, which would have required the prior approval of the husband. The available data highlight the fact that women rarely exercise this right. Less than 0.2 percent of divorces in 2011 were instituted by spouses on the basis of clauses contained in their marriage contract.

Women are generally favored when it comes to the award of physical custody of children, while men generally retain legal custody. For the most part, the prevailing system on child custody favors the award of physical custody of children up to the age of 15 years to mothers. Once in their custody, mothers must satisfy their children's basic needs. In the event of divorce, fathers or, in their absence, other male family members, retain legal custody of minor children. This obliges the father to continue to provide for the financial maintenance of the family members through support payments to the mother until the children cease to be minors, that is, generally at 18 years of age for boys and until marriage for girls. Legal custody means that the father is entitled to make all important decisions on the well-being of the child, and obliges divorced women to obtain the authorization of their ex-husbands, particularly in relation to decisions on their children's education and health. In addition, a divorced woman cannot travel with her child outside Morocco without the consent of her former husband. The Family Code reforms have introduced a level of flexibility in the recognition of rights on child custody matters, by allowing judges to take into consideration the best interests of the child. However, there are no statistics on the frequency with which this process is utilized.

Divorced women often depend on the payment of child support but face a number of challenges in securing compliance with court decisions. This places them in a precarious financial position. Once they are awarded physical custody of children, women then find themselves dependent on child support payments to meet household needs. Such payments are particularly important in view of the low level of women's participation in the workforce and their limited control over economic assets. Yet, despite the 2015 revision of the Fonds d'entraide familiale (Family Support Fund) law dealing with the delays in the implementation of judicial provisions on child support payments, many women continue to find it extremely challenging to have the decision of the courts on custody of children and mechanisms for their protection enforced.

Women who have children out of wedlock, and their children, continue to suffer greatly from legal discrimination. Sexual relations outside of marriage is a criminal offense for both men and women. However, the consequences of transgression are more serious for women than men. Pregnancy outside of wedlock represents irrefutable proof of the crime committed by women and, outside of very specific, exceptional circumstances, abortion is illegal. As a result, unmarried women who become pregnant find themselves without legal recourse. The Family Code recognizes paternity in the context of marriage only. The law does not clearly establish whether a single woman can obtain a *livret de famille* that includes her children. In this scenario, the provision of the *livret de famille* is left to the discretion of the administration. The very act of requesting a *livret de famille* exposes single women to criminal proceedings on the grounds of sexual relations outside of marriage. In addition, single mothers are deprived of the support for themselves and children payable by the Family Support Fund. Children born out of wedlock also suffer from discrimination. Their fathers are not required by law to pay any kind of maintenance to help support them financially and they have no right of inheritance from their fathers. Consequently, the mother must assume the responsibility for all expenses, a particularly difficult proposition for poor women. In extreme cases, some women may even feel compelled to abandon their offspring. Children born to unwed mothers are deprived of the right to take their father's name and must adopt the patronym "Abdi" at the Civil Registry, which identifies them as illegitimate and exposes them to discrimination throughout their lives.

There is a high level of violence against women in Morocco, including psychological, physical, and sexual violence and attacks on their individual freedoms. The 2009 national survey on violence against women revealed that 62 percent of women between the ages of 18 and 64 years had suffered some form of violence in the twelve months preceding the survey (HCP 2009). The most common forms of violence include psychological violence (48 percent), violent opposition in the exercise of their rights under the Family Code (17 percent), and physical violence (15 percent). Almost one-third of women mentioned violations of personal freedoms. While domestic violence is generally viewed by society as negative, the perception varies greatly by gender: only 55 percent of men (versus 77 percent of women) believe that violence against women is never justified (World Values Survey 2007).

With the adoption by the government in March 2016 of the draft law on ending violence against women, Morocco should soon have a legislative framework that can more effectively address the question of violence against women. The draft law stipulates the actions and behaviors that could be classified as acts of violence against women. It also establishes the criminal nature of such acts and forms of behavior, and sets out the mechanisms for caring for women who are victims of violence. Pending the adoption of this law, domestic violence continues to be dealt with under the framework of the general provisions on assault contained in the Criminal Code. Sexual assault and rape are treated as crimes, but the legislation does not clearly stipulate whether acts committed by a husband against a wife are covered under these provisions. In January 2014, the Criminal Code was amended to fill a very important gap in relation to the protection of women. A man who perpetrates an act of rape can no longer escape criminal proceedings by marrying the victim. However, the weight of social norms, the reputational risks, and the lack of adequate support programs induce some victims to accept marriage.

Inequalities in the Application of Law, Arising from Social Norms

In addition to legal forms of discrimination, the limited implementation of legislation is a problem for women and restricts their freedom of action. Legislation is poorly implemented owing to weak institutional capacity and selective application of legislation by the responsible officials who are influenced by social norms. In addition to the legal obstacles faced by women, their freedom of action is often curtailed by social norms. These norms exist due to a combination of societal and family pressures and the practice of self-censorship that women observe in order not to risk generating controversy by their actions. These norms help explain the low rate of women's participation in the labor market and in political life, as well as the disparities in relation to control of economic assets. In Morocco, social perceptions about the roles of women vary greatly between men and women and are defined differently, depending on the issue in question. Men tend to believe that they should enjoy priority over women when jobs are scarce. They also consider themselves to be better at business and politics. It appears that there is a greater level of agreement between men and women on the importance of women having a higher level of education. The views of men and women are also more closely aligned when it comes to disapproval of single mothers (World Bank 2015). The 2007 World Values Survey reveals, nevertheless, that women are twice as likely as men (60 percent vs. 30 percent) to believe that equality between men and women is an important attribute of democracy.

The delivery of public services meant to help women enjoy access to justice also continues to be influenced by social norms. Both men and women are affected by the difficulties of Morocco's justice system, but women continue to find it particularly difficult to access justice, owing in particular to their relatively low level of control over economic assets and because of social norms that dissuade them from filing a complaint. These obstacles persist despite the efforts of the Higher Magistrate's Institute to promote basic and advanced training in gender equality. In general, data on court proceedings are not disaggregated by gender. As a result, it is not easy to identify the particular needs of women or to focus effectively on reducing discrimination in the delivery of specific services. It also makes it difficult to effectively evaluate these services and to measure the broader impact of the reforms. One may, nevertheless, infer from the scant data available that the judicial services are not sufficiently effective to guarantee respect for the rights of women. The 2009 national survey on violence against women revealed that about half of eligible women were not receiving, on a regular basis, the support payments to which they were entitled. One-quarter of eligible women received no support payments whatsoever, underlining the unjust situation that penalizes young women. Data from the Ministry of Justice and Liberties confirm the low rate of implementation of court judgments on support payments. In 2011, only 60 percent of complaints regarding support payments were decided by the courts; and after the decisions were pronounced, only 60 percent of them were enforced.

Strengthening Women's Economic Participation and Autonomy

As in many countries, the fastest track for strengthening social capital in Morocco would be to promote the full and equal participation of men and women and boys and girls at all levels of Moroccan society.

Public policies can be designed to both combat gender inequalities and promote economic growth. Economic and legal inequalities between the sexes and social norms and gender biases tend to reinforce each other in explaining women's low access to economic opportunities as well as women's low bargaining power. Modeling these interactions could help quantify the impact on growth of an integrated approach aimed at reducing gender bias in the labor market, reallocating the time that mothers devote to their daughters and increasing the bargaining power of women within the family (Agénor, Berahab, and El Mokri 2017). In the case of Morocco, the combined effects of these policies on economic growth could reach up to 2 percentage points on an annual basis (see box 6.3).

There is still a great deal of work to be done to improve women's empowerment and access to economic opportunities in Morocco. The policies could revolve around three principal axes: (a) increasing economic opportunities for women by removing the obstacles to their participation in the labor market and by developing entrepreneurship; (b) reducing the gender gap in terms of expression and freedom of action, by supporting the participation of women in political life and protecting their rights inside the home as well as in society more broadly; and (c) mainstreaming gender into political action in order to modernize its practice and change mentalities and cultural norms.

Box 6.3 Evaluation of the Impact of Public Policies on Gender Inequalities and Growth in Morocco

The impact of public decisions on gender equality and economic growth could be quantified by a computable overlapping generations and gender-differentiated model (Agénor 2012, 2017). Such a model was developed and calibrated in the case of Morocco on the basis of the 2014 General Population Census, employment surveys, and the 2012 national survey on the time budget of the High Commission for Planning (Agénor, Berahab, and El Mokri 2017). The model is designed to capture the dynamics among social norms, gender inequalities within the family and the labor market, women's bargaining power in family decisions, spousal time allocation, and economic growth (see figure B6.3.1).

The variables used for the analysis are families, domestic production, commercial production, human capital accumulation, government activity, women's bargaining power, social norms and gender inequalities.

In a first simulation, the government implements measures to fight against women discrimination in the labor market (hiring parity, awareness campaigns, for example). The consequences are multiple: increase in family income, which leads to higher private savings and investment and then higher economic growth and tax revenues. The latter can then be used to increase education spending and promote human capital accumulation, also contributing to economic growth. In addition, these measures affect the time allocation between women and men by strengthening the women bargaining power within the family. By improving their income,

Figure B6.3.1 Social Norms, Gender Bias, and Bargaining Power

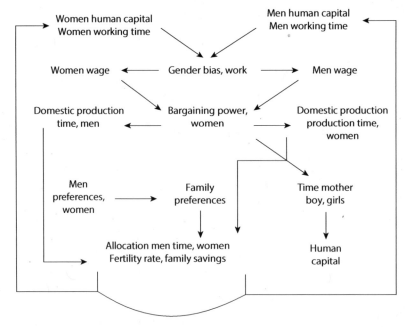

Source: Agénor, Berahab, and El Mokri 2017.

box continues next page

Box 6.3 **Evaluation of the Impact of Public Policies on Gender Inequalities and Growth in Morocco** *(continued)*

women reduce the amount of time spent on domestic tasks (compensated by an increase in that of men). The time freed by women is then allocated between child rearing, participation in the labor market, human capital accumulation or leisure. In the case of Morocco, the model calibration leads to a reduction in the time that men spend on the labor market, as well as the time devoted to human capital accumulation and leisure, and an increase in the time dedicated to the production of domestic goods. In terms of the effect on growth, they are both positive and negative as women and men allocate their time in the labor market in opposite ways.

The second simulation focuses on the reallocation of mothers' time to their daughters, as a result of an awareness campaign, for instance. In this case, economic growth is positively affected by women's human capital increases. Finally, a third simulation examines the effects of an improved bargaining power of women within the household. This leads to three changes: (1) women allocate less time to domestic tasks, unlike men; (2) because of the lower preference of women for current consumption, the saving rate increases, leading to an increase in investment and physical capital; and (3) given the preference of mothers for the education of children, the time spent by women in raising children increases to the detriment of their participation in labor market and their own accumulation of human capital, but to the benefit of the children accumulation of human capital.

Overall, the positive impact of pro-gender measures on economic growth rate would be in the order of 0.2 to 1.95 percentage point on an annual basis depending on the scenarios (Table B6.3.1).

Table B6.3.1 Morocco: Policies' Effect of Reducing Gender Inequalities on the Rate of Economic Growth
percentage points

	Reduced gender bias in the labor market	Increased time dedicated by mothers to girls	Increased women's bargaining power in the family	Integrated program
Allocation of women's time with endogenous leisure	0.2	0.6	1.0	1.95

Increasing Economic Opportunities for Women

Women can make a significant contribution to economic growth in Morocco, provided that the obstacles they face in gaining employment in high productivity sectors and obtaining decent jobs are lifted. In the manufacturing sector alone, young export companies recruit five times more women than nonexporting enterprises. The development potential is even greater in the services sector. Consequently, the government should focus on reforms (discussed in the previous chapters) designed to accelerate the structural transformation of the economy, encourage private sector investment, and stimulate economic growth so as to promote opportunities for women to move out of agriculture and other low productivity sectors and occupations. In order to expand the category of jobs accessible to women, particularly in the most productive sectors such as information and communications technologies or financial services, it is essential not only to improve women's access to economic opportunities but also to remove the legal and social obstacles that discourage employers from hiring women and dissuade women from accepting the jobs available. The government can also work to lift the statutory prohibitions and other barriers, such as transport insecurity, lack of childcare and pre-school facilities, limited access to finance, and the like., that currently prevent women from participating actively in the economy. Enhancing the opportunities for women to establish and develop their own enterprises would also help to increase innovation, growth, and employment in the country. This is particularly critical for women, given the challenges that they face to find work in the formal sector.

Encouraging the Emancipation of Women, Their Freedom of Action, and Empowerment

The government of Morocco has taken a number of important steps to reduce legal forms of discrimination. Nevertheless, the overall consistency of the legislative framework, including at the constitutional level, could be strengthened. It is true that some commitments have been made to the promotion of gender equality through high-level reforms to the legal framework, including the Constitution itself. Nevertheless, discriminatory provisions have not been removed from the basic legal framework or from the Constitution, which makes reference to "respect for the immutable values of the Kingdom and its laws." In addition to promoting equality, it is necessary to effectively guarantee respect for women's freedom of action by adopting effective provisions to combat unequal sociocultural practices, starting with violence against women, particularly domestic violence, and by implementing safeguard measures to protect vulnerable women such as household workers and unmarried mothers.[6] To that end, the draft legislation on combating violence against women adopted by the government in 2016 should be strengthened.

Steps must be taken to enhance women's control over their economic assets. Female entrepreneurs find it difficult to access credit, owing to individual rights provisions that limit the possibility of women owning family assets. The factors underpinning the practice of differentiated access by gender must be targeted in the new policy prescriptions. The new policies must also create a level playing field by strengthening women's property rights, eliminating bias in service delivery institutions, and improving the functioning of credit markets. In return, a greater rate of women's participation in the labor market would serve to enhance their control over their economic assets, including salaries, pensions, and other job-related benefits. Better control over their own salaries could allow women to exercise a greater level of freedom of action, both within and outside the household, particularly as perceptions of the ability of women to manage their own assets are largely positive.

Steps could also be taken to equalize the distribution of economic assets linked to marriage and work. Other than marriage acts, very few married couples sign agreements outlining the framework for managing economic assets during marriage.

The use of such contracts could be encouraged by making available model agreements with provisions for equal rights for husbands and wives. The Family Code provisions that oblige men to assume the financial responsibility for the maintenance of their families could be amended to introduce a greater degree of balance in the responsibilities of men and women, thereby paving the way for women to contribute to household income. Salary-based family benefits disbursed by the CNSS should be made equally accessible to men and women with children, in keeping with the legislative changes that now recognize shared responsibility for the household.

Greater equality of rights in relation to marriage and divorce would help to enhance women's freedom of action and promote better sharing of responsibilities. Women should have the right to a unilateral divorce on the same conditions as men. They should also have the same rights as men in relation to marriage to non-Muslims. The laws on transmitting nationality to a spouse should be standardized to prevent women from having to navigate through complex bureaucratic procedures to achieve this end. Women should be provided with *livrets de famille* on the same conditions as men. This would allow women to carry out administrative tasks connected with family life and promote a better environment for responsibility sharing and time management.

Gender Mainstreaming into Public Policies and Ongoing Promotion of Attitudinal Changes and Legal Reform

It is necessary to mainstream gender into public policies to achieve real gender equality and women's empowerment. A number of policies, programs, and initiatives have been implemented in Morocco to address different aspects of gender inequality, but these measures remain generally insufficient and poorly coordinated and are, therefore, not very effective.[7] This means that there is considerable scope for improving the situation of Moroccan women, including by the application and implementation of existing laws and the promotion of an egalitarian model characterized by greater women participation and a strengthened role for them in the decision-making process within the nation's political, administrative, and professional institutions. The new Budget Framework Law (LOLF), which will come into effect in 2017, could serve to enhance the coherence of public actions to promote gender equality, insofar as it will integrate gender mainstreaming into the programs of Ministry departments, as well as into their monitoring and evaluation procedures.

Looking beyond the prevailing laws, there is some leeway, including in the essence of the spiritual message of Islam, for continuing to modernize the legal framework, shaping mentalities and sociocultural norms, and establishing true social equality between men and women (Lamrabet 2015). The frame of reference for communicating gender-related issues should therefore be revised in order to break with notions of inequality and affirm and disseminate messages of parity and equality that are consistent with the precepts of justice espoused by Islam, the Sunnah tradition, and the profoundly humanist and secular values of Moroccan society. This entails undertaking a review of the ways in which various ideas and values are disseminated, such as through political discourse, media, education, religious teaching, and the like. Building on the favorable reaction to the 2004 Family Code (*Moudawana*) reform, particularly by a large majority of Moroccan women (Prettitore 2014), the country could continue to position itself at the forefront of the Arab world by continuing the modernization of its legal framework. As Islam is an increasingly consequential sociocultural marker, transforming the religious perspective would not only change the male-female dynamic, but result in deep societal changes.

Fostering Interpersonal Trust and Civic Responsibility

Social capital is built on the quality of interpersonal relations. It is a function of the relations between men and women, but depends more broadly on the level of trust that people have in each other, as well as the degree of civic engagement and volunteerism of citizens, and their sense of civic responsibility. As was seen in the previous section, the norms on which social life are founded have far-reaching effects on economic and social development. The mental and cultural models that influence what attracts people's attention, what they perceive, and what they understand (or do not understand) play an increasingly important role in the realization that the economic and social sciences are predicated on economic and social behaviors (World Bank 2015). In particular, the extent of interpersonal trust, civic engagement, and the norms of civic cooperation have long been recognized as essential elements of a country's social capital (Putnam 1993; Keefer and Knack 2002) and economic well-being (Knack and Keefer 1997; Knack and Zak 1998; Knowles and Weatherston 2006). In the absence of interpersonal trust, social cooperation, and civic responsibility, the codes of good conduct between individuals and honest and respectful forms of behavior tend to be confined to small groups of interconnected persons. In a closed or compartmentalized society, opportunistic or selfish behavior tends to be viewed as natural or morally acceptable outside of a tight network. The economic consequence of this phenomenon is that the more a society practices ostracism the less it will be able to promote long-term economic opportunities. Furthermore, when individuals lack trust in each other or do not respect public governance and government affairs, the supply of public goods and services tends to be inadequate and subject to nepotism or corruption. Open societies have a very different experience, in that the general rules of good conduct tend to apply across a wide range of social situations, and not only within families or narrow circles of acquaintances. When individuals are motivated to succeed, and understand that their economic success depends as much on their own choice as on the relations of trust with others and respect for common rules, they are more likely to work hard, save, invest, innovate, and initiate. For Coleman, social capital is quite simply the capacity of individuals to work together for a common goal within different groups or organizations (Coleman 1988).

Social Capital in Morocco

Social capital is essentially the product of cultural factors as defined not only by entrenched customs, values, and attitudes, but also skills and talents that, as previously explained, have a direct bearing on economic outcomes. If there is one important fact to be learned from the history of economic development, it is that the differences in performance between nations can be attributed primarily to cultural differences (Landes 2000; Sowell 2015). In particular, the exploitation of natural resources is of little or no value without the cultural conditions for transforming these resources into real wealth. The comparison of the levels of intangible capital in Morocco and Algeria outlined in chapter 2 demonstrates this point. Even accumulated physical capital is of limited utility in the absence of the necessary cultural conditions that are required to make these assets work effectively or to maintain them and obtain the best returns. Looking at cultural differences between societies, the degree of "receptivity" toward other cultures may well turn out to be decisive in understanding the historical trajectories of different groups, nations, and civilizations (Sowell 2015). Cultural isolation makes it more difficult to achieve the progress and advances that other cultures have made across the range of disciplines linked to human development (scientific, technical, humanities, etc.). In this way, cultural isolation can have the same impact on economic development as geographical isolation.

The cultural dimensions of social capital are not generally confined within the borders of particular countries. They often go beyond the nation-state to encompass far wider civilizational spaces. Morocco is a country with a multifaceted heritage (African, Berber, Arab, among others) in which Islam plays a predominant role. As the magazine *The Economist* put it in 2014: "a thousand years ago, the great cities of Baghdad, Damascus and Cairo took turns to race ahead of the Western World. Islam and innovation were twins. The various Arab caliphates were dynamic superpowers—beacons of learning, tolerance and trade. Yet today the Arabs are in a wretched state." This wretched state may be explained by the relative lack of openness and receptivity of this region in comparison to the rest of the world. This is indicated revealingly in the extent to which Arab populations are exposed to ideas and knowledge from outside sources. With a population of around 300 million people, spread over more than 20 countries, the total number of foreign books translated into Arabic throughout history is around 10,000, or one-fifth of the number of books translated by Greece alone, with a population of 11 million. Over a five-year period, the Arab world translates less than one book per million inhabitants, as compared with Spain with 920 (UNDP 2003). In other words, Spain translates more books into Spanish per year (per inhabitant) than the entire region of the Middle East and North Africa has translated into Arabic in a thousand years. If we focus only on the contemporary period, we see that the extent to which Spain was exposed to, and receptive of, ideas coming from abroad contributed to its rapid economic convergence at the end of the 20th century.

In view of its rich history and heritage, characterized by a certain openness and receptivity to the rest of the world, it appears that Morocco is in a better position than other countries in the region to experience growth in the formation of human capital and to become, in the process, the first non-oil-producing North African country to join the ranks of upper-middle-income countries. In this connection, this Memorandum will accord due importance to interpersonal trust, civic engagement, and civic responsibility. Indeed, the pursuit of the common good will largely require the building of institutions that seek to reconcile, to the greatest possible extent, the interests of the individual and the society as a whole (Tirole 2016).

Interpersonal Trust

One of the most important aspects of social capital is trust in others. Interpersonal trust is deemed to exist in a given society when individuals feel that they can count on people they have never met and when others reward this trust by adopting initiatives of cooperation and reciprocity and by undertaking voluntary commitments. In economics, the concept of trust is defined as imperfect information on the reliability and preferences of others. The existence of standards of reciprocity and trust facilitates the reduction of transaction costs, promotes collective action, and helps individuals to attain their personal goals. If a lack of trust increases transaction costs, then by the same token, interpersonal trust must be considered a key component of economic and social life. As posited by Nobel Prize winner for Economics Kenneth Arrow (1972): "every commercial transaction has within itself an element of trust, certainly any transaction conducted over a period of time. It can be plausibly argued that much of the economic backwardness in the world can be explained by the lack of mutual confidence" (Arrow 1972). In particular, the level of interpersonal trust within corporations has significant implications for the quality of the industrial economy that societies are able to create (Fukuyama 1995).

While efforts to evaluate the contribution of social capital are still at an early stage, the findings of the World Values Surveys and the Arab Barometer provide significant insights into the values upheld by countries, their progression over time, and their impact on social and political life.[8] Based on the responses provided to the question "in general, can most people be trusted?" it is clear that, in Morocco, the level of social trust is generally quite low, not only in relation to the rest of the world, but also in comparison with other developing countries. An examination of the average responses to the question on societal trust in surveys over the past 15 years (so as to minimize the possibility of errors associated with the sample chosen for the surveys) reveals that the general level of trust in Moroccan society is low and actually below the average for lower-middle-income countries (see figure 6.5). Furthermore, all World Values Surveys conducted since 2000 point to the fact that not only is there a low level of societal trust in Morocco, but that it has actually diminished over time. In addition, while societal trust used to be considered a stable feature of societies, recent studies have shown that this is not in fact the case, with the level of trust rising and falling over time, depending on developments in the rule of law as well as the robustness of social networks and the security

Figure 6.5 Response to the Question: "In General, Can Most People Be Trusted?"
(percent)

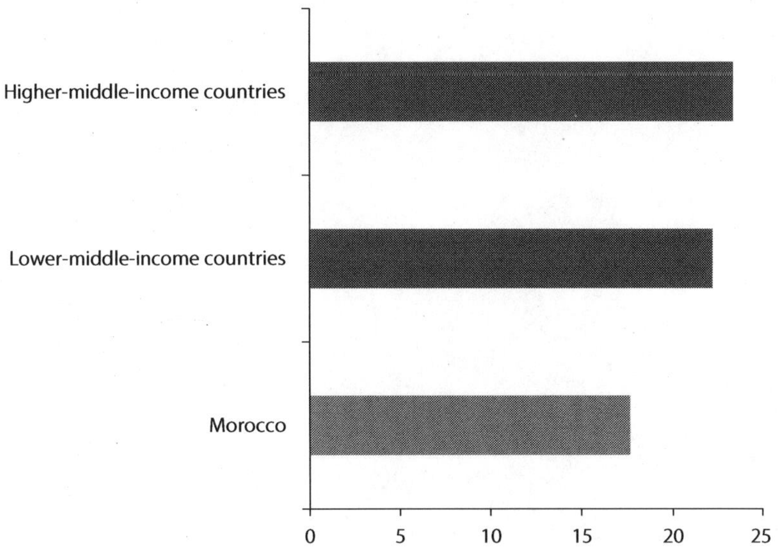

Source: World Values Surveys. Series 4–6, based on average data between 2000 and 2014.

of property (Almond and Verba 1963; Putnam 2000; Welzel 2013). Based on the findings of the Arab Barometer for 2012–14, only 13 percent of Moroccans surveyed believed that people can be trusted.

National surveys confirm a low level of personal trust in Moroccan society. Based on the 2012 survey on social cohesion in Morocco conducted by the Royal Institute for Strategic Studies (IRES), less than 10 percent of Moroccan citizens would be prepared to trust the majority of people (see figure 6.6). In a number of emerging countries, the proportion of people who believe that "in general, people can be trusted" has gone down, while the number of those who affirm that "one can never be too careful when it comes to trusting others" has, for its part, increased. This trend is consistent with the worrying development in the Middle East and North Africa, where personal trust that used to be higher than the world average in 2000 has subsequently slipped below this level. The deterioration of the situation in Morocco should therefore be analyzed in the context of a broader regional transformation.

How can Morocco's poor results with regard to interpersonal trust within the society be explained? This may be partly explained by the distinction between bonding social capital and bridging social capital (see box 6.4). Studies on the "radius of trust" are among the ways in which the level of trust among individuals may be specifically or general assessed (Delhey, Newton, and Welzel 2011). Instead of being asked about their overall level of trust in others, persons surveyed were given a list with different categories of people, ranging from those they knew best (such as friends and family members) to people they met

Figure 6.6 Morocco: Response to the Question, "As a General Rule, Do You Trust Most People?"
(percent)

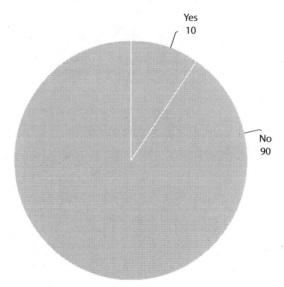

Source: Royal Institute of Strategic Studies 2012. Report of the National Survey on Social Cohesion in Morocco.

Box 6.4 Notions of Bonding Social Capital and Bridging Social Capital

Theories on social capital as it relates to economic development have often drawn a distinction between bonding social capital and bridging social capital. Bonding social capital refers to horizontal ties developed among individuals with shared demographic characteristics, such as members of the same family, friends, neighbors, office colleagues, and people from the same social circle. Bridging social capital, on the other hand, refers to ties that develop across vertical and parallel strata of the population, crossing economic, social, and regional boundaries; for example, divisions of social class, ethnic group, gender, religion, or nationality. Bonding social capital describes a specific type of trust that exists within small communities of people who know each other personally. In contrast, the characteristics of bridging social capital are essential for generalized trust within complex societies with countless daily interactions between people who know each other very little or not at all (Nannestad 2008). By bringing together individuals from different social backgrounds, bridging ties can help to reduce discrimination and ease conflicts between social groupings, increase social mobility, and facilitate the dissemination of information within society, thus engendering large-scale collective action and leading to a more inclusive social structure. Sociological studies have shown that tenuous links existing within vast networks of people are more effective for social insertion than strong ties within small nuclear groups of individuals (Granovetter 1979).

While the importance of bridging social capital is often highlighted, bonding social capital also plays a key role in mitigating risks and bolstering those in need of support.

box continues next page

Box 6.4 Notions of Bonding Social Capital and Bridging Social Capital *(continued)*

While stronger ties within communities are not an absolute good in and of themselves and may inhibit economic development by preventing individuals from moving out of their social milieu, forming ties outside of their habitual groups or engaging in entrepreneurial risks (Narayan 1999), close ties help individuals to survive the consequences of external shocks, such as natural disasters and economic restructuring. Consequently, the ties of bonding social capital are essential for preventing poverty and social exclusion by ensuring that individuals facing difficult times are not excluded from the system. In the absence of such ties, they are more exposed to the risk of definitive social exclusion (Rose 1995).

only occasionally or not at all (e.g., strangers or people of another nationality). In this way, one can assess not only the "degree" of trust, but also the "radius" of trust, that is, the extent to which each individual is willing to engage in reciprocal and voluntary cooperation outside of his or her familiar space, for example, with individuals not known to him or her and whom he or she has no reason, a priori, to treat favorably. Questions on the radius of trust were first tested on the ground as part of the 6th World Values Survey in 2005 and used for the first time in Morocco in 2011.

In Morocco, social ties are disproportionately formed within closed circles, beginning with the family and extending to friends and neighbors, to the detriment of more open and distant relationships, such as with foreigners or persons belonging to a different identity group. While a lower level of trust within open groups is a phenomenon common to most countries, regardless of their income level, Morocco represents a special case in point. The level of trust in persons of another religion, nationality, or in those with whom acquaintance is formed for the first time is lower in Morocco than in other developing countries. These findings indicate that in Morocco more than anywhere else, social ties are firmly anchored in close relationships—the family, and to a lesser extent, one's friends and neighbors—but that the networks that cut across traditional social categories to forge new links between individuals remain weak, or even nonexistent (see figure 6.7). This is demonstrated in weak collective ties in terms of social interaction and civic engagement (see box 6.5). It appears that in societies where the lifestyle is less centered around the family, there exists a greater spirit of cooperation and higher levels of interaction (Heinrich, Boyd, Bowles, Camerer, Fehr, Gintis, and McElreath 2001).

Civic Engagement

Moroccan society may also be characterized by a low level of civic engagement. Based on the results of the World Values Survey, which helps to measure the attachment of those surveyed to a whole range of civil society groups and associations, such as religious organizations, sports clubs, trade unions, professional associations, or political parties, it emerges that the level of civic engagement in Morocco is low when compared to the world level and to that of other

Figure 6.7 Morocco: Radius of Trust

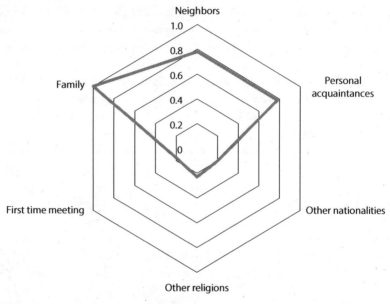

Source: 6th World Values Survey (2010–14). The scale of 0–1 reflects the proportion of persons surveyed who feel "moderate" or "great trust" in each of the groups identified.

Box 6.5 Status of Social Cohesion in Morocco

According to the national survey on social cohesion conducted by the Royal Institute of Strategic Studies, the family is the nucleus of social cohesion in Morocco, while ties of friendship, relationships with coworkers, neighbors, and other members of one's identity group appear to be more nuanced and ambivalent. Political and civic ties, for their part, appear to be weak.

- **The family: the strong nucleus of social cohesion**. However, in the face of multiple elements of change, family ties are becoming increasingly restricted to one's immediate family circle. Moreover, strong cohesiveness within the family decreases vis-à-vis more distant relatives and in-laws. While the majority of those surveyed sought to strengthen family ties through harmony and understanding rather than obedience, and by equal rights and responsibilities of both spouses and mutual dialogue rather than inequality and domination, an appreciable minority continues to believe that the ideal of family cohesion should be built on obedience; notably the obedience of the wife to her husband, in relation to her freedom of movement and right to work outside the home.
- **Friendships, relationships with neighbors and at the workplace: mixed social cohesiveness**. Friendships in Morocco appear to be based more on natural affinity, rather than choice. Friends are not chosen first and foremost from among neighbors, classmates, or work colleagues, but rather from within the family. The most ambivalent and nuanced social ties seem to be formed within the neighborhood, especially in urban areas. Good neighborliness and

box continues next page

Box 6.5 Status of Social Cohesion in Morocco *(continued)*

solidarity are always appreciated, but the level of trust in one's neighbors is far lower than the trust one has for one's friends. Socializing at the workplace is rarely practiced and is infused with mistrust. Personal affinities at work rarely lead to strong and lasting friendships.

- **Politics, civic engagement, and living together in harmony: fragile collective relationships.** The level of trust in institutions is relatively low, particularly in the government, police, the gendarmerie, the courts, public administration, political parties, and the Parliament. There is also limited acceptance of shared principles and common rules for collective civic life. Community life seems far more rooted in religious sentiment and a sense of national belonging than an adhesion to civic values. Collective solidarity is more valued from the religious, rather than from the civic dimension. All in all, there is ambivalence toward the concept of living together in harmony, where liberty is only weakly defended and authoritarianism is only partially rejected, while the factors that determine one's identity (Islam, one's country) are overwhelmingly accepted.

Source: IRES 2012.

developing countries. Individuals surveyed admitted to maintaining very few voluntary ties with groups of this nature (see figure 6.8). This result is corroborated by the Arab Barometer 2012–14, as well as by the national survey on social cohesiveness, which indicates that, in the 12 months leading up to the survey (IRES 2012), an overwhelming majority of persons interviewed (90 percent or more) had not taken part in any individual or collective protest action or activities to defend common interests. One of the paradoxes that strongly emerged from this survey was that although visible social movements that are peaceful and organized, such as the Movement for the Defense of Human Rights, are viewed very positively, there is very little effective mobilization in support of such movements.

The low level of civic engagement has its corollary in the high expectations regarding the redistributive role of the state. When asked the question "to what extent is the redistributive role of the State a characteristic of democracy?" more Moroccans consider this to be an essential feature of democracy than citizens of other countries (see figure 6.9). In countries with a high level of volunteerism and civic engagement, such as the United States or Japan, redistribution by the state is not considered as essential for democracy. In these countries, working together, helping others, and any other form of civic solidarity seem to be the most salient aspects of living together in harmony. In Morocco, social movements driven by material concerns (high cost of living, among others) get the strongest support—far more than movements involving societal advocacy, such as the defense of women's rights (IRES 2012).

Civic Behavior

An important dimension of social capital is the willingness of citizens to engage in civic behavior, to observe the rules of living in society, such as showing respect

Figure 6.8 Rate of Voluntary Membership of an Association

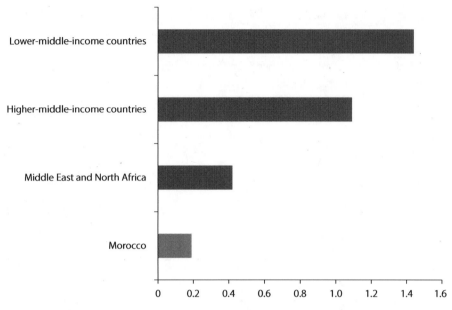

Source: World Values Survey 2010–14 (6th edition). Average level of affiliation to each of the following groups; religious groups, sports clubs, educational or cultural associations, political parties, trade unions, professional associations, environmental associations, women's groups, consumers' groups, and any other groups not mentioned here.

Figure 6.9 To What Extent Is the Statement "The State Should Equalize People's Incomes" Characteristic of a Democracy?
(1: Not an essential characteristic of democracy; 10: Is an essential characteristic of democracy)

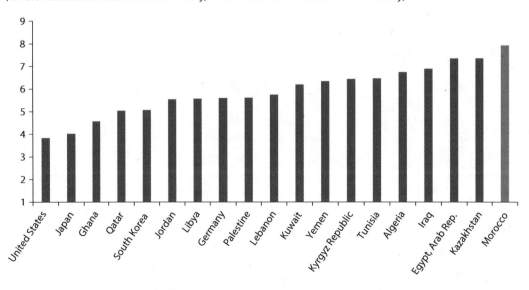

Source: World Values Survey 2010–2014 (6th edition).

for others, for nature (fauna and flora) and for collective property, to refrain from indulging in actions that go against the interests of society, such as corruption, wastage, and other forms of incivility (Herrmann and Thöni 2008). In Morocco, the low level of citizen participation is also reflected in a lack of civic sense and individual responsibility. Judging from the findings of national surveys, it would appear that uncivil conduct is not only widespread but steadily increasing.[9] This lack of civility is particularly striking and may be observed on Morocco's roads, where each year, road code violations exact a heavy toll in road deaths. With more than 200 fatal accidents per year per 100,000 vehicles, the roads of Morocco are some of the deadliest among middle-income countries (WHO 2015). By way of comparison, in the countries of Southern Europe (Spain, France, Italy), there are fewer than eight fatal accidents per 100,000 vehicles, each year, while the average for the Middle East and North Africa was 118 accidents in 2013 (see figure 6.10).

Moroccan society may be described as one in which there is a strong desire to preserve one's "image," with little real attachment to the rules of social coexistence. In, the social world, appearance is usually far more important than reality (Haidt 2012). People are trying harder to look right than to be right. Judging by the replies to the questions in the World Values Survey "do you think that it is sometimes justified to cheat on your taxes or benefits claims or

Figure 6.10 Road Deaths, 2013
(number of fatalities per 100 000 vehicles)

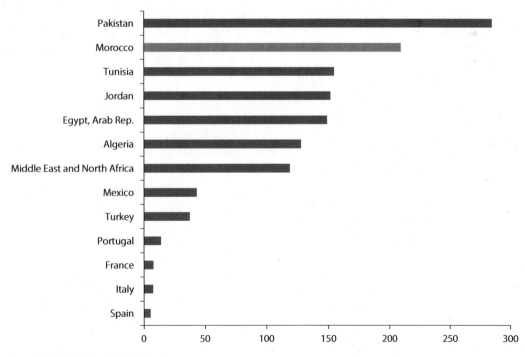

Source: World Health Organization 2015.

Morocco 2040 • http://dx.doi.org/10.1596/978-1-4648-1066-4

to pay bribes?" it would appear that in Morocco there is an extremely high regard for the rules of civic life. Almost everyone surveyed (97 percent) believe that it is "never justified" to resort to many types of socially deviant behavior. In fact, these results seem rather to reflect the fact that in Morocco, there is a deep desire for "social acceptability" and a preoccupation with one's "public image," at a level not comparable to any other country. It appears that voluntary compliance—that is, compliance without any type of coercion—with the rules of social coexistence is, in actual fact, quite limited (Fisman and Miguel 2006). A recent experimental study involving 23 countries arrived at a similar conclusion. Morocco seems to be one of the countries where the lack of honesty (cheating, lying, corruption) is most widespread; however, with the singularity that those persons surveyed said they would avoid telling the most blatant lies in order to conserve an image of honesty and respectability while deriving any potential material benefits (Gächter and Schulz 2016). Moreover, certain forms of cheating appear to be on the rise. For example, reported cases of cheating in the baccalaureate exams have increased tenfold since 2008, to reach 11,000 cases in 2015 (or almost 40 per 1,000 candidates, compared to one case per 1,000 in France, for example).

Realizing the Dividend of Enhanced "Social Capital"

By improving on its social capital, a society can expect to obtain a "dividend" or tangible gain. There are two methods for assessing the scope of such a dividend in a society: one may evaluate the intangible capital, which is the remaining income per capita estimated in terms of intangible assets, such as human or social capital (see chapter 1). One may also conduct an independent estimate on the effect of social capital on economic growth, using the estimate to calculate gains in terms of increased social cohesion and interpersonal trust. An econometric study conducted as part of this Memorandum has concluded that a 10-percentage point increase in interpersonal trust within society in general would mean a 0.6 percentage point increase in the annual growth rate. Year on year, that would translate into a cumulative increase of around 7 percent of economic growth in a decade (Foa 2015). Based on Morocco's 2015 GDP, a strong resurgence of interpersonal trust in Moroccan society would mean an increase on the order of US$7–US$8 billion over the next 10 years. As has been shown by successive World Values Surveys over the past 15 years, Morocco has seen a decline of 9.4 percent in levels of interpersonal trust. The country has therefore rather suffered from a "trust deficit," a fact that would explain why public policies have not necessarily achieved their expected aims.

Apart from measures to improve gender equality and interpersonal trust, countries have rather limited possibilities for radically increasing their social capital. As noted by Moroccan intellectuals Fadma Ait Mous and Driss Ksikes, "to think that 'harmonious coexistence' can be decreed from the top down by policymakers, preachers or demi-gods would be to resurrect, in the form of a benevolent diktat, new forms of totalitarianism."[10] This notwithstanding, a growing body of literature is taking an interest in this question, especially in conjunction with certain measures to strengthen civic consciousness and respect for the rule of law, encourage voluntary engagement, and support the evolution of mentalities. Investing in integrity in a given society is a profitable investment, because where there is loyalty and trust, it is possible to develop a relationship based on integrity. This relationship—this integrity—is an asset that produces economic value (Bernasek 2010). The aim of policy is therefore to nurture a collective culture that is not based on the search for opportunities for short-term economic gain, but rather on opportunities to create wealth in the long term. By developing such a culture based on integrity, one is seeking to promote and put in place clear principles, models of "virtuous" behavior, and sound incentives, notably in terms of access to information and transparency, declarations of conflicts of interest, respect for the law, and accountability. These values should be internalized and transmitted from one generation to the next, so that citizens will gradually learn that serving the interest of the larger community is the best way to serve the vast majority of individual interests in the long term. As noted by the social psychologist Jonathan Haidt, "human life is a series of opportunities for mutually beneficial cooperation. If we play our cards right, we can work with others to enlarge the pie that we ultimately share" (Haidt 2012).

Promoting Greater Respect for the Rule of Law, Civic Responsibility, and Exemplary Behavior

Morocco could take direct measures for strengthening social capital by ensuring greater compliance with the rule of law at all levels of society and by promoting exemplary conduct in all spheres of power by imposing tougher sanctions on behavior that is socially deviant, illegal, or uncivil. Restoring the values of probity, honesty, justice, and openness in society could lead to increased economic growth, through the development of a culture of trust and by allowing all citizens to realize their potential in an equitable, stable, predictable, and transparent environment. A culture of preferential treatment, collusion, and other special privileges tends to undermine interpersonal trust within societies and consequently to hinder the building of social capital needed for realizing common goals. In this regard, the development of information and communications technologies, notably the Internet and social networks, offers a unique opportunity to highlight illicit actions and behavior and foster a culture of greater integrity. Indeed, one important "stimulus to the development of social virtues" is the fact that people are passionately concerned with the "praise and blame of our fellowmen" (Darwin 1871). Last, the principle of exemplarity, which means, among other things, applying to one's self the same standard demanded of others, is a powerful tool for building trust and combating frustration, cynicism, and disengagement. It also serves to prevent counterproductive behavior (corruption, absenteeism, cheating). In view of the fact that one's duty to show exemplary behavior is proportionate to the power that one possesses, it should therefore be an absolute priority for highly placed public servants and officials of the state to live and lead by example.

Encouraging Civic Engagement and the Development of Civil Society

By implementing appropriate public policies, Morocco could also promote all forms of civic and citizen engagement, notably voluntary association, whether through social networks, civil society (associations), or the media (by combating censorship, surveillance, intimidation, etc.). According to the Arab Barometer 2012–14, less than a quarter of those surveyed were of the opinion that freedom of expression is fully guaranteed in Morocco. There is therefore much scope for improvement in this area. With regard to press freedom, Reporters without Borders (2017) has pointed to the slow but steady erosion of press freedoms in Morocco, which in 2017 ranked only 133 out of 180 countries. Citizens' capacity to openly express ideas and opinions can only develop with practice. Whenever collective action is subject to serious restriction, citizens lose confidence, engage in self-censorship, and eventually give up on openly exchanging ideas or working together. The fundamental responsibility of the state is therefore to guard against suspicion and mistrust within the society. The recently adopted draft law on the press and publications is therefore a step in the right direction, especially with regard to the legal recognition of the freedom of electronic media and the establishment of legal protection of the confidentiality of sources of information. However, media professionals consider that further steps could be taken to better protect journalists against the risk of penalties or imprisonment in the exercise of their profession.

Supporting the Development of Sociocultural Norms and Mentalities

Morocco could initiate awareness campaigns to promote new ways of thinking in relation to the values of cooperation, freedom and mutual respect, citizenship, and civic duty. Minor and inexpensive tweaks can be made to the environment to produce big increases in ethical behavior. In this regard, the education policy is one of the best tools available to government for nurturing the development of social norms and a sense of civic commitment (Faour and Muasher 2011; Diwan 2016). The educational system should espouse and apply such values as responsibility, transparency, and accountability. They should be introduced into school curriculums as a matter of priority. Indeed, it is on the basis of their experiences in the school system and later in university that men and women learn how to set up associations, work in teams, and strive toward collective goals. Changes in the academic curriculum can play a positive role, for example, with the inclusion of more creative group work and a more realistic targeting of the requisite administrative and organizational skills, along the lines of proposals set forth in the section on education. Recent studies have demonstrated that in countries where school curriculums tended toward a more collaborative, less hierarchical, and individualistic approach, community life and the attendant values of civic association and engagement have gained in importance (Algan, Cahuc, and Shleifer 2013). In countries where students engage in group work at the primary and secondary levels, such as Sweden, Austria, and the United States, the level of trust within the society is comparatively higher.

Notes

1. In his analysis of Japan's postwar industrialization period Fukuyama (1995) observes that the government and private sector were often at odds and that the Japanese economic miracle came about despite, rather than because of the efforts of the MITI. To consider the Japanese private sector as a mere extension of the State would be to overlook the remarkable capacity of Japanese society to organize itself. For an analysis of the genesis of industrialization in Japan, see Lockwood (1954).

2. Keefer and Knack (1997) estimate that a 10 percent increase in the percentage of people responding "most people can be trusted" to the question posed in the World Values Survey would equate to an increase in growth equivalent to four-fifths of one percentage point.

3. This relates to (1) the adoption of the Organic Law on access to the House of Representatives, which establishes a quota of 60 seats for women out of a total of 395 seats, or 15 percent of the total number; (2) the adoption in 2015 of the Organic Law on the House of Councilors that stipulates that candidates must alternate between men and women in elections. A law was also adopted to amend and complement the Organic Law on the election of members of local and regional governments.

4. Following the signing in 2013 of a memorandum of understanding between the Central Guarantee Fund (CCG) and the Association of Women Entrepreneurs in Morocco (AFEM), a guarantee fund—"Ilayki"—was established to benefit women entrepreneurs seeking to set up their own businesses. In 2015, credits amounting to almost 40 million dirhams were mobilized for 131 approved applications.

5. The project to set up a National Agricultural Register (RNA) was launched in 2016. In the future, it will allow for the establishment of a database with the profiles of farmers and technologies for geo-localization of their farm holdings.

6. A draft law on domestic work adopted by the House of Representatives in July 2016 sets forth the rules governing employment of domestic workers and their working conditions.

7. The new Budget Framework Law, which will come into effect in 2017, underlines the importance of gender mainstreaming in the programs of Ministry departments, as well as in their monitoring and evaluation procedures. This could serve to enhance the coherence of public actions to promote gender equality.

8. http://www.worldvaluessurvey.org/wvs.jsp and http://www.arabbarometer.org/.

9. According to the results of the survey conducted in 14 towns in Morocco by the Association marocaine pour le civisme et le développement (AFAK) (Moroccan Association for Civic Action and Development) in 2009, 66 percent of persons surveyed considered that uncivil behavior was on the rise, 72 percent saw a visible degradation of the environment, 53 percent stated that there was an increase in fanaticism and intolerance, while 61 percent believed that there was growing insecurity.

10. Ait Mous and Ksikes (2016).

References

Acemoglu, Daron, Simon Johnson, and James A. Robinson. 2001. "Colonial Origins of Comparative Development: An Empirical Investigation." *American Economic Review* 91 (5): 1369–1401.

Agénor, P.-R. 2012. "A Computable OLG Model for Gender and Growth Policy Analysis." Discussion Paper Series No. 169. Center for Growth and Business Cycle Research, Economic Studies, University of Manchester, Manchester, UK.

———. 2017. "A Computable Overlapping Generations Model for Gender and Growth Policy Analysis." *Macroeconomic Dynamics* 21: 11–54.

Agénor, P.-R., Rim Berahab, and Karim El Mokri. 2017. "Egalité de genre, politiques publiques et croissance économique au Maroc." In *Evaluation de l'impact des politiques publiques sur les inégalités de genre et la croissance économique au Maroc*. Direction des Etudes et des Prévisions Financières (Ministère de l'Economie et des Finances du Maroc) and OCP Policy Center.

Ait Mous, Fadma, and Driss Ksikes. 2016. "Penser ensemble, tout un cheminement." In *Le tissu de nos singularités: vivre ensemble au Maroc*. Fondation HEM. Casablanca: Les presses de l'Université citoyenne.

———. 2010. *Identity Economics: How Our Identities Shape Our Work, Wages, and Well-Being*. Princeton, NJ: Princeton University Press.

Akerlof, George A., and Rachel E. Kranton. 2010. *Identity Economics: How Our Identities Shape Our Work, Wages, and Well-Being*. Princeton, NJ: Princeton University Press.

Algan, Yann, Pierre Cahuc, and Andrei Shleifer. 2013. "Teaching Practices and Social Capital." *American Economic Journal: Applied Economics* 5 (3): 189–210.

Almond, G. A., and S. Verba. 1963. *The Civic Culture: Political Attitudes and Democracy in Five Nations*. Princeton, NJ: Princeton University Press.

Arrow, Kenneth J. 1972. *Gifts and Exchanges, Philosophy & Public Affairs* 1(4): 343–62.

Bergson, Henri. 1932. *Les deux sources de la morale et de la religion*. Paris: Édition Félix Alcan.

Bernasek, Anna. 2010. *The Economics of Integrity*. New York: HarperCollins.

Beugelsdijk, S., H. de Groot, and A. van Schaik. 2004. "Trust and Economic Growth: A Robustness Analysis." *Oxford Economic Papers* 56: 118–34.

Chaara, Imane. 2012. "Pro-women Legal Reform in Morocco: Is Religion an Obstacle?" Economic Research Forum Working Paper 685, Economic Research Forum, Giza, Egypt.

Coleman, J. S. 1988. "Social Capital in the Creation of Human Capital." *The American Journal of Sociology* 94: S95–120.

Darwin, Charles. 2010 [1871]. *The Descent of Man and Selection in Relation to Sex*. New York: New York University Press.

Delhey, J., K. Newton, and C. Welzel. 2011. "How General Is Trust in "Most People"? Solving the Radius of Trust Problem." *American Sociological Review* 76 (5): 786–807.

Diwan, Ishac. 2016. "Low Social and Political Returns to Education in the Arab World." Economic Research Forum Policy Briefs No. 17, Economic Research Forum, Giza, Egypt.

Faour, Muhammad, and Marwan Muasher. 2011. *Education for Citizenship in the Arab World—Key to the Future*. Beirut: Carnegie Middle East Center.

Fisman, Raymond, and Edward Miguel. 2006. "Cultures of Corruption: Evidence from Diplomatic Parking Tickets." NBER Working Paper 12312, National Bureau of Economic Research, Cambridge, MA.

Foa, Roberto. 2015. "Growing Social Capital for a More Prosperous, Sustainable and Inclusive Society in Morocco." Unpublished report.

Fukuyama, Francis. 1995. *Trust: The Social Virtues and the Creation of Prosperity.* New York: Free Press.

Gächter, Simon, and Jonathan F. Schulz. 2016. "Intrinsic Honesty and the Prevalence of Rule Violations across Societies." *Nature Weekly Magazine*, March 24.

Goumeziane. 2006. "Ibn Khaldoun. Discours sur l'Histoire Universelle (Al Muqaddima), Traduction Vincent Monteil." Commission internationale pour la traduction des chefs-d'œuvre, Beyrouth 1967. Tome II, p. 898.

Goumeziane, Smail. 2006. *Ibn Khaldoun: Un génie maghrébin (1332–1406).* Algiers: Édition EDIF.

Granovetter, Mark. 1979. "The Idea of 'Advancement' in Theories of Social Evolution and Development." *American Journal of Sociology* 85 (November): 489–515.

Haidt, Jonathan. 2012. *The Righteous Mind: Why Good People Are Divided by Politics and Religion.* New York: Pantheon.

Hall, Robert E., and Charles I. Jones. 1999. "Why Do Some Countries Produce So Much More Output per Worker than Others?" NBER Working Paper 6564, National Bureau of Economic Research, Cambridge, MA.

Helliwell, J. F., and R. D. Putnam. 1995. "Economic Growth and Social Capital in Italy." *Eastern Economic Journal* 21 (3): 295–307.

Heinrich, J., R. Boyd, S. Bowles, C. Camerer, E. Fehr, H. Gintis, and R. McElreath. 2001. "In Search of Homo Economicus: Behavioral Experiments in 15 Small-Scale Societies." *American Economic Review Papers and Proceedings* 91 (2): 73–78.

Herrmann, B., and C. Thöni. 2008. "Antisocial Punishment across Societies." *Science* 319 (5868): 1362–67. doi: 10.1126/science.1153808.

High Commission for Planning (HCP). 2009. *Enquête nationale sur la prévalence de la violence à l'égard des femmes.* Morocco.

———. 2012. *La femme marocaine en chiffres, tendances d'évolution des caractéristiques démographiques et socio-professionelles, Journée nationale de la femme.* Morocco.

Ibourk, Aomar. 2016. *Performances en lecture au Maroc: approche par genre.* OCP Policy Center Research Paper RP-16/06, OCP Policy Center, Rabat.

International Monetary Fund (IMF). 2017. *Morocco: 2016 Article IV Consultation-Staff Report.* Washington, DC: IMF.

Keefer, P., and Knack, S. 1997. "Does Social Capital Have an Economic Payoff? A Cross-Country Investigation." *Quarterly Journal of Economics* 112 (4): 1251–88.

———. 2002. "Polarization, Politics and Property Rights: Links between Inequality and Growth." *Public Choice* 111 (1–2): 127–54.

Knack, P. and P. J, Zak. 1998. "Trust and Growth." IRIS Working Paper 219. College Park, MD: University of Maryland.

Knowles, S., and C. Weatherston. 2006. "Informal Institutions and Cross-Country Income Differences." CREDIT Research Paper 06/06, University of Nottingham.

Lamrabet, Asma. 2015. *Les femmes et l'islam: Une vision réformiste.* Série Valeurs d'islam no 8. Paris: La Fondation pour l'innovation politique.

———. 2016. "Lumière sur l'éthique égalitaire du Coran." In *Le tissu de nos singularités: vivre ensemble au Maroc.* Fondation HEM. Casablanca: Les presses de l'Université citoyenne.

Landes, David S. 1998. *The Wealth and Poverty of Nations: Why Some Are So Rich and Some So Poor.* New York: W.W. Norton.

———. 2000. "Culture Makes Almost All the Differences." In *Culture Matters: How Values Shape Human Progress,*" edited by Lawrence E. Harrison and Samuel P. Huntington, 2–13. New York: Basic Books.

Lawlor, Leonard, and Valentine Moulard Leonard. 2013. Henri Bergson. *The Stanford Encyclopedia of Philosophy,* edited by Edward N. Zalta. Stanford, CA: Stanford University. http://plato.stanford.edu/archives/win2013/entries/bergson/

Lockwood, William W. 1954. *The Economic Development of Japan: Growth and Structural Change, 1868–1938.* Princeton, NJ: Princeton University Press.

Marotta, Daniela, Paul Scott Prettitore, and Paolo Verme. 2015. "Gender Inequality, Structural Transformation and Growth: The Case of Morocco." Discussion Paper MFM Global Practice 8, World Bank, Washington, DC.

Ministry of Justice and Liberties, Family Court Statistics. 2011. Morocco.

Moghadam, Valentine. 2005. *Globalizing Women: Transnational Feminist Networks.* Baltimore, MD: Johns Hopkins University Press.

Nannestad, Peter. 2008. "What Have We Learned about Generalized Trust, If Anything?" *Annual Review of Political Science* 11: 413–36.

Narayan, Deepa. 1999. *Bonds and Bridges: Social Capital and Poverty.* Washington, DC: World Bank.

National Science Foundation Meditel. 2007. *World Values Survey.* Morocco.

Nordman, Christophe, and François-Charles Wolff. 2007. "Is There a Glass Ceiling in Morocco? Evidence from Matched Worker-Firm Data." Economic Research Forum Working Paper 720, Economic Research Forum, Giza, Egypt.

North, Douglass. 1990. *Institutions, Institutional Change and Economic Performance.* Cambridge, UK: Cambridge University Press.

Organisation for Economic Co-operation and Development (OECD). 2001. *The Well-Being of Nations: The Role of Human and Social Capital.* Paris: OECD Publishing.

Piccioto, Robert. 1998. "The Missing Development Links: Gender and Social Capital." Paper presented at the Gender and Development Workshop, World Bank, Washington, DC.

Popper, Karl R. 1966 [1943]. *The Open Society and Its Enemies.* Princeton, NJ: Princeton University Press.

Portes, A. 1998. "Social Capital: Its Origins and Applications in Contemporary Sociology." *Annual Review of Sociology* 24: 1–24.

Prettitore, Paul. 2014. "Ten Years after Morocco's Family Code Reforms: Are Gender Gaps Closing?" MENA Knowledge and Learning Note No. 121, World Bank, Washington, DC.

Putnam, Robert D. 1993. "The Prosperous Community: Social Capital and Public Life." *American Prospect* 13: 35–42.

———. 2000. *Bowling Alone: The Collapse and Revival of American Community.* New York: Simon & Schuster.

Putnam, Robert D., Robert Leonardi, and Raffaella Nanetti. 1993. *Making Democracy Work: Civic Traditions in Modern Italy.* Princeton, NJ: Princeton University Press.

Rose, R. 1995. "Russia as an Hour Glass Society: A Constitution without Citizens." *East European Constitutional Review* 4 (3): 34–42.

Royal Institute for Strategic Studies (IRES). 2012. *Rapport de l'enquête nationale sur le lien social au Maroc*. Morocco.

Sen, Amartya. 1999. *Development as Freedom*. New York: Oxford University Press.

Serajuddin, Umar, and Paolo Verme. 2012. "Who Is Deprived? Who Feels Deprived? Labor Deprivation, Youth and Gender in Morocco." Policy Research Working Paper 6090, World Bank, Washington, DC.

Sowell, Thomas. 2015. *Wealth, Poverty, and Politics: An International Perspective*. New York: Basic Books.

Tabellini, G. 2005. "Culture and Institutions: Economic Development in the Regions of Europe." CESifo Working Paper 1492.

Tirole, Jean. 2016. *Économie du bien commun*. Paris: Presses universitaires de France.

United Nations Development Programme (UNDP). 2003. *Arab Human Development Report 2003*. New York: UNDP.

Verme, Paolo, Abdoul Gadiry Barry, and Jamal Guennouni. 2014. "Female Labor Participation in the Arab World: Some Evidence from Panel Data in Morocco." Policy Research Working Paper 7031, World Bank, Washington, DC.

Weber, Max. 1905. *The Protestant Ethic and the Spirit of Capitalism*. London: Allen and Unwin.

Welzel, C. 2013. *Freedom Rising Human Empowerment and the Quest for Emancipation*. Cambridge, UK: Cambridge University Press.

World Bank. 2011. *The Changing Wealth of Nations*. Washington, DC: World Bank.

———. 2012. *Gender World Development Report*. Washington, DC: World Bank.

———. 2015. *Maroc: Équilibrer les chances- renforcer l'autonomisation des femmes pour une société plus ouverte, inclusive et prospère*. Rapport 97778. Washington, DC: World Bank.

World Economic Forum. 2016. Global Gender Gap Index 2016, World Economic Forum, Cologny, Switzerland.

World Health Organization (WHO). 2015. *Global Status Report on Road Safety 2015*. Geneva, Switzerland: WHO.

The Political Economy of Change—
An Essential Transition

"Daring ideas are like chessmen moved forward; they may be beaten, but they may start a winning game."

— Goethe

The political economy of change is no longer concerned with the "what;" it is instead concerned with the "how." How can reforms designed to improve the social well-being of Moroccans, such as those recommended in 2005 to achieve the "desirable Morocco" scenario, be effectively adopted and implemented? In other words, can the balance achieved by the different strata of society drive greater momentum for change and modernization, or is it being driven by stability and preservation? With respect to the current equilibrium in Moroccan society, are the government and the nongovernmental actors (private sector and civil society organizations) participating in the status quo or contributing to progress? In what circumstances, can Moroccan society evolve toward a superior equilibrium? A look at game theory provides answers (at least from a theoretical standpoint) to the issues raised by these key questions at the heart of any in-depth change process (see box E.1).

When applied to political economy, game theory provides an understanding of the numerous equilibria achieved within a society and explains why these equilibria are stable, albeit potentially suboptimal (Grossman and Helpman 2001; Weingast and Wittman 2006; McCarty and Helpman 2007). In game theory terms, therefore, policy formulation is not so much an expression of a long-term cooperative and integrated development strategy, but the result of strategic combinations of circumstances among different players involved in this formulation process (head of state, government, lawmakers, political parties, local and regional elites, religious authorities, enterprise, trade unions, and different and varied interest groups).

This political economy paradigm helps us understand that the limited economic and social convergence being achieved by Morocco with Spain, its closest

Box E.1 Game Theory

Game theory seeks to present and predict the strategies of players who have their own goals and are in a situation of interdependency. In game theory (a game is defined as a formal framework in which players make decisions, with each player cognizant of the fact that the outcome of any decision made is dependent on the decisions of the others), all choices made by several players, who are aware of each other's strategies, are stable when no player can unilaterally modify his or her strategy without weakening his or her own position.

Based on the well-known formula of the famous mathematician and Nobel Prize winner for Economics John Nash, the existence of an equilibrium in a noncooperative game does not mean that this equilibrium is necessarily unique or optimal (Nash 1951). There may be other more cooperative choices involving several players that result in a higher gain for each one. The underlying idea is that it is not possible to predict the result of the choices made by several decision makers if these decisions are analyzed in isolation. Consideration should instead be given to what each decision maker would do, taking the decision-making process of the others into account.

Game theory helps conceptualize the strategic choices of economic players (households, enterprise, the State) in situations where their interests diverge. In this regard, as the Nobel Prize winner for Economics Jean Tirole has noted, game theory can be applied not only to the economy, but also to all social sciences as well as to politics, law, sociology, and even psychology (Tirole 2016).

neighbor to the north, for example, is not due to inadequate potential, but to a suboptimal political economy equilibrium (World Bank 2016). Morocco (as is the case in most countries in an economic catch-up process) has considerable growth potential. Each year, the Moroccan economy earns roughly US$100 billion in goods and services while its estimated post-convergence potential is US$1 trillion. However, the realization of this potential is being severely hobbled by numerous deep-seated suboptimal political economy equilibria that are only evolving very gradually. The behavior that hampers the country's transparency and economic openness and seeks to protect special interests, privileges, and rent seeking is often deeply rooted in the customs, culture, and way of thinking of the elites (Acemoglu and Jackson 2015). Those within the system who benefit from its protection find it normal that the system excludes those who are not a part of this system. While openness to trade and competition usually helps improve the well-being of the great majority, producers facing competition from imports and other well-established producers who feel threatened by these developments will in all likelihood do everything to resist (Krueger 1974; Grossman and Helpman 1994). The administration may itself be "held hostage" by well-organized special interests capable of influencing regulations in their favor at the expense of the public interest (Stigler 1971; Peltzman 1976; Laffont and Tirole 1991). In the long run, these interest groups tend to consolidate their influence, political weight, and capacity to extract wealth for their own gain, making the path to another more inclusive equilibrium difficult to achieve.

From a historical standpoint, several major empires that have been built on "extractive" economic and political institutions can indeed be sustained for a long time (see box E.2). These extractive political systems have been the subject of in-depth research. They are sometimes referred to as "neo-patrimonialism" insofar as political leaders adopt the external form of modern states (bureaucracies, elections, legal systems) but in reality, lead based on private interests (Fukuyama 2014). Other authors speak of "limited access order" whereby a coalition of rent-seeking elites use its political power to impede free competition in both the economic and the political spheres (North, Wallis, and Weingast 2009). As far back as the 14th century, the philosopher Ibn Khaldoun theorized about the formation of the rent-seeking or patrimonial state and the transfer of wealth from productive social categories to the unproductive social categories that this entailed (Goumeziane 2006).

The political economy of change consists of identifying and setting in motion the forces that could contribute to the achievement of a new equilibrium with greater potential to drive social well-being. It should nevertheless be noted that when the political economy equilibrium achieved is stable, it is hard to identify the conditions (see paragraph above relating to the game theory) that could steer players to make different choices in an effort to achieve a new equilibrium when they have no personal interest in doing so. History, as much as geography, contributes to a form of national economic and growth hysteresis (Acemoglu and Robinson 2006).[1] At the same time, history and economic science appear to show that when players are better informed of "the rules of the game" or when these rules change or are effectively implemented and enforced in times of extensive change, then the players review their strategies and make different choices. Another noncooperative, potentially better equilibrium for society then becomes possible.

Box E.2 Characteristics of Extractive and Inclusive Institutions

Extractive economic institutions
- Absence of the rule of law or compliance with it
- Uncertain property rights
- Barriers to market entry and competition distortions

Extractive political institutions
- Concentration of political power in a few hands
- Lack of checks and balances and oversight
- Lack of transparency, information, and accountability

Inclusive economic institutions
- Respect for the rule of law
- Respect for property rights
- Market economy with free and fair competition

Inclusive political institutions
- Broad diversity and equitable representation
- Numerous checks and balances; oversight
- Information, transparency, and accountability

Source: Acemoglu and Robinson 2012.

Improve Information Sharing with Actors

Sharing information and new ideas on policy functioning and outcomes can exert an effect on the political economy equilibrium (Rodrik 2014; Casey 2015). The underlying notion here is that the political economy equilibrium can be determined by the ideas developed by players (especially elites) on the outcomes of the various strategies and by their own vested interests. Special interests are largely the product of mental and social constructs (honor, reputation, respect, power, allegiance, and the like) and are not limited to specific material interests. As the Harvard economist Dani Rodrik notes, human behavior is largely driven by abstract ideals, sacred values, or conceptions of loyalty that cannot be reduced to economic ends (Rodrik 2014). In each social category, persons have a perception of what they are and this perception is tied to beliefs about the way in which they (and others) are supposed to behave. These perceptions play a key role in the way in which economies function (Akerlof and Kranton 2010). Thus, whenever new concepts or ideas change behavior, players may be driven to review their position without compromising their special interests. This helps us understand why, in a number of cases, reforms end up benefiting special interests, which were resisting the most in the first place. Economic history is replete with examples of situations in which information or, more generally, new ideas have shaped a new political economy equilibrium (Leighton and Lopez 2013).

Information and ideas are increasingly important (and have a greater impact) because players are facing increasingly complex games. In most public intervention sectors, a strategy's success hinges on a large number of interdependent economic, social, political, and technological parameters. Globalization is further enhancing this complexity and conditions the relevance of an intervention to external developments, which, by definition, cannot be controlled. Moreover, research in behavioral economics has shown that the reaction of actors to public policy changes is hard to predict (World Bank 2014). All of these factors weaken the capacity of players to anticipate the outcomes of their actions and draw a distinction between "what works" and "what does not." Education actors, for example (such as teachers, parents, and trade unions) must contend with issues for which there are no simple solutions: Should performance-based financial incentives be provided to teachers? Should digital technology be introduced in schools or should cameras be installed in classrooms? Should children begin learning a foreign language in their first year of primary school? What reading methods should be adopted?

In this context marked by complex choices, actors have several options to reduce the uncertainty facing them and potentially help them review their positions: increase the level of knowledge, enhance transparency, and encourage evaluation.

- Increase the level of knowledge through access to information and academic research: all public policies are premised on assumptions regarding the functioning of the economy and the society (if action is taken with respect to A, then B will occur). The role of information and academic research is to provide an objective basis for the selected assumptions. Without information or the benefit of research, decision makers are compelled to rely on subjective opinions or on intuitions that are often biased. Modern public policies are evidence-based; in other words, they are based on empirically proven causal relationships. While the perspective provided by research does not completely eliminate the risk of error, it significantly reduces it.

- Enhance transparency: analysts and decision makers are, like any individual, prone to flawed reasoning and cognitive biases that affect their judgment. The propensity for excessive optimism, the powerful aversion to losses, the sometimes effective but also often counterproductive role of emotions in decision making, selective memory, or even manipulation of one's own beliefs are perfect examples (Tirole 2016). They are often placed at a disadvantage by asymmetric information and cannot know all aspects of a public policy. In these circumstances, transparency in public policy can contribute significantly to the improved quality of public decisions. Consulting the relevant actors makes it possible to gather information so as to better anticipate the outcomes of the planned intervention. Similarly, releasing data and documents on the related policy to the general public helps inform public debate and encourages decision makers to demonstrate the relevance of the selected options.

- Encourage evaluation: the new development economics paradigm advocates the systematic evaluation of public policies, when possible, in order to objectively show their effectiveness (Banerjee and Duflo 2011). This evaluation can be done "ex ante" using tests, or "ex post" using mechanisms to record the reactions of the beneficiaries (feedback loop). The information collected in this manner consistently helps improve public policy design and execution.

These three options, which make it possible to manage the complexity and uncertainty and to make modifications to the positions and strategies of all players by establishing accountability, must be enhanced in Morocco. As things currently stand, the level of information and knowledge that could improve the players' understanding of the "rules of the game" and thus place them in a position of accountability barely increases and does not lead to a steady endogenous shift in political economy equilibria (Bidner and François 2013). Instead of being reactive, the players' position tends to remain frozen as in other emerging countries (Besley and Burgess 2002). However, the issue of information is at the heart of the creation of institutions and the choice of economic policy (see box E.3). It is at the core of the economy for the common good (Tirole 2016).

Moroccan public policies are inadequately informed by academic research. Academic research still plays a limited role in major public policy areas. Where research exists, it is hardly used to inform public policy decisions. Several national plans as well as sectoral strategies adopted in Morocco include few national bibliographical references. National research on crucial issues for the

---

Box E.3 Information Theory

Along with game theory, information theory also represents a major step forward in economic science over the past 40 years and underpins the modern microeconomy. Information theory accounts for the strategic use of insider information by economic players who, as has been observed, have their own goals and are in a situation of interdependence.

According to the Nobel Prize winner for Economics Jean Tirole, this theory is based on one piece of evidence: the decisions of economic players (households, enterprises, the State) are constrained by the limited information in their possession. The consequences of these information limitations are seen everywhere: in the difficulty faced by administrations in understanding and evaluating the policies pursued by their governments; in the difficulty faced by the State in regulating leading banks or enterprises, in protecting the environment or managing innovation; in the difficulty faced by investors in controlling the use of their money by the enterprises they finance; in the internal organizational approaches of our enterprises; in our interpersonal relations; and even in our relationships with ourselves, as when we construct our identity or believe what we want to believe.

In particular, as Jean Tirole has noted, "the State only rarely has the information needed to make decisions on the allocation of resources. That does not mean that the State has no flexibility, but it must humbly accept its limitations. Hubris—excessive confidence in its capacity to make choices regarding economic policy—can, along with the desire to retain control and therefore the power to distribute favors, lead the State to implement harmful policies." In the final analysis, "the necessary compatibility between public policies and the information available has crucial implications for the design of industrial policy or sectoral and banking regulation, employment policies, environmental protection, and so on" (Tirole 2016).

---

country, such as the issue of learning challenges facing Moroccan students in reading, foreign languages, and mathematics, is poor. However, international tests (PIRLS, UNESCO 2014) show that 79 percent of children are not proficient in reading by the age of 10. Limited academic research may be explained by the fact that the work of academic researchers is not sufficiently valued. The central government does not involve researchers in substantive discussions and fails to provide ongoing support to the targeted research programs on public policy issues. More generally, the government does not adequately share the information in its possession. If Morocco does not have sufficient research on the job market, despite the strategic importance of the issue of employment to the country, it is also without a doubt because of limitations on access to comprehensive data from employment surveys. Similarly, there is very limited academic research on taxation in Morocco because detailed tax data are not accessible to researchers, thus hampering, for example, the development of national microsimulation skills. Last, with respect to industry, Morocco does have an annual inventory of all industrial enterprises, which could facilitate a better understanding of sectoral trends. However, these data are highly inaccessible to researchers, hindering the emergence of academic research in this area. In the absence of academic research, the designers of national plans and sectoral strategies are obliged to rely on a limited knowledge base, with a high risk of cognitive bias.

Public policy making is often conducted in a nontransparent manner that does not promote public debate. Morocco has "sectoral roadmaps" in most areas of government intervention designed to share diagnoses, define guidelines, and set goals. Yet, information is often shared piecemeal, with the published documents generally restricted to describing often-ambitious and quantified goals without any rigorous analysis to justify the decision making and choices made. In the absence of precise information, public, academic, or parliamentary debate on the merits of a particular sectoral plan prior to its adoption remains incomplete. However, in an increasingly complex and uncertain world, intellectual debate is critical for the collection of information, correction of possible biases, and, ultimately, enhancement of the quality of public policies. It is important to note that this discussion exercise should also be driven by parliamentary work, particularly in the context of sectoral commissions. A check of the Moroccan Parliament's website in October 2015 did not reveal any information report produced by standing committees. Comparatively, in France and the United Kingdom, the commissions in the two chambers of Parliament produce roughly 100 information reports each year on the various public policies. This underscores the need to assess the output of sectoral plans, their phasing, and overall cohesiveness (CESE 2014). This assessment should be systematic and assume an institutional character through the establishment of mechanisms or dedicated entities to allow for ex-ante analysis and regular and close monitoring to implement the necessary modifications within appropriate timeframes (Bank Al-Maghrib 2016).

Last, public policies are often launched on a large scale, bypassing the necessary pilot test stage. Sectoral policies initiated are generally ambitious and use significant budget resources. A retrospective look, however, reveals that often the development plans initiated in the various sectors (agriculture, industry, tourism, etc.) rarely achieve their objectives. The common element among all these plans is the absence of initial pilot exercises. The execution of pilot projects prior to general implementation would have helped pinpoint difficulties, gain experience, and improve the design of interventions. In this regard, recent economic research recommends the implementation of iterative mechanisms for adapting policies based on the problems encountered (Andrew, Pritchett, and Woolcock 2012). The Chinese experience is an example of how institutionalization of public policy experimentation has helped inform public choices, apprise players of the benefits of the policies implemented (in the case of economic openness), and, ultimately, change the behavior of players and the political economy equilibrium (see box E.4).

Box E.4 Institutionalization of Public Policy Experimentation in China

China has experienced the strongest economic growth in the world over the past three decades. Between 1980 and 2010, the average per capita gross domestic product (GDP) growth rate was 7 percent, resulting in an eight-fold increase in income levels. During this same period, the Moroccan economy grew at an average rate of 2 percent, doubling the per capita GDP. In 1980, Moroccans were twice as wealthy as the Chinese. However, the ratio was reversed in 2010, as Chinese citizens were twice as prosperous as Moroccans. China's economic boom is one of the most extraordinary development experiences in history, despite the fact that the country is now facing a natural slowdown in growth (the other economic miracles have all undergone a similar phase). While China has taken advantage of its low costs to become "the world's factory," it has also successfully upgraded its economy and acquired technological capacity. China now has the highest number of invention patents in the world, with over 500 patents per capita in 2014 (700,000 patents in total) compared to just 9 in Morocco (total of 300 patents).

To achieve these exceptional economic results, China had to implement far-reaching reforms to transform a collectivist economic system into a dynamic and innovative market economy. When Deng Xiaoping initiated the opening-up process in the late 1970s, all economic structures had to be modernized, including the private property system, market regulations, the business environment, openness to the global economy, and the financial system. As is the case in most countries, these types of major reforms provoke spontaneous, stiff resistance in the system as their impact is unknown. Will the reforms succeed? Will they destabilize the political and social order? Who will be the winners and the losers? International experience has shown that these uncertainties typically result in the blocking of the reform process and a continuation of the status quo, a syndrome that the economists Fernandez and Rodrik refer to as "status quo bias" (Fernandez and Rodrik 1991). China has nonetheless successfully overcome this hurdle through an original reform method based on trial and error, experimentation, and pragmatism.

When academic researchers examined China's success in the area of economic reform, they discovered that the vast majority of reforms were first piloted at the local level before being implemented nationwide. Sinologist Sebastian Heilman has demonstrated that since the late 1970s, China has served as a large laboratory for hundreds of pilot projects. This experimental approach, known as *youdian daomian* (literally, from the point to the surface), was institutionalized by the Chinese state to encourage local initiatives, study the results, and actively share good practices (Heilmann 2008). In *China Experiments: From Local Innovations to National Reform* Florini, Lai, and Tan show that this systematic trial and error approach produces radical public policy innovations. The pilot project scope is very wide and can cover such areas as health, transport, public enterprise, the business environment, and social protection. The experimental approach has manifold benefits: (a) it unleashes creativity and encourages innovation at all levels; (b) it verifies the effectiveness of the interventions prior to general implementation; and (c) it defuses resistance to change by showing its beneficial effects (Florini, Lai, and Tan 2012).

box continues next page

Box E.4 Institutionalization of Public Policy Experimentation in China *(continued)*

The growth of the Shanghai free zone is a recent example of experimentation. In the late 1970s, instead of a general opening up of its economy, China implemented special economic zones for the phased testing of the benefits of the market economy. The ensuing success led to the nationwide implementation of the measures. More recently, China recognized the need to launch a new generation of reforms to complete its transition to a market economy. Consistent with this experimental approach, a pilot project—the Shanghai Pilot Free Trade Zone (SPFTZ)—was launched in 2013 to test economic liberalization measures in Shanghai City in the areas of foreign trade (liberalization of imports), foreign investment, capital flows (relaxation of controls), and the financial sector (liberalization of interest rates and facilitation of the entry of foreign players). A "master plan" outlining the experimentation procedures was published. It provides for the establishment of a research center tasked with studying the effects of the measures, with a view to implementation nationwide. A recent independent study reveals that the impacts of the experimentation approach are already beginning to show in the form of capital flows (Yao and Whalley 2015).

Change and Comply with the Rules of the Game

Informing and enlightening players about public policy choices and the rules of the game may not be enough for these players to substantially change their positions. Consideration must therefore be given to actually changing the rules themselves in order to achieve a new political economy equilibrium. The rules can be changed in two ways: introduce and enforce new rules, or ensure that the existing rules (de jure) are effectively implemented (de facto). The economic emergence of the West in the 17th century and of Japan in the late 19th century provide two examples of sweeping changes to the rules of the game. More recently, the changes seen in East Asia and in Central and Eastern Europe attest to the type of historical breaks that can give rise to new political economy equilibria. China opened up in 1978 and moved toward greater economic freedoms, and Central and Eastern European countries transitioned toward a democratic, free market model in the aftermath of the fall of the Berlin Wall in 1989. In both cases, the breaks led to major changes in existing rules of the game. There are several other examples of historical breaks in other countries, for example, in South Africa, Rwanda, Chile, or, more recently, in Myanmar, Vietnam, or Tunisia.

It is also useful to bear in mind that while the introduction of new rules paves the way to new equilibria, there is no guarantee that these equilibria will be superior from the standpoint of growth and collective well-being. Several changes to the rules in Latin America, Asia, and Sub-Saharan Africa led to inferior equilibrium and, in some cases, even resulted in economic meltdowns. However, when these changes improved equilibria, they generally involved transitions toward more open societies, placing greater priority on economic freedoms and civil and political rights. Not only must political players be in a position to make credible commitments, but openness implies that institutions and information systems are in place to enable citizens to hold their leaders accountable for their actions and decisions (Keefer 2011). Political responsibility is indeed a key channel through which social capital can improve the economic well-being and functioning of institutions (Nannicini and others 2013).

In Morocco, the fundamental issue, therefore, is identifying the circumstances that could significantly change the rules in the years ahead so that the pathways to emergence outlined in the Memorandum can be realized. If bottlenecks are fundamentally linked to the culture and internal political economy of countries, solutions cannot mainly come from external players, even if they can clearly play a facilitating and supporting role (Devarajan and Kemani 2016). In this regard, the history of attempts to intervene is largely a history of failures, creating more resentment, offenses, and a heightened sense of nationalist identity than positive results (Landes 1998; Sowell 2015). The best scenario for changing the rules of the game would therefore be the acceleration of the endogenous process of Morocco's transition to an open society, starting with better implementation of existing rules. It should be noted in passing that a society's capacity to implement and enforce common rules is a key element of the social capital of nations, which is discussed in this Memorandum.

It would seem that two exceptional circumstances could trigger the acceleration of Morocco's transition process: the swift and thorough implementation of the spirit and principles of the 2011 Constitution, and the equally swift and thorough implementation of the Advanced Status agreement and a deep and comprehensive free trade agreement (DCFTA) with the European Union. In both cases, the scope and magnitude of the changes could lead to a local, irreversible transition of Morocco's government, economy, and society to a greater equilibrium than the current one. Each circumstance presents an opportunity to significantly strengthen social capital in Morocco and thus realize the country's current potential in the other areas (physical, human, or institutional capital).

The historic constitutional amendments made in Morocco in the wake of political and social turmoil that began in the Arab world in 2011 can generate sweeping changes to the rules of the game (Chauffour 2013). They are thus capable of altering the political economy equilibria, with a view to placing Morocco on a new path of growth and economic convergence (see box E.5). Demand from the Moroccan people for more freedom, human rights, democracy, job opportunities, autonomy, and dignity, and the swift response by Moroccan authorities in the form of a new constitution containing several principles of an open society, present a unique opportunity for Morocco. The country has been presented with a historic opportunity to create a more open, efficient, and accountable state, strengthen economic freedoms and market institutions, and significantly develop its human and social capital. The emergence of the new social contract envisioned in the 2011 constitution could pave the way for the type of historic transformation that has occurred in other regions of the world in recent decades.

Box E.5 New Rules of the Game and the 2011 Constitution

In March 2011, HM King Mohammed VI introduced a series of political reforms that was widely supported by the Moroccan people in the constitutional referendum of July 2011. The new Constitution lays the foundation for a more open and democratic society. It strengthens the country's governance framework through a greater separation and better balance of powers among the King, the government, and the Parliament, and lays the foundation for advanced regionalization and decentralization as a democratic and decentralized system of governance.

The new Constitution strengthens the principles of good governance, human rights, and protection of individual freedoms. It reaffirms a number of fundamental economic, civil, and political freedoms such as the right to own property, the right to enterprise and free competition, the right to freedom of assembly and peaceful protest, the right to free association, and the right to belong to a trade union or political party. It extends a number of rights already contained in 1996; consequently, women are now guaranteed "civil and social equality" with men. Only "political equality" was guaranteed in the past, despite the fact that the 1996 constitution recognized equal rights for all before the law. All citizens have a right to freedom of thought, artistic expression, and creation, while only freedom of opinion, movement, and association had been guaranteed. The new Constitution provides a significant list of civil and political rights that had not been recognized in the 1996 Constitution, including the right to life, the right to security of person, the right to physical or moral integrity, the right to protection of private life, the presumption of innocence and the right to a fair trial, the right to access to justice, the right to access to information, and the right to present petitions. It also recognizes a number of economic, social, and cultural rights such as the right to health, the right to social protection, the right to work, and the right to decent housing.

The new Constitution introduces institutional changes in order to strengthen the separation, balance, and collaboration among the authorities and enhance institutional responsibility and accountability. The main institutional changes pertain to (a) strengthening of the role of Parliament through increased legislative powers and greater oversight of the government; (b) the promotion of the role of the Prime Minister as head of the government appointed by the winning political party in the legislative elections; (c) strengthening of the independence of the courts; and (d) strengthening of oversight institutions, in particular the National Human Rights Council, the Competition Council, and anti-corruption bodies. The constitution also established institutions tasked with guaranteeing equal treatment, parity, and youth participation such as the Parity and Anti-Discrimination Authority and the Youth Advisory Council (Autorité de lutte pour la parité et contre les discriminations et le Conseil consultatif de la jeunesse).

The new Constitution also recognizes the principles of regionalization as a democratic and decentralized system of governance. Far-reaching constitutional amendments were made to enhance the accountability and transparency of local and regional councils, as well as increase citizen participation in the management of local affairs and public services. Particularly noteworthy is the fact that the new Constitution stipulates that regional councils will be elected by direct universal suffrage and that regional affairs will be managed based on the principles of

box continues next page

Box E.5 New Rules of the Game and the 2011 Constitution *(continued)*

administrative autonomy and citizen participation. The presidents of the regional councils—not the governors (or *walis*)—will have the power to implement council decisions. The regional and local councils will be granted expanded powers and the corresponding resources based on the principle of subsidiarity. These major changes will be implemented by means of a revision of the Organic Law on local governments. This will also necessitate the revision and strengthening of the regulatory framework on financial transfers between the central government and local and regional governments, as well as amendments to the Law on local finances.

Source: Madani, Maghraoui, and Zerhouni 2013.

Similarly, the prospects for implementation of the Advanced Status agreement and a DCFTA with the European Union pave the way for potentially establishing new rules of the game with a view to integrating the Moroccan economy into the European Union single market. Introduced in 2008, the Advanced Status agreement ultimately seeks to establish a common economic space between the European Union and Morocco, characterized by a deeper integration of the Moroccan economy into the European Union economy, drawing on standards governing the European Economic Space.[2] Achievement of this objective calls for the implementation of joint actions aimed at convergence of Morocco's legislative and regulatory framework with the *Acquis communautaire* and at complementing and deepening the existing Association Agreement in new areas such as services trade, public procurement, competition policy, investment, intellectual property rights, industrial standards, and sanitary and phytosanitary measures (see box E.6). Despite the absence of European Union accession prospects, Morocco has a unique opportunity to emulate the successful experiences of Central and Eastern European countries in their process of convergence with the European Union, and thus to transform and modernize all of its laws, regulations, and public policies in a single generation. The experiences of Poland, the Baltic States, or more recently Croatia are all precedents for significant changes in national rules, which led to periods of structural transformation and prosperity for the new generations of these countries (Åslund and Djankov 2014). As one enlightened observer already noted in 2005, "from a symbolic standpoint, the signal sent would be even more extraordinary. Morocco would agree, without relinquishing its sovereignty, to being within the sphere of influence of the world's leading economic power" (Berkani 2005).

Morocco stands out as an exception in a turbulent Arab world. It has considerable assets to be able to enhance its distinctiveness and become the first non-oil-producing country in North Africa to join the ranks of emerging countries by the next generation. To this end, Morocco can take up real drivers for change on the political level (the stability of its leadership), the institutional level (the values and principles endorsed by the 2011 Constitution), and the economic, social, and environmental levels (normative convergence with the European Union),

Box E.6 The New Rules of the Game Imported from the European Union

In 1996, Morocco signed the Association Agreement with the European Union, with a view to establishing ongoing political dialogue between Morocco and the European Union, ensuring the phased introduction of a free trade zone, primarily for manufacturing goods, and strengthening economic cooperation in a host of areas (education and training, scientific, technical and technological cooperation, the environment, industrial cooperation, investment promotion and protection, standardization and compliance assessment, agriculture and fishing, transportation and energy), as well as social and cultural cooperation. The Association Agreement was implemented at the beginning of 2000 and supplemented by an agreement on agriculture in 2012.

In 2008, Morocco affirmed its commitment to even greater convergence with the European Union by implementing the Advanced Status agreement. First, the "Réussir le Statut Avancé" (Making a Success of the Advanced Status agreement) program has 10 pillars:

1. strengthening of key institutions in the legislative process;
2. regulatory convergence in the area of standards, technical regulations, and compliance assessment of industrial products;
3. regulatory convergence with European maritime transport safety and security requirements;
4. regulatory convergence with European requirements regarding employment policies and social protection;
5. regulatory convergence with the provisions set forth in the Acquis relating to sanitary and phytosanitary standards;
6. support with the sustainable development and good governance of maritime fishing activities;
7. regulatory convergence with the application of the European framework directive on water;
8. regulatory convergence with the Bologne process (higher education);
9. promotion of consumer protection;
10. and support with the integration into national legislation of the provisions of the conventions of the Council of Europe.

In 2013, Morocco and the European Union launched negotiations for a DCFTA. The DCFTA seeks to supplement and deepen integration between Morocco and the European Union through regulatory and legislative convergence in a number of areas covered by the Acquis communautaire. The Acquis communautaire makes reference to the European Union's entire body of laws; that is, all the legal rights and obligations of the member States. It contains 35 chapters, the first four of which refer to the four fundamental freedoms: free movement of goods, freedom of movement for workers, freedom to provide services, and free movement of capital. Four rounds of negotiations have already taken place but the fifth has been suspended since 2015.

Source: European Union Delegation to Morocco 2013.

in order to build its intangible capital, which is the main source of any future shared prosperity. If there is one lesson to be learned from accrual accounting or capital-based accounting, it is that inclusive sustainable development is essentially based on the accumulation of intangible assets in the form of institutional, human, and social capital. In this age of the knowledge economy and the digital revolution, the wealth of nations is less the outcome of the mere cumulative volume of labor or physical capital than of the quality of institutions, expertise, and knowledge, and collective action standards. Ultimately, these drivers also form the best vectors for strengthening the economic and social cohesion of Morocco and ensuring an organized transition toward economic emergence.

Notes

1. Hysteresis is the phenomenon by which a system (political, economic, social, etc.) tends to remain in a particular state after the disappearance of the cause of that state.

2. Joint European Union + Morocco document on strengthening bilateral relations/Advanced Status.

References

Acemoglu, Daron, and Matthew O. Jackson. 2015. "History, Expectations, and Leadership in the Evolution of Social Norms." *Review of Economic Studies* 82 (1): 1–34.

Acemoglu, Daron, and James A. Robinson. 2006. "De Facto Political Power and Institutional Persistence." *American Economic Association Papers and Proceedings* 96 (2): 325–30.

———. 2012. "Why Nations Fail: The Origins of Power, Prosperity, and Poverty." Crown Business.

Akerlof, George A., and Rachel E. Kranton. 2010. *Identity Economics: How Our Identities Shape Our Work, Wages, and Well-Being*. Princeton, NJ: Princeton University Press.

Andrew, Matt, Lant Pritchett, and Michael Woolcock. 2012. "Escaping Capability Traps through Problem-Driven Iterative Adaptation (PDIA)." Center for Global Development, Working Paper 299, Center for Global Development, Washington, DC.

Åslund, Anders, and Simeon Djankov. 2014. *The Great Rebirth: Lessons from the Victory of Capitalism over Communism*. Washington, DC: Peterson Institute for International Economics.

Banerjee, Abhijit V., and Esther Duflo. 2011. *Poor Economics: A Radical Rethinking of the Way to Fight Global Poverty*. New York: Public Affairs.

Bank Al-Maghrib (BAM). 2016. *Rapport Annuel*. Morocco.

Berkani, Ahmed B. 2005. *Le Maroc à la croisée des chemins*. Paris: L'Harmattan.

Besley, Timothy, and Robin Burgess. 2002. "The Political Economy of Government Responsiveness: Theory and Evidence from India." *Quarterly Journal of Economics* 117 (4): 1415–51.

Bidner, Chris, and Patrick François. 2013. "The Emergence of Political Accountability." *Quarterly Journal of Economics* 128 (3): 1397–448.

Casey, Katherine. 2015. "Crossing Party Lines: The Effects of Information on Redistributive Politics." *American Economic Review* 105 (8): 2410–48.

Chauffour, Jean-Pierre. 2013. *From Political to Economic Awakening in the Arab World: The Path of Economic Integration*. Washington, DC: World Bank. https://openknowledge .worldbank.org/handle/10986/12221.

Devarajan, Shantayanan, and Stuti Khemani. 2016. "If Politics Is the Problem, How Can External Actors Be Part of the Solution?" World Bank Policy Research Paper 7761, World Bank, Washington, DC.

Easterly, William, and Ross Levine. 2013. "The European Origins of Economic Development." No. w18162, National Bureau of Economic Research, Cambridge, MA.

Economic, Social, and Environmental Council (CESE). 2014. *Cohérence des politiques sectorielles et accords de libre-échange: Fondements stratégiques pour un développement soutenu et durable*. Auto-saisine No. 16. Morocco.

The Economist. 2014. "The Tragedy of the Arabs." July 5, p. 9.

Fernandez, Raquel, and Dani Rodrik. 1991. "Resistance to Reform: Status Quo Bias in the Presence of Individual- Specific Uncertainty." *The American Economic Review* 81 (5): 1146–55.

Florini, Ann M., Hairong Lai, and Yeling Tan. 2012. *China Experiments: From Local Innovations to National Reform*. Washington, DC: Brookings Institution Press.

Fukuyama, Francis. 2014. *Political Order and Political Decay: From The Industrial Revolution to the Globalization of Democracy*. New York: Farrar, Straus and Giroux.

Goumeziane, Smail. 2006. *Ibn Khaldoun: Un génie maghrébin (1332–1406)*. Algiers: Édition EDIF 2000.

Grossman, Gene, and Elhanan Helpman. 1994. "Protection for Sale." *The American Economic Review* 84 (4): 833–50.

———. 2001. *Special Interest Politics*. Cambridge, MA: MIT Press.

Heilmann, Sebastian. 2008. "Policy Experimentation in China's Economic Rise." *Studies in Comparative International Development* 43 (1): 1–26.

Keefer, Philip. 2011. "Collective Action, Political Parties, and Pro-Development Public Policy." *Asian Development Review* 28 (1): 94–118.

Keefer, Philip, and Stuti Khemani. 2014. "Radio's Impact on Preferences for Patronage Benefits." Policy Research Working Paper 6932, Washington, DC: World Bank.

Krueger, Anne O. 1974. "The Political Economy of the Rent-Seeking Society." *The American Economic Review* 64 (3): 291–303.

Laffont, Jean-Jacques, and Jean Tirole. 1991. "The Politics of Government Decision-Making: A Theory of Regulatory Capture." *Quarterly Journal of Economics* 106: 1089–127.

Landes, David S. 1998. *The Wealth and Poverty of Nations: Why Some Are So Rich and Some So Poor*. New York: W.W. Norton.

Leighton, Wayne, and Edward Lopez. 2013. *Madmen, Intellectuals, and Academic Scribblers: The Economic Engine of Political Change*. Stanford, CA: Stanford University Press.

Madani, M., D. Maghraoui, and S. Zerhouni. 2013. *The 2011 Moroccan Constitution: A Critical Analysis*. Stockholm: International IDEA.

McCarty, N., and A. Meirowitz. 2007. *Political Game Theory*. Cambridge, UK: Cambridge University Press.

Nannicini, Tommaso, Andrea Stella, Guido Tabellini, and Ugo Troiano. 2013. "Social Capital and Political Accountability." *American Economic Journal: Economic Policy* 5 (2): 222–50.

Nash, John. 1951. "Non-cooperative Games." *The Annals of Mathematics* 54 (2): 286–95.

Newsletter of the European Union Delegation in Morocco. 2013. "Trait d'union." No. 198, Delegation of the European Union in Morocco, Rabat, Morocco.

North, Douglass C., John Wallis, and Barry R. Weingast. 2009. *Violence and Social Orders: A Conceptual Framework for Interpreting Recorded Human History.* New York: Cambridge University Press.

Peltzman, Sam. 1976. "Toward a More General Theory of Regulation." *Journal of Law and Economics* 19 (2): 211–40.

Rodrik, Dani. 2013. "Unconditional Convergence." NBER Working Paper 17546, National Bureau of Economic Research, Cambridge, MA.

———. 2014. "When Ideas Trump Interests: Preferences, Worldview, and Policy Innovations." *Journal of Economic Perspectives* 28 (1): 189–208.

Sowell, Thomas. 2015. *Wealth, Poverty, and Politics: An International Perspective.* New York: Basic Books.

Stigler, George. 1971. "The Theory of Economic Regulation." *The Bell Journal of Economics and Management Science* 2 (1): 3–21.

Tirole, Jean. 2016. *Économie du bien commun.* Paris: Presses universitaires de France.

United Nations Development Programme (UNDP). 2003. *Arab Human Development Report 2003.* New York: UNDP.

Weingast, B., and D. Wittman. 2006. *Oxford Handbook of Political Economy.* Oxford: Oxford University Press.

World Bank. 2014. *Rapport sur le développement dans le monde: "Pensée, société et comportement."* Washington, DC: World Bank.

———. 2016. *Making Politics Work for Development: Harnessing Transparency and Citizen Engagement.* Policy Research Report. Washington, DC: World Bank.

Yao, Daqing, and John Whalley. 2015. "The China (Shanghai) Pilot Free Trade Zone: Background, Developments and Preliminary. Assessment of Initial Impacts." NBER Working Paper 20924, JEL No. F49, National Bureau of Economic Research, Cambridge, MA.